ON FALCON W

THE F-16 STORY

Lindsay Peacock

ON FALCON WINGS
The F-16 Story

Published by:
The Royal Air Force Benevolent Fund Enterprises,
Building 15, RAF Fairford, Glos, GL7 4DL, England
Publishing Director: Paul A. Bowen
Publishing Manager: Cheryl Clifton

Written by: Lindsay Peacock
Compiled & Edited by: Peter R. March
Contributing Author: Neil R. Anderson,
formerly Chief Test Pilot General Dynamics
and International VP, Lockheed Martin Tactical Aircraft Systems
Additional material: Lt Col William C. Diehl, USAF;
Capt William F. Andrews, USAF and Capt John F. Hunnell, USAF;
reproduced by kind permission of Eric Hehs, the Editor of *Code One*,
house magazine of Lockheed Martin Tactical Aircraft Systems
Appendices by: Mike Crutch,
Howard Curtis, Peter R. March,
Lindsay Peacock and Martyn Swann

Assistant Editor: Brian Strickland
US Consultant: Bob Dutton
Design: Graham Finch

Photographs courtesy: Lockheed Martin Tactical Aircraft Systems (LMTAS),
and Bob Archer, Larry Davis, Graham Finch,
Jeremy Flack/Aviation Photographs International,
Peter R. Foster, Andrew March, Daniel March, Peter R. March,
David Menard, PRM Aviation and as otherwise credited
Cover photograph: LMTAS

The Royal Air Force Benevolent Fund Enterprises is indebted to Karen Hagar,
Communications Secretary and Joseph W. Stout, Director of Communications, Lockheed Martin
Tactical Aircraft Systems, for their invaluable assistance with the production of this book.

ISBN 1-899808-01-9

© The Royal Air Force Benevolent Fund Enterprises 1997

Printed in Hong Kong

PETER R MARCH

Contents

Introduction

United States Air Force F-16C

LMTAS

Without doubt the world's most successful multi-role jet aircraft, the General Dynamics (now Lockheed Martin) F-16 Fighting Falcon is the product of a flexible design approach rather than a fighter developed to meet a tight military specification. General Dynamics' visionary design team looked at the basic issues and came up with a relatively straightforward solution making the most of its wide experience from established projects. The use of a modular approach, digital systems technology and a single turbofan engine became fundamental to the success of the new aircraft, keeping the weight and cost down while allowing for the continued introduction of the most advanced technologies in order to keep pace with the threat. The result is that today's F-16 contains the same technologies as those multi-role fighters still in development. Examples include digital fly-by-wire flight controls, low observable technology, and capability to utilize all the emerging weapons to the full extent of their capability. There is a clear message to be learnt from the fact that the F-16, starting from a simple, uncomplicated design, has been an unqualified technical and operational success, and provided a flexibility for development way beyond the original concept.

With production set to continue well into the new millennium, the F-16 is firmly established as the world's largest multi-role aircraft programme. Today it performs the full range of multi-role fighter missions in addition to several roles previously served by dedicated or special mission aircraft, such as US air defence, active defence suppression, close air support and airborne forward air control. In 1997, Fighting Falcons comprise 57% of the USAF's 20-wing general fighter force, and this percentage

ANDREW MARCH

Belgian Air Force F-16A

Royal Netherlands Air Force F-16B

PETER R MARCH

will hold until about the year 2010 or so, when JSFs begin to enter service in quantity. They also comprise 70% of the ten-squadron dedicated air defence force of the USA. With an original purchase of 650 aircraft, by 1997 the USAF had already taken delivery of 2200 F-16s.

Overseas, Fighting Falcons equip more NATO fighter squadrons than any other type. They are operated by eight of the 16 member nations and constitute 100% of the fighter forces of Belgium, Denmark and The Netherlands.

Air National Guard F-16A

PETER R FOSTER

Royal Norwegian Air Force F-16A & F-16B

GRAHAM FINCH

All five Central European countries seeking NATO membership are seriously evaluating the F-16 to begin replacing their Soviet supplied fighter squadrons.

Currently on the front-line strength of 18 air arms, operating in 20 countries, the F-16 is flown from over 80 air bases on five continents world-wide. This is inevitably in a variety of climates and operating tempos, with differing logistic support arrangements and sizes of fleets. Despite these varying conditions it has achieved an impressive operational and safety record. In fact the F-16 holds the distinctions of being the safest multi-role fighter and safest single-engine fighter in USAF history. The safety record still continues to improve as enhancements are incorporated. The USAF F-16 fleet passed five million flying hours in December 1996 and the world-wide fleet exceeded seven million flying hours in February 1997.

Continuing the superlatives, the Fighting Falcon has proved itself to have the best service reliability, maintainability, mission capable rates and ease of support of all US fighters. The USAF's squadrons have demonstrated the F-16's impressive sortie surge capability on many occasions. The highest sortie rate achieved to date was by a squadron deployed to Turkey. In a 12-hour surge and after flying a heavy schedule for 16 days, the unit averaged eight sorties per aircraft, with one F-16 flying 13 sorties. The limiting factor was pilot and not aircraft availability.

It is not surprising that with its low initial procurement cost, high reliability and maintainability and relatively low fuel consumption, the Fighting Falcon has the lowest life cycle costs among all US combat aircraft. Underlining this, the F-16's world-wide popularity and user satisfaction is evident from the fact that 12 overseas air arms have made follow-on purchases, totalling some 800 aircraft, after their initial order. The Lockheed Martin F-16 Fighting Falcon has proved itself to be the top multi-role jet fighter of the last two decades of the 20th century and looks set to take that title well into the new millennium.

Genesis

Lockheed Martin F-16s in the liveries of the first five air arms to operate the fighter – Belgium, Denmark, Netherlands, Norway and the USA. LMTAS

Lockheed Martin's F-16 Fighting Falcon can justifiably lay claim to be the most successful fighter of its generation, as well as a most fitting successor to the mighty McDonnell Douglas F-4 Phantom II. If further proof of that statement is needed, it is provided by the fact that the Fighting Falcon is now in service with, or has been selected by, no fewer than 19 air arms scattered throughout North and South America, Asia, Europe, the Middle East and the Far East. Moreover, now that the Cold War has come to an end, there is every prospect that the F-16 will one day carry the national insignia of some of those nations that were once considered as potential adversaries. Demonstrations have been made to the Czech Republic, Hungary and Poland, all of whom have shown considerable interest and which may go on to take advantage of the favourable terms that are on offer.

In view of these and other notable achievements, one might reasonably assume the process of development that culminated in the Fighting Falcon to have been relatively straightforward. However, such an assumption would be wide of the mark, for the origins of the F-16 were far from straightforward. Indeed, it had to surmount numerous difficulties while making the transition from being a promising idea to a superlative reality. Nor does today's warplane bear much relationship to the original concept.

Changing requirements were instrumental in that, with

these being largely responsible for bringing about the transformation from a relatively inexpensive machine optimised for use solely by day to one that is much more complex and capable of undertaking various roles by both day and night. Such a transformation held the potential for a disastrous outcome, but the finished article actually emerged none the poorer. It is evident that the changes made during the development process were key factors in the ensuing success story.

Evolution of the Fighting Falcon was far from simple and it is necessary to look back to the mid-1960s to find the germ of the seed that was eventually to lead to the contemporary F-16. At that time, the US expected to achieve a fairly rapid resolution of the conflict in Vietnam, but there were already some warning signs, particularly for US air power, with both the Navy and Air Force beginning to take the first casualties of what was to become an ever expanding list. Nonetheless, confidence was high – after all, the US had not previously lost a war and there was no reason to assume that this latest conflict would finish in anything but victory for the superpower.

In 1965, the doctrine 'big is beautiful' seemed to hold sway in the American military. That was certainly true as far as the USAF was concerned, since the air arm was in the process of taking delivery of the mighty F-4 Phantom and

The versatile F-16 has proved a worthy successor to the heavyweight McDonnell Douglas F-4 Phantom II. USAF

General Dynamics produced the large and very complex F-111 for the USAF before designing the new lightweight fighter. DANIEL MARCH

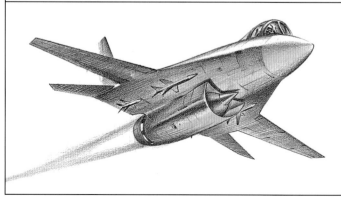

Three of the many General Dynamics designs for the Advanced Day Fighter (ADF) Competition in the mid-1960s that was won by the McDonnell Douglas F-15. BOB CUNNINGHAM

was also pressing ahead with plans to deploy the even larger and very much heavier General Dynamics F-111. Both were potentially formidable warplanes but both were extremely costly to buy as well as complex to operate, requiring the co-ordinated efforts of two crew members in order to function at optimum efficiency.

Standardisation on fewer types of warplane, and the resultant economies of scale, may have held out the promise of substantial savings in the short term. However, rising costs in the areas of training, maintenance and technical support could not be overcome so easily and it is interesting to note that it was the Air Force itself which first made efforts to address these problems by initiating the ADF (Advanced Day Fighter) study of 1965.

Despite representing an early attempt to get away from the vicious spiral of increasing cost and complexity, the odds were heavily stacked against the ADF from the very outset. It was radical and that was always likely to make it a target for hostility from those who prefer the safety of tradition. For

The appearance of Russia's heavyweight MiG-25 Foxbat *in 1967 effectively killed off the US ADF project.* PETER R MARCH

example, at just 25,000 lb (11,340 kg), it was a real lightweight when compared with many of the warplanes then in US service and there were many of conservatives who argued it would not be able to 'punch its weight'. For them, the appearance of the Soviet MiG-25 *Foxbat* in 1967 came at just the right moment, effectively killing off any lingering hopes of a drastic change in USAF fighter procurement policy.

Furthermore, the ADF was intended to be a low-cost aircraft which could be obtained in relatively large quantities. While that idea would undoubtedly find support from accountants and book-keepers, it was never likely to win any friends or influence those who believed that cost is directly proportional to quality. It is probably true to say that most of the time, you get what you pay for, but just occasionally, there are bargains to be had and the ADF proposal *might* have been one, had it been allowed to proceed.

While the ADF foundered, that was certainly not the case with the other major fighter proposal to emerge in the mid-1960s. This evolved from the FX (Fighter Experimental) design study and ultimately led to the McDonnell Douglas F-15 Eagle, which entered service with the USAF in the early 1970s as an uncompromised air superiority fighter. However, as was the case with the abortive ADF, not everyone in the Pentagon hierarchy was wholeheartedly in favour.

The principal focus of opposition was a group of individuals who were collectively known as the 'Fighter Mafia'. While they may not have been able to wield much power at the outset, they included some respected figures, including Major John Boyd and Lieutenant Colonel Everest Riccioni of the USAF and the weapons systems analyst Pierre Sprey.

Even as development of what evolved into the F-15, began to accelerate, the 'Fighter Mafia' was actively promoting a proposal referred to as the 'F-XX' by Sprey. This was basically a revamp of the earlier ADF and was envisaged as a low-cost answer to the Air Force's need to bolster its tactical fighter force. Once again, the attractions of an inexpensive solution were pushed, although they also suggested it could be a useful fall-back in the event of the F-15's radar and other key systems being late or, worse still, inadequate.

Yet again, the proposal met with a fair amount of opposition and hostility, but it also began to find support amongst some of those responsible for planning and making policy. Notable amongst them was Deputy Secretary of Defense David Packard, who was appointed to the Pentagon during 1969, and who quickly endorsed the philosophy being pushed by the 'Fighter Mafia'. In addition, he also favoured the concept of competitive 'prototyping', whereby

The McDonnell Douglas F-15 Eagle was spawned by the USAF's FX design study. MCDONNELL DOUGLAS

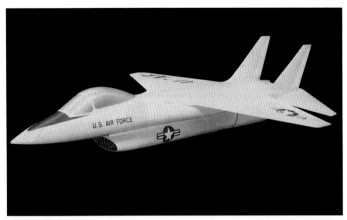

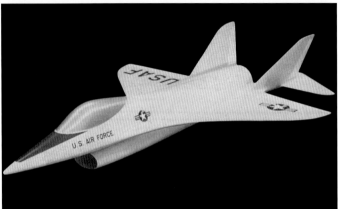

General Dynamics' Light Weight Fighter (LWF) designs developed naturally from the ADF. The last of these (LWF-401-16B) closely resembled the eventual YF-16. LMTAS

the best pair of proposals for a specific design contest would be rewarded with development contracts. Normally for no more than two aircraft, these would be completed and used for a comparative evaluation, after which the most promising machine would be selected for quantity production.

Having resulted in the selection of such types as the A-10 Thunderbolt II and the new Lockheed Martin F-22 and also expected to lead to a definitive Joint Strike Fighter, this is now standard procedure for major projects, but it certainly was not in favour then. Nevertheless, the contest that was won by the Fighting Falcon was amongst the first to employ competitive prototyping, although it was to be a few more years before the proponents of 'light is right' won the day and secured funding for their ideas.

In the meantime, the 'Mafia' kept pushing, supported by some far-sighted individuals in companies like Lockheed, Northrop and Vought. Their persistence was eventually rewarded during 1971 when some $200 million was set aside from the FY 1972 budget appropriations specifically for new Air Force prototypes. Having secured Congressional approval for a limited programme, including construction and flight testing of prototypes of each of the most promising contenders, a sizeable chunk of that money was allocated to the so-called Light Weight Fighter (LWF) project.

This led to a formal Request for Proposals (RFP) being issued to the US aerospace industry on 6 January 1972. Not surprisingly, the RFP incorporated many of Pierre Sprey's original ideas, such as outstanding manoeuvrability, a high thrust-to-weight ratio and the ability to tolerate 6.5g load factors. Where it differed was in stipulating that the optimum gross weight was to be of the order of 20,000 lb (9,072 kg), which was much lighter than the earlier ADF and F-XX proposals.

Despite the fact that there appeared little likelihood of the LWF project resulting in large scale orders, the RFP brought a fair response, with five companies submitting designs during February 1972. The initial review was undertaken by the Air Staff which, in March 1972, announced that its most favoured candidate was the Boeing Model 908-909. Second place went to the General Dynamics Model 401, followed by the Northrop P-600 with the Lockheed and Vought proposals bringing up the rear.

As it transpired, further study of the designs resulted in that decision being overturned by the Source Selection Authority (SSA), which demoted Boeing to third place after General Dynamics and Northrop. This decision was made official in April 1972, when it was announced that contracts had been awarded to the two winning contenders to cover the manufacture, assembly and flight testing of two prototypes of each design. In the case of General Dynamics, whose Model 401 would henceforth be known as the YF-16, it was worth $37.9 million, while Northrop received the slightly larger sum of $39.8 million for the P-600 or YF-17. Programme planning anticipated the maiden flight of both contenders early in 1974, to be followed by a 300-flying hour evaluation at the Air Force Flight Test Center (AFFTC) at Edwards AFB, California.

Encouraged by this, the 'Fighter Mafia' continued to press their claims for the concept with considerable zeal, winning increasing support in the process. Nevertheless, there was still much resistance from the military hierarchy, although it appears that few opponents felt sufficiently motivated or threatened to campaign actively against the LWF programme. This may have had its roots in complacency, with many adversaries presuming that the 'big is beautiful' philosophy would hold sway and that the LWF project would simply fade into oblivion once the test results had been analysed.

The first YF-16 nearing completion in the 'sensitive building' at Fort Worth in September 1973. LMTAS

In this they were much mistaken and advocates of the LWF won a significant victory, in early 1974, when the idea of mutually complementary fighters emerged. This envisaged a high-cost/low-cost force mix, composed of the F-15 Eagle and the winning LWF. In essence, that is what happened, although the cost benefits originally anticipated were overtaken by later developments, with the production F-16 being considerably more sophisticated and a far more potent and costly machine than was first proposed.

Against that background, production of the YF-16 prototypes by General Dynamics continued at Fort Worth, Texas. On 13 December 1973, the first of them (72-01567) was formally rolled out in a handsome red, white and blue colour scheme, this machine being airlifted to the Edwards

The YF-16 prototype was rolled-out in a smart red and white colour scheme at Fort Worth in December 1973. LMTAS

The YF-16 and the design/test team at Fort Worth after roll-out, before it was taken to Edwards AFB, CA on 8 January 1974 by C-5A Galaxy. LMTAS

test base aboard a C-5A Galaxy on 8 January 1974.

Following reassembly and some ground testing, it took to the air for the first time on 20 January 1974, with test pilot Phil Oestricher of General Dynamics at the controls. In fact, the maiden flight was entirely unplanned and was originally scheduled to be nothing more than a high-speed taxi test along the Edwards runway. Unfortunately, at some stage during the proceedings, the pilot encountered violent lateral rocking which would have resulted in the YF-16 slewing off the runway and almost certainly sustaining serious damage before it could be brought to a halt. Faced with that far from desirable situation, Oestricher chose to make an unscheduled take-off and went on to complete a circuit of the traffic pattern before terminating the surprise sortie with an uneventful landing some six minutes later.

Post-flight examination of the YF-16 revealed minor damage to the starboard tailplane which had struck the runway during one of the more extreme oscillations. Otherwise, the aircraft was in good shape and repairs were quickly effected, clearing the way for an official first flight. This took place on 2 February 1974 and lasted some 90 minutes, Oestricher commenting afterwards that it was "a most enjoyable experience". The maiden flight of the second YF-16 (72-1568) was rather less eventful, taking place on 9 May 1974, with General Dynamics' test pilot Neil Anderson.

As for the opposition, the first YF-17 (72-1569) ventured skywards in June 1974, by which time it was evident that the competitors were playing for very much higher stakes. Although some debate had already centred around acquiring the LWF as a low-cost fighter, that idea was soon overtaken by events. The most significant of these came in April 1974, when Secretary of Defense James Schlesinger made it known that the Department of Defense was considering the acquisition of a derivative of the LWF.

The second YF-16 was flown for the first time on 9 May 1974, in the hands of GD test pilot Neil Anderson. VIA LARRY DAVIS

One of the more obvious indications of change was the decision to adopt a different name for any version that might be ordered into quantity production. This resulted in the appearance of the so-called Air Combat Fighter (ACF), but the new title was far from being just an exercise in semantics designed to overcome Air Force resistance. This latest manifestation would be a much more capable warplane indeed.

Nevertheless, opposition from within the USAF persisted, with the service being particularly anxious to avoid having to curtail orders for the F-15, which was the air defence fighter that it really wanted. However, this opposition was largely overcome when Schlesinger made it known that any new fighter which might result from the on-going LWF programme would be purchased *in addition* to the Eagle and not, as many had expected, instead of it.

That news undoubtedly did much to allay any remaining fears, but the icing on the cake was the revelation that Schlesinger intended to provide sufficient hardware to equip no fewer than five full-sized USAF Tactical Fighter Wings. At the very least, that meant about 360 aircraft, although if reserves and attrition were taken into account, it was likely to handsomely exceed the 400 mark. Once this became known, most of the hostility simply melted away and USAF enthusiasm for the LWF/ACF project rose appreciably.

Formal confirmation that the winning design would be built for the USAF came on 11 September 1974, at which time the respective LWF contenders were deeply immersed

The Northrop YF-17 was flown in June 1974, by which time it was clear that neither design would be put into production as just a basic low-cost fighter. PETER R MARCH

in flight testing. In the case of the YF-16, the pair of prototypes completed 330 sorties during the fly-off phase, accumulating some 417 flight hours, which was considerably in excess of the original target. The YF-17 sortie tally was rather less, but was still a respectable 268. During the evaluation, both types undertook simulated air-to-air combat against various front-line USAF aircraft as well as the MiG-17 and MiG-21 (from the 4477th TES), although they never went head-to-head.

Subsequent study of test results and other equally important criteria confirmed that the YF-16 was superior in many respects. In terms of performance, it possessed greater combat radius and acceleration, could withstand higher load

The first YF-16 at Edwards AFB in September 1974, being prepared for another test/evaluation flight. VIA LARRY DAVIS

The two YF-16s had, by September 1974, completed 330 sorties during the fly-off phase. LMTAS

factors and had better endurance. In financial terms, it had a projected unit flyaway cost which was some $250,000 lower than the YF-17 and was also cheaper to operate.

Not surprisingly, therefore, the General Dynamics contender was chosen to fulfil the USAF's ACF requirement, with a formal announcement to that effect being made by Secretary of the Air Force John McLucas on 13 January 1975. Given previous statements about the LWF/ACF programme, that was far from startling, but the news that at least 650 aircraft would be involved did come as a great surprise to many, since it confirmed that the extent of the programme encompassed rather more than just the five Wings referred to by Schlesinger.

One aspect which may have been a factor in prompting such a large US Air Force order was its export potential. Overseas sales were by no means conditional upon USAF selection, but customers were always likely to look more favourably upon a type which was in use by the home forces. That was certainly true of the four NATO air arms which collectively were involved in what was repeatedly touted as the 'sale of the century', since they deliberately delayed the process of reaching a decision until after the USAF had made its mind up.

The search for a new warplane to replace Lockheed F-104G Starfighters in service with the air arms of Belgium, Denmark, the Netherlands and Norway effectively began in the early 1970s and ran parallel with the 'Fighter Mafia's' struggles to promote the LWF for much of the time, although it is doubtful if it was initially viewed as a serious candidate. Transformation from the LWF to the ACF, however, meant it could no longer be overlooked.

At the outset, these four countries worked independently, but in late 1973, they began to consider the possibility of

acting collectively and took the first steps to formalise the arrangement in early 1974 when they formed the Multi-national Fighter Programme Group (MFPG). This included representatives from each country and met formally for the first time in May 1974, with the initial objective being to draw up terms of reference.

In the early 1970s, some NATO air arms were looking to replace their F-104G Starfighters, like this Royal Netherlands Air Force F-104G (top) and Royal Danish Air Force TF-104 (above). PETER R MARCH

The main European contenders for the four-nation F-104 fighter replacement were the French Mirage F1 (above) and the Swedish derivative of the Saab Viggen (left). ANDREW MARCH/PETER R MARCH

One of the first decisions centred around agreement that no unilateral decision would be taken before the evaluation process ended, this being scheduled to occur in September of the same year. In addition, it was stipulated that each of the four MFPG member states would adopt the chosen type in quantity; that licence production would be undertaken within Europe of at least 80% of the capital value of the project; and that long-term support guarantees would be sought from the government of the winning vendor.

With well over 300 aircraft certain to be ordered, this deal was always going to be hotly contested – and so it proved, although some of the allegations that were made by the various competitors seemed more appropriate to a political campaign. Charges of bribery, corruption and even CIA involvement emerged, but with around two billion dollars at stake, that probably is not too surprising, although it is doubtful if many of those most closely associated with the decision-making process expected it to be quite so acrimonious.

US candidates for this order initially included both of the designs in contention for the LWF/ACF project, plus the

Northrop P-530 Cobra which was a private venture that was similar in appearance to the YF-17. Of these, the Cobra was eliminated at a fairly early stage in the proceedings. From Europe, there were also three proposals, namely France's Dassault-Breguet Mirage F1, the Anglo-French SEPECAT Jaguar and Sweden's SAAB Eurofighter derivative of the Viggen. Again, one was rejected at an early point, this being the Jaguar.

Throughout the summer of 1974, a 30-strong team that included test pilots, engineers and legal experts, conducted a thorough study of the four proposals that remained in contention. This naturally looked at technical aspects and operational potential of the various types under consideration, since the objective was first and foremost to buy a warplane. However, the team's brief was rather more wide-ranging than that and focused closely on a variety of

The Anglo-French SEPECAT Jaguar, another contender for the F-104 replacement, was eliminated at an early stage. ANDREW MARCH

financial considerations, with a good deal of effort devoted to the study of price structures, offset proposals and production schedules.

Keeping track of the current status of the various offers was probably a difficult business in itself, for the companies involved in bidding were all desperately trying to upstage their rivals by producing the most attractive deal in order to secure the contract. This resulted in frequent changes, especially in the late summer of 1974, while the French at one point began to question the commitment of the MFPG member states to European ideals, a charge that was probably greeted with incredulity by the respective governments.

By early 1975, however, it was already apparent that the General Dynamics proposal was superior on technical merit and unit cost, even if it lagged behind in so far as offsets were concerned. Further negotiations ensued, leading to a satisfactory compromise being reached and clearing the way for its selection as the winning contender, with a formal announcement to this effect being made on 7 June 1975. This may well have resulted in much gritting of teeth in France, for it took place at the Paris Air Show, an event which also marked the European début of the General Dynamics fighter with Neil Anderson showing off the first YF-16 at Le Bourget.

Although by no means as dramatic as the earlier announcement by the USAF, European selection was based on the initial procurement of close to 350 aircraft. Under the co-production plan that was drawn up, there would be two European assembly lines - one in Belgium and the other in The Netherlands, with each responsible for producing a half-share of the total number of aircraft to be procured. In addition to 104 F-16As and 12 F-16B two-seaters for its own use, Belgium would complete 46 F-16As and 12 F-16Bs for Denmark, with all of these undergoing final assembly at SABCA's Gosselies factory. In neighbouring Holland, Fokker would produce the rest at Schiphol, with its share comprising 80 F-16As and 22 F-16Bs for Dutch use, plus 60 F-16As and 12 F-16Bs for Norway.

1975 proved to be very much a make-or-break year for the F-16 and General Dynamics. While it may have begun with some uncertainty, any doubts that lingered over the future of the programme were dispelled during the first half of the year, initially by the unexpectedly large USAF order and then by the collective NATO decision.

However, while the order book was already encouragingly full, those successes merely marked the start of an intensive period of hard work. In the first instance, a good deal of development work still needed to be done, along with extensive flight testing, before the production aircraft could begin to enter service. Further complications stemmed from the need to establish new assembly lines in Europe. Between them, challenges like these were to sorely tax the minds of everyone associated with the project, but nobody doubted that the effort would ultimately prove worthwhile.

Making its European début at the Paris Air Show in June 1975, the General Dynamics YF-16 was announced as the winning contender for the fighter replacement aircraft. R L WARD

Prototype to Production

The first FSD aircraft featured a redesigned, larger tailplane, ventral fins and nose radome. LMTAS

Following just six months after the announcement that several hundred F-16s would be delivered to the USAF, the decision of the four European NATO air arms to obtain a substantial number also, meant that virtually 1,000 examples of the new General Dynamics fighter were certain to be built even before the first production machine had made its maiden flight. In the short term, however, much

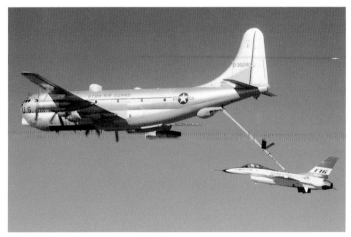

The YF-16s continued to contribute to the development programme alongside the FSD aircraft. Here YF-16 72-01568 is being refuelled from a Boeing KC-97 tanker of the Utah Air Guard. LMTAS

work would be needed to transform what was still little more than a very promising prototype into a true multi-role fighter. One of the initial steps in facilitating the transformation process was taken when General Dynamics was rewarded with the first of several lucrative contracts.

The initial one was by no means as large as those that came later, but still accounted for $417.9 million of FY 1975 funds. It was intended to cover additional design work, plus the production of a batch of 15 Full-Scale Development (FSD) F-16s, earmarked to undertake the wide range of flight trials that are a necessary precursor to service introduction.

As their title implied, the FSD machines would approximate more closely to the definitive production aircraft and would incorporate many new features such as the Westinghouse multi-mode radar and additional hardpoints for the carriage of ordnance and other external stores. Most of the FSD aircraft were to be completed as single-seat F-16As but four examples of the two-seat F-16B version were included. It is significant that the latter was always intended to be fully combat-capable.

In the event, the number of FSD aircraft on order was soon cut by almost half, to just six F-16As and two F-16Bs, and the task of building them got under way at Fort Worth shortly before the end of 1975. It was these machines that bore the brunt of the flight test effort from late 1976

The first FSD 'Full Scale Development' F-16A at Fort Worth after roll-out on 20 October 1976. R ALEXANDER VIA R L WARD

First flown on 3 May 1977, the third F-16A FSD had the full avionics suite. LARRY DAVIS

Above and right: The two-seat F-16B (75-0751) was flown for the first time on 8 August 1977. VIA R L WARD

onwards, with the first of the single-seaters (75-0745) being rolled out at Fort Worth amidst due ceremony on 20 October 1976. This underwent extensive ground testing before it flew for the first time on 8 December.

Since these aircraft were assigned to different aspects of the test programme, they were by no means built to a common configuration. For instance, the first example with the planned avionics suite was in fact the third FSD F-16A (75-0747) to emerge and this made its maiden flight on 3 May 1977. Turning to the two-seat F-16B combat-capable trainer model, the first of these (75-0751) completed its initial flight on 8 August 1977 and was immediately assigned to the test programme.

By mid-summer of 1978, all eight FSD aircraft had flown and been delivered into the hands of the Air Force Flight Test Center's F-16 JTF (Joint Test Force) at Edwards AFB, California. In the normal course of events, a Joint Test Force is composed of test pilots drawn from AFFTC as well as the prime contractor and the major USAF command that will operate the type. Accordingly, representatives from General Dynamics and Tactical Air Command (TAC) formed part of the team that was assembled at Edwards, but the F-16 JTF was unusual in that it also included pilots from some, if not all, of the European customer nations that had signed up to buy.

Between them, these skilled aircrew set about completing a comprehensive evaluation of various aspects of the F-16. These included basic handling qualities, expansion of the flight envelope, weapons carriage and separation trials and

All eight F-16 FSD aircraft together with the second YF-16 (top right) on the apron at Edwards AFB in 1978, before commencing a busy day's test flying. LMTAS

assessment of avionics systems capabilities. Although perhaps the best known location associated with the test programme, Edwards was far from being the only base to support the F-16 project, for specialised facilities at other bases also had a key part to play.

This meant that FSD aircraft were despatched to Eglin AFB, Florida; Howard AFB in the Canal Zone and Eielson AFB, Alaska in order to assess the aircraft's performance in extremes of climatic conditions. It would also verify that the F-16 would be able to function equally efficiently in tropical heat and humidity as well as in near-Arctic chill. In addition, Eglin was also the site for a series of specialised weapons carriage and delivery trials accomplished by the Armament Development and Test Center.

Four of the FSD machines (three F-16As and an F-16B) also ventured much further afield, paying a fairly lengthy visit to Europe in order to complete an environmental and operational test project. They were in fact present for several weeks and one of the F-16As had been fitted with an extended tail fairing which contained a braking parachute, as specified by Norway for its Fighting Falcons. Missions were flown from several of the air bases that would eventually be home to operational aircraft and this tour was deemed to be most successful.

Finally, as well as the trials mentioned above, the new fighter was given a very thorough shake-down by an organisation which rejoiced in the rather grand title of Multinational Operational Test and Evaluation (MOT&E) force. This opened in 1979 at about the same time as deliveries got under way, and it eventually completed almost 5,000 sorties from Hill AFB, Utah (the first operational USAF base) and airfields in Belgium, Denmark, the Netherlands and Norway.

The principal objective of MOT&E was to smooth the path to operational deployment and a total of nine F-16s was used. Responsibility for overseeing this programme was entrusted to Detachment 16 of the 57th Fighter Weapons Wing. Some 18 pilots were assigned to MOT&E, with the USAF contributing the lion's share (ten), while the four European customers provided two each. Trials examined a range of aspects such as aircraft performance as well as

logistics support, ground handling and maintenance, all of which were vital to ensuring smooth operations on a daily basis.

While it cannot be denied that flight testing the F-16 was a matter of crucial importance, there were other equally important matters to be resolved before its entry into service could be contemplated. Some of these hurdles were relatively easy to clear, but the safe negotiation of one or two others called for great care and diplomacy.

Arguably one of the most important of these was the satisfactory resolution of the matter of spreading the work equitably between the different partners in the co-production programme. Almost inevitably, this raised its fair share of problems and generated considerable discussion. On the surface though, there was seldom evidence of discord, despite the fact that quite a few political and practical difficulties had to be surmounted, any one of which taken in isolation could have caused serious delay or even stalled progress altogether.

In Belgium, the politicians were anxious to provide equal shares in the work associated with this project to the French-speaking south and the Flemish-speaking north. That was an understandable ambition as well as a laudable one, even if it was primarily motivated by the desire to avoid presenting government opponents with political capital. Unfortunately, the realities of the situation were not so easily circumvented, for Belgium's aviation industry actually had little room for manoeuvre, since the main centre of activity was located at Gosselies, near Charleroi, in the southern half of the country.

Similar difficulties arose in meeting Danish aspirations, although the outcome was much less satisfactory on the grounds of an inability to achieve predicted job-creation figures. In fact, less than 300 new jobs resulted from Danish involvement in the production programme, which was woefully short of the original estimate of around 8,000. Despite that, considerable progress was made and the partners were agreed that these problems were not the fault of the machine that lay at the heart of the entire programme. Indeed, the consensus was that the F-16 was the right aircraft at the right time.

Looking at the manufacturing programme in greater detail, it is not perhaps widely realised that it was very much a joint effort and thus fully deserving of description as co-production, rather than just licence-assembly. Therefore, as the pace of activity accelerated throughout the late 1970s, key components and assemblies began flowing across the Atlantic Ocean. Initially, most of this traffic was from west to east, with General Dynamics starting to supply tools and raw materials to its partners towards the end of 1976. Subsequently, once the European contribution to the manufacturing process began to pick up, it became a two-way movement.

As the design authority General Dynamics was responsible for a substantial portion of the manufacturing process. It produced key assemblies such as the forward fuselage and horizontal tail surfaces for the assembly line in Fort Worth as well as those in Europe, while also turning out

The fifth single-seat FSD aircraft visited Europe with the Joint Test Force, here photographed at RAF Alconbury, UK. R L WARD

The second production F-16A (78-0002) with the 388th TFW at Hill AFB, Utah. VIA LARRY DAVIS

fin and centre fuselage sections for its own use. The flow of component parts certainly did not go in just one direction, for General Dynamics also received major sub-assemblies from its partners in the manufacturing effort.

SABCA and SONACA in Belgium, for instance, fabricated aft fuselage sections and wing assemblies which were shipped out for integration into the production lines at Schiphol and Fort Worth. In similar fashion, Fokker turned out centre fuselage sections and flaperons for its own line, plus those at Gosselies and Fort Worth, while Per Udsen in Denmark assembled vertical fin boxes using components provided by SONACA. As for the F100 engines which powered the production aircraft, those earmarked for USAF F-16s came directly from Pratt & Whitney, while their European counterparts were fitted with licence-built engines originating from Fabrique Nationale in Belgium.

The official launch of co-production came on 1 July 1977, when personnel at Fokker began the process of machining the first bulkhead plate. Thereafter, milestones came and went thick and fast as the pace of the programme accelerated. For example, the first major shipment of European components to arrive in Texas reached General Dynamics in mid-November 1977 and that was followed by an even more significant event in January 1978 when the first complete F-16 fuselage was shipped to Europe, enabling workers at the Gosselies factory in Belgium to begin final assembly of the first European Fighting Falcon on 15 February 1978. Less than two months later, on 11 April, Fokker's line was also established and by the middle of that year, the two-way flow of major components was building satisfactorily towards its peak.

In the following summer, the first set of European-built

wings (from Belgium) were fitted to an F-16 at Fort Worth, but an even more important development was the maiden flight and formal acceptance by the USAF of the first production F-16A (78-0001) in August. Five months later, on 6 January 1979, the 388th Tactical Fighter Wing at Hill AFB, Utah became the first unit anywhere in the world to begin the process of transition to the newest Air Force fighter when it took delivery of its first F-16. This marked the start of a re-equipment programme that was to see the F-16 initially complement the McDonnell Douglas Phantom with tactical units in the USA, Europe and the Far East – ultimately, the Fighting Falcon was to usurp the dominant position that had once been occupied by the mighty F-4.

Meanwhile, great strides were also being made on the other side of the Atlantic and these bore fruit in Belgium, on 11 December 1978, when the first European-built aircraft made its initial flight from Gosselies. This particular machine (F-16B FB-01/78-0162) was delivered to the Belgian Air Force on 26 January 1979, while the first Belgian-built example to join the Royal Danish Air Force (F-16B ET-204/78-0204) was handed over on 18 January 1980.

Eventually, the SABCA/SONACA team was to complete a total of 222 aircraft. The bulk of this total was made up by the initial purchases for Belgium and Denmark, but follow on contracts were later placed for 40 more F-16As and four F-16Bs for domestic use, as well as four F-16Bs for the USAF.

By the time the first Belgian aircraft was delivered, work at Fokker's Schiphol factory was also forging ahead and the first Dutch aircraft (F-16B J-259/78-0259) made its maiden flight on 3 May 1979. Once again, little more than a month elapsed before the first aircraft was handed over to the customer, with deliveries to the Royal Netherlands Air Force

First F-16B (FB-01) delivered to the Belgian Air Force in 1979, photographed at Brustem on the 10th anniversary of service. ANDREW MARCH

The first Dutch-built aircraft, F-16B J-259 for the Royal Netherlands AF, was flown on 3 May 1979 and delivered a month later. ANDREW MARCH

The Royal Danish Air Force received its first aircraft, Belgian-built F-16B ET-204, on 18 January 1980. PETER R MARCH

getting under way on 6 June, although the first machine to be accepted was actually an F-16A (J-212/78-0212). Fokker was also responsible for producing aircraft for Norway, whose initial example (F-16B 301/78-0301) was delivered on 15 January 1980.

While the line at Schiphol may have lagged slightly behind the Belgian one, it was eventually to produce a total of 300 aircraft, with later orders more than doubling home consumption. In fact, Holland added 97 F-16As and 14 F-16Bs to its original buy. In addition, a re-order from Denmark accounted for another eight F-16As and four F-16Bs, with the total being rounded out by a pair of F-16As for the USAF and one F-16B for Egypt.

By the start of the 1980s, therefore, the F-16 was firmly established in quantity production, with factories at Fort Worth, Gosselies and Schiphol turning out aircraft for the original five customers. In addition, prospects for the future were looking particularly bright, as other orders were starting to come in. The production line at Fort Worth was not surprisingly the source of these aircraft and that situation has pretty much persisted ever since, although manufacturing agreements have resulted in F-16s also emerging from factories in South Korea and Turkey.

Iran had been the first non-participating nation to decide to purchase the F-16. In an announcement that accompanied the formal signature of a letter of intent on 27 October 1976, it was revealed that Iran planned to buy an initial batch of 160 aircraft. At the same time, it was also stated that the total Iranian purchase might eventually rise as high as 300, which was particularly good news for General Dynamics. In the event, history intervened in 1978, when the Shah was ousted from power and departed to exile in Paris.

The RNethAF's first F-16A (J-212) was also the first F-16 handed over, on 6 June 1979. DAVID MENARD

Norwegian F-16s were also built by Fokker, with their first aircraft, F-16B 301, being delivered in January 1980. PETER R MARCH

Customers' national flags applied to the nose of the second prototype YF-16. At the time, the flags included that of Iran. LMTAS

Not long afterwards, the Iranian deal was cancelled by the Revolutionary Council led by Ayatollah Khomeini. Inevitably, this decision had a number of consequences, most of which were very unwelcome. It was undoubtedly a severe blow to General Dynamics, although the company's fortunes were soon to recover as other potential buyers and interested parties began beating a well-worn path to Texas. It

also had some impact on unit cost, which rose immediately, but it was good news for Israel, which had placed an order for 75 aircraft in August 1978, for it allowed them to take delivery at a rather earlier stage than might otherwise have been the case.

So, despite the loss of the Iranian deal, it is fair to say that the future looked quite encouraging at the start of 1980, which turned out to be a significant year for the F-16 in several ways. The air arms of Denmark and Norway both accepted their first F-16s at the start of 1980 and they were joined by Israel on the very last day of January, although it was not until July that the first examples were ferried from the USA to Israel. Nevertheless, those contracts were already secure and General Dynamics was understandably much more concerned with the business of winning fresh orders.

In that respect, the company's fortunes received a most welcome boost in June, when Egypt concluded negotiations for the supply of a batch of 40 aircraft. This was an important breakthrough for the US in general, for the deal just would not have been possible less than a year earlier. Prior to the Camp David peace agreement of July 1979, Egypt had traditionally looked to the Soviet Union for backing and arms, while Israel had relied on the US for material and moral support. Furthermore, there was a history of acrimonious relationships between these two countries. This had periodically erupted into full-scale warfare, with the most recent such occurrence happening in 1973.

After the 1979 agreement, all that changed, paving the way for US restrictions on arms transfers to be greatly

Colourful F-16A of the 388th TFW based at Hill AFB. VIA LARRY DAVIS

The 474th TFW at Nellis AFB, NV was the third Tactical Air Command unit to receive F-16As. VIA LARRY DAVIS

relaxed, although this was apparently a bit of a mixed blessing for the Egyptians. One sign of the new regime was the hurried delivery of a batch of former USAF F-4E Phantoms, but these aircraft were plagued by poor serviceability at the outset and it took quite some time before Egyptian technicians were able to master the Phantom's complex systems. Another sign, of arguably much greater significance, was allowing Egypt to sign-up for the F-16, which was much more 'user-friendly', despite being technologically more advanced than the Phantom.

Finally, 1980 was also notable in that the latest fighter to enter service with the USAF was at last given a name, officially being called the *Fighting Falcon* with effect from 20 July. Perhaps typically, this name does not seem to have been greeted with a great deal of enthusiasm by USAF pilots, who evidently prefer the appellation *Viper*. Irrespective of the name, there can be little doubt that the single most significant event of 1980 was the attainment of an Initial Operational Capability (IOC) by the 388th Tactical Fighter Wing (TFW) in October 1980 and the unit at Hill AFB followed up by undertaking the first overseas deployment when it despatched 12 aircraft to Norway in March 1981.

By then, two more Tactical Air Command (TAC) wings had begun the lengthy process of transition, these being the 56th Tactical Training Wing at MacDill AFB, Florida and the 474th TFW at Nellis AFB, Nevada. However, these were merely the forerunners of many more front-line units, for the Fighting Falcon was destined to become a familiar sight not only in the USA with TAC, but also at overseas bases with the Pacific Air Forces and the United States Air Forces in Europe commands. In addition, second-line elements of the Air National Guard and Air Force Reserve have also since standardised on the F-16, which is now by far the most numerous warplane in the USAF inventory.

An F-16A of the 56th Tactical Training Wing flying from MacDill AFB, FL. JEFF ETHELL

While the massive assembly hall at Fort Worth has continued to manufacture Fighting Falcons of various sub-types virtually uninterrupted for some two decades, the company responsible for the manufacture of those aircraft has experienced a number of changes of name. This is especially true of the 1990s, with General Dynamics becoming just another example of the increasing list of famous names that have disappeared. The sale of General Dynamics Fort Worth Division to Lockheed resulted in overall responsibility for the F-16 programme being entrusted to the Lockheed Fort Worth Company with effect from 1 March 1993. However, even that tenuous link with the past was to disappear in 1995 when the name was changed again, to Lockheed Martin Tactical Aircraft Systems, which is the organisation that now has charge of developing, building and marketing the Fighting Falcon today.

Testing Times

Former General Dynamics test pilot **Neil R Anderson** gives his personal account of the early F-16 test program. Writing in the third person, he uses the same objective, analytical approach that characterized the hundreds of pilot's reports he produced while testing the F-16.

During the design and fabrication phases of the YF-16 program in 1972 and 1973, the flight test program was conceptualized, coordinated and revised several times. Pat Malloy was the original Manager of Flight Test while the selected Flight Test Engineers were Gordon Smith and W. B. Zimmerman. The $38 million USAF contract for the YF-16 included a six-month test program as part of the fly-off against the competing Northrop YF-17.

Phil Oestricher and Neil Anderson were the two assigned experimental test pilots representing General Dynamics/Fort Worth Division. Phil and Neil were long time colleagues from USMC reserve days in FJ-4 and F8U squadrons, as well as six years of company flight testing in all F-111 models. Both combined extensive engineering experience with tactical backgrounds and much more important, an excellent working relationship with the YF-16 design groups. That engineering relationship proved most useful throughout the F-16 program as flight related problems arose and group solutions were developed.

Of all the design innovations in the YF-16 (blended wing/fuselage, large bubble canopy, side stick, and 30 deg tilted seat – to name a few), the fly-by-wire flight control system proved to be the most significant as well as the most challenging. In these pioneering days of flight simulations, the flight control simulator was used extensively to develop rates, gains, damping parameters and multiple other flying quality determinants. George Sanctuary, a former USN pilot and handling qualities expert, shared hundreds of hours in this simulator with the two project pilots.

In late 1972, GD invested considerably to provide a 'cloistered' environment for the YF-16 design and test group. The close working relationship, similar to the Lockheed Skunk Works, yielded focused attention to those problems affecting several design groups and consequent liaison engineering tasks as the prototype hardware was assembled. An interesting sideline is the number of company presidents, vice-presidents and directors who emerged from this cloistered group in later years.

During 1973, the US Air Force leadership directed increased uniformed participation in Flight Testing decisions, piloting, test engineering and data collection, in comparison to previous fighter programs. The rationale for such 'jointness' was ostensibly flight safety and high testing costs; doubtless a more honest rationale was the paucity of test projects at Edwards AFB, and the USAF desire to provide challenging assignments for dozens of under-utilized pilots

Heading photograph: In line with its intended air superiority role, the YF-16 was equipped with Sparrow pylons on the lower fuselage, demonstrated here by the second prototype. LMTAS

The YF-16's 30 deg tilted seat and side control stick are noticeable in this cockpit shot. R L WARD

and engineering test personnel. On the other hand, Edwards AFB is the finest test location in the world, with ranges and test facilities found nowhere else. The appropriate destiny of successful flight testing at Edwards lies in the test management office which ideally would be independent of both contractor and USAF parochialism.

The first YF-16 was transported to Edwards in November of 1973 by C-5A – the Galaxy pilot rightfully proclaiming the journey as the first YF-16 flight. The Edwards AFB Joint Test Team concept included Major Jim Rider as the leader. Jim's deputy was Major Bob Ettinger while the Tactical Air Command was represented by Major M B 'Duke' Johnston and Captain Dean Stickell. Ground tests, instrumentation calibration, test plan co-ordination, contractor personnel relocation and office staffing were some of the preparations for the first YF-16 flight in mid-January, 1974.

One of the preparatory tests before first flight was to be a high-speed taxi test by Phil Oestricher. Fortunately for all involved, the aircraft was fully readied for flight even though taxi speeds were to be targeted for 110 to 120 kt. The intention was for Phil to accelerate to a speed where the YF-16 was light on the oleos, apply a roll input to check response and damping, then decelerate well before the end of the 14,000 ft runway was neared. At the 110 kt indicated air speed point (KIAS), Phil reduced power to a level he felt would check the acceleration. As he applied the roll input, Phil estimated his speed in the 130 KIAS area. The aircraft responded instantly to the roll motion and then Phil's reaction in the opposite direction, quickly building into rapid roll oscillations out of phase with the pilot's stick inputs. Phil was quickly confronted with a wingtip and opposite horizontal tail striking the ground while the aircraft was veering to the left off the side of runway 22. In a brilliant and certainly appropriate snap decision, Phil simultaneously added power to the F100 turbofan and applied back stick force to fly away in the midst of the roll oscillations. Once safely airborne, the roll motions soon damped and Phil flew a race track pattern to a final landing on the same runway 22. This feat of airmanship has been frequently described as

the most significant single flight in the YF-16 program; in any event, it was certainly an impressive beginning.

The YF-16 test program proceeded rapidly through the first half of 1974, with the second aircraft joining the program in May and a first flight by Neil Anderson. The competing Northrop YF-17 fighters began their flights in June and much of the Edwards test engineering, ranges and evaluation pilots' attention was focused on the Northrop aircraft – and a few missions where the two aircraft were flown together. The basic test program for the YF-16 was expanded during the second half of 1974 to include high altitude pressure suit missions, tactical engagements against a myriad of opponent aircraft. It also involved asymmetric stores and foreign stores carriage and delivery, aerial gunnery against several types of towed targets and evaluation flight checkouts for multiple US and foreign pilots.

The Edwards AFB community did a good job of separating the YF-16 and YF-17 teams both physically and in minimizing the test data exchange. The YF-16 contractor team was consistently working 60 to 80 hour weeks and thus had little time to carefully monitor the other group's detailed activities. However, even casually noting the flight durations, the relatively low flight rates and the press releases from Northrop management, we were fairly certain the YF-16 was doing well in the competition. At year-end, 1974, when Air Force Secretary Schlesinger announced the YF-16 as the fly-off winner due to lowest cost and highest performance, all the long hours and General Dynamics investment were vindicated in the minds of company personnel.

The second phase of YF-16 testing began in early 1975 as

Neil Anderson in the cockpit of the second YF-16 that he flew for the first time in May 1974. LMTAS

YF-16 No 1 being prepared for a high-altitude test flight. Pilot Neil Anderson is wearing a standard USAF pressure suit for the supersonic flight above 60,000 ft in August 1974. LMTAS

Inverted over Edwards AFB in August 1974, the YF-16 gets the USAF's previous fighter type, the F-4 Phantom, in its gunsight. LMTAS

the prototype lessons were factored into the design of the production F-16A. Additionally, and just as importantly, the European (Belgium, Denmark, Netherlands and Norway) competition for a new fighter aircraft was entering its final phase. Called 'The arms deal of the Century', due to the 348 aircraft initial quantity, considerable emphasis was placed on maintenance costs, inter-operability with US aircraft, growth for new weapons and especially the industrial co-operation of the aircraft industries in the four countries. The other two competitors were the Saab Viggen and the Dassault Mirage F-1E, both single-engine, single-seat advanced fighter aircraft.

General Dynamics and the USAF developed plans to demonstrate the YF-16 at several USAF and European

fighter bases, with an initial appearance at the Paris Air Show in late May 1975. The three demonstration pilots developed a six-minute air show (as required by Paris Air Show officials) and flew several practice sessions each at Edwards and Fort Worth. During one of these practice sessions, Neil Anderson finished a practice routine at Fort Worth before a large gathering of news media, only to find the right landing gear was wedged in the retracted position and refused to extend. The resolve to save this precious prototype was evident to those in the audience, who watched nervously as 9g manoeuvres and other recommended attempts to dislodge the stuck gear all failed. Some observers recommended flying the aircraft to a safe location and ejecting, since no refueling aircraft were available in the area. The ultimate decision to land the YF-16 in the grass alongside the runway, with all wheels retracted, was made by Neil and Zim Zimmerman, the talented flight test engineer and the other, ground-based half of the contractor test team on every test mission. Neil and Zim agreed (and still agree) the aircraft damage would be lessened in the grass, the impact might be softer and, most importantly, the danger of sparks igniting the remaining fuel vapours might be less.

Since the F100 engine was not turning at impact and full flight control operation was provided by the hydrazine emergency power unit, the landing approach was slow (approximately 110 kt) and touchdown was relatively soft. Later engineering analysis disclosed a subsequent bounce g level above 17g, which resulted in moderate aircraft and engine damage. To its credit, General Dynamics, under flight line chief Bill Plumlee, had the aircraft and engine back in the air within two months. Obviously, the air show sequence was modified to remove the causative manoeuvre.

The 1975 Paris Air Show was a public relations challenge for the three competing companies and their supporting governments. The General Dynamics overall marketing plan was carefully orchestrated by Corporation Chairman David Lewis and F-16 Program Director Lyman Josephs. Each day's

The three pilots on the F-16 European Tour – (left to right) Lt Col Jim Rider, Neil Anderson and Lt Col M B (Duke) Johnston. LMTAS

flight operation was widely reported as the European fighter competition drew toward a climax. As the air show neared its conclusion, the announcement of the F-16 selection was a monumental event for General Dynamics and the USAF participants in this multi-national program.

F-16 participation at air shows around the world has been reported as a major sales aspect of this 4000+ aircraft program. Farnborough, Singapore, Dubai, Ankara, Berlin, Prague, Mildenhall, Gilze-Rijen, Rygge, Copenhagen and Santiago are but a few of the show sites in the years since the F-16's first appearance at Le Bourget.

The European participating countries provided additional F-16 requirements, weapons, test pilots, production facilities and certainly management challenges during the F-16A development years. In addition to the larger wing area, the production aircraft was to incorporate a new Westinghouse

The shape of things to come. The YF-16 making its European debut at the Paris Air Show in June 1975. R L WARD

After the 1975 Paris Air Show, the first YF-16 returned to Fort Worth and was modified as the YF-16 CCV (Control Configured Vehicle). It first flew in this form on 16 March 1976, and the flight test programme lasted until 31 July 1977 after 87 sorties and 125 flying hours. LMTAS

Two F-16A FSDs (nearest the camera) and the two YF-16s (with the prototype modified to CCV configuration), on the flight test line in 1977. LMTAS

The first launch of the GBU-10 on 9 January 1979 from the prototype YF-16 72-01568. LMTAS

radar, more internal fuel, many avionics advances and design challenges in the two seat or 'family model' F-16B.

Certainly the greatest success of the early years was the superb management of a unique five country design/manufacturing program. This executive-level co-operation and unselfish efficiency was accomplished by such leaders as Lyman Josephs, Herb Rogers, USAF Colonel Bill Thurman, and others from the European industry and air forces. Only through their efforts was it possible to fly the first full-scale development F-16A aircraft in 1976, and the first production delivery aircraft in 1978.

In conclusion, the YF-16 experimental flight testing of 1974-1980 yields reflections of state-of-the-art design challenges, successful incorporation of requirements generated to meet worldwide customer needs, a fast paced flying program covering a huge test spectrum, and opportunities for contractor and military testers to excel without claiming overall ownership of program authority. The F-16 is a world class fighter in use around the world: much of the credit for that success goes to the test community of pilots, engineers, managers and technicians.

Development of new technologies and systems for the F-16 continues today as the aircraft is prepared for service in the 21st century. To date, F-16 aircraft have logged more than 40,000 hours of test flying at Edwards AFB alone, not to mention Fort Worth and many other sites around the world.

I am honored to have been a participant in the early years. The F-16 program has proven itself as a model for all fighter aircraft development programs to come.

Neil Anderson has earned a reputation as the consummate aviator through years of test and evaluation flying in more than 250 types of aircraft, including numerous high performance fighters. Since retiring from test flying, amongst many aviation activities, he restores vintage aircraft and has participated in the National Air Races at Reno, NV, in which he holds an Unlimited Class title.

Variations on a theme

The second FSD F-16B, here powered by a GE J79 afterburning turbojet (F-16/79), flying with the first F-16A FSD re-engined with the GE 101 DFE turbofan (F-16/101) and a standard P&W F100-powered F-16A. LMTAS

The majority of the 4,000 or so examples of the Fighting Falcon now in service or on firm order are standard F-16A/B/C/D models. Not surprisingly numerous variations on the basic aircraft have also emerged over the years. Some of these variations, such as the AFTI/F-16, NF-16D and F-16/79, were very much 'one-off' in nature and were only ever intended to undertake test projects. In contrast, some others, like the F-16A ADF, have found wider applications, as they arose from modification programmes intended to satisfy specific missions.

Finally, there were numerous proposals that were considered for possible production but which failed to make the grade for one reason or another. Well in excess of 100 design studies were based on the original F-16A and F-16B models and more have undoubtedly emerged since. Most of these failed to progress beyond the 'paper' stage.

YF-16: The original two prototypes of the General Dynamics Model 401 proposal for the USAF's Lightweight Fighter (LWF) contest were allocated the designation YF-16. The first made a brief and unplanned maiden flight on 20 January 1974, followed by a longer, scheduled, 90-minute sortie on 2 February, while the second made its initial flight on 9 May 1974. After extensive testing during the remainder of 1974, the YF-16 was considered to be superior to the competing Northrop YF-17, with the 13 January 1975 announcement to that effect also revealing that at least 650 examples of the production Air Combat Fighter (ACF) would be obtained for service with the USAF.

Although similar to the resulting production Fighting Falcon, the YF-16s featured some noteworthy differences. It had only seven stores stations, two fewer than on subsequent aircraft. In terms of dimensions the span was identical, but the YF-16's wing area was slightly smaller (280 sq ft compared with 300 sq ft) and it was more than one-foot

The second YF-16 being towed out for public display at Edwards AFB in November 1975. LARRY DAVIS

The first YF-16 was modified as a Control Configured Vehicle and was first flown as such on 16 March 1976. LMTAS

shorter, measuring some 48 ft 5 in (14.75 m) from nose to tail; the height to the fin-tip was also slightly less. Other detail differences centred around the nose radome, which was much more slender and which did not in fact contain a radar antenna; the ventral fins, which were smaller; and the nosewheel door arrangement, which was very different, in that the YF-16s had double doors, whereas all subsequent F-16s had only one, hinged to starboard.

Between them, these differences combined to give the

The YF-16 'CCV Fighter' featured these very large, movable ventral control surfaces. VIA LARRY DAVIS

YF-16 a gross take-off weight of the order of 27,000 lb (9,798 kg). The following F-16 was some 25% heavier and since the YF-16 was fitted with the same Pratt & Whitney F100-PW-200 turbofan engine as the production aircraft, it resulted in performance benefits.

On completion of the LWF competition, further testing ensued, although the second aircraft was damaged in a landing mishap at Carswell AFB, Texas in May 1975. It was repaired within two months, flew for several more years and became the flying test bed for F-16 avionics prior to delivery of the F-16A FSD aircraft with full avionics. Struck off charge on 3 May 1980, it ended up being used for ground-based electronic tests with the Rome Air Development Center at Griffiss AFB, New York, where it is now displayed.

The first YF-16 was modified as a Control Configured Vehicle (CCV) not long after it appeared at the 1975 Paris Air Show. Featuring large movable control surfaces beneath the air intake, the YF-16 CCV flew for the first time in modified form on 16 March 1976. Investigation of unconventional methods of flight control, including decoupled manoeuvring, kept it busy during a test programme that ended abruptly when it was damaged in a hard landing at Edwards AFB.

It next went to Wright-Patterson AFB, Ohio for use in the development of an escape module that was once considered for the F-16. In the event, this proposal failed to reach fruition. The YF-16 prototype was struck off charge on 31 October 1981 and was restored to its original configuration for display as one of the most up-to-date artifacts in the Virginia Air & Space Center at Hampton Roads, VA.

The first FSD F-16A appeared in the same colour scheme as the YF-16 prototypes. It was subsequently re-engined to become the F-16-101. LMTAS

F-16A: The first version to enter operational service, this was eventually superseded in production for the USAF by the improved F-16C during the course of 1985, but is still available for export customers.

The first F-16As to appear were part of the batch of eight Full-Scale Development (FSD) aircraft ordered in January 1975, when the USAF selected the General Dynamics machine to satisfy its future fighter needs. They were, in fact, rather more than just a 'half-way house' between the YF-16 prototypes and the definitive F-16A, for they approximated closely to the definitive production standard by virtue of featuring radar, larger ventral fins and vertical tail surfaces and a redesigned nosewheel door arrangement.

The initial example (75-0745) made its maiden flight on 8 December 1976. Subsequently, it was joined by five more single-seaters, with these being used for company and service trials and playing an important part in smoothing the path to operational service. In later years, most of the FSD F-16As were adapted for further development tasks

including the evaluation of alternative engines and wing configurations as well as radar trials, with projects such as these making them amongst the most modified of all the Fighting Falcons.

Fitted with Westinghouse AN/APG-66 radar and the Pratt

The second F-16A FSD photographed in March 1977 in a multi-role configuration. LMTAS

Big nose – the sixth F-16A FSD modified to carry the APG-65 radar, as on the F/A-18 Hornet. LMTAS

& Whitney F100-PW-200 augmented turbofan engine, the initial production F-16A (78-0001) flew for the first time from Fort Worth on 7 August 1978. By then, further orders had been placed by the European members of the co-production team, but it was the USAF that became the first air arm to accept delivery of the new multi-role fighter on 6 January 1979. The aircraft concerned was assigned to the 388th Tactical Fighter Wing at Hill AFB, Utah which immediately set about achieving combat-ready status. Subsequent highlights included formal adoption of the name Fighting Falcon on 21 July 1980, but an even more important event took place less than three months later, when elements of the 388th TFW declared themselves operationally ready, at the beginning of October 1980.

The 21st production F-16A Block 1 (78-0021), one of the aircraft that first entered service with the 388th TFW at Hill AFB, Utah in 1979.
LARRY DAVIS

Block 10 F-16A 79-0337 was one of the 174th TFW aircraft that was originally equipped to carry the Pave Claw gun pod, although the combination was not a great success. LMTAS

Initial production aircraft (of Block 1 and 5 standard) were later updated to Block 10 configuration, embodying minor internal changes, but retaining the original square-tipped small horizontal tail surfaces. With effect from Block 15, however, this gave way to a larger assembly with cropped tips. This version also incorporated some detail changes to the radar and introduced the *Have Quick* UHF secure voice radio system.

Block 15 was introduced in November 1981. It was the first version of the F-16 Multinational Staged Improvement Program (MSIP). It featured inlet hard points for sensor pods, strengthened wing hard points for greater stores carriage at each station, and structural, wiring and cooling provisions for a more advanced cockpit and avionics when these became available. There were also provisions for the AIM-7 radar missile. In 1987, the F-16A/B Operational Capabilities Upgrade (OCU) program delivered its first retrofit kit to upgrade F-16A/B avionics, which included expanded memory on fire control processors, new software, a radar altimeter and a data transfer unit. Eventually all F-16A/B operators incorporated this low-cost upgrade and it became the production baseline for all F-16A/Bs delivered in

A pair of Block 15 F-16As photographed in 1984. This, the main production version of the F-16A, introduced the Multinational Staged Improvement Program. IAN C JACOBS

Photographed in August 1985, this colourful F-16A Block 10 (aircraft No 187) served as a test aircraft at Hill AFB, hence the tail lettering. LMTAS

F-16A Block 15s from the four European nations – The Netherlands (above), Belgium (right), Norway (middle right) and Denmark (bottom right). PETER R MARCH/ANDREW MARCH

1988 and subsequently. Another upgrade that was standard on FMS F-16A/Bs delivered from this point was the wide-angle HUD, the same as introduced in the Block 25 F-16C/D.

The most recent and on-going modernisation, the so-called Mid-Life Update (MLU) project, will result in more than 300 European F-16A/Bs being reconfigured to Block 20 standard. This will give these older aircraft a cockpit layout that stands comparison with that of the F-16C/D, with the wide-angle HUD and compatibility with Night Vision Goggles. Additional changes include substitution of a modular mission computer in place of the existing three computers, plus fitment of AN/APG-66(V2A) fire control radar, BAe Terprom digital terrain system, new colour displays, GPS and other systems. Furthermore, inlet hardpoints and wiring for FLIR systems will be added to Block 10 aircraft, while both the Netherlands and Norway have signed up for optional helmet mounted display and Hazeltine AN/APX-111 IFF interrogator/transponders.

This programme was at one time intended to involve no fewer than 533 F-16s drawn from the USAF (130), Belgium (110), Denmark (63), The Netherlands (172) and Norway (58). Post-Cold War force reductions and attrition have resulted in cuts in the scale of the project, with the USAF electing to drop out altogether, although it has ordered 223 modular computer retrofit kits for fitment to F-16C Block 50/52 aircraft. Quantities for European nations have also fallen, with Belgium now expected to modify 72, Denmark 61, the Netherlands 136 and Norway 56, although they have options to increase these numbers.

The latest F-16A/Bs in production, the Block 20 Fighting Falcons for Taiwan, which began delivery in mid-1996, also incorporate the MLU avionics package, the F100-PW-220 engine and certain structural components from the F-16C/D

Block 50/52 - such as wings and aft fuselage, for production commonality reasons.

Trials with the first of five prototype conversions (one each from the four European air arms, plus a USAF example) began in the USA in 1995 and in Europe in 1996, although the latter were subject to some delay due to problems experienced with sub-standard wiring harnesses. Nevertheless, depot modifications were scheduled to commence in January 1997 and the upgrade effort is planned to continue until 1999, thus extending the effective service lives of these aircraft until well into the next century.

F-16A ADF: Introduced to replace the F-4 Phantom and F-106 Delta Dart interceptors with dedicated air defence units of the Air National Guard (ANG), the ADF modification program was for 270 aircraft (245 F-16As and 25 F-16Bs);

226 F-16A Block 15 aircraft were actually adapted to this standard and all 25 F-16Bs. Modification work included upgrading the radar to enhance small target detection capability and provide continuous-wave illumination so as to permit it to carry and fire radar-guided AIM-7 Sparrow missiles. In addition, an AIM-120 AMRAAM data link was also incorporated, along with a Bendix/King AN/ARC-200 HF/SSB radio (F-16A only), Teledyne/E-Systems AN/APX-109 advanced IFF and a Grimes night identification light to port. Despite being optimised for air defence tasks, the F-16A/B ADF version remains fully capable of air-to-ground missions.

Work on this version began in autumn 1986, but it was not until February 1989 that the first modified aircraft began to reach the Air National Guard (ANG), which is the only element of the USAF to have employed this version

A quartet of F-16As built as Block 15 aircraft, and here serving with the 347th TFW, all subsequently modified as 'Air Defence Fighters' for the Air National Guard. LMTAS

With the reduction in US forces, this F-16A/ADF, here flying with the Illinois ANG in mid-1994, has been replaced by an F-16C and is now stored at Davis Monthan. JEREMY FLACK/API

operationally. Initial deliveries went to the training unit at Kingsley Field, Oregon, with the first squadron to achieve an operational capability being the 194th Fighter Interceptor Squadron at Fresno, California in the autumn of 1989. Subsequent conversions resulted in several additional Guard squadrons making the transition to the ADF, but the end of the Cold War and diminishing fear of air attack resulted in many squadrons sending their aircraft to storage in the early to mid-1990s, with the replacement type often being later F-16C model Fighting Falcons made available by a run-down in the size of the front-line USAF.

F-16A(R): This designation applies to a batch of about two dozen Fighting Falcons that are in service with No 306 Squadron, Royal Netherlands Air Force. These have been configured to carry the Oude Delft Orpheus reconnaissance pod on the centreline stores station, but they still retain offensive capability and are therefore also tasked with air defence duties.

GF-16A: Approximately 18 examples of the initial production model of the Fighting Falcon have been assigned to instructional duties with the 82nd Training Wing of the Air Education and Training Command (AETC) at Sheppard AFB, Texas. Relegation to these tasks has been accompanied by redesignation as the GF-16A, with the prefix letter indicating they have been permanently grounded.

A Royal Netherlands Air Force F-16A(R) of No 306 Sqn, fitted with the Oude Delft Orpheus reconnaissance pod. DANIEL MARCH

Retired from flying, this GF-16A is one of at least 18 of the type used by the 82nd Training Wing at Sheppard AFB, TX. PETER R MARCH

AFTI/F-16: Originally the sixth and last FSD single-seater, the sole AFTI/F-16 (75-0750), sometimes incorrectly referred to as the NF-16A, ranks amongst the most extensively modified of all Fighting Falcons. It has also been labelled as the AFTI/F-16 DFCS (digital flight control system), AFTI/F-16 AMAS (automated manoeuvre and attack system) and AFTI/F-16 CAS (close air support), according to the modifications made for the respective projects being undertaken by this aircraft. Apart from the specialised equipment detailed below, the AFTI/F-16 was very much a hybrid aircraft. Evidence of this is provided by the fact that although early trials were undertaken with the original horizontal tail, and it has since acquired the 'big tail' that was introduced on the F-16A Block 15, as well as the wing structure of the F-16C Block 25 and F-16C Block 40 avionics.

After playing a full role in the development of the basic fighter aircraft (FDS), it was adapted to serve as the Advanced Fighter Technology Integration (AFTI) testbed and first flew in modified form on 10 July 1982. The most visible evidence of its new role were the movable outward-canted chin canards, ventral surfaces that protruded downward from the air intake adjacent to the nosewheel bay. Additional avionics were also contained in a much enlarged dorsal spine that is similar to, but by no means as large as, those fitted to some Israeli F-16Ds.

A major feature of the AFTI/F-16 was the asynchronous triplex digital flight control system which replaced the analog flight control system in the original F-16. This system featured a backup analog system that was never used in flight other than for test purposes. The various control modes were 'task tailored' providing different control laws for specific flight conditions including take-off and landing, aerial refuelling, air-to-air combat, air-to-ground attack, as well as normal 'up-and-away' flight. A sensor pod was installed in the left wing strake with the initial modification of the aircraft. A forward-looking infrared (FLIR) sensor with an integral laser target designator and tracker were added to the aircraft to accomplish the automated manoeuvring attack phase of the programme.

Initial testing was accomplished under NASA auspices from the Dryden Flight Research Facility at Edwards AFB between July 1982 and July 1983, with the movable ventral fins permitting direct side force to be applied, thus allowing the pilot to rapidly point the nose off-axis. From time to time, this machine has returned to the manufacturer for further modification in order to participate in more advanced phases of testing under the AFTI programme. These have included examination of automatic manoeuvring and attack

The Advanced Fighter Technology Integration (AFTI) F-16 had large outward-canted, movable ventral surfaces, additional electronics in an enlarged dorsal spine and many other modifications. LMTAS

F-16B FSD (75-0751), the first two-seat F-16, being prepared for its first flight on 8 August 1977. LARRY DAVIS

systems; voice-actuated arming of systems; various day/night navigation, target designation and attack options; automatic ground collision avoidance systems and a pilot-activated low-level pilot disorientation recovery system.

It was during the course of these later trials that the CAS (Close Air Support) appellation was acquired. At this time the aircraft had its chin canards removed, trading them for further excrescences in the form of attack sensors. One was installed in each wing root, with two more being fitted directly ahead of the cockpit. All four are associated with the attack mission, with those ahead of the cockpit having the capability to be steered by movement of the pilot's head. Also in 1991 the aircraft was modified with a production quadruplex digital flight control system that had become the standard for later block F-16 aircraft. The production digital flight control system was a direct outgrowth of the pioneering work performed by the AFTI/F-16 in the mid-1980s.

Ensuing trials have included investigation of potential SEAD (suppression of enemy air defences) applications. As part of these, the AFTI/F-16 launched an AGM-88 HARM (High-Speed Anti-Radiation Missile) for the first time in May 1994, when it participated in a demonstration in which sensor data from satellites was received and correlated by a support aircraft (a US Navy EA-6B Prowler) and then passed to an attack aircraft (the AFTI/F-16) by Improved Data Modem.

By February 1997 the AFTI/F-16 had completed 700 sorties and flight testing is currently being conducted on the auto ground collision avoidance system. Auto GCAS is a function of the digital terrain system and there is much interest from the Federal Aviation Administration and civilian airlines, as well as various elements of the military, in this safety device.

An early production F-16B Block 1, subsequently modified to Block 10 and then Block 15 standard, photographed at Selfridge ANGB in August 1991. J R HEILIG

F-16B: The F-16B is fundamentally a two-seat derivative of the F-16A, with identical overall dimensions and retaining full combat capability, albeit at some range penalty, due to lower fuel capacity arising from installation of a second cockpit in tandem. Two aircraft were produced as part of the Full-Scale Development batch, with the first (75-0751) getting airborne for its maiden flight on 8 August 1977. Both subsequently undertook a great variety of test projects, with the second aircraft (75-0752) still being operated by Lockheed Martin today. In general terms the F-16B's development history, production configurations and post-production upgrade projects parallel those for the F-16A.

This early F-16B ADF conversion is still used as a test aircraft at Edwards AFB. LMTAS

F-16B ADF: Approximately two dozen Block 15 F-16Bs were adapted to ADF standard in the late 1980s and early 1990s for service with Air National Guard units tasked with the interception mission. Configuration is broadly similar to the F-16A ADF and is discussed more fully in that entry, although the two-seaters do not feature the bulged area at the base of the fin that is associated with the hydraulic rudder actuation system. Most of these aircraft have now been retired.

F-16B-2: Following a period of use as the F-16/79 test bed, the second FSD two-seater (75-0752) was used for a series of test projects as the F-16B-2. Funded privately by General Dynamics and with the standard Pratt & Whitney F100 engine restored in place of the J79, it was used to evaluate a variety of close air support and night/adverse weather attack systems. One of the most interesting items of equipment tested on the F-16B-2 was the Falcon Eye head-steered FLIR, the sensor for which was located in a small turret directly ahead of the forward cockpit. Others are known to have included the digital TERPROM (Terrain Profile Matching) navigation system; an automated target hand-off system; GEC-Marconi Cat's Eyes night vision goggles, while trials were also conducted with the navigation and targeting equipment systems considered for use in the F-16C and

F-16D models. Martin Marietta's LANTIRN was eventually chosen to satisfy this requirement, fighting off the challenge from the GEC-Marconi Atlantic, but testing was also undertaken of the Lockheed Martin Pathfinder derivative of LANTIRN.

This Edwards-based F-16B has the LANTIRN navigation and targeting pods on development trials in competition with the GEC-Marconi Atlantic system. VIA PETER R FOSTER

The F-16B-2 (75-0752) after conversion from F-16/79 test bed, flying in June 1987 at the start of close air support evaluation and trials. LMTAS

The first F-16Cs nearing completion on the Fort Worth production line early in 1984. LMTAS

GF-16B: This designation refers to about five F-16B two-seaters that have been permanently grounded for instructional duties with the 82nd Training Wing at Sheppard AFB, Texas.

F-16C: This can legitimately claim to be a second-generation version of the Fighting Falcon, as it introduced a number of new features when production was launched in the first half of the 1980s. Benefiting from measures arising out of the second phase of the Multinational Staged Improvement Program (MSIP II), the first version to appear was the Block 25, with the initial F-16C (83-1118) venturing aloft for its maiden flight from Fort Worth in June 1984. Amongst the most important of the changes was a switch to the Westinghouse AN/APG-68 radar, while it was also compatible with the AGM-65D version of the Maverick air-to-surface missile. A new wide-angle HUD was foremost amongst improvements to the cockpit and other changes included increased capacity of electrical and air conditioning systems.

Block 25 F-16Cs were delivered with the F100-PW-200 version of Pratt & Whitney's turbofan, which was common to all F-16s around that time. After problems with this powerplant the USAF hopes to replace the entire inventory of F100-100/200 engines by improved F100-220Es. Priority in the first instance has been given to retrofitting the F-16 Block 25s and by the end of 1996 the task had been completed. The main improvements in the 220/220E over the -200 engine are: the Digital Electronic Engine Control (DEEC). that includes self-diagnostics and fault reporting, an improved life core, gear-driven main full pump and improved anti-ice system. Benefits are in reliability, maintainability, durability, operability, safety, life cycle cost and performance. Although the uninstalled static thrust at sea level is slightly less than for the -200, the actual thrust of delivered engines is higher, and the thrust in most of the envelope is higher (up to 15% in some instances) because of greater efficiency of the DEEC.

All of the Block 25 aircraft went to USAF units. Subsequent similar versions have also been supplied to export customers such as Bahrain, Egypt, Greece, Israel, South Korea and Turkey. As with the USAF's Block 25s they have seen the end of Pratt & Whitney's position as sole engine supplier for the F-16 family. The first such derivative to appear was the Block 30, which made its initial flight in June 1986. This was the first production Fighting Falcon to be equipped with General Electric's F110 engine, it also introduced the so-called common engine bay as a means of production efficiency, to accommodate either the F100-PW-220 or F110-GE-100 turbofan. The two engines were the result of the 'Great Engine War' that allowed the USAF to have a competition between P&W and GE for its F-15/F-16 engine buys. The engines are too different to be interchangeable, so unique production installation kits were designed to accommodate the differences.

As a consequence operating practice (apart from in test organisations and units) has discriminated between versions of the Fighting Falcon fitted with the different engines. In the case of the USAF, this has resulted in specific Fighter Wings operating one or other version (but not both) and it is also worth noting that most of the General Electric-powered aircraft (Block 30, 40 and 50 configurations) have been assigned to overseas commands, while the Pratt & Whitney-powered machines (Block 32, 42 and 52 configurations) are allocated to US-based units. As far as export customers are concerned, they generally – but not invariably – opt for just one type of engine.

The first F-16C (83-1118) on a test flight from Fort Worth in June 1984. LMTAS

F-16C 84-1298, the 1,500th F-16 to be built, was a Block 25E aircraft. LMTAS

F-16C 87-0292, a Block 30 aircraft, the first production variant to be powered by the GE F110 turbofan. LMTAS

Another aspect that misleadingly hinted at standardisation between P&W and GE-powered aircraft was the inaccurately named modular common inlet duct which made its début during production of the Block 30 aircraft. In fact, this is a unique spin-off from adoption of the General Electric engine, which demands a greater air mass flow to the turbine face if it is to operate at its most efficient. Colloquially referred to as the 'Big Mouth', the inlet is larger, though not excessively so and perhaps the most visible recognition feature of the GE-powered aircraft is the shorter and more rounded exhaust nozzle. P&W-powered F-16C/Ds continue to use the original small inlet duct arrangement of the F-16A/B models.

Progressive improvements have been incorporated throughout the production run of the F-16C, with the latest standard being Block 50/52. However, with manufacture continuing at Fort Worth and elsewhere and with further major revisions a possibility, if not exactly a probability, it is quite conceivable that Block 60/62 examples may yet appear in due course, in either new-build or retrofit form – if there is demand from the customer.

Considering past improvements in more detail, changes made during Block 30/32 production include provisions for the AIM-120A AMRAAM, adhesive sealing of centre and aft fuselage fuel tanks, fitment of radar warning receiver antennae on the leading-edge flap on both wings to give better coverage of hostile emitters in the forward hemisphere (these were subsequently retrofitted to many earlier aircraft) and installation of additional chaff/flare dispensers.

Block 40/42 enhancements reflect the increasing capability of this fighter, for these are sometimes referred to as 'Night Falcons' in recognition of the fact that they have a wide-angle holographic HUD, AN/APG-68(V) radar, a fully upgraded fire control computer, a digital flight control system, automatic terrain following and full GPS (Global Positioning System). Structural enhancements included a beefed up wing and fuselage and heavyweight landing gear (48,000 lb maximum take-off gross weight capacity), USAF certified to 42,300 lb as opposed to the 37,500 lb capability

The Block 40 'Night Falcon' featuring LANTIRN, upgraded fire control computer, digital flight control, GPS and other improvements. LMTAS

The improved cockpit of the F-16C block 40/42 features a wide-angle holographic head-up display (HUD). LMTAS

on Block 25/30/32 and late model FMS Block 15 aircraft. The aircraft also had full Group A provisions for advanced internal electronic warfare (EW) systems and carried the all-important Martin Marietta LANTIRN (Low-Altitude Navigation and Targeting, Infra-Red for Night) pod system.

The LANTIRN package is carried on pylons on either side of the air inlet and consists of two pods, that to port being the AN/AAQ-13 navigation unit, which includes a FLIR and terrain-following radar. On the starboard side, there is the AN/AAQ-14 targeting pod, which contains a FLIR sensor as well as a boresighted laser designator. In addition, since the Block 40/42 aircraft and the subsequent Block 50/52 versions have increased empty and operating weights, they introduced bigger wheels, struts, tyres, brakes and bulged undercarriage doors.

Block 50/52 improvements are the latest to have been introduced, with initial deliveries of aircraft to this standard being made in 1991. They are not configured for LANTIRN and therefore do not require the Block 40/42 HUD, instead being fitted with the same unit as the Block 30/32 aircraft, albeit with digital instrumentation. In both cases, new versions of the basic engine are installed, with the Block 50 having General Electric's F110-GE-129 IPE (Increased Performance Engine) while the Block 52 uses Pratt & Whitney's equivalent F100-PW-229 IPE, both of these powerplants having a maximum augmented thrust rating of 29,000 lb (13,154 kg).

The first F-16C Block 50D aircraft (91-0360), the variant that introduced the ASQ-213 HARM Targeting System (HTS) for the SEAD (suppresion of enemy air defence) role. LMTAS

Further work on the radar results in them utilising the AN/APG-68(V5) version which offers enhanced signal processing capability, while they also have AN/ALR-56M Advanced RWRs in lieu of the AN/ALR-69 which was installed in earlier aircraft. These versions do have the Texas Instruments AN/ASQ-213 HARM Targeting System (HTS), which was added with effect from Block 50D/52D. Housed in a pod on the starboard intake station, the HTS gives increased capability in the suppression of enemy air defences (SEAD) role. Block 50D also included an improved data modem, ring laser gyro INS, an upgraded programmable display generator, advanced HARM capability and a major software upgrade. These systems were subsequently retrofitted to earlier USAF Block 50 aircraft.

The SEAD mission, that has been undertaken for some time, saw the F-16 functioning as part of a 'hunter-killer'

team. Under this method of operation, the F-4G *Wild Weasel* version of the ubiquitous Phantom was the 'hunter', being mainly responsible for detecting and classifying hostile radars. Although the F-4G did also possess the ability to attack radar sites, it was more commonplace for the F-16 to work as the 'killer' element, using the Texas Instruments AGM-88 HARM (High-Speed Anti-Radiation Missile) to engage targets.

Age eventually caught up with the *Wild Weasel* Phantom, however, and this proven warhorse was progressively retired during the early to mid-1990s. By then, the advent of HTS enabled suitably configured F-16s to take on increasing responsibility for the SEAD task, by virtue of allowing them to autonomously detect, classify and engage hostile radars.

Export aircraft generally conform to US configurations, but do sometimes embody features that are not standard items on USAF Fighting Falcons. These include the identification light fitted to Greek F-16s; the drag chute housing on aircraft operated by Greece, Israel and Turkey; and the bulged spine on Israeli F-16Ds that accommodates additional avionics. On the other hand USAF F-16s, apart from the ADF, do not currently have an advanced IFF (interrogator/transponder), but this is a popular feature on current FMS F-16s (Block 20/50/52).

That just about completes the picture as far as the present F-16C (and F-16D) models are concerned. However, there are a number of developments planned. Weapons to be integrated on the F-16 by 1999 include AGM-154 JSOW, GBU-31 Joint Direct Attack Munition (JDAM), CBU-103/104/105 WCMD. The next smart weapon to be integrated will be the Joint Air-to-Surface Stand-off Missile. Included in a Block 50+ package (retrofit and potentially production) are: modular mission computer, flat panel colour multifunction displays, Link 16, helmet-mounted

The former 'hunter-killer' team of F-4G Wild Weasel *Phantom and F-16C has now been replaced by HARM Targeting System (HTS) equipped F-16s.* PETER R MARCH

The third production F-16D, used for Digital Flight Control System development flying at Edwards AFB, photographed in June 1986. LMTAS

cueing system, AIM-9X AAM and common missile warning system. Unfortunately the synthetic aperture radar mode and internal FLIR targeting system have been dropped due to USAF budget constraints. Upgrades to LANTIRN and HARM targeting systems are likely.

Although no firm configuration has yet been revealed by Lockheed Martin, for the proposed Block 60/62 development, it might reasonably be expected to include, in addition to the Block 50+ improvements, agile beam radar, internal FLIR targeting system, data fusion, advanced cockpit, enhanced survivability features, advanced automatic features and conformal fuel tanks.

GF-16C: To date, at least seven F-16Cs have been assigned to instructional duties with the 82nd Training Wing at Sheppard AFB, Texas. All are permanently grounded and they include examples of aircraft with the Pratt & Whitney and General Electric engines.

F-16D: In general terms, this version is closely comparable to the F-16C, although it obviously features a second cockpit in tandem. Inclusion of this impinges on fuel capacity, with the result that unrefuelled range and/or endurance characteristics are slightly inferior to those of the single-seater. Flown for the first time from Fort Worth in mid-September 1984, the initial production example of the F-16D Block 25 (83-1174) was fitted with the standard Pratt & Whitney engine. Subsequently, the General Electric F110 was installed on a number of F-16Ds; and this version has also benefited from the progressive changes in weaponry, avionics systems and capability in accordance with production Block variations detailed in the entry for the F-16C.

A late production F-16D Block 50D powered by the GE F110 turbofan and fitted with the HTS, as the F-16C Block 50D aircraft. ANDREW MARCH

NF-16D: As the prefix to its designation suggests, this is another of the surprisingly small number of Fighting Falcons that have been permanently modified for test tasks. However, in this instance, the aircraft concerned (86-0048) is unique in being the only member of the Fighting Falcon family that has replaced a Lockheed T-33A.

Often referred to as VISTA (Variable-Stability In-Flight Simulator Test Aircraft), the NF-16D incorporates special flight control computers that allow it to replicate flying qualities of other aircraft. It is also the only Fighting Falcon with an additional conventional centre-mounted control stick, which can be used when operating in VISTA mode. The more familiar side-stick, as fitted to all other F-16s, is retained and both of these control sticks in the front cockpit can be programmed to replicate the feel of the system

VISTA NF-16D as it was returned to flying in 1993 as the MATV test bed. LMTAS

undergoing test in the VISTA mode. Only the side stick can be used in the F-16 mode.

Modification of the NF-16D was a protracted process and entailed the incorporation of new features such as the Calspan variable-stability flight control system, programmable cockpit controls and displays, flight test data recording systems and additional computers. In its definitive VISTA form, the NF-16D made its maiden flight on 9 April 1992 and was delivered soon afterwards, only to be placed in storage after just five flights due to a shortage of funds.

In 1993, it was returned to flight status in order to serve as the test-bed for the MATV (Multi-Axis Thrust Vectoring) project. At this time, it retained the original General Electric F110-GE-100 engine, but this powerplant was fitted with an AVEN (Axisymmetric Vectoring Exhaust Nozzle) in order that the NF-16D could undertake a series of trials to examine combinations of pitch and yaw thrust vectoring as well as flight at high angles of attack. Computer equipment associated with the VISTA configuration was removed so as to bring the aircraft's weight back to a figure similar to that of a standard F-16D.

As the NF-16D MATV, 86-0048 returned to flying on 2 July 1993 and was involved in a variety of USAF and NASA research programmes throughout the remainder of 1993 and much of 1994. At the end of that interlude, it reverted to VISTA standard, albeit with a standard F110-GE-100 engine without MATV.

In future, the NF-16D is expected to be operated by Calspan, with whom it has replaced a similarly configured NT-33A of early 1950s vintage. In VISTA guise, the Fighting Falcon is expected to be made available to customers who wish to use it as a research tool or to train test pilots and who have the necessary funds to pay for flying time. Early test projects included development work in support of the USAF's F-22 and India's Light Combat Aircraft programmes. The aircraft entered another modification phase in July 1996 to allow it to accept the F100-PW-229 engine with a multi-axis thrust vectoring nozzle, but four months later this was put on hold indefinitely due to funding constraints. This would have allowed full envelope thrust vectoring and post-stall stability investigation.

Another modification is the programmable display system that includes a helmet-mounted sight with sensor cueing capability. It is expected that the VISTA/F-16 will be used to support the US Joint Helmet-Mounted Cueing System and AIM-9X development programmes. The aircraft is expected to return to flight status in mid-1997.

F-16D Recce/'RF-16D': There is in fact no such Fighting Falcon variant as the RF-16D, although one F-16D was tested at Edwards AFB, California with pod-mounted sensors at a time when consideration was being given to using it to replace the long-serving RF-4C Phantom. During these trials, the aircraft concerned (84-1330) carried the legend 'F-16 Recce' on its fin and had the system been adopted operationally it is possible that the RF-16D designation would have been used. Commencing with a first flight on 13 June 1986, various sensors (including infra-red linescan and conventional cameras) were evaluated in the centreline pod, before the test project came to an end. Thoughts of adapting the Fighting Falcon for the reconnaissance role were then put on hold for the best part of a decade, only to emerge again in the mid-1990s, when the retirement of the RF-4C Phantom meant that the USAF had no manned tactical reconnaissance capability.

More recently, some aircraft of the Air National Guard have acquired a reconnaissance capability, with a Lockheed Martin designed package. Known as TARS (Theater Airborne Reconnaissance System), this makes use of the conformal belly pod from the earlier test project, with the sensor system comprising a USAF-supplied KS-87 camera with an electro-optical video back rather than wet film. Lenses of 76-mm, 152-mm and 304-mm focal length may be fitted, with the resulting data stored on an AMPEX Corporation DCRsi-240R digital data recorder, although it is intended to provide a facility whereby this can be transmitted to ground stations via data link. A TERMA Elektronik cockpit control device is also installed.

Flown for the first time on 26 April 1995, the new system was initially tested on an F-16D (85-1572) of the Virginia ANG's 149th Fighter Squadron during the summer of that year, although TARS may also be carried by the single-seat F-16C. Having taken delivery of a total of four TARS pods between May 1995 and February 1996, the 149th FS subsequently deployed five F-16Cs with four pods and a ground exploitation station to Aviano, Italy in order to provide reconnaissance support to elements engaged in Operation *Joint Endeavour*. Operational use of TARS confirmed the value of the system and it is presently planned to buy sufficient pods and associated exploitation equipment to equip four more ANG squadrons. However, since aircraft configured to operate with this system retain full multi-role potential, it is not planned to adopt the RF-16 designation.

Some Danish Fighting Falcons have also been adapted to carry the Per Udsen MRP (Modular Reconnaissance Pod) which can utilise wet film and electro-optical sensors. Once again, though, these retain the basic fighter designation. This system was successfully tested by the Air National Guard Test

The reconnaissance pod fitted to the F-16 Recce was tight on ground clearance. The small slit was for a linescan system. LMTAS

Center at Tucson, Arizona in 1996 and might well be adopted. A similar MRP has been purchased by the Belgian Air Force for its F-16s.

F-16E: This designation was allocated to the F-16 candidate in the USAF's Dual Role Fighter (DRF) competition. The F-16E was a two-seat version using the F-16XL planform. The sole example (F-16XL-1 75-0749) took part in a USAF-sponsored fly-off competition that was intended to culminate in a suitable aircraft to augment the F-111. The contest pitted the General Dynamics contender against the McDonnell Douglas F-15E Strike Eagle and came to an end during 1984. Both contenders displayed excellent capabilities, but the Strike Eagle eventually won out on grounds of a very slight performance advantage and industrial base continuity (keeping the MD/F-15 production line open). Although the F-15E had a lower development cost than the F-16E, the latter had a significant recurring cost advantage over the 400-aircraft programme, which also gave it a total programme cost advantage. After the competition the Air Force pursued the F-16XL in a single-seat version (see F-16F).

F-16ES: Arising from a General Dynamics proposal to develop a two-seat version of the Fighting Falcon with greater range, the F-16ES ('Extended Strategic') is based on the standard F-16C/D model, but is recognisable by virtue of having large conformal fuel tanks situated on the upper surface of the wing/fuselage blend. It emerged in November 1993 in the wake of Israel's selection of the F-15I Eagle and is reportedly still on offer from Lockheed Martin Tactical Aircraft Systems, being one of several Fighting Falcon proposals made to the United Arab Emirates Air Force which has stated a need for up to 80 interdictor aircraft.

Flight testing of the conformal tank arrangement envisaged for the F-16ES was undertaken by the third production F-16C (83-1120). Normally assigned to the Air Force Flight Test Center at Edwards AFB, modification of this aircraft took place during the latter half of 1994 and it made its first flight in F-16ES configuration from Fort Worth on 5 November. Shapes representing the 24 ft (7.32 m) fuel tanks were affixed on each side and a total of 21 test flights was made in order to explore handling qualities and the effect of the tanks on aircraft performance. On any production examples that may result, fuel capacity would be increased by some 1,000 US gallons (3,786 litres), which should confer a combat radius of over 1,000 miles (1,610 km).

Other features were also examined in the flight evaluation project, with the most visible relating to fitment of simulated FLIR sensor turrets above and below the nose section ahead of the cockpit. Initially, only the upper sensor was added, but later flights featured both sensor pods and some sorties were flown with auxiliary fuel tanks, 2,000 lb (907 kg) laser-guided bombs, AIM-120A AMRAAMs and wingtip AIM-9 Sidewinders.

On completion of the short test programme at the beginning of 1995, the tank shapes were removed and the aircraft reverted to normal F-16C configuration, being flown back to rejoin the Air Force Flight Test Center on 23 January 1995.

F-16F: This was to be the designation for a single-seat multi-role F-16 using the F-16XL platform. The complimentary two-seat operational trainer version would have been the F-16G. Neither model designation was ever officially assigned.

F-16N: Had it conformed to standard US military nomenclature practice, this version should properly have been referred to as the F-16E or F, which was the next available designation suffix letter available for a production aircraft. Instead, the suffix letter 'N' was adopted, simply to

A US Navy F-16N in its role as an adversary aircraft. Stripped of much operational equipment, the F-16Ns are the highest-performing of the service variants. LMTAS

This F-16N, the only one to carry US Marine Corps titles while operated from the 'Top Gun' School at Miramar. LARRY DAVIS

indicate assignment to the US Navy. The designation 'F-16N' had previously been used for the 1975 Navy Air Combat Fighter proposal, but was never officially adopted.

Based on the F-16C Block 30 and powered by the General Electric F110 engine, the F-16N was specifically developed to satisfy the Navy's need for a dedicated 'adversary' aircraft and featured a number of notable differences when compared with standard USAF F-16Cs. Since it was only ever intended to equip specialist second-line training units, it was not fully combat-capable. It had the wiring, but the Navy did not buy any alternate mission equipment (AME) such as pylons, racks, launchers and external fuel tanks. The F-16 wing-tip launchers are considered part of the aircraft, and not AME, so AIM-9 Sidewinder acquisition rounds and air combat manoeuvring instrumentation pods were routinely fitted on the wing-tip rails. The AN/ALR-69 radar warning receiver was fitted and the F-16N also featured reflectors on the air intake sides to increase radar cross-section for BVR (beyond visual range) interception exercises.

Some weight and cost savings accrued from adoption of Westinghouse AN/APG-66 radar in place of the 100 lb heavier but more capable AN/APG-68 unit and it was also decided to delete the Vulcan M61A1 rotary cannon with its associated magazine. Between them, these changes resulted in a lighter aircraft with superior performance, thereby making it a more capable dog-fighter for simulated aerial combat. Some strengthening of the airframe was also done, but repeated exposure to high-g manoeuvring flight inevitably resulted in fatigue problems which led to the imposition of at least one grounding order. Coupled with the high cost of maintaining and operating such a small fleet during a period of major force reductions, this raised questions over their long-term future.

A total of 22 F-16Ns was produced for service with four

Navy adversary units, with the variant's maiden flight taking place from Fort Worth on 24 March 1987. In 1994-95, however, the 20 survivors were withdrawn from use, with all but a few preserved aircraft being placed in long-term storage at Davis-Monthan AFB, Arizona.

TF-16N: Basically equivalent to the F-16D Block 30, this two-seat derivative embodied the same changes as those incorporated in the F-16N. Although mainly used by the US Navy to train and validate pilots destined to fly the single-seater with adversary units, the TF-16N also undertook its fair share of duty as an adversary in air combat training exercises. Four aircraft were built, with the first flight taking place on 25 March 1988. Their US Navy service closely paralleled that of the F-16N, with all four being withdrawn and sent to Davis-Monthan for storage in 1994-95.

F-16U: This was a proposed two-seat version featuring extended range and many of the features first evaluated on the F-16XL, that was offered to the United Arab Emirates in the early 1990s. After detailed study, it was subsequently rejected, although other Fighting Falcon configurations are still under consideration by the UAE Air Force which is searching for a new interdictor aircraft to equip first-line combat elements. Had the go-ahead been given, the F-16U would have made use of a delta-wing planform similar to that of the F-16X.

F-16X: In 1993, Lockheed Martin proposed development of a new version of the Fighting Falcon to be known as the F-16X, with a projected service-entry date of 2010. This derivative would be stretched by some 5 ft (1.42 m) and would incorporate a delta-wing planform based on that of the F-22, but featuring increased leading-edge sweep.

Existing engine options would be retained by the F-16X, albeit in developed form, with internal fuel capacity rising by around 80% in order to eliminate the need for external tanks during most combat missions.

Lockheed Martin's proposal also embodies conformal carriage of the Hughes AIM-120 AMRAAM and cost estimates prepared by the manufacturer claim that new-build examples of the F-16X could be purchased for about two-thirds the price of the improved F/A-18E Super Hornet. In the current climate and with the F-22 and Joint Strike Fighter apparently well set to satisfy the USAF's combat requirements for the foreseeable future, there appears to be little likelihood that the F-16X will ever progress beyond the drawing board.

F-16XL: One of the most radical redesigns of the Fighting Falcon yet undertaken, the F-16XL incorporated a 'cranked arrow' wing planform of compound sweep that included composite materials to reduce weight penalties. It was also significantly longer than the standard tactical fighter versions, with a 2 ft 2 in (0.67 m) plug added just aft of the mainwheel well rear bulkhead and a 2 ft 6 in (0.77 m) plug directly ahead of the forward fuel cell. Other alterations involved deletion of the ventral fins; provision of additional hardpoints - raising the number to 17, giving no fewer than 29 stations for the carriage of ordnance. Both aircraft eventually acquired braking parachute fairings to reduce their landing runs.

Funding was initially undertaken by General Dynamics and this proposal emerged at the beginning of the 1980s,

The two F-16XLs over California show their distinctive 'cranked arrow' wing shape. LMTAS

when the company sought authorisation to adapt two of the FSD aircraft. NASA subsequently also joined in, at which time the new version became known as SCAMP (Supersonic Cruise and Manoeuvring Prototype), although it was usually more familiarly referred to as 'The Wedge' or 'Cranked Falcon' in recognition of its distinct shape. Clearance was

During 1994, F-16XL-1 75-0749 was assigned to NASA and repainted as NASA 849 for further aerodynamic flight trials. LMTAS

The intake ramp of the F-16-79 was greatly extended to improve the airflow into the J79 engine. The modified aircraft is seen here carrying an MBB reconnaissance pod on the centreline. LMTAS

forthcoming and the first example (75-0749) was duly modified, making its first flight as the F-16XL from Fort Worth on 15 July 1982. In the meantime, modification of the second aircraft (75-0747) was pressing ahead. This featured a number of notable differences when compared with its predecessor. Most obvious was the fact that it emerged as a two-seater, but it also relied on a different engine, being fitted with a General Electric F110. In this form, it joined the F-16E Combined Test Force at Edwards AFB, California in October 1982.

With the decision not to go ahead with the F-16E proposal, the F-16XL-1 was placed in storage at Fort Worth from 1985 to 1989, emerging from this period of inactivity to join the NASA trials fleet at the Dryden (Edwards) base as NASA 849. With NASA, it has since proved a useful research tool, being employed to investigate such diverse areas as laminar flow, take-off performance and engine noise levels.

Testing of the second aircraft converted to this configuration (F-16XL-2 75-0747) closely paralleled that of the F-16E/F-16XL-1 and it also took part in the DRF fly-off, before a period of storage which ended in 1989 when it too joined NASA for test tasks from Dryden (Edwards), initially as NASA 846 and then as NASA 848. As with the 'F-16E', this aircraft has undertaken numerous research taskings with NASA, including laminar flow investigations and high-lift devices like vortex flaps.

F-16/79: The second FSD F-16B two-seater (75-0752) served as the prototype of the F-16/79 derivative and emerged in response to President Jimmy Carter's February 1977 arms policy revision which basically anticipated calling a halt to supplying top-of-the-line US military hardware to America's allies. By then, of course, the four NATO air arms were already preparing to receive the standard F-16A, but it was evident that future customers would not enjoy the same privilege under this new dictat. Since it was anxious to secure further orders, General Dynamics had little option but to consider developing a simpler version of the Fighting Falcon specifically for overseas markets. The F-16/79 was the result, but the outcome was far from ideal, since simplification was only accomplished at the cost of significant penalties in terms of both payload and performance.

Flown for the first time on 29 October 1980, it featured a different powerplant, with the rather less powerful General Electric J79-GE-119 afterburning turbojet installed in place of the F100 turbofan, hence the new designation. Modifications necessary to accommodate the J79 included redesign of the intake splitter plate, which was enlarged in order to provide a smoother flow of air to the engine. In addition, the aft fuselage section was extended by some 18 inches (46 cm) so as to allow the longer J79 to fit and it was also necessary to incorporate a 2,000 lb (907 kg) steel heat shield to protect the airframe structure in the vicinity of the engine bay.

By itself, the extra weight was far from welcome. However, the fact that it was combined with less thrust made the result a far from winning combination. While it might have pleased the occupant of the White House, the F-16/79 did not generate a great deal of enthusiasm on the part of any of the 20 or so air arms that received presentations on this version. As it transpired, President Carter eventually relaxed this policy before leaving office and his successor, Ronald Reagan, had no qualms at all about making the standard versions available, following his election in 1980.

Despite that, the F-16/79 remained on offer until well into the 1980s, but the only customer that appears to have been tempted to sign up was Singapore, which very quickly amended its order and eventually received F-16A/B models.

F-16/101: The F-16/101 DFE (Derivative Fighter Engine) programme was the second instance of re-engining to occur and once again involved one of the FSD aircraft. This time it was a single-seater that was selected to serve as a test-bed/demonstrator for the General Electric 101 DFE, a derivative of the F101 engine used to power the B-1 bomber. Impetus for the trials project came from the engine manufacturer, which was then going through a lean period, having lost out to Pratt & Whitney with regard to providing engines for the latest generation of US fighters. That process had begun with the F-14 Tomcat and F-15 Eagle and now included the F-16.

Nevertheless, General Electric was pressing ahead with the development of the improved version of the F101 and sought authorisation to demonstrate this on the F-16. This was granted and modification of the aircraft concerned (75-0745) duly took place, with the maiden flight occurring on 19 December 1980. Eventually, about 75 flying hours were accumulated before the trials programme came to an end in July 1981. A couple of minor technical problems emerged but these were soon fixed and subsequent results were highly encouraging, with the GE 101 DFE displaying none of the teething troubles that were then besetting the Pratt & Whitney engine.

Unfortunately for General Electric's aspirations, it was decided to continue with the Pratt & Whitney F100 as the engine of choice on production aircraft for the immediate future. Nevertheless, the idea of finding an alternative powerplant had taken root and this eventually culminated in adoption of the General Electric F110-GE-100 with effect from the mid-1980s. However, rather than simply give General Electric a monopoly, it was decided to continue to install the F100 in some F-16s and to fit the F110 in others with effect from FY 1985 procurement. Arising directly out of the earlier DFE programme, the F110 made its début in the F-16C Block 30, with the initial production example (85-1398) venturing aloft under General Electric power for the first time at Fort Worth on 12 June 1986. A few weeks later, on 30 July, the first F-16D (85-1509) followed suit.

LTV Aerospace Model 1600/1601/1602: Having already beaten the Northrop YF-17 in the contest to provide the USAF with a new fighter, those associated with the F-16

development programme might well have been optimistic about their chances of again emerging victorious when the US Navy turned its attention to selecting a new warplane for service aboard its aircraft carriers. It was to satisfy this requirement that LTV teamed up with General Dynamics in the mid-1970s. Both companies had major production facilities in the Dallas area, so it was a logical pairing, although not in the end a successful one.

The Model 1600 was at the heart of this co-operation and was fundamentally a navalised version of the Block 10 F-16A as used by the Air Force. Structural strengthening figured prominently in the proposal to adapt the basic aircraft for carrier operations and it would also have incorporated other features, such as an arrester hook, a more robust undercarriage and a revised nosewheel including the standard nose-tow link for catapult launch. At least one design study also envisaged fitting body-mounted AIM-7 Sparrow missiles with AIM-9 Sidewinders on the wing-tip rails. Body-mounted AIM-7s were test launched from pylons on the main landing gear doors on YF-16 No 2 in a demonstration programme in 1977.

Alternative engine installations were also considered, with the Model 1600 having the General Electric F404 (as used by the successful F/A-18 Hornet); the Model 1601 having an improved Pratt & Whitney F100; and the Model 1602 relying on the General Electric F101. In each case, however, the fact that it was a single-engined aircraft militated against the LTV submissions and this was an important factor in persuading the Navy eventually to select the Hornet, which was considered far more suitable for 'blue water' operation by virtue of having two engines.

Had it gone ahead, LTV would have been responsible for the Navy version, while GD continued producing F-16s for the Air Force and export customers. In the event, it was announced on 2 May 1975 that the Navy had chosen the F/A-18 proposal put forward by McDonnell Douglas and Northrop, which was itself based on the previously unsuccessful YF-17.

Artists impression of the proposed LTV Model 1600 – a navalised version of the F-16A. LMTAS

The prototype Mitsubishi F-2 on an early test flight. VIA LMTAS

Mitsubishi F-2 (FS-X): Intended to replace the Mitsubishi F-1 tactical support fighter and the T-2 advanced trainer with the Japan Air Self-Defence Force (JASDF), the F-2 is fundamentally similar to the F-16C, from which it was evolved. Many modifications have been made, however, with the most visible changes centring around replacing the existing wing by a new composite wing of greater span, area and chord at root; fitting new horizontal tail surfaces of increased area and revised planform; lengthening the nose and forward fuselage to house more avionics including the Mitsubishi Electric active phased-array radar; adopting a revised cockpit canopy featuring a bow frame; lengthening the aft-fuselage section and providing two additional underwing hardpoints for the carriage of external stores. Plans to fit canard foreplanes were abandoned on grounds of cost.

These and other alterations result in gross take-off weight being significantly greater than the F-16C, at about 48,720 lb (22,100 kg), but few details have emerged regarding performance. In JASDF service, the F-2 is expected to use a number of familiar weapons such as the AIM-7 Sparrow and AIM-9 Sidewinder, but will also be compatible with Mitsubishi ASM-1 and ASM-2 anti-ship attack missiles.

Selection of the F-16 to provide the basis for the FS-X programme occurred in October 1987, with Mitsubishi being chosen as prime contractor for the programme in November 1988. Lockheed Martin is the principal sub-contractor in the US. Government-to-government agreements specify that US industry receives 40% of the development work and approximately 40% of the production work. Initial design contracts for the airframe and the radar were awarded in March 1989 and February 1990 respectively. Subsequently, the General Electric F110-GE-129 Increased Performance Engine was specified in December 1990, with parts of the engine being manufactured under licence by Ishikawajima-Harima Heavy Industries. Adoption of the F-2 designation occurred on 15 December 1995, when the Japanese government approved production.

A total of four prototypes has been completed for the flight test programme, plus fatigue and static test articles. The first pair of flyable airframes emerged as XF-2A single-seaters, with the initial prototype (63-0001) being rolled out on 12 January 1995. This made its maiden flight on 7 October 1995 and was formally delivered to the Japan Defence Agency (JDA) on 22 March 1996. Subsequently, the second XF-2A (63-0002) and both of the XF-2B two-seat prototypes were also flown and delivered to the JDA between April and September 1996, the same month that production began.

If current plans are followed through to completion, the JASDF will eventually receive a total of 83 F-2As and 47 F-2Bs, with initial operational capability (IOC) due to be reached in 2000. However, the extent of the programme has already been slightly curtailed, since the initial desire by the Japan Defense Agency was to purchase 141 aircraft, and it is possible that some further reductions could occur, especially in view of the fact that unit cost for the first batch of aircraft is likely to be around the $120 million mark. Current estimates expect that figure to fall by about a third if the full 130-aircraft programme is completed, but that will still be significantly more than the $26.6 million unit cost for the six standard F-16Cs ordered by the USAF in FY 1996.

In US Service

Based at Aviano, Italy, the 31st FW has played an important part in the peace-keeping effort over the former Yugoslavia. This aircraft, a Block 40 F-16C, is from the 555th Triple Nickel *Fighter Squadron.* PETER R MARCH

Although the F-16 had been flying with various test-dedicated organisations since early 1974, the acid test as far as the USAF was concerned came almost five years later, when the first examples were delivered to an operational unit. As mentioned elsewhere, the unit that was chosen to have the distinction of introducing the new fighter to regular service was the 388th Tactical Fighter Wing (TFW) at Hill AFB, Utah. Preliminary training and preparation paved the way for the start of the transition from the F-4D Phantom and this effectively began on 6 January 1979, when the 16th Tactical Fighter Training Squadron (TFTS) took

At Hill AFB in June 1979, this F-16B was one of the first aircraft to equip the 16th TFTS of the 388th TFW. VIA LARRY DAVIS

delivery of its first aircraft amidst appropriate fanfare. As its title implies, the 16th TFTS was tasked with instructional duties, but subsequent deliveries went to truly front-line squadrons in the form of the 4th, 34th and 421st Tactical Fighter Squadrons (TFSs).

The selection of Hill to accommodate the first operational unit was in fact no coincidence, for this large base was (and still is) also home to the Ogden Air Logistics Center, which has held responsibility for F-16 depot-level maintenance work right from the first day of the Fighting Falcon's operational career. In 1979, of course, the priority was less concerned with maintenance tasks than with bringing the 388th TFW up to speed and this inevitably took time. Nonetheless, a major milestone was passed in October 1980 when the Hill-based unit achieved Initial Operational Capability (IOC).

Five months after the IOC another significant step was successfully negotiated, when 12 aircraft were despatched to Norway, marking the F-16's overseas début in regular service. Six aircraft from the 388th went on to secure top honours in the RAF Tactical Bombing Competition held at RAF Lossiemouth in June 1981. The team scored 98% of all possible points. All sorties were on-target, on-time with 100% bombing effectiveness. In addition the F-16 strike aircraft achieved 88 air combat victories against defending RAF fighters, while suffering only one loss.

By the time of the first overseas deployment, the F-16 had

One of the many F-16Bs that was used by the 56th TTW at MacDill AFB, FL; this one being operated by the 63rd TTS in December 1988. VIA LARRY DAVIS

been given the name Fighting Falcon and two more US-based units of Tactical Air Command (TAC) had also taken delivery of their first examples. The 56th TFW followed the lead set by the 388th TFW within a year, for it accepted its initial F-16 on 22 October 1979. Resident at MacDill AFB on the outskirts of Tampa, the second unit to convert had also previously been equipped with the F-4D Phantom. However, similarities between it and the 388th TFW more or less ended there, for the 56th TFW enjoyed the rather balmier climate of Florida and functioned from the outset as a dedicated training unit, being formally redesignated as the

56th Tactical Training Wing (TTW) in July 1982. Accordingly, it had a greater proportion of F-16B two-seaters distributed amongst its four subordinate squadrons (61st, 62nd, 63rd and 72nd TFS/TFTSs).

While both of the first two units had training obligations to fulfil, that was not the case with the next Wing to convert. Nellis AFB in Nevada was the location involved and, once again, the transition process involved disposing of the F-4D Phantom, with the first F-16 being taken on charge by the 474th TFW on 14 November 1980. Like most of the US-based elements that were eventually to convert to the General Dynamics machine in the early 1980s, the 474th TFW directed the activities of a trio of subordinate squadrons (428th, 429th and 430th TFSs).

Recent force reductions and the establishment of several multi-purpose organisations have resulted in a number of Air Combat Command (ACC) units operating a mix of types and very few active Wings now possess as many as three F-16 squadrons. Then, however, the three-squadron, single-type, Wing was the basic tactical formation at least as far as the USA was concerned, although some overseas-based elements were smaller.

That was most certainly true of the fourth unit to commence transition to the F-16, for the 8th TFW had just two squadrons assigned (35th and 80th TFSs). Stationed at Kunsan AB, South Korea, it was part of the Pacific Air Forces (PACAF) command and had previously been operating the F-4D Phantom. Delivery of the first Fighting Falcon on 15 September 1981 marked the start of overseas deployment of

Initially equipped with F-16As, the 8th TFW at Kunsan AB, South Korea, was operating F-16Cs by 1987. PETER R FOSTER

A pair of the first F-16A Block 15s to be based with the 50th TFW, USAFE at Hahn AB, West Germany in 1982. PETER R MARCH

USAF aircraft on a permanent basis and the 8th TFW was initially given some F-16A/B Block 10 aircraft, although these were soon replaced by the Block 15 'big tail' aircraft.

F-16 Block 15s were also assigned to the second overseas-based unit to transition to the Fighting Falcon. In this case, the United States Air Forces in Europe (USAFE) command was the beneficiary, although the advent of the new fighter probably had marginally less impact, by virtue of the fact that it was already well established in service with four other air arms in Europe. The 50th TFW at Hahn AB, West Germany was the recipient, with transition from the F-4E Phantom effectively being launched in July 1982 when the first F-16 arrived from the USA. Eventually, all three squadrons (10th, 313th and 496th TFSs) were fully equipped with approximately 72 aircraft and a similar number was also assigned to the 401st TFW at Torrejon AB, Spain within a year, for this unit commenced conversion from the F-4D Phantom to the F-16A/B Block 15 in April 1983.

Thereafter, although at least one other TAC unit was to acquire the initial production version of the F-16, attention switched to elements of the Air Force Reserve (AFRes) and the Air National Guard (ANG). Some more modern equipment had been taken on strength and the ANG in

particular had even accepted new aircraft direct from the production line, though this was still very much the exception, rather than the rule.

Accordingly, many units were still 'second-class citizens' in so far as they continued to rely on hardware of 1950s and 1960s vintage, with types like the Republic F-105 Thunderchief, Convair F-106 Delta Dart and McDonnell Douglas F-4 Phantom II forming the backbone of the second-line combat echelons. Today, of course, those three types (and the marginally more modern A-7 Corsair II) have entirely disappeared from the inventory and the Fighting Falcon is the most dominant type with these combat-capable elements. Nevertheless, the build-up that was to bring about this situation was by no means rapid.

At the start of the transition programme, in 1983-84, only one AFRes and one ANG squadron was allocated F-16s and there then followed quite a long hiatus which only ended in 1986. Since then many more units have equipped with the Fighting Falcon, to the extent that it now equips a handful of AFRes squadrons and has seen service with close to 40 squadrons of the ANG. As far as the re-equipment process was concerned, it was greatly accelerated by a couple of factors – one of which was quite normal, while the other was quite extraordinary.

In the first instance, large-scale procurement of the much improved F-16C and F-16D versions of the Fighting Falcon enabled units of the front-line force to progressively re-equip from about the mid-1980s onwards. In the majority of cases, the units concerned upgraded to the newer models, which inevitably resulted in large numbers of the less capable F-16A and F-16B becoming available for reassignment. As had been the case with earlier warplanes, these were passed to selected AFRes and ANG squadrons. Most were allocated to tactical roles as replacements for the long-serving F-105 and F-4, but a substantial quantity was adapted to serve as the F-16A ADF in the air defence role. This was an ANG speciality in which they replaced the elderly F-106 and still more F-4s.

This F-16A was based with the 401st TFW at Torrejon AB, Spain from 1983. PETER R MARCH

The second instance might best be described as one of those happy accidents of history. Wide-scale deployment of the F-16C/D was accomplished against a background of ever more harmonious international relationships. Nowhere was this more evident than in Europe, where the front-line of the Cold War disappeared more or less overnight as democracy took hold amongst those nations that had previously comprised the Warsaw Pact.

The so-called 'peace dividend' was the outcome. The fall-out of this process may not have been welcomed too warmly by many of the military personnel who were declared surplus to requirements as post-Cold War force reductions took hold on each side of the former 'Iron Curtain'. In Europe, USAFE was quite badly affected, shrinking to just a fraction of its former size in little more than three years from 1991. Amongst the units that departed were two full Wings of Fighting Falcons, while TAC/ACC also experienced cuts in the size of its F-16 fleet. It was not all bad news though, for the drawdown in the size of the front-line force materially improved the lot of second-line elements in the USA, with aircraft made surplus as a consequence of unit inactivations cascading down to the benefit of the 'weekend warriors' of both the AFRes and ANG.

AFRes received its first batch of Fighting Falcons in January 1984, when the 419th TFW's 466th TFS converted from the F-105D Thunderchief. In some ways, history can be said to have repeated itself, for the first AFRes unit was stationed at Hill AFB and most of the F-16As that were initially assigned came directly from the co-located 388th TFW, which had been responsible for introducing the type to operational service exactly five years earlier.

An early production F-16A Block 5 that operated with the 466th TFS AFRes at Hill AFB from 1984. VIA LARRY DAVIS

The F-16s allocated to the 419th TFW were drawn from early production Block 1, 5 and 10 aircraft and they remained in use for the best part of a decade, before being replaced by Block 30 F-16Cs in 1994. The fact that the first AFRes F-16 unit shared ramp space with the first regular USAF F-16 unit was not the only aspect in common, for a pilot of the 466th TFS emulated the 388th TFW's feat in winning the *Gunsmoke* competition in 1987 and 1993 by claiming the top individual score in the contest soon after receiving the Fighting Falcon.

No further AFRes unit acquired the Fighting Falcon until June 1987, when the 944th TFG's 302nd TFS was equipped

An F-16C Block 30 that replaced an early model A with the 466th FS/419th FW AFRes in 1994. PETER R FOSTER

The South Carolina ANG (the Swamp Foxes*) was the first ANG unit to receive F-16As in 1983.* GRAHAM FINCH

at Luke AFB, Arizona. In this case, the transition was more dramatic. Firstly, the 302nd had previously flown the CH-3 helicopter and secondly, it was given the very latest model of the Fighting Falcon and claimed the distinction of being the first AFRes or ANG unit to receive brand new aircraft, taking delivery of a batch of F-16C/D Block 32s directly from the factory at Fort Worth.

Other AFRes units followed over the next few years, with the size of the force reaching a peak of eight squadrons in 1992. As it transpired, this level was maintained only briefly, with two units disposing of the F-16 in 1994, when the squadron at Wright-Patterson AFB, Ohio (89th FS) converted to the C-141B while the squadron at Tinker AFB, Oklahoma (465th FS) acquired the KC-135R. Subsequently, the 704th FS at Bergstrom also relinquished it's F-16s, although in a further change in 1997 it received F-16Cs from the 706th FS at New Orleans that has re-equipped with OA-10s.

The Air National Guard got its hands on the Fighting Falcon fully six months before the Air Force Reserve, when South Carolina's 157th TFS (the *Swamp Foxes*) began to convert from the A-7D Corsair II at McEntire ANGB, in July 1983. The model involved was the F-16A Block 10 and these aircraft were still on charge almost eight years later when the South Carolina unit was one of two ANG squadrons to utilise the Fighting Falcon in combat during the Gulf War. Since then, it has re-equipped with late production F-16C Block 52 aircraft.

More than two years were to elapse before the second ANG unit converted, but thereafter the pace of transition accelerated as the front-line force contracted. The second unit was the 182nd TFS of the Texas ANG at Kelly AFB,

which received F-16A Block 15 aircraft as replacements for the long-serving F-4C Phantom in early 1986. Even as the Texans were getting to grips with the complexities of the Fighting Falcon, the ANG took the first steps towards establishing its own training unit in March 1986, when elements of the Arizona ANG's 162nd TFG began to take delivery of the F-16 at Tucson.

Today, like all other ANG Groups, this unit has been given elevated status as a Fighter Wing, but it continues to function in the training role, not only for other ANG units, but also in support of overseas air arms earmarked to utilise the F-16A. In that regard, the complement of aircraft assigned to the 162nd did for a time include a number of Dutch single- and two-seaters, which were operated in

The second ANG squadron to convert to the F-16 was the 182nd TFS Texas ANG at Kelly AFB – one of its 'SA'-coded Block 15 aircraft is shown here in 1992. PETER R MARCH

An F-16A of the Arizona ANG (162nd FW) in October 1988. PETER R FOSTER

USAF markings throughout the first half of the 1990s; these have now left, but the F-16A/B International Military School remains to help satisfy the training requirements of foreign customers. In addition, the 162nd FW parents the unique ANG/AFRes Test Center which is a small but important organisation that is tasked with operational trials work, and which can call upon examples of all the primary Fighting Falcon versions that are presently in ANG and AFRes service.

Attention then switched to the air defence-dedicated units, with Florida's 159th Fighter Interceptor Squadron (FIS) leading the way when it began converting in September 1986. In early 1987, it was followed by Montana's 186th FIS, with a third interceptor unit being added in summer 1987 in the form of the Vermont ANG's 134th FIS. This squadron had in fact started to transition back in April 1986 as a tactical unit, only to be redesignated as an FIS on 1 July 1987. In each case, the initial equipment was the F-16A Block 15 and these aircraft were amongst the number later modified to F-16A ADF standard.

At the beginning of 1997, amongst the 30 ANG squadrons equipped with Fighting Falcons, only three operational Air Defense Squadrons fly the F-16 ADF, plus one training squadron at Kingsley Field, Klamath Falls, OR. There are two general purpose (the word 'tactical' is no longer used) fighter squadrons still flying F-16A/Bs – one flies F-16A Block 15s and the other a mix of Block 15s and ADFs. All of the squadrons flying F-16A/Bs in the US are assigned to the ANG except for those used at the two test centres (Edwards and Eglin). At least four squadrons are due to step up to F-16C/D models within the next year or so and it is likely that the others will follow suit.

The Thunderbirds *have been displaying F-16s since 1982.* PETER R MARCH

No survey of USAF Fighting Falcon operating units would be complete without some mention of the US Air Force Air Demonstration Squadron at Nellis, Nevada. More familiarly known as the *Thunderbirds* it is actually part of the USAF Weapons and Tactics Center's 57th Wing. The team had a long tradition of flying front-line, combat-capable types like the F-84, F-100 and F-105, but this eventually came to an end in 1974, when it re-equipped from the F-4E Phantom to the T-38A Talon.

As it transpired, the Talon was to remain on strength for more than a decade, before a tragic accident brought about a reappraisal in 1982. It was decided to adapt a small number of F-16A Block 15 aircraft as display mounts (plus at least one F-16B for demonstration flights). The first *Thunderbirds* show season using the Fighting Falcon was 1982 and they were retained until November 1991, when they gave way to Pratt & Whitney-engined Block 32 F-16Cs, for the 1992 season, in company with two F-16D Block 32s. F-16s have now served the *Thunderbirds* for over 14 years, the longest of any type in the team's 35-year history. They have given over 1,000 shows before 100 million spectators and have made five overseas tours.

Major reorganisation has taken place within the USAF since the F-16 entered service and the current structure bears only a passing resemblance to that which existed in 1979. For much of the Fighting Falcon's career, aircraft assigned to front-line and training units of the regular Air Force were under the overall control of Tactical Air Command, an organisation which was supplanted by Air Combat Command on 1 June 1992.

The latter agency now reigns supreme as the USAF's principal combat-dedicated echelon and accordingly has command jurisdiction over all of the US-based, first-line Wings that are equipped with the F-16. However, with regard to the training role that was once a prime function of selected TAC units, responsibility for this has passed to the Air Education and Training Command (AETC), which

Retired Arizona ANG F-16Bs 79-430 and 79-422 are both now re-designated as GF-16Bs with the 82nd TW at Sheppard AFB, TX. PETER R MARCH

currently has a large fleet of F-16Cs and F-16Ds under the control of the 56th FW at Luke AFB, Arizona. In addition, AETC has a much smaller number of permanently grounded GF-16A, GF-16B and GF-16C aircraft with the 82nd Training Wing at Sheppard AFB, Texas, where they are used for technical training.

Moving overseas, the major commands of PACAF and USAFE are still in existence, but even here there has been major change. As already mentioned, USAFE has experienced significant reductions as part of the aftermath of an end to the Cold War, to the extent that it bears just a superficial resemblance to the formidable and formidably powerful force that once existed.

The 523rd FS of the 27th FW was operating this F-16C Block 30 from Cannon AFB, NM in October 1996. BOB ARCHER

Both F-16Cs (top) and F-16Ds (above) are operated by the 23rd FS with the 52nd FW, USAFE at Spangdahlem AB, Germany. PETER R MARCH

Furthermore, second-line echelons of the ANG and AFRes have not escaped entirely from the cuts that have been implemented in the past five years or so. In these cases, however, reductions have generally been accomplished by a process of unit shrinkage, rather than by wholesale inactivations; in consequence, while most squadrons still exist, they have fewer aircraft on strength. Indeed, about the only unit that has escaped the reduction process more or less unscathed is the *Thunderbirds* – but one could hardly expect this team to put on a performance full of vim, vigour and impact if its complement of aircraft was cut by up to half, as has been the case elsewhere.

Despite all these cuts, today F-16s comprise 57% of the USAF's 20-wing general purpose fighter force and is likely to remain at this level for at least the next 12-14 years. Fighting Falcons also comprise 70% of the ten squadrons dedicated to home air defence in the US, although this force structure could change slightly as a result of the 1997 Quadrennial Defense Review.

United States Navy

US Navy use of the Fighting Falcon was limited, as the service only obtained a total of 26 aircraft (including four TF-16N two-seaters) and these did not have a front-line role. Despite that, they did make a worthwhile contribution to combat readiness, by virtue of all being assigned to the 'adversary' training units that functioned in support of front-line fighter squadrons of both major fleet organisations.

Delivery of the F-16N commenced in April 1987, when the first example joined VF-126 at NAS Miramar, California and this base was also home to the Navy Fighter Weapons School (NFWS) which acquired its initial aircraft a couple of months later, in June. More familiarly known as 'Top Gun', the NFWS fleet was eventually to number seven F-16Ns (including one adorned with Marines titles) and one TF-16N. Like all the other units, these featured a variety of colour schemes, although the NFWS machines were perhaps more exotically marked than most.

Attention then switched to the Atlantic Fleet, with VF-45 at NAS Key West, Florida taking delivery of the first of ten F-16Ns in October 1987, these subsequently being joined by two TF-16Ns. As it transpired, half of the VF-45 complement passed to VF-43 at NAS Oceana, Virginia on a loan basis with effect from June 1988, although this arrangement came to an end in mid-1989 when these aircraft were officially transferred to the control of VF-43. This action resulted in all three of the VF units standardising on a fleet of five F-16Ns and one TF-16N.

Although it performed admirably in the dissimilar air combat training role, the Fighting Falcon's career in Navy service was short-lived and not entirely free of problems. The most serious of these came in 1991 when all of the aircraft were grounded following the discovery of structural fatigue, which occurred despite the fact that the Navy Fighting Falcons had been strengthened in order to withstand the added stress and strain of repeated high-g manoeuvring. These fatigue problems were eventually eradicated, but the end was in sight as force reductions across the front-line fleet resulted in F-14 Tomcats and F/A-18 Hornets becoming available for assignment to the specialist 'adversary' units.

This sounded the death knell for the F-16N, although its cause was not helped by the fact that the Navy had barely two dozen aircraft on charge, and thus found it hard to justify their continued operation on the grounds of economy. As a result, the four units began to dispose of the Fighting Falcon in the summer of 1994 and by early January 1995 the last aircraft had been sent for storage at Davis-Monthan AFB, Arizona. There, they remain, alongside a very large number of Air Force F-16A/Bs to await their fate.

F-16N 163268 whilst in service with the Navy Fighter Weapons School (NFWS) at NAS Miramar, CA. All the F-16Ns have been retired and are now stored at Davis-Monthan. PETER R FOSTER

The *Fighting* Falcon

A New York ANG F-16A equipped with the centreline-mounted GPU-5/A Pave Claw *30-mm cannon, operating from Al Kharj, Saudi Arabia during the Gulf War.* VIA PRM

When considering the F-16's operational career, the Gulf War of 1991 ranks as the high point, as *Desert Storm* witnessed the type's combat début in USAF service. Despite the fact that the F-16 possesses genuine multi-role capability, and could therefore have contributed to the task of maintaining continuous combat air patrol (CAP) cover throughout the war, this mission was entrusted to dedicated air superiority fighters like the F-15 Eagle. Their exploits quickly resulted in the threat posed by Iraqi interceptors being all but eliminated during the first few days of the aerial onslaught, which in turn meant that the F-16 was employed predominantly on air-to-ground missions throughout the conflict.

In the process, it made a significant contribution in preparing the way for the hugely successful and stunningly swift ground war that culminated in the liberation of Kuwait and also decimated Iraq's future potential to wage effective warfare. With almost 250 examples operating from a handful of bases in the Gulf region and Turkey, the F-16 was by far the most numerous USAF tactical aircraft in the theatre and it is hardly surprising that it won the distinction of being described as both the 'workhorse' and the 'backbone' of the Coalition air effort.

While it may not have claimed any aerial victories in the 1991 confrontation, subsequent developments in the Gulf area have resulted in further shows of strength and US warplanes have been called into action several times. These periodic altercations have given the Fighting Falcon and its American pilots opportunities to display their prowess in aerial combat and those opportunities have certainly not been spurned.

However, when it comes to the art of knocking adversaries from the sky, the Israeli Defence Force/Air Force (IDF/AF) has repeatedly demonstrated that it has few peers, with most informed sources acknowledging that at least 45 aircraft and helicopters have fallen victim to F-16s flown by personnel of the IFF/AF since 1982, although the tally may be even greater than that.

An F-16C from the Torrejon-based 401st TFW is bombed up for another Gulf War mission at Doha, Qatar. VIA LARRY DAVIS

In view of the fact that it has been at loggerheads with one or other of its neighbours for most of its existence, Israel is understandably quite conscious of national security and is not noted for publicising the exploits of its airmen. This is a matter of some regret, for Israel has accumulated a wealth of combat experience with the four basic production versions of the Fighting Falcon – or Netz/Hawk (F-16A/B), Barak/Lightning (F-16C) and Brakeet/Thunderbolt (F-16D) as they are known locally – since the first aircraft entered service in 1980 and there must surely be many interesting tales and exploits to recount.

Unfortunately, few details of any of these exploits have emerged, although it is known that IFF/AF aircraft claimed the distinction of being the very first F-16s to engage in combat. That event occurred less than a year after the first examples were delivered to Israel and just a matter of months after an Initial Operational Capability (IOC) was attained.

Since it involved a surprise attack on a nuclear reactor being built at Osirak near Baghdad in Iraq, the precision strike that took place on 7 June 1981 naturally dominated newspaper headlines around the world. Equally naturally, many of those headlines were hostile to Israel, though it is doubtful if too many individuals in the political hierarchy were bothered by that, for they would have been well used to verbal flak by then.

As for personnel of the IFF/AF, they would most probably have professed themselves well satisfied with the outcome of the mission and more than happy that all eight F-16As returned safely to Israel on conclusion of, what was by all accounts, a stunningly successful attack. Nevertheless, they would have been far more guarded when invited to comment on how the aircraft managed to penetrate so far into Iraq and strike with relative impunity at a target at the heart of what was undoubtedly a formidably defended area.

An Israeli F-16C Barak (Lightning). LMTAS

A formation of Israeli Defence Force/Air Force F-16A/Bs, locally named Netz (Hawk). LMTAS

A dual-marked MiG-23, that had defected from the Syrian Air Force, being escorted by an Israeli F-16B. VIA TIM RIPLEY

Thereafter, opportunities to further test the mettle of the F-16 in combat seemed to come thick and fast, with the newest warplane to join Israel's already potent inventory playing a key role in the support of ground forces operating in Lebanon during 1982. Again, not too many details have emerged, but most sources seem to agree that IFF/AF F-16s accounted for over 40 hostile aircraft and helicopters (mostly of Syrian origin) in a series of aerial battles in the skies above the Bekaa Valley – and some of those victories were scored by aircraft engaged on air-to-ground strike missions, while at least one encounter is reported to have resulted in a single pilot claiming four kills during one sortie.

If information on Israeli combat experience is hard to come by, the same cannot be said of Pakistan, which has been much more forthcoming. Although it has been denied the chance to acquire additional Fighting Falcons, the Pakistan

Air Force (PAF) has nevertheless made good use of the 40 examples (28 F-16As and 12 F-16Bs) that were delivered from 1983 onwards, using some of these to rack up a number of kills during 1986-88. This was a time when Afghan and Soviet military aircraft frequently violated Pakistani airspace in pursuit of Mujahideen rebels, who were themselves not excessively concerned with observing the sanctity of national borders, and who engaged in cross-border forays into Afghanistan from sanctuaries within Pakistan.

The full story of this period has still to emerge and there is also some confusion as to exactly how many aircraft were destroyed by PAF Fighting Falcons. Publicity material originating from Lockheed Martin states that more than 16 intruders were shot down, while another source (based on interviews conducted with some of the pilots involved) speaks of no more than eight such victories. Either way, there's no doubting the fact that the PAF was the second air arm to commit the F-16 to combat – and also the second to score an aerial victory with the Fighting Falcon.

The first kill was claimed in May 1986, by which time the war in neighbouring Afghanistan had been under way for some seven years. The period leading up to the first victory was a time of great frustration for PAF fighter pilots, since the rules of engagement (RoE) that were in force stipulated that only fighter aircraft could be engaged – and then only if the wreckage was certain to fall on Pakistani territory. The upshot of those restrictions was that while many interceptions were attempted with fighters like the F-86 Sabre, Shenyang F-6 and Mirage III, none of them resulted in authorisation being given to open fire.

With regard to the airspace violations, while these were obviously unwelcome, the PAF concluded that they were usually unintentional and stemmed mainly from Soviet and Afghan operating procedures. These almost invariably involved strict control being maintained from the ground, with the result that Russian and Afghan pilots seldom had a clear picture of precisely where they were. Furthermore,

Photographed in 1991, Pakistan AF F-16B Block 15 84607 was originally delivered to 11 Squadron/38 Wing at Sargodha. PETER R FOSTER

since the combat aircraft that were in use lacked mapping radar and since maps were hardly ever carried, the risk of unwittingly straying across the border and violating Pakistani airspace was ever present.

By 1986, the Fighting Falcon was just about fully operational with the PAF and the years of frustration were soon to end. The first PAF unit to equip with the F-16 was No 11 Squadron at Sargodha, which took delivery of its initial aircraft in January 1983. Functioning as both an operational and a training unit, No 11 was not involved in any of the subsequent aerial encounters, but can probably claim some of the credit for the ensuing success by virtue of being responsible for training pilots destined to join the two other units that transitioned to the F-16. No 9 Squadron came first, during 1984, and remained at Sargodha. The programme was completed in 1986 by No 14 Squadron which moved to a new base at Kamra in October of that year.

By that time, the newest PAF warplane had opened its air combat account, with Squadron Leader Hameed Qadri using a mix of gun and missile armament to knock down a couple of Afghan Su-22 *Fitters* near Parachinar on 17 May 1986. At the time, he was serving with No 9 Squadron, although there is some doubt as to whether he did indeed succeed in destroying both. As far as one of his victims is concerned, of that there is no doubt, for the wreckage fell on the Pakistani side of the border and later examination revealed the presence of fragments of an AIM-9L Sidewinder missile. The fate of the other *Fitter* is a bit more contentious, for this succeeded in regaining Afghan airspace despite being badly damaged and on fire after apparently taking hits from the M61 cannon. As a consequence, no wreckage was found to substantiate Qadri's claim.

Just under a year later, on 30 March 1987, Wing Commander Abdul Razzaq added to No 9 Squadron's tally when he destroyed an Antonov An-26 *Curl*. Few details are known of the circumstances and weaponry employed in this encounter. However, there is some reason to believe that the

transport aircraft had been adapted to gather electronic intelligence and was 'ferreting', which does not sit comfortably with the previous comment that border violations were unintentional, nor that the Mujahideen guerillas were the principal targets.

At that point in the saga, No 14 Squadron entered the picture and it was this unit that was responsible for all of the other five confirmed kills, accumulating these over a period of about 18 months in 1987-88. The first of them actually came barely two weeks after No 9's last success and again involved an Su-22 *Fitter*, with Squadron Leader Badar knocking this aircraft down on 16 April 1987.

At least four hostile aircraft were detected by Pakistani radar, although two may have been MiG-23 *Floggers* providing air cover and it was also reported that the unfortunate *Fitter* had been strafing villages before it was destroyed. For Badar and his wingman, the engagement began when they were informed by ground controllers that a border incursion was in progress, with a follow-up message alerting him to the presence of four hostile aircraft at a range of some 22 miles. Badar's initial attempt to establish radar contact with the intruders was unsuccessful, but he soon locked-on to a

Block 15 F-16A 82701, the first Fighting Falcon to enter service with 11 Squadron, Pakistan AF at Sargodha in 1983. LINDSAY PEACOCK

A Pakistan AF F-16A of 14 Squadron on alert at Kamra, equipped with AIM-9L/9P Sidewinders. LINDSAY PEACOCK

contact at a range of 21 miles, only to experience the frustration of seeing it turn away and head for sanctuary across the border.

The frustration was short-lived, for a further message from the ground advised Badar that two other hostile aircraft were still within Pakistani airspace. Badar immediately turned on to a new heading and very quickly established radar contact, accelerating in pursuit and starting to hear the audible tone of a Sidewinder seeker head at a range of about six miles. He was still outside missile launch parameters, so continued to close the gap, before eventually firing an AIM-9L at a range of just over three miles. A few seconds later, when the distance between Badar and his target had fallen to just under three miles, he let fly with another missile. This was probably an AIM-9P, but it was not needed, for the first weapon homed satisfactorily, striking its target, which burst into flames and began spiralling down, even as the surviving intruder turned tail and hastened back to Afghanistan.

The PAF then had a considerable wait before it was able to claim its next victim, although the interval was probably not as quiet as it may appear at first glance, for it is likely that incursions continued to be frequent occurrences. In the context of previous encounters, the late summer and autumn of 1988 was a quite hectic time and it began explosively enough, when Squadron Leader Athar Bokhari got his kill near Miranshah on 4 August.

For Bokhari, it was obviously a day to remember, but it was also unique in another way, in that his victim was a Soviet pilot in an Su-25 *Frogfoot*. On the evening in question, Bokhari was on alert duty and was ordered aloft to investigate four radar contacts. By the time he reached the Miranshah area, all was quiet, so he began patrolling and had been airborne for just under an hour when he was advised by controllers on the ground of the presence of further 'trade'. At this time, radar confirmed that the 'hostiles' were still on the Afghan side of the border, but that a violation was on the cards.

Sure enough, they continued heading east, flying in pairs with about five miles lateral separation between each pair as they pressed on into Pakistan where Bokhari waited. Aware that they were approaching, he moved to forestall the threat, which resulted in them approaching more or less head-on and then used his own radar to lock-on to one of the intruders at a range of about 18 nautical miles. By this time, the range was diminishing rapidly and at seven miles Bokhari became aware that one of his Sidewinders was tracking a target although it was still outside launch parameters.

What happened next must have astonished the Pakistani pilot, for one of the hostile aircraft made a rapid right turn more or less directly in front of him. In so doing, the Soviet airman (a Colonel Alexandrov) surrendered the tactical advantage to Bokhari at a stroke – and Bokhari wasted no time in capitalising on his good fortune, by himself turning left and manoeuvring to slide in behind the Su-25 at a range of about three miles. With launch criteria satisfied, Bokhari fired a single AIM-9L and watched it all the way to the target before breaking away and setting course back to Kamra, enduring a few anxious moments when he saw what he thought were missiles being fired at him. With hindsight, he decided these were almost certainly infra-red decoy flares ejected by other aircraft in the enemy formation.

As for Colonel Alexandrov, he wasted no time in ejecting from his damaged aircraft and was subsequently taken prisoner by the Pakistan Army, which was perhaps just as well, for I doubt that he would have fancied his chances had he fallen into the hands of the Mujahideen. The inevitable interrogation ensued before he was handed back to the Soviet authorities, little the worse for his experience. During questioning, he revealed that his first thought on being hit was that his aircraft had suffered some sort of catastrophic technical problem and it was only later that he accepted he had been shot down. Despite that, he continued to insist that he must have fallen victim to a radar-guided weapon launched from a head-on pass rather than a heat-seeking missile fired from behind.

'Fighting Fourteen's' reputation was enhanced still further during the next couple of months when Flight Lieutenant Khalid Mahmood twice had the good fortune to be in just the right place at just the right time. In the process, he accounted for three more Afghan aircraft, starting off in spectacular fashion by bagging a brace of MiG-23 *Floggers* on 12 September. That was good by any yardstick, although in conversation he revealed that he felt he could have done better – by destroying four more enemy aircraft in the same sortie.

That sortie opened when two F-16s were scrambled from Kamra and told to head towards Nawagai, ground radar having detected the presence of two hostile contacts that seemed certain to cross the border. On reaching the area, Mahmood and his wingman were informed that the contacts had changed course and were now flying a roughly parallel track on the Afghan side of the border. Both of the F-16s then also changed course, taking up an easterly heading, but within a few seconds they were alerted to the presence of three more hostile contacts, so they reversed track and headed towards them.

At this point, Mahmood used his own radar, which revealed the presence of four enemy aircraft and he immediately locked-on to the number four, while accelerating and climbing in company with his wingman. RWR indications betrayed the fact that the hostiles were MiG-23s, Mahmood passing word to ground control just moments before catching sight of the four-strong formation at a distance of about seven miles. While all that was going on, the original pair of MiGs had also reversed track and these were now also heading towards the F-16s.

Although they were rapidly overtaking the leading four, Mahmood felt confident that they would not be able to intervene in time and chose to continue closing with the larger group, which was now looming up fast. At a range of less than two miles, Mahmood fired an AIM-9L, which homed accurately, and then looked around for the first pair in time to see them overshoot the four-ship. Judging that they offered no threat, he again focused his efforts on the larger group, locking-on to the third aircraft at a distance of less than three miles.

Simultaneously, he conceived an ambitious plan that would result in him destroying all six aircraft. Like all the best plans, it was simple in conception, for it basically entailed using his remaining missiles (an AIM-9L and two AIM-9Ps) to knock down the remaining three aircraft of the four-ship, before switching to 'guns' mode to go after the other two. Seconds later, an AIM-9P was homing unerringly towards one of the MiG-23s and Mahmood switched his attention to the next potential victim.

Unfortunately for Mahmood, he never got the chance to put the rest of his plan into action, fate intervening when ground control broke in with a warning call instructing him to break right. It was, in fact, a false alarm, but he had no way of knowing that and therefore responded immediately. By the time he realised that no threat existed, it was too late to regain the advantage, for the remaining four hostile aircraft were straining every sinew as they hurtled back towards Afghanistan and safety. Nonetheless, it had not been a totally wasted day, for Mahmood had destroyed two MiG-23s, with wreckage of both later being found by the Pakistan Army.

Seven weeks later, on 3 November, Khalid Mahmood was again in the thick of it, flying as number two in a two-ship combat air patrol mission near Kohat. Word was passed from ground control that half-a-dozen enemy aircraft were approaching the border from the Afghan side and a later message verified that three of the six had entered Pakistani airspace, whereupon the F-16s moved to intercept.

Both F-16 pilots were able to establish radar contact, with Mahmood managing to lock-on to the number two aircraft as they continued closing. At a range of about eight miles, both the number two and number three turned tail and headed back towards Afghanistan. The leader of the Afghan contingent kept coming for some reason, allowing both F-16 pilots to obtain visual contact at a range of about seven miles and positively identify the intruder as an Su-22 *Fitter* which was flying some 7,000 ft higher.

Seconds later, as the F-16s began climbing, the pilot of the

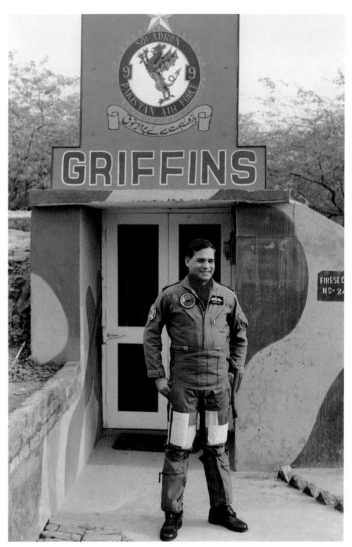

Pakistan Air Force F-16 pilot Flt Lt Khalid Mahmood (top), who shot down three Afghan Air Force aircraft in two encounters in late 1988 while flying with 14 Squadron. One of the F-16As he flew was 84717 (above). LINDSAY PEACOCK/PETER R FOSTER

Fitter obviously realised his predicament and started to turn for home skies, perhaps as a result of a warning from his own controllers. Unfortunately, he had left it too late and Mahmood's leader moved to attack, although his initiative was forestalled when the Afghan pilot turned to face the threat. In so doing, he became vulnerable to attack from Mahmood, who pounced eagerly, getting off an AIM-9L at a range of 2.7 nautical miles in a head-on pass.

Meanwhile, the lead F-16 pilot had been trying to get into

Photographed in 1991, Pakistan AF F-16B Block 15 84607 was originally delivered to 11 Squadron/38 Wing at Sargodha. PETER R FOSTER

position for a gun attack from the classic six-o'clock position, but Mahmood's Sidewinder arrived first, disabling but not destroying the *Fitter*. Aware that he had inflicted damage, Mahmood launched a second AIM-9L to administer the *coup de grace*. This had only been in flight for a moment or two when the enemy pilot ejected, which was timely, for the second missile also scored a direct hit, causing the Su-22 to break in two and plunge earthwards in flames.

That just about concludes the combat saga of the Fighting Falcon in PAF service, although Flight Lieutenant Mahmood did experience some further excitement on the night of 31 January 1989, during a solo scramble mission to investigate a border incursion in the vicinity of Bannu. The intruder turned out to be an Antonov An-24 *Coke* and was therefore not considered a legitimate target, but Mahmood kept shadowing it and was able to report to his controller that it looked as if the transport aircraft was preparing to land.

As he watched, the An-24 began to make an approach to a dried-up river bed, with its crew possibly believing that they were about to land on a properly surfaced runway. It was indeed a bad mistake to make, although for a few moments it looked as if they might get away with it. Then, the Antonov struck a tree, subsequently cartwheeling out of control and being destroyed by a massive explosion.

In the case of Pakistan, opportunities to test the mettle of the F-16 in combat have been fleeting and few. In the case of the USAF, no such opportunities presented themselves during the first decade of front-line service. However, when the chance finally did arrive, it was answered with massive force, for the Fighting Falcon eventually completed approximately 13,500 combat sorties and delivered somewhere in the region of 20,000 tons of ordnance against a variety of targets, in both Kuwait and Iraq, during the Gulf War of 1991.

Iraq's invasion of Kuwait on 2 August 1990 precipitated the crisis, but it may be fair to say that it was the apparent threat of a further attack on Saudi Arabia that provoked the United Nations response which eventually culminated in the creation of the massive allied Coalition. It was the USA which formed the core of that Coalition and it also spearheaded it, deploying its first fighter aircraft and ground forces to the Gulf within a week of Iraqi forces crossing the border into Kuwait.

F-15 Eagles from the appropriately numbered 1st Tactical Fighter Wing led the way, with their arrival in Dhahran, Saudi Arabia generating considerable publicity. US Navy carriers moved to the adjacent waters of the Red Sea and Arabian Gulf and also made headline news, as did further USAF deployments of B-52s and F-117s. In contrast, even though they were despatched to the region within a couple of days of the F-15s, the build-up of the F-16 contingent attracted little in the way of media attention and was seemingly accomplished by stealth. The 17th TFS from Shaw AFB, SC was the first US air-to-ground capable unit deployed, going to Al Dhafra, Sharjah, UAE to form part of the 363rd TFW

363rd TFW F-16C on a mission from its Gulf base at Al Dhafra, United Arab Emirates. VIA TIM RIPLEY

The first USAFE F-16C unit deployed, the Torrejon-based 401st TFW's 614th TFS, operated from Doha, Qatar from August 1990. VIA TIM RIPLEY

Al Dhafra AB in Sharjah alongside the 17th TFW. The other squadron came from USAFE, whose 401st TFW at Torrejon sent the 614th TFS to Doha in Qatar.

No more F-16s arrived until the winter months, when it was becoming apparent that Saddam Hussein was not going to back off. With effect from November, deployment of further squadrons resulted in the force expanding more than threefold in readiness for the onset of combat operations. The next unit to arrive was also from USAFE, with the 50th TFW's 10th TFS moving from Hahn to Al Dhafra in November, to join the 363rd TFW (Provisional).

Thus far, only the F-16C version had been sent to the Gulf, but the next contingent operated the F-16A and was also unusual in being from the Air National Guard (ANG). As the first ANG unit to convert to the Fighting Falcon, South Carolina's 157th TFS was a logical choice and it was joined by New York's 138th TFS, with both squadrons taking up residence at Al Kharj, Saudi Arabia in December 1990. There, they formed the F-16 Division of the 4th TFW (Provisional), which was also equipped with F-15E Strike Eagles.

Fighting Falcon deployment was completed in January, just days before *Desert Shield* evolved into *Desert Storm* and involved a further five squadrons, all of which were equipped with the F-16C. TAC provided three of them, with the 388th TFW at Hill AFB, Utah despatching the 4th TFS

(Provisional). It was on alert within 24 hours of arrival, following a 16-hour, non-stop flight from the USA on 9 August 1990.

During the initial phase of the operation that was known as *Desert Shield*, two other squadrons moved to the Gulf. Unlike the F-15s, they went to neighbouring states and this may well explain the lower levels of publicity that they received. Tactical Air Command (TAC) provided a second squadron from the 363rd TFW, despatching the 33rd TFS to

The 388th TFW from Hill AFB provided two of the three squadrons of F-16Cs based at Al Minhad in Abu Dhabi. VIA LMTAS

Based at Incirlik, Turkey, the 52nd TFW's 23rd TFS operated SEAD missions with its F-16Cs, alongside the F-4G Wild Weasels. JEREMY FLACK/API

and the 421st TFS to form the core of the 388th TFW (Provisional) at Al Minhad AB in Abu Dhabi. The remaining element in this provisional organisation was the 69th TFS which came from the 347th TFW at Moody AFB, Georgia.

Finally, a potent contingent was also assembled in Turkey for *Proven Force*, which was tasked with operations against targets in northern Iraq. This organisation was almost entirely composed of USAFE elements under the overall control of the 7440th Composite Wing (Provisional) at Incirlik AB. Inevitably, the F-16 had a part to play in this force, with the 401st TFW contributing the 612th TFS, while Spangdahlem's 52nd TFW sent the 23rd TFS to undertake the SEAD mission with a mixed fleet of F-4G *Wild Weasels* and F-16Cs.

This, then, was the line-up that resulted in close to 250 examples of the Fighting Falcon being available for action when the air war commenced on 17 January – and they were in the thick of it pretty much from the moment that the shooting started, right up to the ceasefire on 28 February. The mission was predominantly air-to-ground, but this catch-all description actually covers the multitude of possibilities embraced by the 'Battlefield Air Interdiction' nomenclature.

Accordingly, tanks and other armoured fighting vehicles, barrack blocks, SAM sites, troop concentrations, POL (petrol, oil, lubricants) dumps, munitions storage sites, roads, railways, bridges and convoys were just a few of the disparate objectives that were attacked. When engaged in interdiction, the F-16 invariably operated at medium altitude so as to be outside the lethal envelope of smaller calibre anti-aircraft artillery (AAA) pieces. At the start, operations were undertaken independently, but once the air threat had been virtually eliminated, the airborne forward air control (FAC) concept came back into favour, with attacking forces being directed to targets in much the same way as early generations of USAF pilots had been during the Vietnam War.

Offensive ordnance that was employed included 'dumb' general purpose bombs, cluster bomb units and missiles like the Maverick and HARM, while defensive weaponry was generally restricted to the AIM-9L/M Sidewinder, with AN/ALQ-184 or AN/ALQ-131 pod to provide defensive ECM. The integral Vulcan cannon was also used for strafing, it being common to fire a short burst when pulling out of a dive-bombing attack, while the New York ANG F-16As made very limited use of the centreline-mounted GPU-5 30-mm gun pod, although this was stopped when it was apparent that there was a real danger at low level from ground fire and hand-held SAMs. After the first few days of the war, rules for USAF fighters were not to go below 10,000 ft in combat areas unless really necessary. Another unusual 'munition' carried was the M-1209 leaflet dispenser.

Other missions included road and rail reconnaissance and the F-16 was also pressed into service in the so-called 'Scud Hunt' that occupied the attentions of the Allies for some time. In the event, a considerable amount of energy was expended in the search for Iraq's missile launchers.

A Tactical Munitions Dispenser (TMD) being loaded onto a 401st TFW/614th TFS F-16C at Doha. VIA TIM RIPLEY

Unfortunately, this was usually to little avail, since these devices were highly mobile and fairly easily hidden. In conjunction with the size of the area in which they were active, this made them hard to find – and even when a missile was found, it was more often the case that by the time attacking forces arrived on the scene, the Scud had been fired and the launch vehicle had left the area.

When it comes to summing up the part played by the Fighting Falcon during the Gulf War, it is perhaps fair to say that it did an impressive job, but that it could have done an even better one had the circumstances been different. For instance, the medium altitude that was adopted militated against getting the best value from the LANTIRN navigation pod, while the absence of the associated targeting pod automatically denied the chance to use precision laser-

Fully armed F-16A of the 138th TFS New York ANG over the oilfields during Desert Storm *– one of 250 Fighting Falcons involved in the conflict in January 1991.* USAF

Bombs are prepared for loading onto a line of 388th TFW F-16Cs in Abu Dhabi. VIA PRM

The end of the Gulf War was by no means the end of action for USAF F-16s over Iraq, with the 363rd FW involved in several subsequent actions, including attacks on Iraqi SAM sites. VIA LMTAS

guided munitions. Consideration was being given to employing the GBU-12 LGB in conjunction with 'spiking' (laser-target designation) by the F-111F, but hostilities ended before this could happen. Furthermore, the aircraft's bombing system was optimised for use in low-level operations and suffered to some extent from accuracy deficiencies at medium altitude, which made it difficult to engage small targets such as armoured vehicles.

Despite that, it acquitted itself more than satisfactorily and also came through the war reasonably well with only five aircraft lost. In fact, there were only four F-16 combat losses – three to SAMs and one due to a premature bomb; the fifth aircraft had an engine fire. In all cases the pilot was able to successfully eject. Three other aircraft were lost to non-combat related causes during the build-up and the post-conflict period, involving one fatality. The F-16 came out of the war with one of the lowest loss rates amongst Coalition strike aircraft – 0.023% or 0.23 losses per 1,000 sorties.

Although the USAF contingent of F-16s was far and away the largest involved in carrying the war to Iraq, one other member of the coalition force was also equipped with the Fighting Falcon. This was Bahrain, which had taken delivery of eight F-16Cs and four F-16Ds during 1990. Stationed alongside a much larger number of US Marine Corps F/A-18 Hornets and A-6E Intruders at Sheikh Isa Air Base, Bahrain's modest force of F-16s played a fairly minor part in the conflict, but were involved in both defensive and offensive operations. In conjunction with a similar quantity of Bahraini F-5 Tiger IIs, they joined the fray for the first time about a week after the start of *Desert Storm*, but little is known about the precise nature of the missions undertaken.

Since then, not a year has passed without at least some examples of the Fighting Falcon engaging in combat, although the extent of these activities pales into insignificance when compared with the effort expended in *Desert Storm*. Nevertheless, they are all part of the continuing saga and do merit brief mention, especially since the post Gulf War period has been notable in allowing the USAF to score its first kills with the F-16.

That milestone was accomplished above Iraq on 27 December 1992, when F-16D 90-0778 of the 363rd FW's 33rd FS encountered an Iraqi MiG-25 *Foxbat* that had infringed the UN-enforced southern no-fly zone during one of the periodic bouts of sabre-rattling indulged in by Saddam Hussein. As often seems to be the case, the worst consequences of Hussein's actions befall others, with this particular MiG-25 pilot having the misfortune to tangle with an AIM-120 AMRAAM fired by the Fighting Falcon. In fact, this was a double first for the USAF, for not only was it the first confirmed kill to be credited to an F-16, it was also the first kill to be achieved with the AIM-120.

Earlier that same day, an F-15E Strike Eagle of the 4th Wing had also been threatened ineffectually by a *Foxbat* and a further encounter occurred on 2 January 1993, when yet another MiG-25 attempted to intercept a U-2R, only to beat a hasty retreat when some 33rd FW F-15Cs intervened. Then, the transfer of mobile missile sites into the disputed area to the south of the 32nd Parallel prompted yet another UN ultimatum being given to Iraq.

This was not so much a case of 'use it or lose it', but more one of 'move it or lose it'. The deadline set by the UN for withdrawal of the missile sites was 6 January 1993 and, as usual, it was ignored, although it was to be a further week before armed force was employed. Eventually, allied patience ran out and on 13 January a co-ordinated raid was staged against a number of targets in southern Iraq. Eight F-16Cs of the 363rd FW were involved in the mission, which featured a total of just over 80 warplanes drawn from the USAF, US Navy, French Air Force and Royal Air Force. Further strikes followed in the next few days, which were perhaps most significant in witnessing the second kill to be credited to a USAF Fighting Falcon.

This time, the area of interest was over northern Iraq, which also had its own UN-enforced no-fly zone, although this one was patrolled by aircraft operating from Incirlik, Turkey. Responsibility for the kill rested with the 52nd FW's 23rd FS, although there are conflicting reports as to just what the victim was, with some sources describing it as a MiG-23 *Flogger* while others allude to a MiG-29 *Fulcrum*. What was undeniable was that the AIM-120 AMRAAM was again the weapon employed, but this time the Fighting Falcon was a single-seat F-16C (86-0262).

Further attacks on Iraqi SAM sites were made during April, but things quietened down thereafter for a while and the next spot of action faced by the Fighting Falcon came in a very different theatre, albeit in rather similar circumstances. Again, the aircraft involved were patrolling a no-fly zone imposed by the United Nations, but this was in Europe, over war-ravaged Bosnia-Herzegovina. On 28 February 1994, a group of six Serbian-manned Soko J-1 Jastrebs were detected in the vicinity of Banja Luka by an RAF E-3D Sentry AEW1 AWACS which promptly ordered four F-16Cs to investigate.

Arriving in the area, the first pair of Fighting Falcons spotted the intruders and followed the standard *Deny Flight* procedure by broadcasting radio warnings over a period of

An 86th TFW F-16C flying over Kurdistan in May 1991, at the start of the long-running enforcement of the 'no-fly' zones. TIM RIPLEY

about 15 minutes in which they advised the Jastreb formation to withdraw. The warnings were ignored and the leader of one pair of F-16Cs (in aircraft 89-2137) then opened fire, quickly knocking down three of the hostile contacts with an AIM-120 AMRAAM and two heat-seeking AIM-9M Sidewinders. In the process, he became the first USAF pilot to score three confirmed victories in a single sortie since the Korean War, thus emulating the feat achieved by Cunningham and Driscoll of the US Navy in the Vietnam

Aviano-based F-16Cs were involved in shooting down four Serbian Jastrebs on 28 February 1994, three of the 'kills' accounted for by this aircraft (89-2137) with an AMRAAM and two Sidewinder missiles.
TIM RIPLEY

The Royal Netherlands Air Force had its F-16As operating from Villafranca during Operation Deny Flight. JEREMY FLACK/API

War. Close by, in F-16C 89-2009, another unidentified pilot also had an interesting day. He succeeded in destroying a fourth Jastreb with an AIM-9M, but the other two managed to escape after the Dutch fighter controller on the AWACS ordered the F-16s to disengage, as they were approaching the boundary of the 'no-fly' zone.

Further active missions followed, with F-16Cs using 500-lb Mk 82 bombs against Bosnian Serb ground targets on 10 April 1994. However, the exchange was not entirely one-way, as Captain Scott O'Grady of the 31st FW's 555th FS learned to his cost on 2 June 1995. While engaged in patrolling the no-fly zone in the proximity of Banja Luka, his F-16C (89-2032) was struck by an SA-6 *Gainful* SAM and subsequently crashed in flames. Fortunately, O'Grady was able to eject and then spent six days on the run inside Bosnia before he was retrieved from near Mrkonjic Grad by a Marine Corps CH-53E helicopter in a highly successful rescue mission.

Continuing Bosnian Serb provocations such as the seizure of the so-called 'safe areas' of Zepa and Srebrenica in July; the devastating mortar attack on Sarajevo of 28 August 1995 in which almost 40 civilians died; and the increasing threat to personnel of the UN Protection Force (UNPROFOR) finally goaded the allied forces into positive action. *Deliberate Force* was the name given to the operation in which NATO air power was committed to combat between 29 August and 20 September 1995 and this short but bruising campaign was instrumental in bringing about the eventual ceasefire.

Just over a fifth of the 3,500 sorties flown in that three-week period were specifically targeted on Bosnian Serb military forces, with missile defences, command and control centres, ammunition and weapons dumps and associated infrastructure taking a real battering from NATO resources provided by France, Germany, Holland, Italy, Spain, Turkey, the United Kingdom and the USA. Not surprisingly, examples of the F-16 figured prominently in the action from start to finish, with aircraft of the USAF's 31st FW being joined by others from Holland and Turkey in logging over 350 sorties. It undertook bombing attacks with both 'dumb' and 'smart' weapons; it flew combat air patrols; it helped

The Turkish Air Force has also been involved in the UN/NATO operations over Bosnia. An F-16A is here being refuelled by a USAF KC-135 while on a Deliberate Guard *patrol.* JEREMY FLACK/API

suppress enemy air defences with AGM-88 HARMs; it performed reconnaissance sorties; and it accomplished high-speed FAC duties, all with near equal facility.

If any further proof of the F-16's versatility is needed, it must surely have been provided by *Deliberate Force*, for the process of carrying out these disparate tasks once again offered ample confirmation of the Fighting Falcon's formidable multi-role potential.

In terms of its invaluable flexibility, F-16s were (in April 1997) still involved in three UN peacekeeping operations: *Deliberate Guard* over Bosnia (USAF, Netherlands, Belgium, Turkey all flying F-16s out of bases in Italy); *Northern Watch* over northern Iraq (USAF deployed units flying out of Turkey), and *Southern Watch* over southern Iraq (USAF deployed units flying out of Gulf states).

As for the Fighting Falcon's achievements as a fighter, Lockheed Martin claims that the F-16 had, by 1997, a worldwide aerial combat record of 69:0 (kills:losses). F-16s have achieved all six aerial victories by US fighters since the end of the Gulf War. Three of these have been with the new AIM-20 AMRAAM, being the only combat kills with this new weapon.

A Belgian Air Force F-16A taxying out for a Deliberate Guard *mission from Villafranca in December 1996.* TIM RIPLEY

Into *Desert Storm*

F-16 Fighting Falcons provided "the backbone of the Air Force effort", US Defense Secretary Dick Cheney announced after the Gulf War had been brought to a successful conclusion; Gen Colin Powell, Chairman of the Joint Chiefs of Staff said, "the people who designed and made ...M1 tanks and F-16 aircraft...gave our troops the decisive edge". The following three accounts from F-16 pilots underline the impact that the Fighting Falcon had on the conflict.

Lt Col William C Diehl, USAF, *then Commander of the 17th Tactical Fighter Squadron based at Shaw AFB, SC, looks back at the deployment to Al Dhafra, Sharjah, UAE, where his squadron formed part of the 363rd TFW (Provisional).*

On 7 August 1990 we were alerted for deployment to Southwest Asia. We began deploying our people and equipment two days later on C-5 Galaxy and C-141 Starlifter aircraft, with intermediate stops en route to the Persian Gulf. As for deploying the aircraft; 24 of our jets took off at 5 o'clock in the afternoon for a long 16 plus hour non-stop flight with ten air refuelings. The sun went down as we began flying across the Atlantic and came up as we entered the Mediterranean at Gibraltar. We flew south over Egypt and across Saudi Arabia before landing at our destination, just prior to sunset.

Our deployment was unprecedented for a large-scale movement of fighter aircraft. We broke several records; never before had a fighter squadron successfully launched and recovered all its aircraft, without any air spares, on this long a flight. Prior to our deployment the F-16 aircraft had never flown this long a mission. It was truly a challenge for both man and machine. I wish you could have seen our pilots climbing out of their jets after this gruelling flight and helping each other chock and pin the aircraft with a look of exhaustion yet excitement in their eyes. We were the first from the Wing in-country and had to park, bed-down, and secure the jets ourselves. The rest of our people started arriving the next day. Eight days after Saddam's troops invaded Kuwait, our squadron was in place, loaded, and on alert.

Now for the WAR. On the morning of 16 January, we got the word that we were to execute Operation *Desert Storm* early the next morning. It was not at all a surprise, but we all swallowed hard when told that we were actually going to do it. The Wing could not have been better prepared. We had started planning the first day's missions four and a half months earlier. To accomplish the mission planning, we had a top secret room built within our intelligence office, only an absolute limited number of our people were briefed on what was going on, and not a word was mentioned about this

Heading photo: Munitions being loaded onto a Fighting Falcon at the height of Operation Desert Storm *in early 1991.* VIA LARRY DAVIS

operation outside the top secret room. We conducted three different conferences with representatives from all the different units throughout the theatre to co-ordinate the most minute of details concerning the first missions of the operation.

The Wing practised flying these missions on ranges in Saudi Arabia some 12 times. The majority of our pilots were not told they were practising the mechanics of the mission they would soon be called upon to fly for real. We had actually briefed the 'day one' afternoon mission during four separate general officer visits and to the Secretary of the Air Force. Finally, one week before the war, we briefed the Chief of Staff of the Air Force. Following the briefing, he called CINCCENTAF and told him we were the most combat-ready and best prepared Wing in the Command. That was a real confidence builder for us as we prepared for what we would soon have to do. Although we didn't think so at the time, our being over here five months early was a real blessing. It enabled us to do intensive training, studying, and design of theatre specific tactics for large force employment that we would have never been able to do at home.

On 17 January, our morning package took off hours

A 363rd TFW (Provisional) F-16C landing back at Al Dhafra after a mission over Iraq. VIA LMTAS

before sunrise for a night rendezvous with their cell of tankers and their F-15 air-cover. The sun was just starting to light the horizon as the package crossed the Iraqi border. At sunrise, our bombs were smashing their targets, letting Saddam's military know 'the fight was on.' The morning attack was a complete success. I can't describe the almost overwhelming feeling of pride all of us on the ground felt as we watched the formations of aircraft return to base and pitch out overhead for landing. It seemed that the entire base turned out to welcome the morning pilots. Our afternoon fliers didn't have time to hear the combat stories for we had to immediately start our own mission briefing. We took off at mid-afternoon and rendezvoused with our numerous other airborne assets. Our target was located deep in the heart of enemy territory.

The package pushed across the Iraqi border a half hour before sunset. Ten minutes across the border our airborne warning and control (AWACS) aircraft warned us of our first enemy reaction – two MiG-29 *Fulcrums* airborne, turned towards our formation. Within a few minutes our pre-strike sweep of F-15s were on them and blew them out of the sky. As we made our last turn and headed for our target, the on-board radar warning receiver started lighting up and indicated an array of surface-to-air missile systems (SAMS) and anti-aircraft artillery (AAA) covering both front quadrants – they knew we were coming. Although there was a broken cloud layer below, we were able to pick out our individual targets at around ten miles. SA-2s and SA-3s SAMS were launched to the left of our formation. As we rolled in on our target, I informed our trailing flights that the weather was good enough for our primary attack plan, meaning that they wouldn't have to use a weather backup radar attack.

Following release of our weapons, we checked back to see if anything was coming up from the target after us. Tremendous explosions were going off at all our assigned target locations and the sky was filling with 37 mm AAA white puffy airbursts. By the time our last aircraft pulled off target they said you could have gotten out and walked on the layer of flak left by the AAA. Sometimes it's good to be in and out first! Our package reformed and raced out of the enemy territory. We rendezvoused with post-strike tankers and returned home at night for another super welcoming. The mission went exactly as we had planned, briefed, and practised.

The rest of the week was pretty much the same as that first day. During Vietnam, I thought I witnessed some great air battles over Hanoi, but the intensity of our first week exceeded anything I remember.

I completed my 100th combat hour in the F-16 on 12 February 1991. Completing 100 combat-hours in less than a month was quite an accomplishment for me, but even more says a lot for the aircraft and our aircraft maintenance folks. In the last 27 days, I flew 28 missions without a single ground or air abort, or even late takeoff. Twenty of the flights returned with a code one, discrepancy-free aircraft and believe me, the aircraft was really being worked out in the target area.

Laden with bombs and fuel tanks, an F-16C of the 363rd TFW waits to taxi out for another night mission from Al Dhafra. VIA PRM

In this second account we reproduce extracts from the diary of **Capt William Andrews,** *of the 10th Tactical Fighter Squadron, whose Gulf War journal begins on the eve of 1991. Andrews and his fellow members of the 50th Tactical Fighter Wing from Hahn AB, Germany had just arrived in the Middle East to join forces with the 363rd TFW from Shaw AFB, SC.*

31 December 1990
New Year's eve in the Middle East. Could anyone at Hahn have anticipated this a year ago? Definitely not me! But you know something? I definitely wouldn't want to spend New Year's with any other group (besides my wife and family) than a bunch of Americans about 8,000 miles from the United States. Being so far away from home really gives one a sense of purpose. I know we can't hold a candle to the boys from Shaw (who have been here for five months), but we're all glad to be here for the show.

2 January 1991
Got 'The Plan' and my heart soared. The guys that wrote this plan have put together an incredible air campaign. I was worried that when push came to shove, the right people weren't going to be in the places where they'd be needed. I am not nearly as apprehensive as before.

4 January
First flight today. Severe rust. Couldn't handle the radio, but at least stayed in formation.

7 January
I felt real confident in the guys in the flight today. Everybody did a good job.

8 January
I flew a CAS mission about 50 miles from Kuwait this eve. Wow! It was busy. We did well, but it was a real workout. We flew northwest through the Persian Gulf. That felt strange – you could clearly see Iran to the east and Saudi Arabia to the west. The radios were full of American voices. The ships below were part of American fleets. You could hear the US Navy challenging unidentified aircraft and ships on the Guard frequency. An American F-18 intercepted and identified us. After getting to our CAS target, I was damn sure glad I'm not in the Army. Those guys are on the surface of the moon, about 1000 miles from civilisation. I continue to pray for peace and hope for tomorrow, but expect the worst.
(CAS – Close Air Support. Air missions to support ground troops; Guard frequency – an open emergency radio frequency that could be heard over other frequencies in the cockpit).

Captain Bill Andrews, who flew with the 363rd TFW in Desert Storm. VIA LMTAS *CODE ONE*

13 January
No peace hopes. Just a question of when does it start?

15 January
Deadline's gone.

16 January
Tensions are running high – everybody is doing a lot of thinking and are kind of quiet – subdued. How about grim determination?

17 January
Went to bed last night knowing that B-52s were on their way and the Stealth fighters were briefing. It was hard to get much sleep. We heard the first takeoffs from the wing go at about four am. They came low over tent city with afterburners cooking. A lot of guys went outside and cheered. When the news of the attack hit the radio. It sounded like the Stealths, Beagles, Varks, and Tomahawks kicked ass. Our Sabres who went downtown had big eyes when they talked about all the SAM launches all around them, how the RWR scope was filled, and how the SAMs seemed unguided.
(Beagles – F-15E Strike Eagles; Varks – F-111 Aardvarks; Sabres – other pilots from the 10th TFS; Downtown – Baghdad; SAM – Surface-to-Air Missiles; RWR – Radar Warning Receiver).

18 January
Hit Tallil airfield at sunset. I led the last eight ships of a 40-plane strike force. The target area popped up suddenly. I found it on radar and took my best guess where our target –

the wing headquarters – was. Joey and I let our 2000-pounders fly. The RTB was exciting, zooming out on top of the clouds at 40,000 ft in afterburner. Like a drag race, weaving and billowing white contrails behind.
(RTB - Return to Base).

23 January
The package plan was still good from yesterday and our support was eight Eagles, four *Weasels*, and two Ravens. The briefing was short and standard so I had a lot of extra time in the cockpit before start. I thought, this sure looks like war (Mk-84s, chaff, flares, gun, ECM pod), but it doesn't feel like war. It seemed like a normal day at work. The flight went as if on rails. The *Weasels* and EF-111s joined us en route – perfectly. Inbound from the IP, we saw many HARMs streaking inbound. They were great. We got a bit of RWR from a SAM and an anti-aircraft gun. Tail-end Charlie got a steady SAM lock-on and four launches. He jettisoned everything and survived a ninety-second SAM engagement. He's still pulling seat cushion out of his backside! I saw the target from about ten miles out (or more). The roll in was exciting, finally hitting something we could see.
(Weasels – F-4G Wild Weasels *equipped with anti-radar missiles; Ravens – EF-111s; Mk-84 – a 2000-lb conventional bomb; IP – Initial Point, the final navigation point before the target; HARM – High Speed Anti-Radiation Missile; Tail-end Charlie – the last plane onto target, in this case piloted by Capt Kelly Parkinson).*

28 January
Our orders were to press north from the neutral zone towards Tallil, looking for surface defences. Then we were supposed to turn eastward and fly to the Tigris-Euphrates basin and fly down the river to Kuwait. It was an eerie tour. We passed over several Iraqi fighter bases. We looked hard for MiGs in the open or in the sky. However, we didn't see

Return to base – With its 2000lb Mk 84 bombs gone, a 363rd FS F-16C taxies in to dispersal. VIA LMTAS

An F-16 is refuelled on its return from a mission before going to dispersal for re-arming. VIA TIM RIPLEY

anything. Some of the fields had dozens of bomb craters. I also saw some Tab-Vs cracked wide open and scorched black. They looked like split-open clamshells.
(Tab-Vs – Hardened aircraft shelters).

2 February

Flew our four ship into Kuwait. We went in over a cloud deck and then we were between cloud decks. I was sweating the clouds on the way into the target, but they co-operated and we flew out from the undercast about three miles from the target. Joey and I went in first. We hit an MRL battery dug in by the coast. I then directed Ivan (Capt Evan Thomas) and Pete (Capt Pete McCaffrey) onto the HQ area inside a deep berm. They plastered it. All four of Pete's CBUs hit inside the berm. Setter 41 hit some launchers at the site ten minutes later with Mk-82s. They said the headquarters was scorched and the MRL battery was still burning.
(MRL – Multiple Rocket Launcher; Berms – protective barriers of dirt and sand; CBU – cluster bomb; Setter 41 – callsign of subsequent flight over the target area; Mk-82s – 500 lb conventional bombs).

8 February

We flew three missions today, carrying four Mk-84s each on every sortie – quite a manly load. The jet just looks awesome with that bomb load (four 2000 pounders and no drop tanks). It does, however, really make you sweat the gas. We went to southern Iraq and hit some lightly held positions. RTB was to an A-10 base in the middle of nowhere. It looked quite Godforsaken. The ramp, nothing more than a parallel taxiway, was littered with fuel blivets, bombs, Mavericks, and ammo loaders. What a target it would be!
On Sortie No 2, we flew to the Kuwait City-Basra autobahn for road recce. Our goal was to stop trucks. The bombs going off in Kuwait are awesome. You can see two or three areas getting hit at all times. Sortie No 3 was more of the same.
(Mavericks – air-to-surface missiles guided by electro optical or infra-red systems).

13-15 February

Worked as the night chief of mission planning. The night shift stinks, but I was glad not to be shot at. I really don't

relish being shot at whatsoever. But one thing stands out – when I'm down the chute, it doesn't matter what's out there. I'm 100% in the HUD, on the bomb fall line, and in the pipper! I'll worry about the AAA after I feel the clunk.
(Down the chute – in the final bomb run; HUD – Head-Up Display; Pipper – bombsight cue on the HUD; AAA – anti-aircraft artillery); Clunk – sound made in the cockpit by a bomb release).

18 February

A thick black cloud was hanging over Kuwait, as if it were a doomed place. Columns of thick smoke boiled up from many fires. What a ravaged land. It's tough finding a place to bomb that looks like it hasn't been hit yet. God help the Kuwaitis – that place is a ravaged wasteland. We describe where our troops are from blown up things, bomb marks and craters.

22 February

A busy three-sortie day. We flew over the 7th Corps and part of the 18th Airborne Corps – awesome! What a juggernaut poised at the border. Battalion laagers in every shape as far as you could see! The big vehicles were M-lA1 Abrams main battle tanks. We saw one entire armoured division poised: hundreds of thousands of troops waiting to go over the top in the big push.

The Iraqis are trashing Kuwait. The oil wells were torching brightly all over eastern Kuwait. The black pall went up to about 15,000 ft. Visibility was 1000 ft in the smoke. The clouds were billowing black columns, joining a solid black overcast. Flames twinkled brightly 30 miles away.

27 February

Because of recent events, this entry was made on 7th March. I have much to catch up on....

Our mission for the day was a Push CAS *(a type of mission launched with no prescribed target. Once in the air, the air liaison officers on the ground would provide target assignments according to the rapidly changing needs of the ground forces).* We were assigned to the 18th Airborne Corps. We came off the tanker almost 200 miles from the Iraqi border. We came in hanging on the edge of a stall at 28,000 ft with our heavy load of four CBU-87 500lb conventional bombs each, our best anti-armour weapon. We contacted the 18th Corps, but they handed us off to a Forward Air Control aircraft already heading home. We switched back to the Airborne Battlefield Command, Control and Communication (ABCCC) aircraft (in this case an EC-130E) who gave us some co-ordinates to recce.

It was undercast with a few holes. Joey (Lt Joey Booher) and I dropped down through one of them, leaving Pete and Ivan on top. I made about a 270 degree turn and then another 90 degree turn and saw almost nothing on the ground besides some dilapidated vehicles in a truck park and two movers on a north-south road. I had been under the clouds for less than a minute and was considering whether to get

Pete McCaffrey, Joey Booher, Ivan Thomas and Bill Andrews with a 'DS' (Desert Storm) coded F-16 at Al Dhafra. Note the bomb symbols below the cockpit denoting successful missions. VIA LMTAS-CODE ONE

permission from ABCCC to hit the movers when I was hit.

The hit was sudden and unbelievably violent. My plane felt like it was wrenched out of my grasp. The nose pitched very hard down, yawed right, and rolled right all at once. The view was incomprehensible. I couldn't interpret or understand what I was seeing. I recall seeing a lot of lights. The cockpit was out of focus. There was a bright pink and orange glow over the entire canopy.

I knew my machine was totally uncontrollable. It felt like it had been totally blown apart. I made no attempt at the radio: I didn't think it would work, and didn't think I could delay my ejection for an instant. I looked down and grabbed for the handle with both hands. If the G forces were too severe for a safe ejection, it didn't matter. I was literally grabbing for my life. Every fraction of a second counted.

I found the handle, closed my eyes, and pulled with both hands. I felt a tremendous force. According to the flight manual, the canopy blows off and is followed a fraction of a second later by the seat. I don't remember any of these details. I just felt an extreme wind rush and a tremendous suction that pulled me out of the aircraft. I kept my eyes closed. When free of the aircraft, I felt a great flutter around me. My classified materials, authenticators, charts, list of contact points, and line-up cards were being blown off me. (I also lost my glasses and visor.)

A moment later, I felt the chute open. I was in a different world. I opened my eyes and heard the blowing wind and the sounds of battle-fire from numerous machine guns and AAA pieces. I felt motionless, as if permanently suspended above the Iraqi desert. I reached into my G-suit and pulled out my spare pair of glasses and my radio. I hit the emergency beeper and then called, 'Mayday. Mayday. Mayday. This is Mutt 41 on Guard.'

I described my surroundings to my mates – a hardball east-west road, a burning factory, another burning item (which turned out to be my jet). I did a four-line jettison and tried to steer downwind to cover the most distance. But there wasn't much wind. I probably did about two 360s without covering much ground.

About this time, I realised that the Iraqi troops were shooting at me. Some big 23-mm tracer rounds came zipping by from behind. I then heard all kinds of rounds shooting through the air around me. I started to scream on my radio: "They're firing at me in the straps. They're shooting at my canopy!" I kept describing my position. I saw some Iraqi ground troops close by and looked away from them.

The ground came up damn quick after being so far away for so long. It smacked me hard. From the hit, I knew my right leg was broken. I released my chute and tried to move, but no dice. I described my position on the radio from some big explosions to my northeast. A couple of Iraqi soldiers were coming at me and firing their AK-47s. I called over the radio, "They're close. They're attacking me!" Their shots became more accurate as they approached. When they were about 100 feet away from me, I decided I'd better try to see what I could do to get them to stop shooting. So I dropped the radio and raised my hands. They stopped shooting and motioned me to get up. I shook my head that I couldn't, and they closed upon me.

Postscript: *Capt Andrews managed to escape from his captors during the confused Iraqi retreat, despite having a broken leg, but was recaptured after the ground war had ceased and taken to Basra on the following day. On 2 March he was placed on a bus with other POWs and driven to Baghdad, where he was interrogated at length and placed in a small prison cell. He and most of the other POWs in the jail were released to the Red Cross on 5 March and flown to Saudi Arabia the next day.*

Capt Andrews received the Air Force Cross, the Purple Heart and the Prisoner of War Medal, for his mission on 27 February.

Capt John F Hunnell *of the 347th TFW, who flew 33 F-16 combat missions, mostly at night, wrote the following letter describing his first operational sortie in the Gulf.*

I was part of a fairly large strike against some factories in the greater Baghdad area. CNN would later report that 'the damage was so extensive we know that it was B-52s.' I guess I'll take that as a compliment.

When I was some 50 miles out from the target, the first bombs of our strike began to hit. Unfortunately, this gave the Iraqis notice that they should be shooting at us. My radar warning receiver immediately began beeping and squeaking the enemy radars were searching for us. We accelerated to ten miles per minute by selecting afterburner. My fuel consumption doubled. Flak started bursting in the skies ahead, just like in the movies, only silently. There are no 'combat sounds' or explosions in a fighter jet; just the sounds of your radio, radar warning receiver and the low roar of your engine.

We started a weaving ballet of manoeuvres designed to

One of the Moody AFB, GA F-16Cs of the 347th TFW that deployed to Al Minhad, UAE, making a dusk take-off. MICHAEL MONTFORD

make it more difficult to track or shoot us. Suddenly, the intensity picked up. Two missiles were being launched at us. They streaked in front of us to explode in two dirty-brown fireballs – both misses. An F-16 called to report that he was 'engaged defensively with a missile.' Another missile launch was called, then another blared over the radio. Suddenly the words 'Magnum, Magnum' were heard. A friendly aircraft had launched a missile against those sites shooting at us. Magnum, Magnum – such sweet words – I think I will name my next child Magnum.

We continued to scream in upon our target, raining our bombs, dropping chaff, weaving to the left, launching missiles, weaving to the right, dodging flak and missiles. The threat calls started coming so fast I couldn't keep track of all the missile launches.

My turn came to roll in. I pointed my nose to the ground at over 500 knots. God, tell those below on the ground to duck. Suddenly, my aircraft shuddered, sending a shot of adrenaline through me. Then I realised, no, I had not been hit; it was just the bombs leaving the aircraft. 'Oh God, don't let me screw up.' As I climbed off the target, I checked my fuel – I had just enough to make it home – not enough for afterburner. My chaff – I never checked it before in flight – I noticed it was gone, all used up. My two best defences against missiles – chaff and speed – were gone. 'Oh Lord! Grant me a goodly exit!'

As I zoomed back to altitude, I began to hear the radio again – I was concentrating too intently on releasing the bombs. I found my wingman, and we turned toward home.

But before I could get halfway into the turn, my radar warning receiver screamed at me, an ear-splitting sound. The electronic hand of a missile had grabbed me and locked onto my jet. I broke hard left in a six-G turn, selecting afterburner. I thought, 'I don't have enough gas for this. I can't see a missile. I can't find it!'

Over the warning receiver came three loud beeps. A missile was being launched at me. I double-checked – I was in full afterburner – my fuel flow was four times what I could afford. That last turn had cost me 150 knots of air speed. Another six-G pull. Another 150 knots of speed was gone. The warning receiver went silent – the missile was going to miss. I rolled out and accelerated from the virtual standstill I had put myself in, back to a good safe manoeuvring speed and cancelled afterburner.

The leader of this strike called for everyone to check in. I held my breath – which friends would not be coming home? Slowly, surely, everyone counted off – all OK – not even a scratch. We called ahead for tankers and to advise 'the world' (ie, friendly defences) that we would be coming back higher and slower than planned to save on gas. It looked like a World War II movie with all the contrails streaming home - Jimmy Stewart would have loved it.

That's when the fear set in. When it was all happening, I'd been too busy for it. I still shudder remembering this scene. I never want my children to know this much fear. The bravest thing I ever did was to get back in a jet the next day.

We learned our lesson from this mission. We changed our tactics and have never been threatened like that again.

F-16s Around the World

Early success in selling the F-16 to four NATO countries boosted its worldwide sales potential. ANDREW MARCH

Even though it has faced intense rivalry for overseas orders from the F/A-18 Hornet and other modern warplanes, the F-16 began life with a near priceless advantage, that of having been selected for service with four European air arms at an early stage in its development. Buoyed up by that impressive boost to its long-term prospects, the Fighting Falcon has gone on to emulate many of the achievements of its illustrious forerunner, the McDonnell Douglas F-4 Phantom II, which it largely replaced in US Air Force service.

When it comes to considering the relative success of these two types on the export market, the Phantom's record of serving with 11 overseas air arms has already been surpassed by the F-16, although the Fighting Falcon still has a considerable way to go before it can match the 31 nations that have flown versions of the Northrop F-5 family. Nevertheless, the F-16 is now either in service with, or on order for, close to 20 overseas operators and there is every probability that the list will continue to grow in the years to come.

Ironically, amongst the brightest prospects for future sales are several nations that were formerly viewed as being firmly in the 'enemy camp', by virtue of their membership of the Warsaw Pact alliance. Prior to the early 90s, the possibility of selling modern US military hardware to countries like the Czech Republic, Hungary and Poland would have been greeted with derision and suspicion. Today, those countries, and others like them, are being actively courted as future customers.

Prospects are indeed bright and the only real questions concern the funding of these aircraft and their source. Major reductions in defence budgets in the USA and Europe have resulted in many low-houred Fighting Falcons becoming available for disposal on the second-hand marketplace. That can only be good news for potential buyers, although it is perhaps less good for Lockheed Martin, which would obviously prefer any additional operators to acquire newly manufactured aircraft direct from the Fort Worth production line, rather than reconditioned ones from military surplus.

For ease of reference, the various overseas operators of the F-16 are looked at by country in regional area and in alphabetical order. Tabular data, giving details of variant and block number, local serial numbers (where known) and FMS/USAF identities can be found in Appendices B and D.

Belgian Air Force F-16B of the Operational Conversion Squadron lined up for take-off at Beauvechain. PETER R MARCH

EUROPE

BELGIUM

One of the four NATO nations that opted for the F-16 in the much-vaunted 'Sale of the Century', the Force Aerienne Belge/Belgische Luchtmacht (Belgian Air Force) became the first customer outside the USA to take delivery of a production aircraft when it accepted F-16B FB-01 on 29 January 1979. The initial contract called for 96 F-16As and 20 F-16Bs to replace the ageing F-104G Starfighter with Nos 1 and 10 Wings at Beauvechain and Kleine Brogel respectively.

All of the Belgian Fighting Falcons were assembled by the SABCA/SONACA factory at Gosselies. Transition from the F-104 was duly accomplished between 1979 and 1982, with the first unit to achieve initial operational capability being No 349 Squadron at Beauvechain in January 1981. In addition, the Operational Conversion Squadron was also established within No 1 Wing at Beauvechain to undertake transition training – not surprisingly, this was mainly equipped with the F-16B, although some F-16As were also assigned.

In February 1983, it was announced that a follow-on purchase of 40 F-16As and four F-16Bs would permit replacement of the Dassault Mirage V with No 2 Wing at Florennes. Although basically similar to previous examples, F-16As from this batch incorporated extended tail fairings, as first adopted by Norway to contain a braking parachute. However, on the Belgian aircraft this drag chute canister was used to house internal ECM components. It was originally planned to incorporate the *Rapport III* system but it was eventually decided to install *Carapace*. Deliveries took place between March 1987 and 1991, with most of the new aircraft going to No 2 Wing, which began conversion early in 1988.

Thereafter, force distribution remained stable until the spring of 1996, when F-16 squadrons based at Beauvechain were transferred to Nos 2 and 10 Wings, this action resulting in the disbandment of No 1 Wing. In addition, the Force Aerienne Belge/Belgische Luchtmacht has also withdrawn all surviving Block 10 F-16As and a few Block 10 F-16Bs from service. Approximately 45 aircraft were involved and these have been placed in storage at Weelde, although attempts to

An early SABCA/SONACA-built F-16A that entered service with the Belgian Air Force at Beauvechain in 1979. LMTAS

find a purchaser have yet to meet with success and their future is uncertain.

Throughout its service career in Belgium, the Fighting Falcon has been progressively upgraded. The first such effort resulted in early production Block 1 and Block 5 aircraft being brought to Block 10 configuration; later projects involved the installation of tail 'drag chute canisters' with *Carapace* ECM in place of the original equipment on earlier single-seat aircraft. Belgium also committed itself to the ongoing Mid-Life Update (MLU) programme in June 1993, when it announced the intention to submit 48 aircraft to this major modernisation effort. Upgrading is due to be accomplished during the remaining years of this century and Belgium has also taken an option on a further 24 kits, which would be sufficient to permit its entire planned fleet of 72 Fighting Falcons to be modernised.

DENMARK

Also involved in the four-nation NATO deal, Denmark's Kongelige Danske Flyvevaabnet (Royal Danish Air Force) ordered the smallest number at the outset, contracting for 46 F-16As and 12 F-16Bs. These initial aircraft came from the SABCA line at Gosselies and deliveries began in January 1980 with F-16B ET-204. Production of the first Danish batch was completed in 1984, by which time a further order had been placed for eight F-16As and four F-16Bs.

Unlike the first group of aircraft, these were assembled by Fokker at Schiphol, with deliveries getting under way in December 1987. Denmark also intended to procure a third batch of 12 Fighting Falcons, but defence economies precluded this and the only other examples to have been delivered are three ex-USAF machines obtained in July 1994 as attrition replacements.

Royal Danish Air Force F-16A E-600, part of the main production batch built in Belgium. ANDREW MARCH

In Denmark's case, the new fighter was destined to replace two combat types. The first was the F-100 Super Sabre, that equipped two squadrons at Skrydstrup, where the transition programme was launched by Esk 727 at the end of January 1980, with Esk 730 following on 1 January 1981. Attention then switched to Aalborg, which hosted a pair of F-104G Starfighter units. Esk 723 was first to convert to the F-16, starting in January 1983, followed by Esk 726 a year or so later.

Some post-production modification has occurred, including upgrading of initial Block 1 and 5 aircraft to Block 10 standard, while the Esk 726 aircraft were adapted for the reconnaissance role. This task was initially undertaken with *Red Baron* sensor pods previously carried by Drakens, although it has since given way to a slimmer, more aerodynamic pod designed by Per Udsen. Denmark is also a participant in the Mid-Life Update (MLU) project and currently plans to put 61 aircraft through this programme.

Royal Danish Air Force F-16B E-022, built by Fokker at Schipol. PETER R MARCH

The first Greek F-16D Block 30, delivered in November 1988. LMTAS

GREECE

Although Greece made known its desire to add the Fighting Falcon to the Elliniki Aeroporia (Hellenic Air Force) inventory as early as November 1984, it was not until January 1987 that it became the 13th overseas nation to place a firm order. *Peace Xenia* is the code name allocated to Greek purchases of new-build aircraft, of which there have been two to date, with the first contract covering 34 F-16Cs and six F-16Ds. All were to Block 30 configuration with the General Electric F110 engine, but they differ slightly from standard aircraft by virtue of featuring an extended tail fairing containing a braking parachute as well as a nose-mounted searchlight fitted on the starboard side for visual identification of potentially hostile aircraft under cover of darkness.

Delivery began in November 1988 and was completed just under a year later, in October 1989, with all aircraft being assigned to 111 Pterix (Wing) at Nea Ankhialos. Subsequently, a follow-on batch of 32 F-16Cs and eight F-16Ds was ordered and these Block 50 machines are scheduled for delivery to replace the remaining Northrop F-5s during 1997-98, while Greece is also due to take delivery of the Lockheed Martin LANTIRN navigation and targeting pod system which will

Hellenic Air Force F-16C operated by 346 Moira at Nea Ankhialos. PETER R FOSTER

greatly enhance combat effectiveness of the F-16 fleet.

In addition, the Elliniki Aeroporia has reportedly elected to obtain further aircraft from surplus stocks in the USA and elsewhere, although these will be older F-16A and F-16B versions. Up to 80 Fighting Falcons are expected to be acquired in this way, with delivery of the first batch of 40 reportedly set to begin during the course of 1996.

A colourful Royal Netherlands Air Force F-16B, celebrating 316 Squadron's 40th anniversary, accompanied by an F-16A. PETER R FOSTER

THE NETHERLANDS

One of the four European states that gave the Fighting Falcon such an impressive launch platform, the Netherlands originally signed up for 102 aircraft, although subsequent re-orders raised the total number delivered to the Koninklijke Luchtmacht (Royal Netherlands Air Force) between June 1979 and March 1992 to 213.

All of these aircraft originated from the Fokker assembly line at Schiphol, which completed 177 F-16As and 36 F-16Bs for domestic use as replacements for the Lockheed F-104 Starfighter and Canadair (Northrop) NF-5. Introduction to KLu service began at Leeuwarden, where in May 1981 No 322 Squadron became the first of an eventual total of nine squadrons to attain operational status. Today, post-Cold War force reductions have reduced the number of active units to seven, of which one (No 313 Squadron) is dedicated solely to training while another (No 306 Squadron) has a primary reconnaissance mission, with its aircraft being known as F-16A(R)s and are equipped with the Orpheus sensor pod.

Fewer squadrons means that there is a surplus of aircraft and Holland has revealed the intention to reduce the size of its fleet. This process was expected to begin in 1996 with an initial batch of 20 Fighting Falcons being declared surplus, followed by a further 16 after the year 2000. To date however, no potential buyer has been found for the fighters.

As with other operators, Dutch F-16s have been the subject of some updating since they first entered service. One visible sign of this is the extended tailcone which accommodates a braking parachute, while less obvious changes occurred beneath the exterior of Block 15 aircraft courtesy of the Operational Capabilities Upgrade which was launched in 1987. Looking to the future, KLu Fighting Falcons will also figure in the Mid-Life Update (MLU) programme, although the extent of this improvement initiative has been slightly curtailed and will now only involve 156 aircraft rather than the 172 originally envisaged.

NORWAY

The remaining participant in the original NATO purchase, Norway signed up for 60 F-16As and 12 F-16Bs to replace both the F-104 Starfighter and F-5. All of the initial batch of aircraft were produced by Fokker at Schiphol, differing in detail from Dutch aircraft by virtue of being fitted with the extended tail drag chute housing from the outset. Delivery to the Kongelige Norske Luftforsvaret (Royal Norwegian Air Force) began in January 1980 and was completed in June 1984, by which time four squadrons had been equipped, with No 332 at Rygge leading the way.

The second production F-16A and the seventh (of 12) F-16B built by Fokker for the Royal Norwegian Air Force. PETER R MARCH

KNL hopes of acquiring additional aircraft to offset the inevitable attrition losses were partially satisfied during 1987 when two F-16Bs were ordered. These originated from the Fort Worth factory, but a simultaneous request for four F-16As was rejected. With attrition having now accounted for one-fifth of the F-16A fleet, the KNL could well benefit from an infusion of replacement aircraft and may yet seek to obtain some of the second-hand examples now coming on to the market. Norway also has a current study underway to replace its remaining fleet of F-5s. The F-16 has been announced as one of two short-listed candidates, the other being Eurofighter 2000. A final decision is expected in 1999.

In the meantime, unless further accidents make more inroads into the inventory, Norway plans to put a total of 56 aircraft through the Mid-Life Update programme.

PORTUGAL

Portugal became the seventh European operator of the Fighting Falcon in mid-February 1994 when it formally accepted the first examples of the F-16A and F-16B, although it was not until July 1994 that two aircraft of each variant were ferried direct from Fort Worth to Monte Real Air Base for service with Esquadrao 201 of the Forca Aerea Portuguesa (Portuguese Air Force).

Negotiations for the Fighting Falcon purchase predated delivery by more than four years, for it was in June 1990 that Portugal's wish to acquire F-16s was first made known. At that time, the FAP anticipated satisfying its requirement through the acquisition of 20 surplus USAF aircraft.

These were earmarked to replace the A-7P Corsair IIs then in use with Esquadrao 304 at Monte Real in the interception/air defence role, with delivery expected to take place during the course of 1992. As it turned out, this plan changed dramatically, with the most significant alteration concerning the source of aircraft, Portugal eschewing the

second-hand market in favour of new-build machines, fresh from the Fort Worth production line under the *Peace Atlantis* programme. However, a unique feature of this was the fact that second-hand 'used' F100 engines were purchased. They were overhauled and upgraded to the F100-PW-220E configuration prior to installation in the newly-built F-16s.

Portuguese AF F-16A with Esq 201 at Monte Real shows its unique HF fairing on the base of its fin. PETER R FOSTER

The second of three F-16Bs obtained by the Portuguese Air Force and operating with F-16As at Monte Real (Esq 201). PETER R FOSTER

These two F-16Cs were built by General Dynamics and delivered to the Turkish Air Force in 1987. VIA PRM

Turkish Air Force F-16D, used as an operational trainer by 4 Filo at Mürted. ANDREW MARCH

While the source and operating unit may have changed in the intervening period, the quantity of aircraft did not, Portugal eventually obtaining a total of 17 F-16As and three F-16Bs. Since they are primarily tasked with air defence, they embody some of the features incorporated in the specialised Air Defence Variant as used by the US Air National Guard. The most visible of these are the bulged fairing at the base of the fin. Associated with provision of HF radio equipment, this is unique to the F-16A model, while both the F-16A and F-16B are fitted with the nose-mounted identification searchlight forward of the cockpit on the port side.

Further F-16s seem sure to follow, with the USA announcing in June 1996 that it had offered to sell 25 examples to Portugal. Unlike the first batch, these would be second-hand airframes from USAF surplus, with the proposal involving complete refurbishment and re-engining prior to delivery. Portugal's decision is awaited at the time of writing.

TURKEY

Although only the tenth overseas air arm to take delivery of the Fighting Falcon when it accepted its first F-16D in summer 1987, Turkey has more than made up for lost ground in the decade that has passed since then. On current planning, it will eventually possess a fleet surpassed in size only by Israel and the USAF.

Peace Onyx is the programme code name assigned to Turkish procurement, with selection of the F-16 in September 1983 being partly motivated by the aircraft's capability and partly by the wish for TAI (TUSAS Aerospace Industry) to undertake licence production at Murted. Between them, these two factors resulted in an order being placed for 160 aircraft for service with the Turk Hava Kuvvetleri (Turkish Air Force), although this has since been increased to 240 and may yet rise as high as 320.

The first two F-16Cs and six F-16Ds originated from the parent company at Fort Worth, but all aircraft built since then have been produced 'in country' by TAI, which is currently set to turn out some 202 F-16Cs and 30 F-16Ds of various Block numbers for the Turkish Air Force and which

has also secured contracts covering the assembly of 47 F-16C/Ds for Egypt.

Entry into TAF service began in 1987, with the first unit to convert being 141 Filo (Squadron) at Akinci (formerly Murted). Since then, the F-16 has been delivered to combat units located at Balikesir, Bandirma and Diyarbakir. In the process, it has replaced a substantial number of F-5s and F-104s and appears likely to oust the trusty F-4E Phantom in due course. Once that day arrives, Turkey's Air Force will at last be able to rely on just a single combat type after years of having to make do with a miscellaneous collection of largely obsolescent warplanes obtained from a variety of sources.

THE MIDDLE EAST

BAHRAIN

This small but strategically important Gulf state became the 15th nation to acquire the Fighting Falcon when the Bahrain Amiri Air Force accepted delivery of the first of a dozen examples during March 1990. Supplied under the code name *Peace Crown*, the order covered a total of eight F-16C-40s and four F-16D-40s, Bahrain having selected the General Electric F110 turbofan for its aircraft, which now equip a single squadron of its air force at Sheikh Isa Air Base. Additional purchases are a possibility, but it appears that the idea of trading Bahrain's surviving F-5 Tiger IIs for a batch of 18 US Navy F-16Ns that had previously served in the adversary role has been shelved.

One of the Bahrain Amiri Air Force's eight F-16C Block 40s, based at Sheikh Isa AB. GEOFF LEE

This Block 40 F-16D is the first of four newly built for Bahrain. LMTAS

EGYPT

Peace Vector is the programme name allocated to procurement of the Fighting Falcon by Egypt, which became eligible to receive military equipment of US origin in the wake of the historic peace agreement concluded with Israel during 1979. Subsequent to that, formal acceptance of an American offer in June 1980 covering the F-16 paved the way for an initial batch to be supplied to the Al Quwwat al Jawwiya Ilmisriya (Egyptian Air Force). Further orders have followed at regular intervals, allowing Egypt to become one of the major operators of the Fighting Falcon.

The first contract (*Peace Vector I*) involved 34 F-16A single-seaters and six F-16B two-seaters. All were to Block 15 configuration, with the initial examples being handed over at Fort Worth during January 1982 and flown to Egypt some two months later to begin equipping the 232nd Fighter Regiment at An Shas Air Base. As it transpired, the number of aircraft actually supplied was increased slightly, for two additional F-16Bs were delivered, one being diverted from USAF production while the other came from the Fokker factory at Schiphol and was originally intended for the Royal Netherlands Air Force.

The second batch (*Peace Vector II*) accounted for a further 40 aircraft and also gave Egypt the distinction of being the second overseas air arm to receive the improved F-16C and F-16D versions, ahead even of Israel. Some 34 F-16Cs and six F-16Ds were involved, all of which were to Block 32 configuration with the Pratt & Whitney F100 engine.

Delivered to the Egyptian Air Force in 1986, this was the first of 40 Block 32 F-16Cs. LMTAS

Deliveries to the 242nd Fighter Regiment at Beni Suef commenced in October 1986 and were still in progress when still more Fighting Falcons were ordered in October 1987.

This new contract (*Peace Vector III*) encompassed 35 F-16Cs and 12 F-16Ds to Block 40 standard with the General Electric F110 powerplant, which was also specified for the fourth group of aircraft to be purchased (*Peace Vector IIIA*). In the latter case, however, the 35 F-16Cs and 12 F-16Ds originated from a different source, namely the Tusas production facility at Murted in Turkey, with aircraft from these batches being used to equip fighter units at Abu Suwayr and Janaklies.

Procurement is set to continue, for it was revealed in April 1996 that Egypt has placed yet another order, albeit a smaller one which calls for 21 more Fighting Falcons to be delivered during 1999-2000 and it is conceivable that they will not be the last to don Egyptian insignia.

ISRAEL

In view of the close links between the USA and Israel, one might reasonably have expected the latter to be an early recipient of the Fighting Falcon – and so it proved, although the first such request was politely but firmly rejected, before the August 1978 announcement that the sale of a substantial number had been authorised. Prior to that, permission had been granted for Iran to receive the F-16, but the subsequent overthrow of the Shah paved the way for a regime that was nothing if not hostile to the USA. In consequence, Israel claimed the distinction of being the first Middle Eastern air arm to operate the General Dynamics fighter. Ironically, most of the aircraft delivered to the Tsvah Haganah Le Israeli – Heyl Ha'Avir (Israel Defence Force – Air Force) had been laid down for Iran, with the initial batch consisting of 67 F-16As and eight F-16Bs which were supplied under the *Peace Marble* programme.

Known locally as the 'Netz' (Hawk), delivery to Israel of these aircraft commenced in July 1980, with the first unit to undergo transition being No 117 Squadron at Ramat David Air Base. Further batches of new and second-hand Fighting Falcons have followed, permitting the IDF/AF to build a formidable force which currently comprises three squadrons

Showing the effectiveness of its desert camouflage, this Israeli F-16A was originally built for the Iranian AF. LMTAS

Development of the indigenous IAI Lavi project, based on the F-16, was abandoned in 1987. VIA TIM RIPLEY

at each of four major air bases, namely Hatzor (101, 105 and 144 Squadrons), Nevatim (104, 115 and 116 Squadrons), Ramat David (109, 110 and 117 Squadrons) and Ramon (140, 147 and 253 Squadrons).

Acquisition of improved variants began in October 1987, when the first of 51 F-16Cs and 24 F-16Ds were received as the 'Barak' (Lightning) and 'Brakeet' (Thunderbolt) respectively. A further order for new-build examples followed, primarily as a result of the decision to abandon development of the indigenous IAI Lavi multi-role fighter in 1987. This follow-on batch consisted of 30 F-16Cs and 30 F-16Ds which entered service in the early 1990s and there have been reports that the IDF/AF will obtain an additional identical quantity of each variant during 1997-99.

Furthermore, as a kind of *quid pro quo* for not intervening in the 1991 Gulf War despite extreme provocation, and the US supplying F-15 Eagles to Saudi Arabia, Israel obtained 36 F-16As and 14 F-16Bs from surplus USAF stocks during 1994.

The F-16 has been extensively modified in Israeli service, with much locally-produced electronic equipment being fitted, as well as additional chaff/flare dispenser units. This process is perhaps best exemplified by the two-seat F-16D 'Brakeet', since most (probably all) of the 54 examples delivered to the IDF/AF feature a prominent dorsal spine. Incorporated during manufacture at Fort Worth, this fairing is thought to contain avionics (possibly the Elisra SPS 300 ECM jamming system) permitting use in the defence suppression role.

Wearing the markings of 105 Squadron based at Hatzor-Qastina AB, this Brakeet (F-16D Block 40) is fully combat capable. PETER R FOSTER

One of eight Block 15 F-16As in service with No 3 Squadron of the Indonesian National Defence-Air Force. LMTAS

JORDAN

Jordan is presently expected to become the 18th overseas operator of the Fighting Falcon when the Al Quwwat Al Jawwiya Al Malakiya Al Urduniya (Royal Jordanian Air Force) receives 12 F-16As and four F-16Bs under the *Peace Falcon* programme. These aircraft will be operated under the terms of a five-year lease agreement, authorisation for the transfer from surplus USAF stocks being granted in January 1996 as part of a package of military aid valued at approximately $300 million.

Pilot training was due to commence in the USA in January 1997, with delivery of the initial six aircraft to Jordan now expected to take place in December 1997. Further batches of five will follow in January and February 1998, El Azraq having already been selected as the operating base. These are unlikely to be the last F-16s to adopt Royal Jordanian Air Force insignia, for this air arm has expressed a wish to obtain about 72 as replacements for the Northrop F-5E Tiger II and Dassault Mirage F1.

THE FAR EAST

INDONESIA

The final new operator to emerge in the 1980s was Indonesia, with the Tentara Nasional Indonesia – Angkatan Udara (Indonesian National Defence – Air Force) accepting the first of a small batch of Fighting Falcons during October 1989 under the *Peace Bima-Sena* programme. Agreement for supply of these aircraft occurred in August 1986, with the contract covering eight F-16As and four F-16Bs, all of which were delivered to No 3 Squadron at Madium-Ishwahyudi Air Base during 1989-90.

TNI-AU single and two-seat aircraft feature the extended tail cone associated with use of a drag chute and also entered service in a highly distinctive camouflage colour scheme that was predominantly based upon the use of different shades of blue. However, all eight F-16As adopted an even more pronounced guise in 1996. Basically blue overall, relieved by

A Pakistan Air Force F-16B-15 carrying an Atlis II laser targeting pod. LMTAS

yellow trim and displaying the red and white national colours on the fin, they were flown in this scheme by the *Elang Biru (Blue Falcons)* aerobatic display team, although it appears the new finish was destined to be short-lived with the F-16s due to revert to more conventional camouflage after helping to commemorate the TNI-AU's 50th anniversary.

Indonesia has expressed a wish to procure further examples of the Fighting Falcon and has been identified as a potential customer for approximately nine of the 28 embargoed Pakistani aircraft that are presently being held in store at Davis-Monthan AFB, Arizona, pending satisfactory resolution of financial questions concerning repayment of monies already handed over. At one time, it looked as if the sale was about to go ahead, but cash once again appears to be a stumbling block, with Indonesia seeking more advantageous terms from the USA. Assuming those problems are resolved, the TNI-AU could well obtain most of the stored aircraft, for Indonesia has stated the desire to fund and equip a second F-16 squadron under the five-year defence plan that was to be launched in 1996.

PAKISTAN

The honour of being the first Asian air arm to acquire the Fighting Falcon was claimed by Pakistan's Fiza'Ya (Air Force) which reached agreement with the USA for the procurement of 40 aircraft in December 1981. Purchased under the *Peace Gate* programme, the order initially called for 32 F-16As and 8 F-16Bs but these quantities were subsequently amended to 28 and 12 respectively, an action that had only minimal impact on combat potential. Formal acceptance of the first example took place at Fort Worth in October 1982, with deliveries to Pakistan getting under way in January 1983 when an initial quantity of two F-16As and four F-16Bs were

flown to Sargodha. On arrival, they were assigned to No 11 Squadron which had been chosen to function as a dual operational training and combat-ready unit.

By the time deliveries were completed, two further units had been equipped with the F-16, these being No 9 Squadron (also at Sargodha) and No 14 Squadron at Kamra. Both of these units went on to utilise their new equipment to deadly effect when they accounted for a number of Afghan and Soviet aircraft that had violated Pakistani air space between 1986 and 1988.

In September 1989, Pakistan announced that further examples of the Fighting Falcon would be obtained along with new-build Lockheed P-3 Orions. Plans drawn up at that time anticipated delivery of 54 F-16As and 17 F-16Bs and government funds to the tune of some $658 million were handed over to the USA in order to launch production of the new aircraft. Unfortunately, they failed to take into account the so-called 'Pressler Amendment', under the terms of which Congress effectively imposed a ban on the supply

This Pakistan Air Force F-16A (83703) is being flown here by 11 Squadron at Sargodha. PETER R FOSTER

of military hardware to those countries believed to be engaged in development of nuclear weapons. By that time, work on the follow-on order was well advanced, with the result that 28 aircraft (13 F-16As and 15 F-16Bs) were eventually completed and test flown, before being placed in storage at Davis-Monthan AFB, Arizona. There they would stay until the vexed question of their future was resolved, but Pakistan understandably requested the return of the initial payment, although it appears that this money has still to be handed back.

At the time of writing, the embargoed machines are still in store, although efforts have been made to find another buyer. Senator Larry Pressler, who was responsible for the contentious legislation that prevented delivery to Pakistan in the first place, suggested the Philippines and Taiwan as suitable customers, but neither country seemed eager to take up the idea. As a consequence, it now looks as if Indonesia offers the best chance of disposing of at least some of the aircraft involved, assuming that a mutually satisfactory financial arrangement can be reached.

SINGAPORE

Despite its small size, this strategically important state possesses a substantial air arm which includes a modest quantity of Fighting Falcons as its most potent element, with additional examples currently on order. Procurement of the F-16 for service with the Republic of Singapore Air Force began with the placement of an order for eight aircraft in January 1985, simultaneously taking out an option for a further 12. At that time, General Dynamics was promoting the General Electric J79-powered version and it looked for a while as if Singapore would be the first customer for this less capable model.

As it transpired, the original proposal was soon superseded, with the contract being amended in mid-1985 to cover supply of an identical quantity of F100-powered aircraft under the programme name *Peace Carvin*, with the first order being divided equally between single-seat and two-seat machines. Earmarked to replace the veteran Hunter, the first aircraft was formally accepted at Fort Worth

One of the four F-16Bs now operated by 140 Squadron of the RoSAF, from Tengah AB. LMTAS

in February 1988 – and was, coincidentally, the 2000th Fighting Falcon to be delivered.

The remaining aircraft of the initial order soon followed, but these were destined to spend most of the next two years at Luke AFB, Arizona, apart from a brief spell at Nellis AFB, Nevada during November 1989 in order to participate in a *Red Flag* exercise. Not long afterwards, in February 1990, they were finally transferred to Singapore, entering front-line service with No 140 Squadron at Tengah.

Singapore chose not to exercise the 12-aircraft option that it held and it was not until well into the next decade that consideration was given to further purchases to satisfy a stated requirement for 18 new combat aircraft. Before committing itself, however, Singapore undertook a comparative evaluation of later versions of the F-16 and the F/A-18 Hornet, which eventually culminated in the decision to opt for the F-16C/D Block 52D. The resulting order was officially placed in July 1994 and called for a total of eight F-16Cs and 10 F-16Ds, with delivery expected to take place between March 1998 and December 1999. As with the original batch, training will be undertaken at Luke AFB before the new aircraft are transferred to Singapore, although it is possible some will remain in the USA for an indefinite period.

In addition to its own Fighting Falcons, Singapore has made extensive use of USAF aircraft under the terms of a leasing arrangement, whereby Singaporean pilots receive training with the 56th Fighter Wing's 425th Fighter Squadron at Luke AFB. At its height, this involved close to a dozen F-16A and F-16B versions, several of which were still on charge in January 1996. However, transition to the improved F-16C and F-16D models began during November 1995. This arrangement is set to terminate in mid-1998, at which time Singapore intends to implement a new agreement with Lockheed covering the lease of a dozen F-16C/Ds.

SOUTH KOREA

In March 1986, South Korea had the distinction of being the first overseas air arm to acquire enhanced versions of the Fighting Falcon, when it took delivery of the first aircraft ordered under the *Peace Bridge* programme. Some 30 F-16Cs and six F-16Ds were involved in the initial order and in Han-Guk Kong Goon (Republic of Korea Air Force) service, they were used to replace F-4D Phantoms with two squadrons of the 11th Tactical Fighter Wing at Taegu Air Base.

Apart from a small re-order placed in June 1988 which added four more F-16Ds to the fleet, that might well have been the end of South Korean purchases, since the Fighting Falcon failed to overcome the formidable challenge posed by the F/A-18 Hornet in the Korean Fighter Programme competition of the late 1980s. This was based on co-production, but not long after the December 1989 announcement of the intent to obtain 120 Hornets, irreconcilable differences over funding and offsets brought about a change of heart on the part of the Korean authorities, who promptly switched allegiance to the General Dynamics' Fighting Falcon.

This resulted in 80 F-16Cs and 40 F-16Ds being ordered. Delivery of these Block 52 aircraft began in December 1994,

The second RoK AF F-16C Block 52 built by Lockheed Martin at Fort Worth in 1994. LMTAS

the terms of the agreement specifying that the first 12 (probably two F-16Cs and 10 F-16Ds) would be manufactured and flown by Lockheed Martin at Fort Worth before delivery to the customer. The next 36 (probably 26 F-16Cs and 10 F-16Ds) would be supplied in knocked-down kit form for assembly by Samsung Aerospace in Korea. This company rolled-out its first F-16C in November 1995. Finally, the remaining aircraft (52 F-16Cs and 20 F-16Ds) would be built under licence by Samsung.

TAIWAN

President Nixon's celebrated visit to the People's Republic of China heralded a shift in US foreign policy which culminated in it being accorded most favoured nation trading status, although subsequent events like the Tiananmen Square massacre eventually forced a rethink. In the meantime, the USA's long-time ally in this volatile region, Taiwan, was no longer viewed quite so warmly and in fact became the victim of an unofficial embargo concerning the sale of military hardware.

For a nation that had traditionally been dependent upon the USA as a source of its front-line military equipment, this was a potentially devastating situation. One result of American reluctance to supply modern combat aircraft was Taiwan's decision to develop the indigenous Ching-Kuo fighter. As it turned out, plans to procure 250 examples of the Ching-Kuo have been cut back by almost half, but Taiwan has not been reluctant to look elsewhere, having turned to France and ordered 60 Dassault Mirage 2000-5s to satisfy at least one of its requirements.

At about the same time, negotiations for the purchase of the Fighting Falcon culminated in the *Peace Fenghuang* programme, which covers the eventual supply of the unique new-build Block 20 F-16As (120) and F-16Bs (30) to the Chung-Kuo Kung Chuan (Republic of China Air Force) by the year 2000. Handover of the first Taiwanese Fighting Falcon took place on schedule at Fort Worth in July 1996, with the aircraft involved being one of a number that are to be retained in the USA for pilot training. In consequence, deliveries to Taiwan did not commence until 1997, to equip the 4th Tactical Fighter Wing (TFW) at Chia Yi Air Base and the 8th TFW at Hualien.

THAILAND

Thailand's interest in obtaining the Fighting Falcon to modernise its air arm was revealed in the spring of 1985. At that time, it appeared the version to be offered in response to the formal request for 12 aircraft would be the F-16/79. Not surprisingly, Thailand was far from enthusiastic about this 'poor relation' of the Fighting Falcon family and was eventually allowed to receive the rather more potent F110-powered aircraft. Delivery of the first of eight F-16As and four F-16Bs to be supplied under the *Peace Naresuan* programme took place at Fort Worth in May 1988.

By then, however, permission had been granted for the Royal Thai Air Force to add six more F-16As to the initial purchase, with a formal agreement to that effect being reached in December 1987. These extra aircraft were completed between December 1990 and March 1991, being delivered from April to July 1991, allowing No 103 Squadron at Korat to boost its complement to 18. By some odd quirk of the USAF/FMS serial system, these were actually given FY 1991 identities.

Negotiations for the third batch were not finalised until fully four years later, with a contract covering 12 F-16As and six F-16Bs being signed in January 1992. Delivery to the Royal Thai Air Force began in September 1995, with the latest arrivals being assigned to No 403 Squadron at Takhli.

Further updating of combat echelons appears likely in the mid-term future, although the recent Thai order for eight F/A-18 Hornets means that Lockheed Martin must expect to face vigorous opposition from its prime competitor when it comes to future orders for new fighters.

The first F-16A for the Thai Air Force that was handed over at Fort Worth in May 1988. VIA PRM

SOUTH AMERICA

VENEZUELA

Unique in being the only Latin American nation to operate the Fighting Falcon, Venezuela concluded an agreement to purchase 24 aircraft in May 1982. In fact, this sale almost failed to go ahead, for the US government initially offered the J79-powered version which was considered unsuitable by the Fuerza Aerea Venezolana (Venezuelan Air Force). Eventually, the US relented and cleared the way for the F100-powered F-16A and F-16B models to be supplied. Quantities involved were 18 and six respectively and these aircraft were destined to replace the Dassault Mirage.

Acceptance of the first example supplied under the *Peace Delta* programme took place at Fort Worth in September 1983, with deliveries to Venezuela commencing two months later, when six aircraft were flown south to El Libertador Air Base. Once there, they began to equip the two squadrons of Grupo Aereo de Caza No 16 (16th Fighter Air Group).

Venezuela's Fighting Falcons are distinctive by virtue of being the only examples of this fighter to utilise brown and green tactical camouflage and they also feature the braking parachute installation first used by Norway. Some updating has occurred since delivery, with all the surviving machines benefiting from the Operational Capability Upgrade, while late 1995 saw the start of a project to install the Honeywell ring laser gyro inertial navigation system across the fleet.

The second Venezuelan Air Force F-16A-15 on a test flight prior to delivery. LMTAS

The Falcon described

As far as its basic appearance is concerned, the Fighting Falcon has not changed all that much during the course of the past 20 years, with the result that the F-16C and F-16D of today do not look dissimilar to the early production F-16A and F-16B versions that emerged from the Fort Worth factory back in 1978. Beneath the surface appearance, however, it is a very different aircraft, with many significant improvements having been made throughout the intervening period. Most of those detailed improvements have been considered elsewhere and the following is intended to provide a broad overview of the characteristics of the design. When it first appeared the F-16 was considered quite radical, but today many of the features of the original YF-16 prototypes (and the competing Northrop YF-17) are now commonplace.

The basic design utilises a cropped delta planform incorporating wing/fuselage blending, as well as sharply swept vortex control strakes that extend forward from the wing root leading edge to a position adjacent to the front of the cockpit canopy. These generate extra lift and bestow increased directional stability when operating at high angles of attack that might occur in aerial combat. The F-16's wing features a NACA 64A-204 section and embodies 40 degrees of sweep at the leading edge.

On single-seat versions, the pilot is accommodated in a pressurised and air-conditioned cockpit, beneath a single-piece bird-proof forward canopy section that is made of polycarbonate advanced plastics material and designed to offer exceptional visibility. Two-seater F-16s have separate cockpits in tandem, with instrumentation and systems in the rear cockpit essentially duplicating those of the forward one. It is, therefore, fully combat-capable from either station. On both versions, the canopy is hinged at the rear, although the two-seater has a two-piece, single-enclosure canopy with a metal bow frame at the mid-point and therefore has a marginally inferior field of view.

Emergency egress is provided by the McDonnell Douglas ACES II ejection seat which has zero/zero capability and which is canted 30 degrees aft, with a higher heel line.

The fourth production (FSD) F-16A (top) photographed in 1977 is little different in overall appearance from this 20th FW Block 50 F-16C (above) pictured nearly 20 years later. VIA LARRY DAVIS/DANIEL MARCH

The F-16's characteristic cropped delta wings and tail, and strakes forward from the wing root, are clearly seen on this RNethAF F-16A.
PETER R MARCH

Ostensibly, the reason for this is to increase pilot tolerance to g forces and there is no doubt that it does do that; however, there are those who claim that the real reason for this novel aspect is simply that the seat would not fit in the cockpit any other way!

Another very distinctive feature of the Fighting Falcon is the air intake, which gives the aircraft a particularly predatory appearance. Indeed, this layout may well have been influential in the adoption of the nickname *Viper* for the F-16 by USAF aircrew. The name was in fact coined from the movie *Star Wars* in which the fighter aircraft of the good forces is named *Millennial Viper*. The term *Viper* also had a lethal connotation, particularly in relation to rattlesnakes that are much feared in many parts of the US. The air intake is situated below the fuselage, beneath the aft end of the cockpit, and is basically a very simple arrangement, incorporating a fixed-geometry inlet, with a boundary layer splitter plate directly above.

Although not readily apparent at first glance, the inlet does in fact provide one of the more subtle differences between aircraft that have General Electric's F110 engine when compared with those that use the Pratt & Whitney F100. Alternative engine installations were introduced by the Block 30 (General Electric) and Block 32 (Pratt & Whitney) models in the mid-1980s, with the General Electric-powered aircraft able to accommodate increased mass air flow and therefore benefiting from a larger intake. As it turned out, although the new engine was adopted straight away, the revised inlet took a while longer to appear and did not make its début until the 368th F-16C (Block 30D 86-0262). This and all subsequent GE-powered examples of the Fighting Falcon have an inlet that is some 15cm (6in) wider than their P&W-powered counterparts, hence the fact that they are more familiarly known by the unflattering appellation of 'big mouth' although it is only 6% larger in frontal area.

The Fighting Falcon also broke new ground in other ways, not least of which was the adoption of fly-by-wire control

The F-16's cockpit is covered by a single piece moulded polycarbonate canopy. DANIEL MARCH

The F-16B/D has two separate cockpits with controls and instruments in each, covered by a single-enclosure canopy with a metal frame at mid-point. ANDREW MARCH

systems, being the first operational aircraft to incorporate this capability. Analog computer technology was at the heart of the system on all F-16A/B blocks up to and including 32 and is still in production today for the Block 20s. The F-16 Block 40/42 models introduced a four-channel digital system. As for the flight control surfaces, these have also

With its control column on the right-hand console, reclining ejector seat and head-up display, the F-16's cockpit broke new ground. PETER R MARCH

been subjected to change over the years, most notably with effect from the F-16A/B Block 15 which was the first to feature the so-called 'big tail'.

The flight controls are otherwise quite conventional for today and comprise wing-mounted flaperons for roll control; fully-variable monobloc tailerons for pitch control; full-span, automatic, wing leading-edge flaps that are programmed to operate as a function of Mach number and angle of attack; a rudder; and split upward and downward-opening air brakes with a maximum deflection of 60 degrees situated inboard of the tailerons adjacent to the engine exhaust nozzle.

Conventional rudder pedals are provided, but the F-16 was much less standard in other areas. For a start, it made use of the HOTAS (Hands On Throttle And Stick) philosophy, allowing the pilot to keep his head out of the cockpit and thus focus his attention on the developing tactical situation. Of greater significance is the fact that it also did away with the familiar control column – and this was truly revolutionary, for the F-16 pilot actually flies his aircraft with a side-stick controller that protrudes from a console that is conveniently positioned for the pilot's right hand.

On the YF-16 prototypes, this control device was completely rigid, with command inputs in pitch and roll being generated in response to the amount of force applied by the pilot. However, when it comes to production aircraft, some stick movement is possible, but this is extremely limited – about three-sixteenths of an inch aft, less than one hundredth of an inch forward and just three thirty-seconds

of an inch to both left and right. That is by no means a lot, but it is sufficient to provide a measure of 'feel' for the pilot, giving the impression of having positive and reactive control.

While the F-16 cockpit arrangement could arguably be described as 'hand-ist', by virtue of apparently favouring those who are right-handed, it has not posed any great difficulty for left-handed pilots. Indeed, the only reservations that have been voiced about this layout originated with the Israelis and were related to a pilot's continued ability to fly the aircraft in the event of sustaining injury to the right hand.

Moving on to the basic structure, the wing is mainly composed of light alloy materials built up around 11 spars and five ribs with single-piece upper and lower skins and also serves as a fuel tank. Wing-fuselage attachment is by machined aluminium fittings. The hydraulically-actuated leading-edge flaps are one-piece bonded aluminium honeycomb, as are the flaperons, while the fin is of multi-spar, multi-rib construction with graphite epoxy skin. Aluminium honeycomb is also used for the twin ventral fins. Tailerons incorporate a corrugated aluminium sub-structure, with a leading edge of aluminium honeycomb and graphite epoxy laminate skins. Attachment is by a single pivot point, allowing maximum deflections of 21 degrees up or down, measured at the leading edge. In addition, the flaperon and taileron assemblies are interchangeable to port and starboard.

Mensaco is responsible for the tricycle undercarriage units, which are hydraulically actuated, with each unit having a single wheel. The steerable nosewheel rotates through 90 degrees as it retracts aft to lie flat in a well situated beneath the air intake ducting, while the mainwheels retract

The large tailerons allow a 21 deg deflection up or down. PETER R MARCH

Single wheels on the tricycle undercarriage units are hydraulically activated. PETER R MARCH

forwards and are housed in the lower fuselage sides. Many of the components of the mainwheel assemblies are interchangeable and may be fitted to port or starboard and these units also feature brake-by-wire and anti-skid systems. For emergency situations, an arrester hook is fitted under the aft fuselage between the ventral fins and many aircraft also feature an extended fairing at the base of the fin which contains a drag chute; this is fitted on F-16s operated by Greece, Indonesia, the Netherlands (retrofitting), Norway, Taiwan, Turkey (except Block 50s) and Venezuela, but has not been adopted by other air arms. Belgian F-16s have the extended fairing, but it is used to house internal ECM boxes.

While all F-16s are single-engined, not all of them have the same powerplant installed. At the outset, Pratt & Whitney enjoyed a monopoly position in providing all engines for the

Although Belgian F-16As have the tail canister, it is used to house ECM equipment rather than a drag-chute. PETER R MARCH

Fighting Falcon, with the 23,830 lb st F100-PW-200 being fitted as standard to F-16As and F-16Bs up to Block 15 and the F-16C/D Block 25. However, one noteworthy change did occur during the course of production of the F-16A/B series, with new-build examples of the Block 15 OCU (Operational Capabilities Upgrade) version having the 23,770 lb st F100-PW-220, which was also installed in the F-16C/D Block 32 and 42. While giving only a marginal increase in thrust over most of the flight envelope, the Dash 220 engine offered increased levels of reliability arising from the adoption of a Digital Electronic Engine Control unit that also allows much more 'carefree' handling by reducing the risk of engine stalls.

Modification of the basic F100-PW-200 on existing aircraft has produced the comparable F100-PW-220E engine. This retrofit is programmed for all remaining F-16s (and

A Dutch F-16A deploying its fin-base mounted braking parachute.
DANIEL MARCH

The Pratt & Whitney F100-PW-200 turbofan was standard on all F-16A/Bs up to Block 15 and F-16C/D Block 25 aircraft. VIA LARRY DAVIS

The second F-16B FSD was used as the test aircraft for the upgraded F100-PW-220 engine. PETER R MARCH

has taken full advantage of the belated opportunity and has accounted for the lion's share of recent production. This is particularly true with regard to aircraft bought by the USAF over the past decade, for this service is due to take delivery of almost 900 GE-powered machines as opposed to barely 300 with Pratt & Whitney engines. Furthermore, GE's F110 has also been specified for those aircraft purchased by Bahrain, Egypt, Greece, Israel and Turkey.

Fuel may be carried both internally and externally, with the former being housed in the wing and in five seal-bonded fuselage cells. Normal internal capacity of the single-seat versions is 1,053 US gallons. In the case of the F-16B and F-16D two-seat derivatives, provision of a second cockpit reduces the space available in the fuselage for fuel and maximum capacity falls to 871 US gallons. However, both single- and two-seat versions are fitted with in-flight refuelling receptacles behind the cockpit in the upper centre-fuselage section, for the 'flying boom' system.

In addition, up to three external tanks may be carried to extend ferry range or combat radius. The most commonly used option – which is currently favoured by the USAF and all but one of the export customers – comprises a 300 US gallon tank on the centreline (station 5), plus a pair of 370 US gallon tanks on the inner wing pylons (stations 4 and 6),

F-15s) in the USAF inventory, starting with Block 25 F-16C/Ds. Most F-16A/Bs in the ANG, and particularly the ADF aircraft have not received this engine modification because it is planned to retire all of these aircraft soon after the turn of the decade.

With effect from the F-16C/D Block 30, General Electric was also given the chance to provide engines for the Fighting Falcon. The first such aircraft was delivered in the mid-1980s and was fitted with the F110-GE-100 turbofan. This engine was also installed in the F-16C/D Block 40 versions. However, the F110-100 engine with the original inlet was restricted on air flow and only developed 25,725 lb st maximum thrust. Modified with a larger inlet the engine was improved to provide 28,984 lb st in maximum afterburner.

Thereafter, the GE and P&W powerplants were further modified, which resulted in the appearance of the Increased Performance Engine (IPE) versions. In the case of GE, this resulted in the F110-GE-129, which is fitted to the F-16C/D Block 50 and is rated at 29,588 lb st; P&W's F100-PW-229 as fitted to the F-16C/D Block 52, produces slightly less power (29,100 lb st) but is a little lighter than the F110-GE-100 and therefore has a slightly higher thrust-to-weight ratio.

While it may have had to wait some considerable time for the chance to power the Fighting Falcon, General Electric

The Block 50 F-16Cs that equip the 52nd Wing at Spangdahlem are powered by the 29,588 lb st GE F110-GE-129 turbofan. DANIEL MARCH

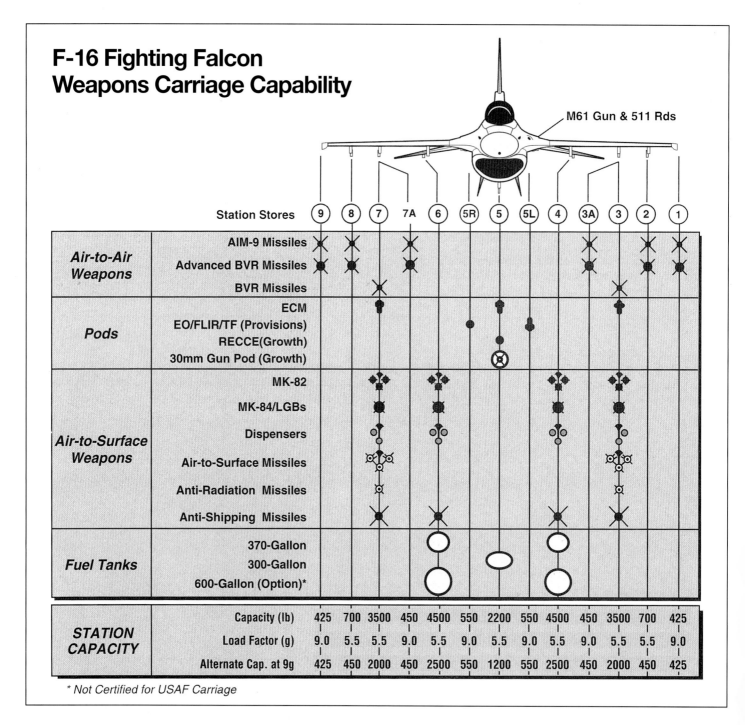

F-16 Fighting Falcon
Weapons Carriage Capability

M61 Gun & 511 Rds

	Station Stores	9	8	7	7A	6	5R	5	5L	4	3A	3	2	1
Air-to-Air Weapons	AIM-9 Missiles	X	●		X							X	X	X
	Advanced BVR Missiles	●	X		●						X	●	X	X
	BVR Missiles			X								X		
Pods	ECM			●								●		
	EO/FLIR/TF (Provisions)						●		●					
	RECCE(Growth)							●						
	30mm Gun Pod (Growth)							⊗						
Air-to-Surface Weapons	MK-82			✦		✦				✦		✦		
	MK-84/LGBs			●		●				●		●		
	Dispensers			●		●				●		●		
	Air-to-Surface Missiles			⊗●⊗								⊗●⊗		
	Anti-Radiation Missiles			☒								☒		
	Anti-Shipping Missiles			X		●				●		X		
Fuel Tanks	370-Gallon					◯				◯				
	300-Gallon							◯						
	600-Gallon (Option)*					◯				◯				
STATION CAPACITY	Capacity (lb)	425	700	3500	450	4500	550	2200	550	4500	450	3500	700	425
	Load Factor (g)	9.0	5.5	5.5	9.0	5.5	9.0	5.5	9.0	5.5	9.0	5.5	5.5	9.0
	Alternate Cap. at 9g	425	450	2000	450	2500	550	1200	550	2500	450	2000	450	425

* Not Certified for USAF Carriage

giving a grand total of 2,093 US gallons (1,911 US gallons for two-seaters). The single exception to date is Israel, which has opted for the ability to hang considerably larger tanks on the inner stations. Each of these tanks has a capacity of 600 US gallons which increases the total uplift to 2,553 US gallons (2,371 US gallons for two-seaters).

The Fighting Falcon has no fewer than nine stores stations (numbered in sequence from port to starboard) and may therefore operate with a formidable array of weapons and other equipment. All F-16 versions have a single integral Vulcan M61A1 rotary cannon and 511 rounds of 20 mm ammunition in the port wing/body fairing. The very wide range of external weapons loads that can be carried by the

F-16 largely depends upon the nature of the mission to be undertaken.

For combat a heat-seeking AIM-9 Sidewinder missile is usually carried on each of the two wing-tip rails (stations 1 and 9), irrespective of the nature of the task, for these offer a defensive capability in the event of being 'bounced' by hostile fighters when engaged in air-to-ground missions. When tasked with air superiority or interception roles, the F-16 may carry up to six missiles, with the AIM-7 Sparrow and AIM-120 AMRAAM also figuring in the air combat equation. There is probably no such thing as a typical load, for the weapons fit would be driven by the nature of the threat.

In an ideal world, the most desirable solution would be

Edwards F-16C test aircraft carrying an ALQ-131 ECM pod, AIM-120 AMRAAM BVR missiles and an AGM-130 rocket-boosted glide bomb. It has an anti-spin parachute canister attached to the tail. LMTAS

347th TFW F-16C in the standard 'three-tank' long-range USAF configuration. PETER R FOSTER

An Edwards Test Center F-16A ADF launches an AGM-65A Maverick air-to-surface missile. LMTAS

simply to load the aircraft with BVR weapons and knock the enemy down long before he got too close for comfort. Unfortunately, in the real world, an enemy is seldom co-operative enough and there may well be occasions when he (or she) displays extreme cunning. In view of that, the weapons chosen are most likely to include a mix of heat-seeking and beyond visual range (BVR) missiles so as to enable hostile aircraft to be engaged effectively across the broad spectrum of the air combat arena.

In the normal course of events, missile armament is carried on the wing-tip rails and the outer pair of under-wing hardpoints on each side (stations 2, 3, 7 and 8) with this configuration allowing manoeuvring up to the maximum 9 g load factor. However, when external fuel tanks are fitted, the maximum permissible load factor falls to 5.5 g, although they may always be jettisoned.

When it comes to air-to-surface ordnance, there are many more options available and these weapons are usually carried on the inner pair of hardpoints on each side (stations 3, 4, 6 and 7), often in conjunction with missiles. Typical combinations include three 500 lb Mk 82 bombs on each station, for a total of 12; one 2,000 lb 'slick' (Mk 84) or a laser-guided bomb (LGB) of similar weight on each station, for a total of four; two sub-munitions dispensers (cluster bombs) on stations 3 and 7, plus three on stations 4 and 6, for a total of 10; three air-to-surface missiles such as the AGM-65 Maverick on stations 3 and 7, for a total of six; one anti-radiation missile such as the AGM-88 HARM on stations 3 and 7, for a total of two; and one anti-ship attack missile such as the Norwegian Penguin on each station, for a total of four. The F-16 is also cleared for the use of the AGM-84 Harpoon. There is a current programme to certify four-

A 20th FW F-16C equipped with AIM-9 Sidewinders and AGM-88 HARM missiles. LMTAS

A test F-16 carrying Norwegian Penguin Mk 3 anti-shipping missiles under each wing, in 1983. LMTAS

An F-16A with standard drop tanks, wing-tip Sidewinders and an AN/ALQ-131 jamming pod. VIA LARRY DAVIS

station (wing stations 3,4,6 and 7) carriage of large missiles (anti-ship, anti-radiation). Flight-testing of four-station HARM loads commenced in March 1997.

Although the centreline station is not normally used for weaponry, the potential exists to fit a non-jettisonable General Electric GPU-5/A *Pave Claw* gun pod on aircraft dedicated to the close-air support mission. In practice, this item of equipment has only had limited use with just a couple of dozen F-16A/B Block 10 aircraft of the New York ANG's 138th Fighter Squadron reconfigured to carry and use it briefly in the Gulf War. Weighing some 339 lb and containing a four-barrelled GAU-13/A 30 mm cannon, it

was by no means a great success. Subsequently, the modified aircraft assigned to the 138th FS gave way to the F-16C/D versions and were placed in storage at Davis-Monthan AFB, where they remain.

Other items of equipment that can be carried externally comprise a variety of pods and sensors. Carriage of these is again driven by mission requirements, with many of them used for electronic countermeasures. The Westinghouse AN/ALQ-131 and Raytheon AN/ALQ-184 jamming pods in particular are widely used by the USA and overseas air arms; these may be fitted to stations 3, 5 and 7. In the case of the centreline station, another option involves fitment of a reconnaissance pod, although there is no universal standard. Suitably adapted Dutch aircraft carry the Delft Orpheus sensor package, while Danish examples have Per Udsen equipment and those of the Virginia ANG's Richmond-based 149th FS have recently begun using a Lockheed Martin pod.

Finally, there are two further stations on each side of the air inlet (stations 5L and 5R) which are reserved for electro-optical (EO), forward-looking infra-red (FLIR) and terrain following (TF) pods. The best known of these is the LANTIRN (Low Altitude Navigation and Targeting Infra-Red for Night) package as used by the USAF and now available for export. This comprises the AN/AAQ-13 navigation and AN/AAQ-14 targeting pods, which are normally carried to port (5L) and starboard (5R) respectively. However, they are by no means the only options, with the Lockheed Martin Sharpshooter targeting pod (a downgraded version of the

F-16A of the 138th FS during the Gulf War, with GE GPU-5/A gun pod under the fuselage, standard wing-tip Sidewinders and 2,000 lb bombs beneath the wings. LMTAS

A Danish Air Force F-16B reveals its Per Udsen reconnaissance pod as it takes off. DANIEL MARCH

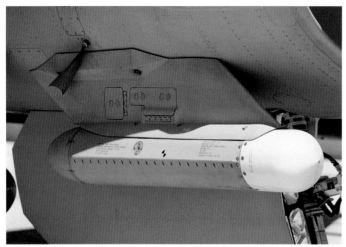

AN/ASQ-213 HARM Targeting System pod carried on the starboard side, just below the engine air intake on this F-16C. DANIEL MARCH

AN/AAQ-14), Thomson-CSF Atlis laser designator pod and Rafael Litening infra-red targeting and navigation pod either already in use or due to be introduced to service in the near future. Last, but by no means least, there is the AN/ASQ-213 HARM Targeting System (HTS) pod which is usually carried to starboard by aircraft configured for and engaged in the suppression of enemy air defences (SEAD) mission.

With all the formidable weapons potential available on the F-16 it is essential that the best use is made of it. This can only be done by ensuring that the various weapons are taken to the right place from which they can be released in order to have the greatest chance of successfully hitting the target or targets, irrespective of whether they are in the air or on the ground. It is in enabling the Fighting Falcon to do this that the avionics come into their own and these are no less formidable in their own unique way.

Foremost amongst them is the multi-mode radar. On the F-16A/B models, this is the Westinghouse AN/APG-66, which remains an impressive system, as it has been up-graded during the course of its service career. Westinghouse was also responsible for the development and production of the AN/APG-68(V) pulse Doppler range and angle track radar. This is used by contemporary F-16C/D models and is

Latest standard Block 50 F-16C of the 52nd FW with wing-tip AIM-120 AMRAAM, AIM-9L on stations 2/8, AGM-88 HARM on stations 3/7, together with a pair of long-range fuel tanks and LANTIRN.
BEN DUNNELL

significantly better, being capable of operating in a variety of air-to-air and air-to-ground modes.

Available with the APG-68 for air-to-air modes are: air combat manoeuvring, long-range search, velocity search with ranging, track-while-scan (as many as 10 targets), raid assessment by cluster resolution, single- and dual-target situation awareness and track retention through notch (when targets can 'disappear' while flying a course paralleling that of the planar antenna array). Air-to-surface modes include ground mapping, Doppler beam sharpening, surveillance of fixed and moving sea targets, acquisition and tracking of surface vessels in varying sea states, fixed and ground moving target track, target 'freeze' after pop-up, beacon, and air-ground ranging.

In conjunction with other mission systems such as LANTIRN, the radar provides a formidable attack capability and the data generated by these sensors is displayed to the pilot via a GEC-Marconi wide-angle holographic electronic head-up display (HUD) and on two Honeywell multi-function displays (MFDs).

In addition to the radar, a host of other avionics items are fitted, although the precise suite of equipment carried does vary according to model and block number. In the case of the latest F-16 Block 50/52 versions, communications apparatus can include an AN/URC-126 Have Quick IIA UHF transceiver, AN/ARC-205 Have Sync Group A VHF AM/FM transceiver, ARC-190 HF radio and an AN/APX-101 IFF (Identification Friend or Foe) transponder, plus government-furnished systems like the National Security Agency KIT-1A/TSEC cryptographic equipment and AN/AIC-18/25 intercom. Other CNI items on Block 50/52 aircraft are the IDM (Improved Data Modem), DTS (Digital Terrain System) and AIFFs (Advanced IFFs).

The IDM is a device that translates digital signals sent across either of the radios to interface with the F-16's core avionics. Typical uses are as an intra-flight data link or targeting messages from the AWACS or Forward Air Controller. The F-16 is the first US aircraft to employ DTS. It involves using radar altimeter inputs, a digital terrain data base and terrain profile matching comparisons. DTS modes include: very accurate reference navigation, ground collision avoidance system, terrain following, obstacle warning and cueing, and passive air-to-ground ranging. The F-16 accommodates several AIFFs (APX-109+ and APX-113) which are used for air-to-air interrogation, identification and location as well as traditional transponding. This is installed in place of an APX-101 transponder. The Block 50 F-16 also has a crash survivable flight data recorder.

Avionics core equipment associated with flight management can vary in order to satisfy a customer's specific requirements, but the Block 50/52 has either a Litton LN-93 or Honeywell H-423 ring laser inertial navigation system, as well as a Collins AN/ARN-108 ILS, Collins AN/ARN-118 Tacan, Gould AN/APN-232 radar altimeter, Honeywell central air data computer, Rockwell Global Positioning System and an Elbit Fort Worth enhanced stores management computer.

A LANTIRN-equipped F-16C Block 40 of the 69th FS from Moody AFB, GA. BOB ARCHER

There are also a number of items of defensive avionics and this is another area where the installed equipment can be, and often is, uniquely tailored to meet customer demand. In the case of the latest Block 50/52 aircraft as supplied to the USAF, these feature a Loral AN/ALR-56M advanced radar warning receiver (RWR) with AN/ALE-47 chaff/flare dispenser units. The AN/ALR-56M RWR is now also available for export and is being fitted to South Korean Fighting Falcons.

Another RWR that is extensively used is the Dalmo Victor AN/ALR-69, while Greek aircraft have the integrated Litton ASPIS self-defence suite which comprises an AN/ALR-93 RWR, Tracor chaff and flare dispensers and Raytheon's AN/ALQ-187 I-DIAS jammer. Other ECM systems currently employed by various operators include external jamming pods (see earlier remarks for details), while internally-housed systems are coming into favour. Noteworthy amongst these are the Dassault Electronique Carapace (Belgium), Northrop Grumman AN/ALQ-162 (Denmark), Loral AN/ALQ-178(V)3 Rapport III (Turkey) and Elta EL/L-8240 (Israel). South Korea is currently proceeding with plans to install ALQ-165 ASPJ on its Block 52 F-16Cs. In view of this diversity, it may be fair to say that while every F-16 operator is anxious to minimise the threat posed by ground-based defensive systems, there appears to be little consensus as to how this can best be accomplished.

Regardless of type of avionics equipment that is installed, complex systems such as those mentioned here are not much use without suitable hydraulic and electrical power sources and environmental systems. In the F-16 they comprise a regenerative 12-kW environmental control system that makes use of engine bleed air to pressurise and cool the cockpit and avionics compartments; dual independent hydraulic systems for operation of flight control surfaces and utility functions; and an electrical system which is powered by an engine-driven Westinghouse 60 kVA main generator and a 10 kVA standby generator.

In addition, the F-16 also has an integral Sundstrand/ Solar jet fuel starter, for self starting in any location, and a Simmonds fuel measuring system. Finally, there is an AlliedSignal emergency power unit that operates off bleed air and/or hydrazine to drive a 5 kVA emergency generator and pump. If the engine is not turning, the EPU operates on 100% hydrazine. This ensures the continued supply of electrical and hydraulic power should the primary systems cease to function, such as might occur in the event of an engine failure.

Two Aviano-based F-16Cs with wing-tip AIM-120 AMRAAM and AIM-9L Sidewinders, and Mk 82 bombs under each wing, together with an AN/ALQ-213 jammer. TIM RIPLEY

Looking Ahead

When it comes to contemplating the future of the Fighting Falcon, the fact that close to 4,000 aircraft have already been ordered means that it is certain to be with us in one form or another for many years yet. This, of course, does not mean that Lockheed Martin is content to rest on its laurels, for the company is vigorously pursuing a twin-track approach that is intended to ensure the Fort Worth production line continues to produce new-build aircraft for the foreseeable future.

One of those tracks involves the continued marketing of existing versions. All four of the basic models that have been built to date are still on offer, although the contemporary F-16C and F-16D Block 50/52 models appear to have been at the heart of recent and ongoing efforts to secure fresh orders. Aggressive sales efforts were rewarded with some success during 1996 in the form of another purchase of 21 aircraft by Egypt, but 1997 may yet turn out to be even better still, for Lockheed Martin awaits a decision from the United Arab Emirates, which currently has a requirement for up to 80 new strike aircraft. The UAE announced in September 1996 that it had shortlisted the F-16 and Rafale, but early in 1997 it added Eurofighter 2000 to its final consideration.

With regard to new orders, 1996 may well have been one of the leanest years for some time. One ray of light amidst

Egypt has ordered 21 further examples of the latest Block 50/52 F-16s. LMTAS

the gloom concerns procurement by the USAF, which seems set to continue for a while longer, even though it was at one time intended to terminate with delivery of the dozen examples obtained with FY 94 appropriations. However, the quantities involved are so small as to appear insignificant when compared with earlier orders, for the latest USAF contract covers just half-a-dozen aircraft with FY 97 funding.

The F-16 was evaluated by the Finnish Air Force in 1996, in keeping with several other European air arms. VIA PRM

Some of the 350 surplus F-16s (mostly As and Bs) stored at Davis-Monthan AFB, AZ awaiting their fate. JEREMY FLACK/API

As far as new markets are concerned, it is probably fair to say the brightest prospects now rest within Eastern Europe, from amongst the former members of the Warsaw Pact alliance. If anyone had suggested in the mid-1980s that before the end of the century the F-16 might appear in the insignia of one of these Eastern European air arms, they would most likely have been laughed at. Today, however, the old order has largely gone, taking with it most of the old certainties and it is this factor that has been responsible for providing Lockheed Martin and other US and European aircraft manufacturers with fresh opportunities to sell their wares. In consequence, sales representatives from those companies are now beating a well-worn path to defence ministries in Eastern Europe in the hope of stealing a march on the competition by securing a firm order, for there is a distinct possibility that whoever makes the first breakthrough might well end up scooping the pool.

Although the idea of selling the F-16 to Eastern Europe had been in prospect for some time, it moved a big step closer to becoming a reality during the course of 1996. At least three former Warsaw Pact air arms have expressed great interest in obtaining military aircraft and equipment from manufacturers that were once considered to be firmly in the enemy camp, but it is one thing to show interest and quite another to take action. In 1996, however, that is exactly what happened, with the Czech Republic, Hungary and Poland all

conducting evaluations of the Fighting Falcon (as well as the F/A-18 Hornet and the Gripen) in the latter half of the year.

To date, these evaluations have yet to be translated into firm contracts for any of the contenders and Lockheed Martin is well aware that it faces stiff opposition from its competitors. Furthermore, even if the Fighting Falcon does emerge victorious, there is no absolute guarantee that it will result in the factory at Fort Worth being called upon to build them, for there is what can only be described as a glut of second-hand aircraft currently available.

This has to be good news for potential buyers, who may well be able to negotiate very favourable terms covering the supply of reconditioned fighters from this source – or perhaps even brand new aircraft from Lockheed Martin. It is much less welcome news for the manufacturer, which is having to come to terms with the very real prospect that it may yet find itself in competition with its own government as well as those of other countries in the battle to secure new sales.

In North America, for instance, somewhere in the region of 350 surplus USAF/USN aircraft of the F-16A/B, F-16A/B ADF, F-16N and TF-16N sub-types were being held in storage at Davis-Monthan AFB, Arizona in March 1997, along with 28 brand-new F-16A/Bs that formed part of the embargoed Pakistan Air Force order. At one time, consideration was being given to selling at least some of those aircraft and using the funds obtained to finance further procurement of

One of the 28 brand new (and unused) embargoed Pakistan Air Force F-16A Block 15s (92734) sitting at Davis-Monthan. MIKE CRUTCH

new-build F-16C/D models, although this idea seems to have fallen by the wayside.

Nonetheless, the stock of aircraft now held at Davis-Monthan represents a substantial investment. Some surplus USAF aircraft have been transferred to Denmark and Israel in recent times and further examples from storage are earmarked for delivery to Jordan and Portugal. In view of what is likely to be an attractive price when compared with that for a 'top-of-the-range' F-16C, it is not beyond the realms of possibility that the Czechs, the Hungarians and the Poles may opt to obtain Fighting Falcons in this way.

Furthermore, efforts to find a customer for some or all of the embargoed Pakistani F-16s have been under way for quite a while. For a time, it looked as if these efforts would yield at least some success, with Indonesia linked to a deal involving nine of them. Negotiations continued for several

It had been hoped that some of the intended Pakistani F-16As might join this aircraft in Indonesia. LMTAS

months in 1996, although the possibility of a sale now appears to have receded, apparently as a result of being unable to agree terms that are satisfactory to both seller and buyer.

Those are by no means the only surplus F-16s that are available at present. In Europe, Belgium and Holland have significantly reduced the size of their respective operational fleets over the past few years. As a consequence, both have spare aircraft that they are quite keen to dispose of, if a mutually satisfactory arrangement can be reached.

Clearly, then, Lockheed Martin might well find it an uphill struggle to secure new orders for the Fighting Falcon in the face of determined sales efforts by other manufacturers and the large number of surplus aircraft.

One of the most imaginative possibilities for the use of redundant F-16s, that is currently being considered by the design team at Fort Worth, is the Unmanned Combat Aerial Vehicle (UCAV). If it goes ahead, this would provide a new capability to the USAF and at the same time make use of some of the large number of F-16s that are now stored at Davis-Monthan. In general terms, the proposal envisages removing the cockpit and associated life-support systems from these aircraft so as to reduce weight, while simultaneously fitting 60 ft span wings and increasing internal fuel load to some 22,000 lbs.

Applications vary, but missions that could conceivably be undertaken by the UCAV include the interception of ballistic missiles during the boost phase immediately after launch and the interdiction of high-threat targets with up to six weapons in the 2,000 lb class, such as the GBU-10 LGB that was extensively used in the Gulf War. Alternatively, the extra fuel is sufficient to allow eight hour combat air patrol (CAP) sorties to be flown.

In addition, however, the design team at Fort Worth is alert to the fact that there are some potential customers who are wary of turning to the second-hand market as a source of hardware, but who also require something that is superior to the current Block 50/52 Fighting Falcon. It is therefore seeking ways and means to expand existing capabilities so as to ensure the product remains attractive to potential customers. In fact, a number of options exist to further improve what is already an outstanding machine.

Some of those options are understandably aimed at existing operators and will take the form of upgrade packages similar to the Mid-Life Update (MLU) that is now being implemented by the four original European customers. In the case of the USAF, plans to adopt the MLU have lapsed, but this service is now working on yet another Multinational Staged Improvement Program (MSIP IV). If it goes ahead, this is expected to result in upgraded aircraft entering service in about the year 2000. Amongst the improvements being considered are a new synthetic-aperture radar, flat-panel colour displays, targeting and navigation systems similar to LANTIRN but contained internally, datalink communications and new precision guided munitions (PGMs).

As far as the latter are concerned, the Fighting Falcon is already playing an important part in the development process, with a pair of Eglin-based aircraft being used as launch vehicles in trials of the Joint Direct Attack Munition (JDAM) that began in November 1996. JDAM is fundamentally a tail-kit which is fitted to the weapon and which comprises dual inertial navigation/global positioning system (INS/GPS) sensors. These offer accuracy levels comparable to those attained with laser-guided bombs, but have the advantage of being able to home autonomously (ie they do not require target designation by either the aircraft that is dropping the bomb or another source). In the Eglin trials, Mk 84 2,000 lb weapons are being used, but the JDAM sensor package can be fitted to several types of conventional bomb, including the BLU-109 penetrator, and will eventually be installed on weapons carried by B-52Hs, B-1Bs, B-2As and F/A-18s as well as the F-16. Operational trials are set to

begin on all of these types during the course of 1997.

Further possibilities that have been mooted for a proposed F-16C Block 50 Plus version include terrain-referenced navigation equipment and passive missile warning systems, while Block 60/62 proposals may yet emerge. There is thus far no guarantee that the latter will progress beyond the design stage and nor has Lockheed Martin said what form they might take. However, it is reasonable to expect that they could well incorporate any or all of the above features, as well as an auxiliary power unit and a larger spine like that fitted to Israeli F-16Ds, but containing additional fuel cells, rather than avionics equipment.

Lockheed Martin is also considering other derivatives, as a kind of fall-back if the Joint Strike Fighter (JSF) project fails to reach fruition. One is the 'Falcon 2000', which would have a bigger delta wing of greater area, a fuselage extension, doubled fuel capacity and no fewer than 20 hardpoints. Another is the so-called F-16X, which has been the subject of design studies with a view to service entry in about 2010. If it goes ahead, this would have a modified F-22 delta wing as well as a fuselage stretch, approximately 80 per cent extra fuel and conformal carriage of the AIM-120 AMRAAM.

These are far from being the only options, nor by any means the only configuration changes under consideration, for Lockheed Martin has already evaluated a number of features that could be adopted, either on new-build aircraft or as a retrofit programme. The conformal fuel tanks that were tested on the F-16ES are one example; nose and wing-root FLIR sensors are another; multi-axis thrust vectoring a third; and it is perhaps not too much of an exaggeration to remark that Lockheed Martin could pursue a 'pick and mix' philosophy in seeking to tailor new models of the Fighting Falcon to satisfy a customer's unique requirements. In summing up the future prospects for the F-16, then, one could almost say that 'the sky appears to be the limit' – but that has also been true for most of the Fighting Falcon's career to date.

FA-46 is one of 30 F-16As now stored by the Belgian Air Force at Weelde awaiting sale. PETER R MARCH

Wing span over launch rails		31 ft 0 in	(9.45 m)
Wing span over missiles		32 ft 9.75 in	(10.00 m)
Length overall		49 ft 4 in	(15.03 m)
Height overall		16 ft 8.5 in	(5.09 m)
Tailplane span		18 ft 3.75 in	(5.58 m)
Wheel track		7 ft 9 in	(2.36 m)
Wheelbase		13 ft 1.5 in	(4.00 m)
Gross wing area		300.0 sq ft	(27.87 m^2)
Flaperon area (total)		31.32 sq ft	(2.91 m^2)
Leading-edge flap area (total)		36.72 sq ft	(3.41 m^2)
Fin area, including dorsal fin		43.10 sq ft	(4.00 m^2)
Rudder area		11.65 sq ft	(1.08 m^2)
Horizontal tail area (total)		63.70 sq ft	(5.92 m^2)
Empty weight	F-16C Block 50	18,917 lb	(8,581 kg)
	F-16C Block 52	18,591 lb	(8,433 kg)
	F-16D Block 50	19,421 lb	(8,810 kg)
	F-16D Block 52	19,059 lb	(8,645 kg)
Maximum internal fuel weight JP-4			
	F-16C	6,846 lb	(3,104 kg)
	F-16D	5,659 lb	(2,567 kg)
Maximum external fuel weight JP-4			
	(2 x 370 gal + 1 x 300 gal tanks)	6,760 lb	(3,066 kg)
	(2 x 600 gal + 1 x 300 gal tanks)	9,523 lb	(4,320 kg)
Maximum external load – full internal fuel			
	F-16C Block 50	15,591 lb	(7,071 kg)
	F-16C Block 52	15,930 lb	(7,224 kg)
Typical combat weight (2 air-to-air missiles, 50% fuel)			
	F-16C Block 50	23,837 lb	(10,813 kg)
	F-16C Block 52	23,498 lb	(10,659 kg)
Maximum take-off weight (2 air-to-air missiles, no tanks)			
	F-16C Block 50	27,099 lb	(12,292 kg)
	F-16C Block 52	26,760 lb	(12,139 kg)
Maximum take-off weight (with external load)			
	F-16C/D Block 50/52	42,300 lb	(19,187 kg)

Max speed at 40,000 ft (12,200 m) exceeds Mach 2.0

Service ceiling exceeds 50,000 ft (15,240 m)

Radius of action

F-16C Block 50 with two 2,000 lb (907 kg) bombs, two AIM-9 Sidewinders, external fuel tanks (retained when empty), hi-lo-lo-hi profile

    – with 1040 US gal external fuel – 676 nm (1252 km)

    – with 1500 US gal external fuel – 802 nm (1485 km)

F-16C Block 50 with two BVR missiles, two AIM-9 Sidewinders, combat air patrol mission, 1040 US gal fuel with external tanks jettisoned when empty

    – 866 nm (1604 km)

Ferry range

F-16C/D Block 50 with drop tanks retained

    – with 1040 US gal external fuel – 1961 nm (3,632 km)

    – with 1500 US gal external fuel – 2276 nm (4,215 km)

Note: F-16C/D Block 50 has F110-GE-129 engine; Block 52 has F100-PW-229

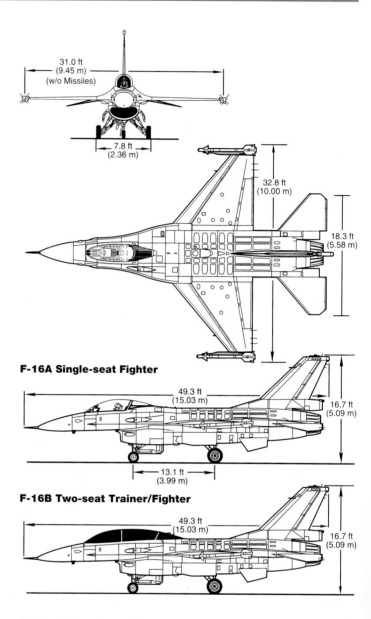

F-16A Single-seat Fighter

F-16B Two-seat Trainer/Fighter

Stores Station Capacities

Station	Pylon Location	Payload (5.5 g)	Payload (9 g)
1	Left Wingtip	425 lb	425 lb
2	Left Outer	700 lb	450 lb
3	Left Centre	3,500 lb	2,000 lb
3A	Left Centre*	450 lb	450 lb
4	Left Inner	4,500 lb	2,500 lb
5	Centreline	2,200 lb	1,200 lb
5L	Left intake wall	550 lb	550 lb
5R	Right intake wall	550 lb	550 lb
6	Right Inner	4,500 lb	2,500 lb
7	Right Centre	3,500 lb	2,000 lb
7A	Right Centre*	450 lb	450 lb
8	Right Outer	700 lb	450 lb
9	Right Wingtip	425 lb	425 lb

* Stations 3A and 7A applicable to dedicated air defence fit

The first YF-16 (72-01567) in June 1976 after conversion to Control Configured Vehicle test aircraft, but without the canards. VIA LARRY DAVIS

1. For the UNITED STATES AIR FORCE

Variant	Serial Numbers	Remarks	Note
YF-16	72-01567 and 72-01568	LWF prototypes	
F-16A	75-0745 to 75-0750	FSD aircraft	
F-16A Block 01	78-0001 to 78-0021	Upgraded F-16A Block 10	
F-16A Block 05	78-0022 to 78-0027	Upgraded F-16A Block 10	
	78-0038 to 78-0076	Upgraded F-16A Block 10	
	79-0288 to 79-0331	Upgraded F-16A Block 10	
F-16A Block 10	79-0332 to 79-0409		
	80-0474 to 80-0540		
F-16A Block 15	80-0541 to 80-0622	Inc conversions F-16A ADF	
	81-0663 to 81-0811	Inc conversions F-16A ADF	
	82-0900 to 82-1025	Inc conversions F-16A ADF	
	83-1066 to 83-1117		
F-16B	75-0751 to 75-0752	FSD aircraft	
F-16B Block 01	78-0077 to 78-0098	Upgraded F-16B Block 10	
F-16B Block 05	78-0099 to 78-0115	Upgraded F-16B Block 10	
	79-0410 to 79-0419	Upgraded F-16B Block 10	
F-16B Block 10	79-0420 to 79-0432		
	80-0623 to 80-0634		
F-16B Block 15	80-0635 to 80-0638	Inc conversions F-16B ADF	
	81-0812 to 81-0822	Inc conversions F-16B ADF	
	82-1026 to 82-1042	Inc conversions F-16B ADF	
	82-1044 to 82-1049	Inc conversions F-16B ADF	
	83-1166 to 83-1173		
F-16C Block 25	83-1118 to 83-1165		
	84-1212 to 84-1318		
	84-1374 to 84-1395		
F-16C Block 25/30	85-1398 to 85-1505		
F-16C Block 30/32	85-1544 to 85-1570		
	86-0207 to 86-0371		
	87-0217 to 87-0349		
	88-0397 to 88-0411		
F-16C Block 40/42	87-0350 to 87-0362		
	88-0412 to 88-0550		
	89-2000 to 89-2154		
	90-0700 to 90-0776		
F-16C Block 50/52	90-0801 to 90-0833		
	91-0336 to 91-0423		
	92-3880 to 92-3923		
	93-0531 to 93-0554		
	94-0038 to 94-0049		

Variant	Serial Numbers	Remarks	Note
	96-0080 to 96-0085		
F-16D Block 25	83-1174 to 83-1185		
	84-1319 to 84-1331		
	84-1396 to 84-1397		
F-16D Block 25/30	85-1506 to 85-1517		
F-16D Block 30/32	85-1571 to 85-1573		
	86-0039 to 86-0047		
	86-0049 to 86-0053		
	87-0363 to 87-0390		
	88-0150 to 88-0152		
F-16D Block 40/42	87-0391 to 87-0396		
	88-0153 to 88-0175		
	89-2155 to 89-2179		
	90-0777 to 90-0800		
F-16D Block 50/52	90-0834 to 90-0849		
	91-0462 to 91-0481		
	92-3924 to 92-3927		2
NF-16D (VISTA)	86-0048		1

Note 1: The NF-16D (VISTA) was adapted from a standard F-16D Block 30 aircraft with the General Electric F110-GE-100 engine at the outset; however, it has since been retrofitted with a Pratt & Whitney F100-PW-229.

Note 2: A further batch of six aircraft has been ordered in FY97; these will be to Block 50 standard.

The 1,000th F-16 built (82-0926) photographed in 1983 on delivery to Hill AFB. LMTAS

2. For the UNITED STATES NAVY

Variant	Serial Numbers	USAF/FMS Identities	Note
F-16N-30	163268 to 163277	85-1369 to 85-1378	3
	163566 to 163577	86-1684 to 86-1695	3
TF-16N-30	163278 to 163281	85-1379 to 85-1382	4

Note 3: Equivalent to USAF F-16C Block 30
Note 4: Equivalent to USAF F-16D Block 30

3. For overseas air arms

Bahrain

Variant	Serial Numbers	USAF/FMS Identities	Note
F-16C Block 40	101 to 115	90-0028 to 90-0035	5
F-16D Block 40	150 to 156	90-0036 to 90-0039	6

Note 5: Only odd serial numbers used in sequence 101 to 115
Note 6: Only even serial numbers used in sequence 150 to 156

Belgium

Variant	Serial Numbers	USAF/FMS Identities	Note
F-16A Block 01	FA-01 to FA-17	78-0116 to 78-0132	7
F-16A Block 05	FA-18 to FA-25	78-0133 to 78-0140	7
F-16A Block 10	FA-26 to FA-46	78-0141 to 78-0161	
	FA-47 to FA-55	80-3538 to 80-3546	
F-16A Block 15	FA-56 to FA-96	80-3547 to 80-3587	
	FA-97 to FA-101	86-0073 to 86-0077	
	FA-102 to FA-112	87-0046 to 87-0056	
	FA-113 to FA-122	88-0038 to 88-0047	
	FA-123 to FA-133	89-0001 to 89-0011	
	FA-134 to FA-136	90-0025 to 90-0027	
F-16B Block 01	FB-01 to FB-06	78-0162 to 78-0167	7
F-16B Block 05	FB-07 to FB-10	78-0168 to 78-0171	7
F-16B Block 10	FB-11 to FB-12	78-0172 to 78-0173	
F-16B Block 15	FB-13 to FB-20	80-3588 to 80-3595	
	FB-21	87-0001	
	FB-22 to FB-23	88-0048 to 88-0049	
	FB-24	89-0012	

Note 7: Surviving aircraft later upgraded to Block 10 standard

Two specially marked Belgian Air Force 75th anniversary F-16As: (top) FA-120 in the colours of 2 Sqn and (above) FA-111 of 1 Sqn, in 1992. PETER R MARCH

Danish F-16A E-191 carried special 40th anniversary markings in 1994. GRAHAM FINCH

Denmark

Variant	Serial Numbers	USAF/FMS Identities	Note
F-16A Block 01	E-174 to E-176	78-0174 to 78-0176	7
F-16A Block 05	E-177 to E-188	78-0177 to 78-0188	7
F-16A Block 10	E-189 to E-203	78-0189 to 78-0203	
F-16A Block 15	E-596 to E-611	80-3596 to 80-3611	
	E-024	82-1024	8
	E-075	83-1075	8
	E-107	83-1107	8
	E-004 to E-008	87-0004 to 87-0008	9
	E-016 to E-018	88-0016 to 88-0018	9
F-16B Block 01	ET-204 to ET-205	78-0204 to 78-0205	7
F-16B Block 05	ET-206 to ET-208	78-0206 to 78-0208	7
F-16B Block 10	ET-209 to ET-211	78-0209 to 78-0211	
F-16B Block 15	ET-612 to ET-615	80-3612 to 80-3615	
	ET-197 to ET-199	86-0197 to 86-0199	9
	ET-022	87-0022	9

Note 7: Surviving aircraft later upgraded to Block 10 standard
Note 8: Attrition replacements obtained from USAF stocks in 1994
Note 9: Fokker-built

Egypt

Variant	Serial Numbers	USAF/FMS Identities	Note
F-16A Block 15	9301 to 9305	80-0639 to 80-0643	
	9306 to 9324	81-0643 to 81-0661	
	9325 to 9334	82-1056 to 82-1065	
F-16B Block 15	9201 to 9205	80-0644 to 80-0648	
	9206	81-0662	
	9207	81-0883	10
	9208	82-1043	11
F-16C Block 32	9501 to 9508	84-1332 to 84-1339	
	9509 to 9534	85-1518 to 85-1543	
F-16C Block 40	9901 to 9902	89-0278 to 89-0279	
	9903 to 9934	90-0899 to 90-0930	
	9935	90-0953	
	9951 to 9978	93-0485 to 93-0512	12
	9979 to 9984	93-0525 to 93-0530	12
F-16D Block 32	9401 to 9406	84-1340 to 84-1345	
F-16D Block 40	9801 to 9807	90-0931 to 90-0937	
	9808 to 9812	90-0954 to 90-0958	
	9851 to 9862	93-0513 to 93-0524	12

Note 10: Fokker-built; diverted from Dutch order
Note 11: Diverted from USAF order
Note 12: Turkish-built
Note 13: In April 1996, Egypt confirmed its intention to obtain another 21 Fighting Falcons during 1999-2000

Greece

Variant	Serial Numbers	USAF/FMS Identities	Note
F-16C Block 30	110 to 143	88-0110 to 88-0143	
F-16C Block 50	TBA	TBA	14
F-16D Block 30	144 to 149	88-0144 to 88-0149	
F-16D Block 50	TBA	TBA	15

Note 14: Total of 32 aircraft for delivery 1997-98
Note 15: Total of 8 aircraft for delivery 1997-98

Indonesia

Variant	Serial Numbers	USAF/FMS Identities	Note
F-16A Block 15	TS-1605 to TS-1612	87-0713 to 87-0720	
F-16B Block 15	TS-1601 to TS-1604	87-0721 to 87-0724	

The first IDF/AF F-16C Block 30 (86-1598) taking off for a test flight at Fort Worth. LMTAS

Israel

Variant	Serial Numbers	USAF/FMS Identities	Note
F-16A Block 01		78-0012	16
		78-0014	16
		78-0018	16
F-16A Block 05		78-0308 to 78-0325	17
		79-0288	16
F-16A Block 10		78-0326 to 78-0354	18
		79-0289	16
		79-0291 to 79-0293	16
		79-0295	16
		79-0297	16
		79-0299	16
		79-0302	16
		79-0304 to 79-0305	16
		79-0319 to 79-0321	16
		79-0325	16
		79-0328	16
		79-0333	16
		79-0339	16
		79-0347	16
		79-0356	16
		79-0358	16
		79-0361	16
		79-0369	16
		79-0377	16
		80-0491	16
		80-0501 to 80-0503	16
		80-0514	16
		80-0516 to 80-0517	16
		80-0532	16
		80-0534	16
		80-0649 to 80-0668	19
F-16B Block 01		78-0086	16
		78-0095	16
F-16B Block 05		78-0106	16
		78-0108 to 78-0109	16
		78-0111	16
		78-0114 to 78-0115	16
		78-0355 to 78-0362	20
		79-0410	16
F-16B Block 10		79-0423 to 79-0425	16
		80-0624	16
		80-0632	16
F-16C Block 30		86-1598 to 86-1612	21
		87-1661 to 87-1693	22
		88-1709 to 88-1711	23
F-16C Block 40		89-0277	24
		90-0850 to 90-0874	25
		91-0486 to 91-0489	26
F-16D Block 30		87-1694 to 87-1708	27
		88-1712 to 88-1720	28
F-16D Block 40		90-0875 to 90-0898	29
		91-0490 to 91-0495	30

Note 16: Ex-USAF aircraft; delivered to IDF/AF in 1994. New identities are understood to be in the '700' (F-16As) and '900' (F-16Bs) sequences, but no further details are known

Note 17: IDF/AF serials are 100, 102, 105, 107, 109, 111-114, 116, 118, 121, 124, 126, 129, 131, 135 and 138 respectively

Note 18: IDF/AF serial numbers are 219, 220, 222, 223, 225, 227, 228, 230, 232, 233, 234, 236, 237, 239, 240, 242, 243, 246, 248-250, 252, 254, 255, 257, 258, 260, 261 and 264 respectively

Note 19: IDF/AF serial numbers are 265-267, 269, 272-277, 281, 282, 284, 285, 287, 290, 292, 296, 298 and 299 respectively

Note 20: IDF/AF serial numbers are 001, 003, 004, 006, 008, 010, 015 and 017 respectively

Note 21: IDF/AF serial numbers are 301, 304, 305, 307, 309, 310, 315, 317, 318, 321, 324, 326, 332, 333 and 337 respectively

Note 22: IDF/AF serial numbers are 340, 341, 344, 345, 348-350, 353, 355, 356, 360, 364, 367, 368, 371, 373, 374, 377, 378, 381, 384, 386, 388, 389, 391, 393, 394, 392, 397, 399, 383, 385 and 376 respectively

Note 23: IDF/AF serial numbers are 359, 313 and 329 respectively

Note 24: IDF/AF serial number is 502

Note 25: IDF/AF serial numbers are 503, 506, 508, 511, 512, 514, 516, 519, 520, 522, 523, 525, 527, 528, 530, 531, 534-536, 538, 539, 542, 543, 546, 547 respectively

Note 26: IDF/AF serial numbers are 551, 554, 557 and 558 respectively

Note 27: IDF/AF serial numbers are 020, 031, 023, 027, 034, 036, 022, 041, 045, 039, 046, 050, 057, 061 and 055 respectively

Note 28: IDF/AF serial numbers are 072, 063, 069, 077, 074, 079, 075, 088 and 083 respectively

Note 29: IDF/AF serial numbers are 601, 603, 606, 610, 612, 615, 619, 621, 624, 628, 630, 633, 637, 638, 642, 647, 648, 651, 652, 656, 660, 664, 666 and 667 respectively

Note 30: IDF/AF serial numbers are 673, 676, 678, 682, 684 and 687 respectively

Jordan

Variant	Serial Numbers	USAF/FMS Identities	Note
F-16A	TBA	TBA	31
F-16B	TBA	TBA	32

Note 31: Identities of the 12 F-16As are not yet known, though all will be former USAF aircraft

Note 32: Identities of the four F-16Bs are not yet known, though all will be former USAF aircraft

The Netherlands

Variant	Serial Numbers	USAF/FMS Identities	Note
F-16A Block 01	J-212 to J-223	78-0212 to 78-0223	33
F-16A Block 05	J-224 to J-237	78-0224 to 78-0237	33
F-16A Block 10	J-238 to J-257	78-0238 to 78-0257	
F-16A Block 15	J-258	78-0258	
	J-616 to J-648	80-3616 to 80-3648	
	J-864 to J-881	81-0864 to 81-0881	
	J-192 to J-207	83-1192 to 83-1207	
	J-358 to J-367	84-1358 to 84-1367	
	J-135 to J-146	85-0135 to 85-0146	
	J-054 to J-063	86-0054 to 86-0063	
	J-508 to J-516	87-0508 to 87-0516	
	J-710	87-0710	
	J-001 to J-012	88-0001 to 88-0012	
	J-013 to J-021	89-0013 to 89-0021	
F-16B Block 01	J-259 to J-264	78-0259 to 78-0264	33
F-16B Block 05	J-265 to J-266	78-0265 to 78-0266	33
F-16B Block 10	J-267 to J-271	78-0267 to 78-0271	
F-16B Block 15	J-649 to J-657	80-3649 to 80-3657	
	J-882	81-0882	
	J-884 to J-885	81-0884 to 81-0885	
	J-208 to J-211	83-1208 to 83-1211	
	J-368 to J-369	84-1368 to 84-1369	
	J-064 to J-065	86-0064 to 86-0065	
	J-066 to J-068	87-0066 to 87-0068	

Note 33: Surviving aircraft later upgraded to Block 10 standard

F-16B (J-068) and F-16A (J-021) operating with 312 Sqn, Royal Netherlands AF from Volkel AB in 1995. DANIEL MARCH

Norway

Variant	Serial Numbers	USAF/FMS Identities	Note
F-16A Block 01	272 to 274	78-0272 to 78-0274	33
F-16A Block 05	275 to 284	78-0275 to 78-0284	33
F-16A Block 10	285 to 299	78-0285 to 78-0299	
F-16A Block 15	300	78-0300	
	658 to 688	80-3658 to 80-3688	
F-16B Block 01	301 to 302	78-0301 to 78-0302	33
F-16B Block 05	303 to 304	78-0303 to 78-0304	33
F-16B Block 10	305 to 307	78-0305 to 78-0307	
F-16B Block 15	689 to 693	80-3689 to 80-3693	
	711 to 712	87-0711 to 87-0712	34

Note 33: Surviving aircraft later upgraded to Block 10 standard
Note 34: Built by General Dynamics at Fort Worth

Pakistan

Variant	Serial Numbers	USAF/FMS Identities	Note
F-16A Block 15	82701 to 82702	81-0899 to 81-0900	
	83703	81-0901	
	84704 to 84719	81-0902 to 81-0917	
	85720 to 85728	81-0918 to 81-0926	
	91729	90-0942	35
	92730 to 92734	90-0943 to 90-0947	35
	92735 to 92738	92-0404 to 92-0407	35
	93739 to 93741	92-0408 to 92-0410	35
F-16B Block 15	82601 to 82604	81-0931 to 81-0934	
	83605	81-0935	
	84606 to 84608	81-0936 to 81-0938	
	85609 to 85612	81-1504 to 81-1507	
	91613	90-0948	35
	92614 to 92617	90-0949 to 90-0952	35
	92618 to 92619	92-0452 to 92-0453	35
	93620 to 93621	92-0454 to 92-0455	35
	94622 to 94623	92-0456 to 92-0457	35
	624 to 627	92-0458 to 92-0461	35

Note 35: Embargoed and stored at Davis-Monthan AFB, Arizona. At least nine of these aircraft may be supplied to Indonesia, if terms can be agreed. A further 41 F-16A Block 15s (742 to 782/92-0411 to 92-0451) and two F-16B Block 15s (628 to 629/92-0462 to 92-0463) were ordered by Pakistan, but will not be built.

Portuguese Air Force F-16A Block 15 15109 is based at Monte Real. PETER R FOSTER

Shown with combined R Thai AF and USAF markings, this F-16A Block 15 now serves with 403 Squadron. LMTAS

Portugal

Variant	Serial Numbers	USAF/FMS Identities	Note
F-16A Block 15	15101 to 15117	93-0465 to 93-0481	
F-16B Block 15	15118 to 15120	93-0482 to 93-0484	

Singapore

Variant	Serial Numbers	USAF/FMS Identities	Note
F-16A Block 15	880 to 883	87-0397 to 87-0400	
F-16B Block 15	884 to 887	87-0401 to 87-0404	

Note 36: A total of eight F-16C Block 52s and 10 F-16D Block 52s is currently on order for delivery during 1998-99. Singapore has also made use of aircraft leased from the USAF for training purposes with the 56th Fighter Wing at Luke AFB, Az; initially, this involved older F-16A/B models, but these were replaced by F-16C/D Block 40 versions delivered during 1995-96. F-16As known to have been used were 81-0663, 81-0667, 81-0670, 81-0676 to 81-0679, 81-0683 and 81-0687. F-16Bs were 80-0638 and 81-0815. F-16Cs include 88-0417, 88-0427, 89-2002, 89-2022 and 89-2034. F-16Ds include 88-0156.

South Korea

Variant	Serial Numbers	USAF/FMS Identities	Note
F-16C Block 32	85-574 to 85-583	85-1574 to 85-1583	
	86-586 to 86-597	86-1586 to 86-1597	
	87-653 to 87-660	87-1653 to 87-1660	
F-16C Block 52	92-000 to 92-027	92-4000 to 92-4027	37
F-16D Block 32	84-370 to 84-373	84-1370 to 84-1373	
	85-584 to 85-585	85-1584 to 85-1585	
	90-938 to 90-941	90-0938 to 90-0941	
F-16D Block 52	92-028 to 92-047	92-4028 to 92-4047	38

Note 37: Additional 52 F-16C Block 52 for delivery 1997-99 from licence production by Samsung Aerospace
Note 38: Additional 20 F-16D Block 52 for delivery 1997-99 from licence production by Samsung Aerospace

Taiwan

Variant	Serial Numbers	USAF/FMS Identities	Note
F-16A Block 20	TBA	TBA	39
F-16B Block 20	TBA	TBA	40

Note 39: Total of 120 new-build aircraft for delivery 1996-99
Note 40: Total of 30 new-build aircraft for delivery 1996-99

Thailand

Variant	Serial Numbers	USAF/FMS Identities	Note
F-16A Block 15	86378	86-0378	
	87702 to 87708	87-0702 to 87-0708	
	90020 to 90031	90-7020 to 90-7031	
	91062 to 91067	91-0062 to 91-0067	
F-16B Block 15	86379 to 86381	86-0379 to 86-0381	
	87709	87-0709	
	90032 to 90037	90-7032 to 90-7037	

Note 41: The Royal Thai Air Force uses its own serialling system, which is based on the Buddhist calendar and incorporates a local designation as well as sequence and year of delivery. Under this scheme, the F-16 is the type BK.19, with aircraft 91-0062 being serialled as BK.19-13/37, indicating it was the 13th Fighting Falcon delivered and was accepted by the RTAF in the Buddhist year 2537. In addition, corrupted versions of the FMS identity are displayed along with a five-digit unit identifying code, an example of the latter being 10309 which is carried by the ninth aircraft assigned to 103 Squadron.

Turkey

Variant	Serial Numbers	USAF/FMS Identities	Note
F-16C Block 30	86-0066 to 86-0072	86-0066 to 86-0072	
	87-0009 to 87-0021	87-0009 to 87-0021	
	88-0019 to 88-0032	88-0019 to 88-0032	
F-16C Block 40	88-0033 to 88-0037	88-0033 to 88-0037	
	89-0022 to 89-0041	89-0022 to 89-0041	
	90-0001 to 90-0021	90-0001 to 90-0021	
	91-0001 to 91-0021	91-0001 to 91-0021	
	92-0001 to 92-0021	92-0001 to 92-0021	
	93-0001 to 93-0014	93-0001 to 93-0014	
	93-0857 to TBA	93-0857 to TBA	42
F-16D Block 30	86-0191 to 86-0196	86-0191 to 86-0196	
	87-0002 to 87-0003	87-0002 to 87-0003	
	88-0013	88-0013	
F-16D Block 40	88-0014 to 88-0015	88-0014 to 88-0015	
	89-0042 to 89-0045	89-0042 to 89-0045	
	90-0022 to 90-0024	90-0022 to 90-0024	
	91-0022 to 91-0024	91-0022 to 91-0024	
	92-0022 to 92-0024	92-0022 to 92-0024	

Note 42: An additional 68 F-16C Block 50 and 12 F-16D Block 50 are on order for delivery during 1996-99

Venezuela

Variant	Serial Numbers	USAF/FMS Identities	Note
F-16A Block 15		82-1050 to 82-1052	43
		83-1186 to 83-1188	44
		84-1346 to 84-1357	45
F-16B Block 15		82-1053 to 82-1055	46
		83-1189 to 83-1191	47

Note 43: FAV identities are 1041, 0051 and 6611 respectively
Note 44: FAV identities are 8900, 0049 and 0678 respectively
Note 45: FAV identities are 7268, 9864, 8924, 8900, 6023, 3260, 4226, 6426, 4827, 9864, 3648 and 0220 respectively
Note 46: FAV identities are 1715, 2179 and 9581 respectively
Note 47: FAV identities are 2337, 7635 and 9583 respectively

4. US production totals by variant

Variant	Total	Cumulative Total (by basic variant)
YF-16	2	2
F-16A (FSD)	6	6
F-16A Block 01	21	
F-16A Block 05	89	
F-16A Block 10	145	
F-16A Block 15	409	664
F-16B (FSD)	2	2
F-16B Block 01	22	
F-16B Block 05	27	
F-16B Block 10	25	
F-16B Block 15	46	120
F-16C Block 25	209	
F-16C Block 30	360	
F-16C Block 32	56	
F-16C Block 40	234	
F-16C Block 42	150	
F-16C Block 50	165	
F-16C Block 52	42	1216 (Note 48)
F-16D Block 25	35	
F-16D Block 30	47	
F-16D Block 32	5	
F-16D Block 40	31	
F-16D Block 42	47	
F-16D Block 50	20	
F-16D Block 52	12	205
NF-16D (VISTA)	1	1 (Note 49)
F-16N-30	22	22
TF-16N-30	4	4
TOTAL		**2242** (Note 50)

Note 48: Further six F-16C Block 50 on order in FY97
Note 49: Modified from F-16D Block 30 prior to delivery
Note 50: Total including aircraft on order is 2248
Note 51: Totals are given as originally built and do not take into account post-production modification programmes

5. Aircraft supplied by variant and manufacturer

		LMTAS	FOKKER	SABCA	TAI	SAMSUNG	SURPLUS	TOTAL
Bahrain	F-16C	8						8
	F-16D	4						4
Belgium	F-16A				136			136
	F-16B				24			24
Denmark	F-16A		8	46			(3)	57#
	F-16B		4	12				16
Egypt	F-16A	34						34
	F-16B	7	1					8
	F-16C	90			34			124
	F-16D	18			12			30
Greece	F-16CG	66						66*
	F-16DG	14						14*
Indonesia	F-16A	8						8
	F-16B	4						4
Israel	F-16A	67					(36)	103#
	F-16B	8					(14)	22#
	F-16C	81						81
	F-16D	54						54
Jordan	F-16A						(12)	12#
	F-16B						(4)	4#
Netherlands	F-16A		177					177
	F-16B		36					36
Norway	F-16A		60					60
	F-16B	2	12					14
Pakistan	F-16A	28						28
	F-16B	12						12
Pakistan (embargoed aircraft)								
	F-16A	13						13
	F-16B	15						15
Portugal	F-16A	17						17
	F-16B	3						3
Singapore	F-16A	4						4
	F-16B	4						4
	F-16C	8						8*
	F-16D	10						10*
South Korea	F-16C	32				78		110*
	F-16D	20				30		50*
Taiwan	F-16A	120						120*
	F-16B	30						30*
Thailand	F-16A	26						26
	F-16B	10						10
Turkey	F-16C	2			202			204*
	F-16D	6			30			36*
USAF	YF-16	2						2
	F-16A (FSD)	6						6
	F-16A	662	2					664
	F-16B (FSD)	2						2
	F-16B	116		4				120
	F-16C	1222						1222*
	F-16D	206						206
US Navy	F-16N	22						22
	TF-16N	4						4*
Venezuela	F-16A	18						18
	F-16B	6						6
Production Lease								
	F-16C	4						4*
	F-16D	8						8*
TOTALS	YF-16	2						2
	F-16A (FSD)	6						6
	F-16A	997	247	182			(51)	1420
	F-16B (FSD)	2						2
	F-16B	217	53	40			(18)	310
	F-16C	1603			236	78		1806
	F-16D	340			42	30		412
	F-16N	22						22
	TF-16N	4						4
GRAND TOTAL		**3103**	**300**	**222**	**278**	**108**	**(69)**	**4011**

* On order or delivery in progress
# Total includes aircraft obtained from surplus USAF stocks, which are not included in final production summary at foot of table

APPENDIX C

US AIRCRAFT STATUS

1. F-16A/B/XL

Serial	Type/Code	c/n	Operator/location
72-1567	YF-16	60-1	Virginia Air & Space Center, Hampton, VA
72-1568	YF-16	60-2	On display, Rome Laboratory, Griffiss, NY
75-0745	F-16A	61-1	Dover AFB Museum, DE
75-0746	F-16A	61-2	Fort Worth, TX (derelict?)
75-0747	F-16A/F-16XL-2	61-3	To NASA as 848 (also 847)
75-0748	F-16A	61-4	On display, USAF Academy, Colorado Springs, CO
75-0749	F-16A/F-16XL-1	61-5	To NASA as 849
75-0750	F-16A/AFTI	61-6	USAF 416th TS/412th TW, Edwards AFB, CA
76-0751	F-16B	62-1	Air Force Flight Test Center Museum Edwards AFB, CA
76-0752	F-16B-2/J79	62-2	Lockheed Martin, Fort Worth, TX
78-0001	F-16A-01	61-7	Preserved at Langley AFB, VA
78-0002	F-16A-01	61-8	USAF Misawa AB, Japan, BDRT
78-0003	F-16A-01	61-9	AMARC, Davis-Monthan AFB, AZ [FG235]; arr 29-Sep-94
78-0004	F-16A-01	61-10	Cr 11-Feb-85 (58th TTW)
78-0005	F-16A-01	61-11	On display, Tucson, AZ
78-0006	F-16A-01	61-12	Cr 01-Oct-79 (388th TFW)
78-0007	F-16A-01	61-13	AMARC, Davis-Monthan AFB, AZ [FG234]; arr 27-Sep-94
78-0008	F-16A-01	61-14	USAF 162nd FW, Arizona ANG, Tucson IAP
78-0009	F-16A-01	61-15	Cr 24-Jan-91 (161st TFTS)
78-0010	F-16A-01	61-16	AMARC, Davis-Monthan AFB, AZ [FG109]; arr 18-Mar-94
78-0011	F-16A-01	61-17	AMARC, Davis-Monthan AFB, AZ [FG059]; arr 27-Jan-94
78-0012	F-16A-01	61-18	To IDF/AF 09-Sep-94
78-0013	F-16A-01	61-19	Cr 06-Apr-81 (388th TFW)
78-0014	F-16A-01	61-20	To IDF/AF 01-Sep-94
78-0015	F-16A-01	61-21	USAF 162nd FW, Arizona ANG, Tucson IAP
78-0016	F-16A-01	61-22	Was in use for BDRT at Hahn AB, Germany
78-0017	F-16A-01	61-23	AMARC, Davis-Monthan AFB, AZ [FG206]; arr 11-Aug-94
78-0018	F-16A-01	61-24	To IDF/AF 09-Aug-94
78-0019	F-16A-01	61-25	AMARC, Davis-Monthan AFB, AZ [FG198]; arr 29-Jul-94
78-0020	F-16A-01	61-26	AMARC, Davis-Monthan AFB, AZ [FG161]; arr 06-May-94
78-0021	F-16A-01	61-27	USAF Misawa AB, Japan, BDRT
78-0022	F-16A-05	61-28	AMARC, Davis-Monthan AFB, AZ [FG170]; arr 20-Jun-94
78-0023	F-16A-05	61-29	Cr 26-Mar-80 (388th TFW)
78-0024	F-16A-05	61-30	AMARC, Davis-Monthan AFB, AZ [FG188]; arr 22-Jul-94
78-0025	F-16A-05	61-31	USAF Nellis AFB, NV, BDRT
78-0026	F-16A-05	61-32	USAF 162nd FW, Arizona ANG, Tucson IAP
78-0027	F-16A-05	61-33	Hill AFB Fire Section
78-0038	F-16A-05	61-34	AMARC, Davis-Monthan AFB, AZ [FG083]; arr 18-Feb-94
78-0039	F-16A-05	61-35	USAF Eielson AFB, AK, BDRT
78-0040	F-16A-05	61-36	USAF Hill AFB, UT, BDRT
78-0041	F-16A-05	61-37	Cr 22-Mar-90 (388th TFW)

Serial	Type/Code	c/n	Operator/location
78-0042	F-16A-05	61-38	On display, Montgomery, AL
78-0043	F-16A-05	61-39	USAF Hill AFB, UT, BDRT
78-0044	F-16A-05	61-40	USAF 162nd FW, Arizona ANG, Tucson IAP
78-0045	F-16A-05	61-41	Cr 22-Mar-90 (388th TFW)
78-0046	F-16A-05	61-42	Cr 05-Aug-81 (388th TFW)
78-0047	F-16A-05	61-43	AMARC, Davis-Monthan AFB, AZ [FG154]; arr 22-Apr-94
78-0048	F-16A-05	61-44	Cr 15-Jan-82 (388th TFW)
78-0049	F-16A-05	61-45	AMARC, Davis-Monthan AFB, AZ [FG112]; arr 23-Mar-94
78-0050	F-16A-05	61-46	USAF Hill AFB, UT, Fire Section
78-0051	F-16A-05	61-47	AMARC, Davis-Monthan AFB, AZ [FG173]; arr 23-Jun-94
78-0052	F-16A-05	61-48	USAF Eielson AFB, AK, BDRT
78-0053	F-16A-05	61-49	USAF Misawa AB, Japan, BDRT
78-0054	F-16A-05	61-50	AMARC, Davis-Monthan AFB, AZ [FG329]; arr 13-Jul-95
78-0055	F-16A-05	61-51	Cr 12-Feb-86 (3246th TW)
78-0056	F-16A-05	61-52	USAF 162nd FW, Arizona ANG, Tucson IAP
78-0057	F-16A-05	61-53	USAF Spangdahlem AB, Germany, BDRT
78-0058	F-16A-05	61-54	AMARC, Davis-Monthan AFB, AZ [FG247]; arr 13-Oct-94
78-0059	F-16A-05	61-55	Selfridge Military Museum, MI
78-0060	F-16A-05	61-56	AMARC, Davis-Monthan AFB, AZ [FG151]; arr 22-Apr-94
78-0061	F-16A-05	61-57	USAF Alabama ANG, Montgomery, BDRT
78-0062	F-16A-05/GF-16A	61-58	USAF TTC/82nd TRW, Sheppard AFB, TX
78-0063	F-16A-05	61-59	AMARC, Davis-Monthan AFB, AZ [FG066]; arr 04-Feb-94
78-0064	F-16A-05	61-60	AMARC, Davis-Monthan AFB, AZ [FG224]; arr 13-Sep-94
78-0065	F-16A-05	61-61	USAF Hill AFB, UT, BDRT
78-0066	F-16A-05	61-62	USAF Hill AFB, UT, BDRT
78-0067	F-16A-05	61-63	Cr 11-May-82 (388th TFW)
78-0068	F-16A-05	61-64	AMARC, Davis-Monthan AFB, AZ [FG082]; arr 18-Feb-94
78-0069	F-16A-05/GF-16A	61-65	USAF TTC/82nd TRW, Sheppard AFB, TX
78-0070	F-16A-05	61-66	AMARC, Davis-Monthan AFB, AZ [FG143]; arr 13-Apr-94
78-0071	F-16A-05	61-67	Cr 25-Jun-80 (388th TFW)
78-0072	F-16A-05	61-68	Cr 19-Jun-84 (56th TTW)
78-0073	F-16A-05	61-69	AMARC, Davis-Monthan AFB, AZ [FG186]; arr 21-Jul-94
78-0074	F-16A-05	61-70	USAF Hill AFB, UT, BDRT
78-0075	F-16A-05	61-71	Cr 10-Oct-86 (388th TFW)
78-0076	F-16A-05	61-72	AMARC, Davis-Monthan AFB, AZ [FG194]; arr 27-Jul-94
78-0077	F-16A-05	62-3	AMARC, Davis-Monthan AFB, AZ [FG054]; arr 21-Jan-94
78-0078	F-16B-01	62-4	Cr 09-Aug-79 (388th TFW)
78-0079	F-16B-01	62-5	AMARC, Davis-Monthan AFB, AZ [FG240]; arr 06-Oct-94
78-0080	F-16B-01	62-6	USAF 416th TS/412th TW, Edwards AFB, CA
78-0081	F-16B-01	62-7	USAF 416th TS/412th TW, Edwards AFB, CA
78-0082	F-16B-01	62-8	AMARC, Davis-Monthan AFB, AZ [FG381]; arr 01-Aug-96
78-0083	F-16B-01	62-9	AMARC, Davis-Monthan AFB, AZ [FG377]; arr 12-Jul-96
78-0084	F-16B-01	62-10	AMARC, Davis-Monthan AFB, AZ [FG406]; arr 10-Jan-97

The second YF-16 (75-1568) photographed at RAF Mildenhall, UK on 29 May 1977 on its European demonstration tour. R L WARD

The first F-16B (72-0751) at the Air Force Flight Test Center, Edwards AFB, CA in November 1977. VIA LARRY DAVIS

Serial	Type/Code	c/n	Operator/location
78-0085	F-16B-01	62-11	USAF 416th TS/412th TW, Edwards AFB, CA
78-0086	F-16B-01	62-12	To IDF/AF 09-Sep-94
78-0087	F-16B-01	62-13	AMARC, Davis-Monthan AFB, AZ [FG397]; arr 08-Nov-96
78-0088	F-16B-01	62-14	USAF 416th TS/412th TW, Edwards AFB, CA
78-0089	F-16B-01	62-15	USAF 416th TS/412th TW, Edwards AFB, CA
78-0090	F-16B-01	62-16	USAF 416th TS/412th TW, Edwards AFB, CA
78-0091	F-16B-01/ADF	62-17	USAF 162nd FW, Arizona ANG, Tucson IAP
78-0092	F-16B-01	62-18	Cr 23-Jul-80 (388th TFW)
78-0093	F-16B-01	62-19	Cr 15-May-95 (162nd FG)
78-0094	F-16B-01/ADF	62-20	USAF 195 FS/162nd FW, Arizona ANG, Tucson IAP
78-0095	F-16B-01	62-21	To IDF/AF 09-Sep-94
78-0096	F-16B-01	62-22	USAF 416th TS/412th TW, Edwards AFB, CA
78-0097	F-16B-01	62-23	USAF 40th TES/46th TW, Eglin AFB, FL
78-0098	F-16B-01	62-24	USAF 416th TS/412th TW, Edwards AFB, CA
78-0099	F-16B-05	62-25	AMARC, Davis-Monthan AFB, AZ [FG325]; arr 05-Jul-95
78-0100	F-16B-05	62-26	USAF 416th TS/412th TW, Edwards AFB, CA
78-0101	F-16B-05/GF-16B	62-27	USAF TTC/82nd TRW, Sheppard AFB, TX
78-0102	F-16B-05	62-28	USAF 40th TES/46th TW, Eglin AFB, FL
78-0103	F-16B-05/ADF	62-29	AMARC, Davis-Monthan AFB, AZ [FG177]; arr 01-Jul-94
78-0104	F-16B-05	62-30	AMARC, Davis-Monthan AFB, AZ [FG335]; arr 25-Sep-95
78-0105	F-16B-05	62-31	Cr 27-Mar-81 (56th TTW)
78-0106	F-16B-05	62-32	To IDF/AF 27-Sep-94
78-0107	F-16B-05	62-33	USAF IAAFA, Kelly AFB, TX
78-0108	F-16B-05	62-34	To IDF/AF 09-Aug-94
78-0109	F-16B-05	62-35	To IDF/AF 27-Sep-94
78-0110	F-16B-05	62-36	Cr 29-Oct-80 (56th TTW)
78-0111	F-16B-05	62-37	To IDF/AF 04-Oct-94
78-0112	F-16B-05	62-38	Cr 23-Mar-82 (3246th TW)
78-0113	F-16B-05	62-39	Cr 25-Jul-83 (56th TTW)
78-0114	F-16B-05	62-40	To IDF/AF Nov-94
78-0115	F-16B-05	62-41	To IDF/AF 27-Sep-94
79-0288	F-16A-05	61-73	To IDF/AF 20-Mar-95
79-0289	F-16A-05	61-74	To IDF/AF 27-Sep-94
79-0290	F-16A-05	61-75	USAF Montana ANG, Great Falls IAP, BDRT
79-0291	F-16A-05	61-76	To IDF/AF 20-Mar-95
79-0292	F-16A-05	61-77	To IDF/AF 18-Nov-94
79-0293	F-16A-05	61-78	To IDF/AF 04-Nov-94
79-0294	F-16A-05	61-79	AMARC, Davis-Monthan AFB, AZ [FG046]; arr 10-Jan-94
79-0295	F-16A-05	61-80	To IDF/AF 04-Nov-94

Serial	Type/Code	c/n	Operator/location
79-0296	F-16A-05	61-81	USAF 162nd FW, Arizona ANG, Tucson IAP
79-0297	F-16A-5	61-82	To IDF/AF 04-Nov-94
79-0298	F-16A-5	61-83	Cr 08-Nov-82 (56th TTW)
79-0299	F-16A-5	61-84	To IDF/AF 04-Nov-94
79-0300	F-16A-5	61-85	AMARC, Davis-Monthan AFB, AZ [FG042]; arr 04-Jan-94
79-0301	F-16A-5	61-86	Cr 20-May-82 (388th TFW)
79-0302	F-16A-5	61-87	To IDF/AF 18-Nov-94
79-0303	F-16A-5	61-88	AMARC, Davis-Monthan AFB, AZ [FG396]; arr 08-Nov-96
79-0304	F-16A-5	61-89	To IDF/AF 04-Nov-94
79-0305	F-16A-5	61-90	To IDF/AF 09-Sep-94
79-0306	F-16A-5	61-91	AMARC, Davis-Monthan AFB, AZ [FG047]; arr 10-Jan-94
79-0307	F-16A-5/GF-16A	61-92	USAF TTC/82nd TRW, Sheppard AFB, TX
79-0308	F-16A-5	61-93	AMARC, Davis-Monthan AFB, AZ [FG045]; arr 10-Jan-94
79-0309	F-16A-5	61-94	USAF Shaw AFB, SC, BDRT
79-0310	F-16A-5	61-95	AMARC, Davis-Monthan AFB, AZ [FG067]; arr 09-Feb-94
79-0311	F-16A-5	61-96	AMARC, Davis-Monthan AFB, AZ [FG326]; arr 06-Jul-95
79-0312	F-16A-5	61-97	AMARC, Davis-Monthan AFB, AZ [FG044]; arr 10-Jan-94
79-0313	F-16A-5	61-98	Cr 29-Jun-81 (388th TFW)
79-0314	F-16A-5	61-99	AMARC, Davis-Monthan AFB, AZ [FG058]; arr 27-Jan-94
79-0315	F-16A-5	61-100	Cr 10-Apr-84 (157th TFS)

This early production F-16B (78-0091) was later converted to ADF standard. PETER R MARCH

F-16A (79-0317) photographed in April 1989 while serving with the South Carolina ANG. PETER R FOSTER

Serial	Type/Code	c/n	Operator/location
79-0316	F-16A-5	61-101	Cr 10-Apr-81 (388th TFW)
79-0317	F-16A-5	61-102	AMARC, Davis-Monthan AFB, AZ [FG074]; arr 14-Feb-94
79-0318	F-16A-5	61-103	Cr 27-Jan-82 (388th TFW)
79-0319	F-16A-5	61-104	To IDF/AF 04-Nov-94
79-0320	F-16A-5	61-105	To IDF/AF 04-Nov-94
79-0321	F-16A-5	61-106	To IDF/AF 04-Nov-94
79-0322	F-16A-5	61-107	AMARC, Davis-Monthan AFB, AZ [FG056]; arr 26-Jan-94
79-0323	F-16A-5	61-108	Cr 07-Feb-85 (157th TFS)
79-0324	F-16A-5	61-109	AMARC, Davis-Monthan AFB, AZ [FG410]; arr 06-Dec-96
79-0325	F-16A-5	61-110	To IDF/AF 04-Nov-94
79-0326	F-16A-5/GF-16A	61-111	USAF TTC/82nd TRW, Sheppard AFB, TX
79-0327	F-16A-5/GF-16A	61-112	USAF TTC/82nd TRW, Sheppard AFB, TX
79-0328	F-16A-5	61-113	To IDF/AF 01-Sep-94
79-0329	F-16A-5	61-114	AMARC, Davis-Monthan AFB, AZ [FG111]; arr 22-Mar-94
79-0330	F-16A-5/GF-16A	61-115	USAF TTC/82nd TRW, Sheppard AFB, TX
79-0331	F-16A-5	61-116	AMARC, Davis-Monthan AFB, AZ [FG016]; arr 05-Aug-93
79-0332	F-16A-10/GF-16A	61-117	USAF TTC/82nd TRW, Sheppard AFB, TX
79-0333	F-16A-10	61-118	To IDF/AF 09-Sep-94
79-0334	F-16A-10/GF-16A	61-119	USAF TTC/82nd TRW, Sheppard AFB, TX
79-0335	F-16A-10	61-120	USAF Davis-Monthan AFB, AZ, BDRT
79-0336	F-16A-10	61-121	AMARC, Davis-Monthan AFB, AZ [FG029]; arr 26-Aug-93
79-0337	F-16A-10	61-122	USAF New York ANG, Hancock Field, Syracuse, BDRT
79-0338	F-16A-10	61-123	Cr 09-Sep-88 (56th TTW)
79-0339	F-16A-10	61-124	To IDF/AF 01-Sep-94
79-0340	F-16A-10	61-125	USAF Aviano AB, Italy, BDRT
79-0341	F-16A-10	61-126	AMARC, Davis-Monthan AFB, AZ [FG128]; arr 01-Apr-94
79-0342	F-16A-10	61-127	AMARC, Davis-Monthan AFB, AZ [FG152]; arr 22-Apr-94
79-0343	F-16A-10	61-128	Cr 27-Dec-82 (474th TFW)
79-0344	F-16A-10/GF-16A	61-129	USAF TTC/82nd TRW, Sheppard AFB, TX
79-0345	F-16A-10	61-130	AMARC, Davis-Monthan AFB, AZ [FG135]; arr 08-Apr-94
79-0346	F-16A-10	61-131	AMARC, Davis-Monthan AFB, AZ [FG108]; arr 18-Mar-94
79-0347	F-16A-10	61-132	To IDF/AF 02-Aug-94
79-0348	F-16A-10	61-133	AMARC, Davis-Monthan AFB, AZ [FG181]; arr 15-Jul-94
79-0349	F-16A-10	61-134	AMARC, Davis-Monthan AFB, AZ [FG014]; arr 04-Aug-93
79-0350	F-16A-10	61-135	Cr 18-Nov-83 (474th TFW)
79-0351	F-16A-10	61-136	USAF Arkansas ANG, Fort Smith ANGB, BDRT
79-0352	F-16A-10	61-137	USAF 162nd FW, Arizona ANG, Tucson IAP
79-0353	F-16A-10	61-138	AMARC, Davis-Monthan AFB, AZ [FG019]; arr 12-Aug-93
79-0354	F-16A-10	61-139	AMARC, Davis-Monthan AFB, AZ [FG191]; arr 22-Jul-94
79-0355	F-16A-10	61-140	AMARC, Davis-Monthan AFB, AZ [FG021]; arr 12-Aug-93
79-0356	F-16A-10	61-141	To IDF/AF 01-Sep-94
79-0357	F-16A-10	61-142	USAF 162nd FW, Arizona ANG, Tucson IAP
79-0358	F-16A-10	61-143	To IDF/AF 04-Oct-94
79-0359	F-16A-10	61-144	AMARC, Davis-Monthan AFB, AZ [FG141]; arr 12-Apr-94
79-0360	F-16A-10/GF-16A	61-145	USAF TTC/82nd TRW, Sheppard AFB, TX
79-0361	F-16A-10	61-146	To IDF/AF 02-Aug-94
79-0362	F-16A-10	61-147	AMARC, Davis-Monthan AFB, AZ [FG399]; arr 22-Nov-96
79-0363	F-16A-10	61-148	AMARC, Davis-Monthan AFB, AZ [FG031]; arr 02 Sep-93
79-0364	F-16A-10	61-149	USAF 162nd FW, Arizona ANG, Tucson IAP
79-0365	F-16A-10	61-150	AMARC, Davis-Monthan AFB, AZ [FG0171]; arr 20-Jun-94
79-0366	F-16A-10	61-151	USAF Mountain Home AFB, ID, BDRT
79-0367	F-16A-10	61-152	Cr 11-Mar-86 (474th TFW)
79-0368	F-16A-10	61-153	USAF 162nd FW, Arizona ANG, Tucson IAP
79-0369	F-16A-10	61-154	To IDF/AF 09-Aug-94
79-0370	F-16A-10	61-155	USAF 162nd FW, Arizona ANG, Tucson IAP
79-0371	F-16A-10/GF-16A	61-156	USAF TTC/82nd TRW, Sheppard AFB, TX

Serial	Type/Code	c/n	Operator/location
79-0372	F-16A-10	61-157	Cr 01-Nov-85 (56th TTW)
79-0373	F-16A-10	61-158	USAF Colorado ANG, Buckley ANGB, BDRT
79-0374	F-16A-10	61-159	Cr 20-May-82 (474th TFW)
79-0375	F-16A-10	61-160	AMARC, Davis-Monthan AFB, AZ [FG382]; arr 01-Aug-96
79-0376	F-16A-10	61-161	AMARC, Davis-Monthan AFB, AZ [FG132]; arr 07-Apr-94
79-0377	F-16A-10	61-162	To IDF/AF 07-Apr-94
79-0378	F-16A-10	61-163	Cr 16-Jun-82 (474th TFW)
79-0379	F-16A-10	61-164	Cr 21-Apr-93 (107th FS)
79-0380	F-16A-10	61-165	USAF Moody AFB, GA, BDRT
79-0381	F-16A-10	61-166	AMARC, Davis-Monthan AFB, AZ [FG049]; arr 11-Jan-94
79-0382	F-16A-10	61-167	USAF Texas ANG, Kelly AFB, BDRT
79-0383	F-16A-10	61-168	AMARC, Davis-Monthan AFB, AZ [FG063]; arr 02-Feb-94
79-0384	F-16A-10	61-169	AMARC, Davis-Monthan AFB, AZ [FG127]; arr 01-Apr-94
79-0385	F-16A-10	61-170	Cr 22-Jun-87 (56th TTW)
79-0386	F-16A-10	61-171	Cr 19-Jan-83 (388th TFW)
79-0387	F-16A-10	61-172	USAF Selfridge ANGB, MI, BDRT
79-0388	F-16A-10	61-173	Preserved at Hill AFB, UT
79-0389	F-16A-10	61-174	AMARC, Davis-Monthan AFB, AZ [FG383]; arr 23-Aug-96
79-0390	F-16A-10	61-175	Cr 04-May-82 (474th TFW)
79-0391	F-16A-10	61-176	Cr 11-Apr-91 (138th TFS)
79-0392	F-16A-10	61-177	Cr 09-Jun-82 (474th TFW)
79-0393	F-16A-10	61-178	AMARC, Davis-Monthan AFB, AZ [FG130]; arr 07-Apr-94
79-0394	F-16A-10	61-179	USAF South Carolina ANG, McEntire ANGB, BDRT
79-0395	F-16A-10	61-180	AMARC, Davis-Monthan AFB, AZ [FG018]; arr 05-Aug-93
79-0396	F-16A-10	61-181	AMARC, Davis-Monthan AFB, AZ [FG030]; arr 27-Aug-93
79-0397	F-16A-10	61-182	Cr 22-Mar-88 (56th TTW)
79-0398	F-16A-10	61-183	Cr 28-Jun-89 (161st TFTS)
79-0399	F-16A-10	61-184	USAF Illinois ANG, Springfield, BDRT
79-0400	F-16A-10	61-185	Cr 13-Jan-91 (138th TFS)
79-0401	F-16A-10	61-186	USAF Indiana ANG, Terre Haute, BDRT
79-0402	F-16A-10	61-187	USAF Museum, Wright-Patterson AFB, OH
79-0403	F-16A-10	61-188	Air-Sea-Space Museum, USS Intrepid, NY
79-0404	F-16A-10	61-189	USAF 162nd FW, Arizona ANG, Tucson IAP
79-0405	F-16A-10	61-190	AMARC, Davis-Monthan AFB, AZ [FG022]; arr 13-Aug-93
79-0406	F-16A-10	61-191	USAF Iowa ANG, Des Moines IAP, BDRT
79-0407	F-16A-10	61-192	USAF Museum, Wright-Patterson AFB, OH
79-0408	F-16A-10/GF-16A	61-193	USN NATTC, NAS Memphis, TN
79-0409	F-16A-10	61-194	AMARC, Davis-Monthan AFB, AZ [FG327]; arr 06-Jul-95
79-0410	F-16B-05	62-42	To IDF/AF 04-Nov-94
79-0411	F-16B-05	62-43	AMARC, Davis-Monthan AFB, AZ [FG385]; arr 10-Oct-96
79-0412	F-16B-05	62-44	USAF 162nd FW, Arizona ANG, Tucson IAP
79-0413	F-16B-05	62-45	USAF 40th TES/46th TW, Eglin AFB, FL
79-0414	F-16B-05	62-46	USAF 162nd FW, Arizona ANG, Tucson IAP
79-0415	F-16B-05	62-47	AMARC, Davis-Monthan AFB, AZ [FG120]; arr 30-Mar-94
79-0416	F-16B-05	62-48	Cr 16-May-85 (56th TTW)
79-0417	F-16B-05/ADF	62-49	USAF 162nd FW, Arizona ANG, Tucson IAP
79-0418	F-16B-05	62-50	AMARC, Davis-Monthan AFB, AZ [FG041]; arr 22-Dec-93
79-0419	F-16B-05	62-51	Cr 14-Nov-91 (466th TFS)
79-0420	F-16B-10/GF-16B	62-52	USAF TTC/82nd TRW, Sheppard AFB, TX
79-0421	F-16B-10/ADF	62-53	USAF 162nd FW, Arizona ANG, Tucson IAP
79-0422	F-16B-10/GF-16B	62-54	USAF TTC/82nd TRW, Sheppard AFB, TX
79-0423	F-16B-10	62-55	To IDF/AF 09-Aug-94
79-0424	F-16B-10	62-56	To IDF/AF 02-Aug-94
79-0425	F-16B-10	62-57	To IDF/AF 04-Oct-94
79-0426	F-16B-10	62-58	AMARC, Davis-Monthan AFB, AZ [FG126]; arr 01-Apr-94
79-0427	F-16B-10/GF-16B	62-59	USAF TTC/82nd TRW, Sheppard AFB, TX
79-0428	F-16B-10	62-60	AMARC, Davis-Monthan AFB, AZ [FG384]; arr 23-Sep-96
79-0429	F-16B-10	62-61	AMARC, Davis-Monthan AFB, AZ [FG387]; arr 17-Oct-96
79-0430	F-16B-10/GF-16B	62-62	USAF Fire Section, Sheppard AFB, TX
79-0431	F-16B-10	62-63	USAF 162nd FW, Arizona ANG, Tucson IAP
79-0432	F-16B-10	62-64	AMARC, Davis-Monthan AFB, AZ [FG408]; arr 31-Jan-97
80-0474	F-16A-10	61-195	AMARC, Davis-Monthan AFB, AZ [FG207]; arr 12-Aug-94
80-0475	F-16A-10	61-196	AMARC, Davis-Monthan AFB, AZ [FG110]; arr 22-Mar-94
80-0476	F-16A-10	61-197	AMARC, Davis-Monthan AFB, AZ [FG062]; arr 02-Feb-94
80-0477	F-16A-10	61-198	Cr 25-Sep-84 (474th TFW)
80-0478	F-16A-10	61-199	Cr 10-Feb-83 (474th TFW)
80-0479	F-16A-10	61-200	AMARC, Davis-Monthan AFB, AZ [FG133]; arr 07-Apr-94
80-0480	F-16A-10	61-201	AMARC, Davis-Monthan AFB, AZ [FG199]; arr 29-Jul-94
80-0481	F-16A-10/GF-16A	61-202	USAF TTC/82nd TRW, Sheppard AFB, TX
80-0482	F-16A-10	61-203	AMARC, Davis-Monthan AFB, AZ [FG131]; arr 07-Apr-94
80-0483	F-16A-10	61-204	AMARC, Davis-Monthan AFB, AZ [FG061]; arr 28-Jan-94
80-0484	F-16A-10	61-205	Cr 27-Nov-91 (121st TFS)
80-0485	F-16A-10	61-206	AMARC, Davis-Monthan AFB, AZ [FG139]; arr 08-Apr-94
80-0486	F-16A-10	61-207	Cr 28-Feb-94 (162nd FG)
80-0487	F-16A-10	61-208	AMARC, Davis-Monthan AFB, AZ [FG138]; arr 08-Apr-94

Serial	Type/Code	c/n	Operator/location
80-0488	F-16A-10	61-209	USAF New Mexico ANG, Kirtland AFB, BDRT
80-0489	F-16A-10	61-210	AMARC, Davis-Monthan AFB, AZ [FG119]; arr 30-Mar-94
80-0490	F-16A-10	61-211	Cr 06-Jul-82 (8th TFW)
80-0491	F-16A-10	61-212	To IDF/AF 01-Sep-94
80-0492	F-16A-10	61-213	AMARC, Davis-Monthan AFB, AZ [FG400]; arr 22-Nov-96
80-0493	F-16A-10	61-214	AMARC, Davis-Monthan AFB, AZ [FG179]; arr 08-Jul-94
80-0494	F-16A-10	61-215	AMARC, Davis-Monthan AFB, AZ [FG084]; arr 23-Feb-94
80-0495	F-16A-10/GF-16A	61-216	USAF TTC/82nd TRW, Sheppard AFB, TX
80-0496	F-16A-10	61-217	AMARC, Davis-Monthan AFB, AZ [FG028]; arr 26-Aug-93
80-0497	F-16A-10	61-218	AMARC, Davis-Monthan AFB, AZ [FG043]; arr 04-Jan-94
80-0498	F-16A-10	61-219	AMARC, Davis-Monthan AFB, AZ [FG048]; arr 11-Jan-94
80-0499	F-16A-10	61-220	USAF 162nd FW, Arizona ANG, Tucson IAP
80-0500	F-16A-10	61-221	AMARC, Davis-Monthan AFB, AZ [FG195]; arr 27-Jul-94
80-0501	F-16A-10	61-222	To IDF/AF 02-Aug-94
80-0502	F-16A-10	61-223	To IDF/AF 27-Sep-94
80-0503	F-16A-10	61-224	To IDF/AF 09-Aug-94
80-0504	F-16A-10	61-225	USAF 162nd FW, Arizona ANG, Tucson IAP
80-0505	F-16A-10	61-226	USAF 162nd FW, Arizona ANG, Tucson IAP
80-0506	F-16A-10	61-227	AMARC, Davis-Monthan AFB, AZ [FG055]; arr 25-Jan-94
80-0507	F-16A-10	61-228	AMARC, Davis-Monthan AFB, AZ [FG146]; arr 20-Apr-94
80-0508	F-16A-10	61-229	AMARC, Davis-Monthan AFB, AZ [FG137]; arr 08-Apr-94
80-0509	F-16A-10	61-230	AMARC, Davis-Monthan AFB, AZ [FG129]; arr 01-Apr-94
80-0510	F-16A-10	61-231	AMARC, Davis-Monthan AFB, AZ [FG015]; arr 05-Aug-93
80-0511	F-16A-10/GF-16A	61-232	USAF TTC/82nd TRW, Sheppard AFB, TX
80-0512	F-16A-10	61-233	AMARC, Davis-Monthan AFB, AZ [FG020]; arr 12-Aug-93
80-0513	F-16A-10	61-234	AMARC, Davis-Monthan AFB, AZ [FG142]; arr 12-Apr-94
80-0514	F-16A-10	61-235	To IDF/AF 27-Sep-94
80-0515	F-16A-10	61-236	AMARC, Davis-Monthan AFB, AZ [FG196]; arr 28-Jul-94
80-0516	F-16A-10	61-237	To IDF/AF 01-Sep-94
80-0517	F-16A-10	61-238	To IDF/AF 02-Aug-94
80-0518	F-16A-10	61-239	AMARC, Davis-Monthan AFB, AZ [FG184]; arr 21-Jul-94
80-0519	F-16A-10	61-240	AMARC, Davis-Monthan AFB, AZ [FG197]; arr 28-Jul-94
80-0520	F-16A-10	61-241	AMARC, Davis-Monthan AFB, AZ [FG079]; arr 15-Feb-94
80-0521	F-16A-10	61-242	AMARC, Davis-Monthan AFB, AZ [FG023]; arr 19-Aug-93
80-0522	F-16A-10/GF-16A	61-243	USAF TTC/82nd TRW, Sheppard AFB, TX
80-0523	F-16A-10	61-244	AMARC, Davis-Monthan AFB, AZ [FG085]; arr 23-Feb-94
80-0524	F-16A-10	61-245	USAF 162nd FW, Arizona ANG, Tucson IAP
80-0525	F-16A-10	61-246	AMARC, Davis-Monthan AFB, AZ [FG033]; arr 10-Sep-93
80-0526	F-16A-10/GF-16A	61-247	USAF TTC/82nd TRW, Sheppard AFB, TX
80-0527	F-16A-10	61-248	USAF 162nd FW, Arizona ANG, Tucson IAP
80-0528	F-16A-10	61-249	AMARC, Davis-Monthan AFB, AZ [FG096]; arr 04-Mar-94
80-0529	F-16A-10	61-250	AMARC, Davis-Monthan AFB, AZ [FG027]; arr 26-Aug-93
80-0530	F-16A-10	61-251	AMARC, Davis-Monthan AFB, AZ [FG024]; arr 19-Aug-93
80-0531	F-16A-10	61-252	AMARC, Davis-Monthan AFB, AZ [FG032]; arr 09-Sep-93
80-0532	F-16A-10	61-253	To IDF/AF 04-Nov-94
80-0533	F-16A-10	61-254	AMARC, Davis-Monthan AFB, AZ [FG157]; arr 29-Apr-94
80-0534	F-16A-10	61-255	To IDF/AF 02-Sep-94
80-0535	F-16A-10	61-256	USAF Wright-Patterson AFB, OH, BDRT
80-0536	F-16A-10	61-257	Cr 24-Jan-91 (161st TFTS)
80-0537	F-16A-10	61-258	Lockheed Martin, Fort Worth
80-0538	F-16A-10	61-259	AMARC, Davis-Monthan AFB, AZ [FG187]; arr 21-Jul-94
80-0539	F-16A-10	61-260	AMARC, Davis-Monthan AFB, AZ [FG174]; arr 23-Jun-94
80-0540	F-16A-10	61-261	AMARC, Davis-Monthan AFB, AZ [FG185]; arr 21-Jul-94
80-0541	F-16A-15/ADF	61-262	AMARC, Davis-Monthan AFB, AZ [FG321]; arr 17-Mar-95
80-0542	F-16A-15/ADF	61-263	AMARC, Davis-Monthan AFB, AZ [FG117]; arr 29-Mar-94
80-0543	F-16A-15/ADF	61-264	AMARC, Davis-Monthan AFB, AZ [FG258]; arr 20-Oct-94
80-0544	F-16A-15/ADF	61-265	AMARC, Davis-Monthan AFB, AZ [FG231]; arr 23-Sep-94
80-0545	F-16A-15/ADF	61-266	AMARC, Davis-Monthan AFB, AZ [FG242]; arr 07-Oct-94
80-0546	F-16A-15/ADF	61-267	AMARC, Davis-Monthan AFB, AZ [FG278]; arr 07-Nov-94
80-0547	F-16A-15/ADF	61-268	AMARC, Davis-Monthan AFB, AZ [FG285]; arr 17-Nov-94
80-0548	F-16A-15/ADF	61-269	AMARC, Davis-Monthan AFB, AZ [FG286]; arr 18-Nov-94
80-0549	F-16A-15/ADF	61-270	AMARC, Davis-Monthan AFB, AZ [FG078]; arr 15-Feb-94
80-0550	F-16A-15	61-271	USAF 416th TS/412th TW, Edwards AFB, CA
80-0551	F-16A-15	61-272	AMARC, Davis-Monthan AFB, AZ [FG189]; arr 22-Jul-94
80-0552	F-16A-15/ADF	61-273	AMARC, Davis-Monthan AFB, AZ [FG073]; arr 14-Feb-94
80-0553	F-16A-15/ADF	61-274	AMARC, Davis-Monthan AFB, AZ [FG156]; arr 29-Apr-94
80-0554	F-16A-15/ADF	61-275	USAF 179th FS/148th FW, Minnesota ANG, Duluth IAP
80-0555	F-16A-15/ADF	61-276	AMARC, Davis-Monthan AFB, AZ [FG317]; arr 03-Mar-95
80-0556	F-16A-15	61-277	AMARC, Davis-Monthan AFB, AZ [FG244]; arr 12-Oct-94
80-0557	F-16A-15	61-278	USAF 416th TS/412th TW, Edwards AFB, CA
80-0558	F-16A-15/ADF	61-279	USAF 198th FS/156th FW, Puerto Rico ANG, Muniz ANGB
80-0559	F-16A-15/ADF	61-280	AMARC, Davis-Monthan AFB, AZ [FG394]; arr 04-Nov-96
80-0560	F-16A-15/ADF	61-281	AMARC, Davis-Monthan AFB, AZ [FG268]; arr 28-Oct-94
80-0561	F-16A-15/ADF	61-282	AMARC, Davis-Monthan AFB, AZ [FG272]; arr 03-Nov-94
80-0562	F-16A-15/ADF	61-283	AMARC, Davis-Monthan AFB, AZ [FG252]; arr 17-Oct-94

Serial	Type/Code	c/n	Operator/location
80-0563	F-16A-15/ADF	61-284	USAF 186th FS/120th FW, Montana ANG, Great Falls IAP
80-0564	F-16A-15	61-285	Cr 01-Dec-82 (50th TFW)
80-0565	F-16A-15/ADF	61-286	USAF 186th FS/120th FW, Montana ANG, Great Falls IAP
80-0566	F-16A-15/ADF	61-287	Cr 18-Sep-92 (179th FS)
80-0567	F-16A-15/ADF	61-288	AMARC, Davis-Monthan AFB, AZ [FG115]; arr 28-Mar-94
80-0568	F-16A-15/ADF	61-289	AMARC, Davis-Monthan AFB, AZ [FG118]; arr 29-Mar-94
80-0569	F-16A-15/ADF	61-290	AMARC, Davis-Monthan AFB, AZ [FG245]; arr 12-Oct-94
80-0570	F-16A-15/ADF	61-291	AMARC, Davis-Monthan AFB, AZ [FG071]; arr 11-Feb-94
80-0571	F-16A-15/ADF	61-292	AMARC, Davis-Monthan AFB, AZ [FG180]; arr 08-Jul-94
80-0572	F-16A-15/ADF	61-293	AMARC, Davis-Monthan AFB, AZ [FG227]; arr 16-Sep-94
80-0573	F-16A-15	61-294	USAF Armament Museum, Eglin AFB, FL
80-0574	F-16A-15	61-295	Cr 20-May-88 (31 TFW)
80-0575	F-16A-15/ADF	61-296	AMARC, Davis-Monthan AFB, AZ [FG403]; arr 17-Dec-96
80-0576	F-16A-15/ADF	61-297	AMARC, Davis-Monthan AFB, AZ [FG316]; arr 10-Feb-95
80-0577	F-16A-15	61-298	AMARC, Davis-Monthan AFB, AZ [FG228]; arr 22-Sep-94
80-0578	F-16A-15	61-299	USAF 179th FS/148th FW, Minnesota ANG, Duluth IAP
80-0579	F-16A-15	61-300	AMARC, Davis-Monthan AFB, AZ [FG144]; arr 15-Apr-94
80-0580	F-16A-15/ADF	61-301	AMARC, Davis-Monthan AFB, AZ [FG093]; arr 25-Feb-94
80-0581	F-16A-15/ADF	61-302	USAF 114th FS/173rd FW, Oregon ANG, Klamath Falls
80-0582	F-16A-15/ADF	61-303	AMARC, Davis-Monthan AFB, AZ [FG226]; arr 16-Sep-94
80-0583	F-16A-15/ADF	61-304	AMARC, Davis-Monthan AFB, AZ [FG294]; arr 01-Dec-94
80-0584	F-16A-15	61-305	USAF 416th TS/412th TW, Edwards AFB, CA
80-0585	F-16A-15/ADF	61-306	AMARC, Davis-Monthan AFB, AZ [FG313]; arr 03-Feb-95
80-0586	F-16A-15	61-307	Cr 22-Oct-85 (50th TFW)
80-0587	F-16A-15/ADF	61-308	AMARC, Davis-Monthan AFB, AZ [FG261]; arr 21-Oct-94
80-0588	F-16A-15/ADF	61-309	AMARC, Davis-Monthan AFB, AZ [FG265]; arr 26-Oct-94
80-0589	F-16A-15/ADF	61-310	USAF 198th FS/156th FW, Puerto Rico ANG, Muniz ANGB
80-0590	F-16A-15/ADF	61-311	AMARC, Davis-Monthan AFB, AZ [FG304]; arr 15-Dec-94
80-0591	F-16A-15/ADF	61-312	AMARC, Davis-Monthan AFB, AZ [FG282]; arr 10-Nov-94
80-0592	F-16A-15/ADF	61-313	AMARC, Davis-Monthan AFB, AZ [FG213]; arr 26-Aug-94
80-0593	F-16A-15/ADF	61-314	AMARC, Davis-Monthan AFB, AZ [FG310]; arr 24-Jan-95
80-0594	F-16A-15/ADF	61-315	USAF 179th FS/148th FW, Minnesota ANG, Duluth IAP
80-0595	F-16A-15	61-316	Cr 25-Jan-84 (50th TFW)
80-0596	F-16A-15/ADF	61-317	USAF 186th FS/120th FW, Montana ANG, Great Falls IAP
80-0597	F-16A-15	61-318	Cr 24-Jul-87 (57th FWW)
80-0598	F-16A-15/ADF	61-319	AMARC, Davis-Monthan AFB, AZ [FG155]; arr 29-Apr-94
80-0599	F-16A-15	61-320	Cr 11-Sep-86 (57th FWW)
80-0600	F-16A-15	61-321	Cr 12-Jan-83 (57th FWW)
80-0601	F-16A-15/ADF	61-322	AMARC, Davis-Monthan AFB, AZ [FG398]; arr 15-Nov-96
80-0602	F-16A-15/ADF	61-323	USAF 198th FS/156th FW, Puerto Rico ANG, Muniz ANGB
80-0603	F-16A-15/ADF	61-324	AMARC, Davis-Monthan AFB, AZ [FG395]; arr 05-Nov-96
80-0604	F-16A-15/ADF	61-325	USAF 114th FS/173rd FW, Oregon ANG, Klamath Falls
80-0605	F-16A-15/ADF	61-326	USAF 186th FS/120th FW, Montana ANG, Great Falls IAP
80-0606	F-16A-15	61-327	Cr 30-Jul-85 (50th TFW)
80-0607	F-16A-15/ADF	61-328	AMARC, Davis-Monthan AFB, AZ [FG266]; arr 27-Oct-94
80-0608	F-16A-15/ADF	61-329	AMARC, Davis-Monthan AFB, AZ [FG380]; arr 25-Jul-96
80-0609	F-16A-15	61-330	USAF 40th TES/46th TW, Eglin AFB, FL
80-0610	F-16A-15/ADF	61-331	Cr 05-May-92 (186th FS)
80-0611	F-16A-15/ADF	61-332	AMARC, Davis-Monthan AFB, AZ [FG229]; arr 22-Sep-94
80-0612	F-16A-15/ADF	61-333	USAF 198th FS/156th FW, Puerto Rico ANG, Muniz ANGB
80-0613	F-16A-15/ADF	61-334	AMARC, Davis-Monthan AFB, AZ [FG125]; arr 31-Mar-94
80-0614	F-16A-15/ADF	61-335	AMARC, Davis-Monthan AFB, AZ [FG267]; arr 27-Oct-94
80-0615	F-16A-15/ADF	61-336	USAF 186th FS/120th FW, Montana ANG, Great Falls IAP
80-0616	F-16A-15/ADF	61-337	AMARC, Davis-Monthan AFB, AZ [FG357]; arr 02-Feb-96
80-0617	F-16A-15	61-338	Cr 20-Jan-83 (50th TFW)
80-0618	F-16A-15/ADF	61-339	AMARC, Davis-Monthan AFB, AZ [FG315]; arr 10-Feb-95
80-0619	F-16A-15/ADF	61-340	AMARC, Davis-Monthan AFB, AZ [FG295]; arr 01-Dec-94
80-0620	F-16A-15/ADF	61-341	AMARC, Davis-Monthan AFB, AZ [FG276]; arr 04-Nov-94
80-0621	F-16A-15/ADF	61-342	AMARC, Davis-Monthan AFB, AZ [FG243]; arr 07-Oct-94
80-0622	F-16A-15/ADF	61-343	USAF 114th FS/173rd FW, Oregon ANG, Klamath Falls
80-0623	F-16B-10	62-65	AMARC, Davis-Monthan AFB, AZ [FG193]; arr 27-Jul-94
80-0624	F-16B-10	62-66	To IDF/ADF 04-Oct-94
80-0625	F-16B-10	62-67	AMARC, Davis-Monthan AFB, AZ [FG017]; arr 05-Aug-93
80-0626	F-16B-10	62-68	AMARC, Davis-Monthan AFB, AZ [FG407]; arr 10-Jan-97
80-0627	F-16B-10	62-69	Cr 11-Jul-83 (56th TTW)
80-0628	F-16B-10	62-70	AMARC, Davis-Monthan AFB, AZ [FG382]; arr 17-Oct-96
80-0629	F-16B-10	62-71	AMARC, Davis-Monthan AFB, AZ [FG176]; arr 28-Jun-94
80-0630	F-16B-10	62-72	USAF 162nd FW, Arizona ANG, Tucson IAP
80-0631	F-16B-10	62-73	USAF 162nd FW, Arizona ANG, Tucson IAP
80-0632	F-16B-10	62-74	To IDF/AF 04-Oct-94
80-0633	F-16B-10	62-75	USAF 416th TS/412th TW, Edwards AFB, CA
80-0634	F-16B-10	62-76	USAF 416th TS/412th TW, Edwards AFB, CA
80-0635	F-16B-15	62-77	USAF 416th TS/412th TW, Edwards AFB, CA
80-0636	F-16B-15/ADF	62-78	USAF 162nd FW, Arizona ANG, Tucson IAP
80-0637	F-16B-15/ADF	62-79	USAF 114th FS/173rd FW, Oregon ANG, Klamath Falls

A Puerto Rico ANG F-16A ADF (81-0709) of the 198th FS, photographed in November 1995. PETER R FOSTER

Serial	Type/Code	c/n	Operator/location	Serial	Type/Code	c/n	Operator/location
80-0638	F-16B-15	62-80	USAF 162nd FW, Arizona ANG, Tucson IAP	81-0711	F-16A-15/ADF	61-392	AMARC, Davis-Monthan AFB, AZ [FG283]; arr 10-Nov-94
81-0663	F-16A-15	61-344	USAF Museum, Wright-Patterson AFB, OH	81-0712	F-16A-15/ADF	61-393	AMARC, Davis-Monthan AFB, AZ [FG351]; arr 24-Jan-96
81-0664	F-16A-15	61-345	Cr 10-May-83 (50th TFW)	81-0713	F-16A-15/ADF	61-394	AMARC, Davis-Monthan AFB, AZ [FG328]; arr 06-Jul-95
81-0665	F-16A-15/ADF	61-346	USAF 178th FS/119th FW, North Dakota ANG, Hector Field	81-0714	F-16A-15/ADF	61-395	AMARC, Davis-Monthan AFB, AZ [FG214]; arr 26-Aug-94
81-0666	F-16A-15/ADF	61-347	USAF 186th FS/120th FW, Montana ANG, Great Falls IAP	81-0715	F-16A-15/ADF	61-396	AMARC, Davis-Monthan AFB, AZ [FG281]; arr 09-Nov-94
81-0667	F-16A-15	61-348	AMARC, Davis-Monthan AFB, AZ [FG356]; arr 01-Feb-96	81-0716	F-16A-15/ADF	61-397	AMARC, Davis-Monthan AFB, AZ [FG051]; arr 13-Jan-94
81-0668	F-16A-15	61-349	AMARC, Davis-Monthan AFB, AZ [FG404]; arr 17-Dec-96	81-0717	F-16A-15/ADF	61-398	Cr 26-Jan-91 (171st FIS)
81-0669	F-16A-15/ADF	61-350	AMARC, Davis-Monthan AFB, AZ [FG080]; arr 15-Feb-94	81-0718	F-16A-15/ADF	61-399	AMARC, Davis-Monthan AFB, AZ [FG091]; arr 25-Feb-94
81-0670	F-16A-15	61-351	AMARC, Davis-Monthan AFB, AZ [FG355]; arr 01-Feb-96	81-0719	F-16A-15/ADF	61-400	AMARC, Davis-Monthan AFB, AZ [FG150]; arr 22-Apr-94
81-0671	F-16A-15	61-352	Cr 14-Sep-89 (186th FIS)	81-0720	F-16A-15/ADF	61-401	AMARC, Davis-Monthan AFB, AZ [FG076]; arr 14-Feb-94
81-0672	F-16A-15/ADF	61-353	AMARC, Davis-Monthan AFB, AZ [FG320]; arr 17-Mar-95	81-0721	F-16A-15/ADF	61-402	USAF Pope AFB, NC, BDRT
81-0673	F-16A-15/ADF	61-354	USAF 114th FS/173rd FW, Oregon ANG, Klamath Falls	81-0722	F-16A-15/ADF	61-403	AMARC, Davis-Monthan AFB, AZ [FG323]; arr 21-Apr-95
81-0674	F-16A-15/ADF	61-355	USAF 186th FS/120th FW, Montana ANG, Great Falls IAP	81-0723	F-16A-15/ADF	61-404	USAF 186th FS/120th FW, Montana ANG, Great Falls IAP
81-0675	F-16A-15/ADF	61-356	AMARC, Davis-Monthan AFB, AZ [FG360]; arr 20-May-96	81-0724	F-16A-15	61-405	Cr 15-Dec-82 (8th TFW)
81-0676	F-16A-15/GF-16A	61-357	USAF TTC/82nd TRW, Sheppard AFB, TX	81-0725	F-16A-15/ADF	61-406	AMARC, Davis-Monthan AFB, AZ [FG075]; arr 14-Feb-94
81-0677	F-16A-15	61-358	AMARC, Davis-Monthan AFB, AZ [FG358]; arr 05-Mar-96	81-0726	F-16A-15/ADF	61-407	AMARC, Davis-Monthan AFB, AZ [FG064]; arr 02-Feb-94
81-0678	F-16A-15/GF-16A	61-359	USAF TTC/82nd TRW, Sheppard AFB, TX	81-0727	F-16A-15/ADF	61-408	AMARC, Davis-Monthan AFB, AZ [FG057]; arr 26-Jan-94
81-0679	F-16A-15	61-360	AMARC, Davis-Monthan AFB, AZ [FG354]; arr 01-Feb-96	81-0728	F-16A-15/ADF	61-409	AMARC, Davis-Monthan AFB, AZ [FG300]; arr 13-Dec-94
81-0680	F-16A-15/ADF	61-361	USAF 186th FS/120th FW, Montana ANG, Great Falls IAP	81-0729	F-16A-15/ADF	61-410	AMARC, Davis-Monthan AFB, AZ [FG068]; arr 10-Feb-94
81-0681	F-16A-15/ADF	61-362	AMARC, Davis-Monthan AFB, AZ [FG352]; arr 30-Jan-96	81-0730	F-16A-15	61-411	Cr 27-Jan-84 (388th TFW)
81-0682	F-16A-15/ADF	61-363	AMARC, Davis-Monthan AFB, AZ [FG164]; arr 13-May-94	81-0731	F-16A-15/ADF	61-412	AMARC, Davis-Monthan AFB, AZ [FG342]; arr 21-Dec-95
81-0683	F-16A-15	61-364	AMARC, Davis-Monthan AFB, AZ [FG353]; arr 01-Feb-96	81-0732	F-16A-15/ADF	61-413	AMARC, Davis-Monthan AFB, AZ [FG343]; arr 21-Dec-95
81-0684	F-16A-15/ADF	61-365	Cr 07-Jan-97 (179th FS)	81-0733	F-16A-15/ADF	61-414	AMARC, Davis-Monthan AFB, AZ [FG290]; arr 22-Nov-94
81-0685	F-16A-15/ADF	61-366	USAF 198th FS/156th FW, Puerto Rico ANG, Muniz ANGB	81-0734	F-16A-15/ADF	61-415	AMARC, Davis-Monthan AFB, AZ [FG147]; arr 20-Apr-94
81-0686	F-16A-15/ADF	61-367	AMARC, Davis-Monthan AFB, AZ [FG072]; arr 14-Feb-94	81-0735	F-16A-15/ADF	61-416	AMARC, Davis-Monthan AFB, AZ [FG065]; arr 02-Feb-94
81-0687	F-16A-15	61-368	USAF 425th FS/56th FW, Luke AFB, AZ	81-0736	F-16A-15/ADF	61-417	AMARC, Davis-Monthan AFB, AZ [FG050]; arr 12-Jan-94
81-0688	F-16A-15	61-369	AMARC, Davis-Monthan AFB, AZ [FG330]; arr 13-Jul-95	81-0737	F-16A-15/ADF	61-418	AMARC, Davis-Monthan AFB, AZ [FG291]; arr 22-Nov-94
81-0689	F-16A-15/ADF	61-370	AMARC, Davis-Monthan AFB, AZ [FG296]; arr 02-Dec-94	81-0738	F-16A-15/ADF	61-419	AMARC, Davis-Monthan AFB, AZ [FG211]; arr 19-Aug-94
81-0690	F-16A-15/ADF	61-371	AMARC, Davis-Monthan AFB, AZ [FG249]; arr 13-Oct-94	81-0739	F-16A-15/ADF	61-420	AMARC, Davis-Monthan AFB, AZ [FG246]; arr 12-Oct-94
81-0691	F-16A-15/ADF	61-372	AMARC, Davis-Monthan AFB, AZ [FG333]; arr 31-Jul-95	81-0740	F-16A-15/ADF	61-421	AMARC, Davis-Monthan AFB, AZ [FG087]; arr 23-Feb-94
81-0692	F-16A-15	61-373	Cr 16-Nov-82 (8th TFW)	81-0741	F-16A-15/ADF	61-422	AMARC, Davis-Monthan AFB, AZ [FG284]; arr 17-Nov-94
81-0693	F-16A-15/ADF	61-374	USAF, 114th FS/173rd FW, Oregon ANG, Klamath Falls	81-0742	F-16A-15/ADF	61-423	AMARC, Davis-Monthan AFB, AZ [FG105]; arr 10-Mar-94
81-0694	F-16A-15/ADF	61-375	AMARC, Davis-Monthan AFB, AZ [FG251]; arr 14-Oct-94	81-0743	F-16A-15/ADF	61-424	AMARC, Davis-Monthan AFB, AZ [FG148]; arr 20-Apr-94
81-0695	F-16A-15/ADF	61-376	AMARC, Davis-Monthan AFB, AZ [FG346]; arr 02-Jan-96	81-0744	F-16A-15/ADF	61-425	AMARC, Davis-Monthan AFB, AZ [FG100]; arr 07-Mar-94
81-0696	F-16A-15/ADF	61-377	AMARC, Davis-Monthan AFB, AZ [FG337]; arr 07-Nov-95	81-0745	F-16A-15	61-426	Cr 01-May-84 (388th TFW)
81-0697	F-16A-15/ADF	61-378	Cr 31-Aug-92 (186th FS)	81-0746	F-16A-15/ADF	61-427	AMARC, Davis-Monthan AFB, AZ [FG090]; arr 24-Feb-94
81-0698	F-16A-15/ADF	61-379	AMARC, Davis-Monthan AFB, AZ [FG134]; arr 08-Apr-94	81-0747	F-16A-15	61-428	Cr 24-Apr-86 (388th TFW)
81-0699	F-16A-15/ADF	61-380	USAF 114th FS/173rd FW, Oregon ANG, Klamath Falls	81-0748	F-16A-15/ADF	61-429	AMARC, Davis-Monthan AFB, AZ [FG104]; arr 10-Mar-94
81-0700	F-16A-15/ADF	61-381	AMARC, Davis-Monthan AFB, AZ [FG262]; arr 21-Oct-94	81-0749	F-16A-15/ADF	61-430	AMARC, Davis-Monthan AFB, AZ [FG159]; arr 06-May-94
81-0701	F-16A-15/ADF	61-382	AMARC, Davis-Monthan AFB, AZ [FG145]; arr 15-Apr-94	81-0750	F-16A-15	61-431	Cr 08-Aug-85 (388th TFW)
81-0702	F-16A-15/ADF	61-383	AMARC, Davis-Monthan AFB, AZ [FG077]; arr 14-Feb-94	81-0751	F-16A-15/ADF	61-432	USAF 186th FS/120th FW, Montana ANG, Great Falls IAP
81-0703	F-16A-15/ADF	61-384	AMARC, Davis-Monthan AFB, AZ [FG392]; arr 01-Nov-96	81-0752	F-16A-15/ADF	61-433	AMARC, Davis-Monthan AFB, AZ [FG149]; arr 22-Apr-94
81-0704	F-16A-15/ADF	61-385	Cr 03-Mar-92 (107th FS)	81-0753	F-16A-15/ADF	61-434	AMARC, Davis-Monthan AFB, AZ [FG103]; arr 10-Mar-94
81-0705	F-16A-15/ADF	61-386	AMARC, Davis-Monthan AFB, AZ [FG241]; arr 06-Oct-94	81-0754	F-16A-15/ADF	61-435	AMARC, Davis-Monthan AFB, AZ [FG230]; arr 23-Sep-94
81-0706	F-16A-15/ADF	61-387	Cr 03-Mar-92 (107th FS)	81-0755	F-16A-15/ADF	61-436	AMARC, Davis-Monthan AFB, AZ [FG339]; arr 12-Dec-95
81-0707	F-16A-15/ADF	61-388	AMARC, Davis-Monthan AFB, AZ [FG314]; arr 03-Feb-95	81-0756	F-16A-15/ADF	61-437	AMARC, Davis-Monthan AFB, AZ [FG236]; arr 29-Sep-94
81-0708	F-16A-15/ADF	61-389	AMARC, Davis-Monthan AFB, AZ [FG158]; arr 06-May-94	81-0757	F-16A-15/ADF	61-438	AMARC, Davis-Monthan AFB, AZ [FG359]; arr 20-May-96
81-0709	F-16A-15/ADF	61-390	USAF 198th FS/156th FW, Puerto Rico ANG, Muniz ANGB	81-0758	F-16A-15/ADF	61-439	Cr 03-Apr-91 (119th FIS)
81-0710	F-16A-15/ADF	61-391	AMARC, Davis-Monthan AFB, AZ [FG305]; arr 15-Dec-94	81-0759	F-16A-15/ADF	61-440	USAF 114th FS/173rd FW, Oregon ANG, Klamath Falls

Serial	Type/Code	c/n	Operator/location
81-0760	F-16A-15/ADF	61-441	AMARC, Davis-Monthan AFB, AZ [FG216]; arr 01-Sep-94
81-0761	F-16A-15/ADF	61-442	USAF 85th TES/53rd Wg, Eglin AFB, FL
81-0762	F-16A-15/ADF	61-443	AMARC, Davis-Monthan AFB, AZ [FG274]; arr 04-Nov-94
81-0763	F-16A-15/ADF	61-444	USAF 198th FS/156th FW, Puerto Rico ANG, Muniz ANGB
81-0764	F-16A-15/ADF	61-445	AMARC, Davis-Monthan AFB, AZ [FG338]; arr 14-Nov-95
81-0765	F-16A-15/ADF	61-446	AMARC, Davis-Monthan AFB, AZ [FG092]; arr 25-Feb-94
81-0766	F-16A-15	61-447	Cr 11-Mar-88 (159th FIS)
81-0767	F-16A-15/ADF	61-448	AMARC, Davis-Monthan AFB, AZ [FG081]; arr 18-Feb-94
81-0768	F-16A-15/ADF	61-449	AMARC, Davis-Monthan AFB, AZ [FG094]; arr 28-Feb-94
81-0769	F-16A-15/ADF	61-450	AMARC, Davis-Monthan AFB, AZ [FG114]; arr 25-Mar-94
81-0770	F-16A-15/ADF	61-451	USAF 114th FS/173rd FW, Oregon ANG, Klamath Falls
81-0771	F-16A-15/ADF	61-452	AMARC, Davis-Monthan AFB, AZ [FG331]; arr 14-Jul-95
81-0772	F-16A-15/ADF	61-453	AMARC, Davis-Monthan AFB, AZ [FG379]; arr 24-Jul-96
81-0773	F-16A-15/ADF	61-454	USAF 178th FS/119th FW, North Dakota ANG, Hector Field
81-0774	F-16A-15/ADF	61-455	USAF 198th FS/156th FW, Puerto Rico ANG, Muniz ANGB
81-0775	F-16A-15/ADF	61-456	USAF 198th FS/156th FW, Puerto Rico ANG, Muniz ANGB
81-0776	F-16A-15/ADF	61-457	USAF 186th FS/120th FW, Montana ANG, Great Falls IAP
81-0777	F-16A-15/ADF	61-458	USAF 179th FS/148th FW, Minnesota ANG, Duluth IAP
81-0778	F-16A-15/ADF	61-459	USAF 179th FS/148th FW, Minnesota ANG, Duluth IAP
81-0779	F-16A-15/ADF	61-460	Cr 11-Sep-93 (169th FS)
81-0780	F-16A-15/ADF	61-461	AMARC, Davis-Monthan AFB, AZ [FG319]; arr 08-Mar-95
81-0781	F-16A-15/ADF	61-462	AMARC, Davis-Monthan AFB, AZ [FG297]; arr 06-Dec-94
81-0782	F-16A-15/ADF	61-463	USAF 178th FS/119th FW, North Dakota ANG, Hector Field
81-0783	F-16A-15/ADF	61-464	USAF 179th FS/148th FW, Minnesota ANG, Duluth IAP
81-0784	F-16A-15/ADF	61-465	AMARC, Davis-Monthan AFB, AZ [FG309]; arr 09-Jan-95
81-0785	F-16A-15/ADF	61-466	USAF 179th FS/148th FW, Minnesota ANG, Duluth IAP
81-0786	F-16A-15/ADF	61-467	USAF 114th FS/173rd FW, Oregon ANG, Klamath Falls
81-0787	F-16A-15/ADF	61-468	USAF 179th FS/148th FW, Minnesota ANG, Duluth IAP
81-0788	F-16A-15	61-469	AMARC, Davis-Monthan AFB, AZ [FG349]; arr 24-Jan-96
81-0789	F-16A-15/ADF	61-470	USAF 178th FS/119th FW, North Dakota ANG, Hector Field
81-0790	F-16A-15	61-471	AMARC, Davis-Monthan AFB, AZ [FG368]; arr 26-Jun-96
81-0791	F-16A-15/ADF	61-472	USAF 178th FS/119th FW, North Dakota ANG, Hector Field
81-0792	F-16A-15	61-473	AMARC, Davis-Monthan AFB, AZ [FG256]; arr 17-Oct-94
81-0793	F-16A-15/ADF	61-474	USAF 179th FS/148th FW, Minnesota ANG, Duluth IAP
81-0794	F-16A-15	61-475	AMARC, Davis-Monthan AFB, AZ [FG225]; arr 14-Sep-94
81-0795	F-16A-15/ADF	61-476	USAF 179th FS/148th FW, Minnesota ANG, Duluth IAP
81-0796	F-16A-15	61-477	USAF 162nd FW, Arizona ANG, Tucson IAP
81-0797	F-16A-15/ADF	61-478	USAF 198th FS/156th FW, Puerto Rico ANG, Muniz ANGB
81-0798	F-16A-15	61-479	Cr 25-May-90 (347th TFW)
81-0799	F-16A-15/ADF	61-480	USAF 179th FS/148th FW, Minnesota ANG, Duluth IAP
81-0800	F-16A-15	61-481	AMARC, Davis-Monthan AFB, AZ [FG219]; arr 09-Sep-94
81-0801	F-16A-15/ADF	61-482	USAF 114th FS/173rd FW, Oregon ANG, Klamath Falls
81-0802	F-16A-15	61-483	USAF 162nd FW, Arizona ANG, Tucson IAP
81-0803	F-16A-15/ADF	61-484	USAF 179th FS/148th FW, Minnesota ANG, Duluth IAP
81-0804	F-16A-15	61-485	USAF 162nd FW, Arizona ANG, Tucson IAP
81-0805	F-16A-15/ADF	61-486	USAF 179th FS/148th FW, Minnesota ANG, Duluth IAP
81-0806	F-16A-15	61-487	USAF 162nd FW, Arizona ANG, Tucson IAP
81-0807	F-16A-15/ADF	61-488	USAF 179th FS/148th FW, Minnesota ANG, Duluth IAP
81-0808	F-16A-15	61-489	Cr 08-Feb-85 (401st TFW)
81-0809	F-16A-15/ADF	61-490	AMARC, Davis-Monthan AFB, AZ [FG163]; arr 13-May-94
81-0810	F-16A-15	61-491	USAF 162nd FW, Arizona ANG, Tucson IAP
81-0811	F-16A-15/ADF	61-492	AMARC, Davis-Monthan AFB, AZ [FG324]; arr 26-May-95
81-0812	F-16B-15/ADF	62-81	USAF 114th FS/173rd FW, Oregon ANG, Klamath Falls
81-0813	F-16B-15	62-82	Lockheed Martin, Fort Worth, TX
81-0814	F-16B-15/ADF	62-83	Cr 09-Jun-91 (111st FIS)
81-0815	F-16B-15	62-84	USAF 162nd FW, Arizona ANG, Tucson IAP
81-0816	F-16B-15	62-85	Preserved at Atlantic City, NJ
81-0817	F-16B-15/ADF	62-86	USAF 416th TS/412th TW, Edwards AFB, CA
81-0818	F-16B-15	62-87	USAF 162nd FW, Arizona ANG, Tucson IAP
81-0819	F-16B-15/ADF	62-88	USAF 186th FS/120th FW, Montana ANG, Great Falls IAP
81-0820	F-16B-15/ADF	62-89	USAF 111st FS/147th FW, Texas ANG, Ellington ANGB
81-0821	F-16B-15	62-90	AMARC, Davis-Monthan AFB, AZ [FG340]; arr 13-Dec-95
81-0822	F-16B-15	62-91	AMARC, Davis-Monthan AFB, AZ [FG232]; arr 23-Sep-94
82-0900	F-16A-15	61-493	AMARC, Davis-Monthan AFB, AZ [FG341]; arr 13-Dec-95
82-0901	F-16A-15/ADF	61-494	USAF 179th FS/148th FW, Minnesota ANG, Duluth IAP
82-0902	F-16A-15	61-495	USAF 184th FS/188th FW, Arkansas ANG, Fort Smith ANGB
82-0903	F-16A-15/ADF	61-496	USAF 178th FS/119th FW, North Dakota ANG, Hector Field
82-0904	F-16A-15	61-497	AMARC, Davis-Monthan AFB, AZ [FG348]; arr 10-Jan-96
82-0905	F-16A-15/ADF	61-498	USAF 178th FS/119th FW, North Dakota ANG, Hector Field
82-0906	F-16A-15	61-499	USAF 162nd FW, Arizona ANG, Tucson IAP
82-0907	F-16A-15/ADF	61-500	USAF 178th FS/119th FW, North Dakota ANG, Hector Field
82-0908	F-16A-15	61-501	AMARC, Davis-Monthan AFB, AZ [FG347]; arr 09-Jan-96
82-0909	F-16A-15	61-502	Cr 10-Feb-88 (57th FWW)
82-0910	F-16A-15/ADF	61-503	USAF 114th FS/173rd FW, Oregon ANG, Klamath Falls
82-0911	F-16A-15/ADF	61-504	USAF 184th FS/188th FW, Arizona ANG, Fort Smith ANGB
82-0912	F-16A-15	61-505	Cr 24-Jul-87 (57th FWW)
82-0913	F-16A-15/ADF	61-506	AMARC, Davis-Monthan AFB, AZ [FG402]; arr 06-Dec-96
82-0914	F-16A-15	61-507	USAF 162nd FW, Arizona ANG, Tucson IAP
82-0915	F-16A-15/ADF	61-508	AMARC, Davis-Monthan AFB, AZ [FG275]; arr 04-Nov-94
82-0916	F-16A-15/ADF	61-509	AMARC, Davis-Monthan AFB, AZ [FG273]; arr 03-Nov-94
82-0917	F-16A-15/ADF	61-510	AMARC, Davis-Monthan AFB, AZ [FG293]; arr 23-Nov-94
82-0918	F-16A-15	61-511	AMARC, Davis-Monthan AFB, AZ [FG205]; arr 08-Aug-94
82-0919	F-16A-15/ADF	61-512	USAF 178th FS/119th FW, North Dakota ANG, Hector Field
82-0920	F-16A-15	61-513	USAF 184th FS/188th FW, Arkansas ANG, Fort Smith ANGB
82-0921	F-16A-15/ADF	61-514	USAF 198th FS/156th FW, Puerto Rico ANG, Muniz ANGB
82-0922	F-16A-15	61-515	AMARC, Davis-Monthan AFB, AZ [FG345]; arr 28-Dec-95
82-0923	F-16A-15/ADF	61-516	AMARC, Davis-Monthan AFB, AZ [FG287]; arr 18-Nov-94
82-0924	F-16A-15	61-517	USAF 184th FS/188th FW, Arkansas ANG, Fort Smith ANGB
82-0925	F-16A-15	61-518	Cr 10-Nov-83 (388th TFW)
82-0926	F-16A-15/ADF	61-519	USAF 178th FS/119th FW, North Dakota ANG, Hector Field
82-0927	F-16A-15	61-520	Cr 17-Dec-93 (184th FS)
82-0928	F-16A-15	61-521	USAF 184th FS/188th FW, Arkansas ANG, Fort Smith ANGB

Block 15 F-16A ADF (82-1000) in the colours of the Houston-Ellington based 147th FW. PETER R MARCH

Serial	Type/Code	c/n	Operator/location
82-0929	F-16A-15/ADF	61-522	USAF 178th FS/119th FW, North Dakota ANG, Hector Field
82-0930	F-16A-15/ADF	61-523	USAF 111st FS/147th FW, Texas ANG, Ellington ANGB
82-0931	F-16A-15	61-524	AMARC, Davis-Monthan AFB, AZ [FG372]; arr 26-Jun-96
82-0932	F-16A-15/ADF	61-525	USAF 198th FS/156th FW, Puerto Rico ANG, Muniz ANGB
82-0933	F-16A-15	61-526	USAF 162nd FW, Arizona ANG, Tucson IAP
82-0934	F-16A-15/ADF	61-527	Cr 12-Jun-94 (169th FS)
82-0935	F-16A-15/ADF	61-528	USAF 179th FS/148th FW, Minnesota ANG, Duluth IAP
82-0936	F-16A-15	61-529	AMARC, Davis-Monthan AFB, AZ [FG344]; arr 21-Dec-95
82-0937	F-16A-15/ADF	61-530	Cr 16-Mar-90 (388th TFW)
82-0938	F-16A-15	61-531	USAF 162nd FW, Arizona ANG, Tucson IAP
82-0939	F-16A-15	61-532	Cr 21-Oct-85 (388th TFW)
82-0940	F-16A-15	61-533	Cr 15-Nov-85 (57th FWW)
82-0941	F-16A-15	61-534	AMARC, Davis-Monthan AFB, AZ [FG350]; arr 24-Jan-96
82-0942	F-16A-15/ADF	61-535	AMARC, Davis-Monthan AFB, AZ [FG334]; arr 31-Jul-95
82-0943	F-16A-15	61-536	Cr 31-Jul-92 (170th FS)
82-0944	F-16A-15	61-537	AMARC, Davis-Monthan AFB, AZ [FG253]; arr 17-Oct-94
82-0945	F-16A-15/ADF	61-538	AMARC, Davis-Monthan AFB, AZ [FG116]; arr 28-Mar-94
82-0946	F-16A-15	61-539	USAF 184th FS/188th FW, Arkansas ANG, Fort Smith ANGB
82-0947	F-16A-15/ADF	61-540	AMARC, Davis-Monthan AFB, AZ [FG269]; arr 28-Oct-94
82-0948	F-16A-15	61-541	AMARC, Davis-Monthan AFB, AZ [FG182]; arr 15-Jul-94
82-0949	F-16A-15	61-542	USAF 184th FS/188th FW, Arkansas ANG, Fort Smith ANGB
82-0950	F-16A-15/ADF	61-543	USAF 178th FS/119th FW, North Dakota ANG, Hector Field
82-0951	F-16A-15/ADF	61-544	USAF 111st FS/147th FW, Texas ANG, Ellington ANGB
82-0952	F-16A-15	61-545	AMARC, Davis-Monthan AFB, AZ [FG307]; arr 15-Dec-94
82-0953	F-16A-15/ADF	61-546	USAF 198th FS/156th FW, Puerto Rico ANG, Muniz ANGB
82-0954	F-16A-15	61-547	Cr 16-Aug-89 (31st TFW)
82-0955	F-16A-15/ADF	61-548	USAF 114th FS/173rd FW, Oregon ANG, Klamath Falls
82-0956	F-16A-15/ADF	61-549	USAF 178th FS/119th FW, North Dakota ANG, Hector Field
82-0957	F-16A-15	61-550	USAF 184th FS/188th FW, Arkansas ANG, Fort Smith ANGB
82-0958	F-16A-15	61-551	AMARC, Davis-Monthan AFB, AZ [FG292]; arr 23-Nov-94
82-0959	F-16A-15	61-552	Cr 21-Nov-84 (401st TFW)
82-0960	F-16A-15/ADF	61-553	AMARC, Davis-Monthan AFB, AZ [FG308]; arr 16-Dec-94
82-0961	F-16A-15/ADF	61-554	USAF 111st FS/147th FW, Texas ANG, Ellington ANGB
82-0962	F-16A-15	61-555	AMARC, Davis-Monthan AFB, AZ [FG217]; arr 01-Sep-94
82-0963	F-16A-15/ADF	61-556	AMARC, Davis-Monthan AFB, AZ [FG250]; arr 14-Oct-94
82-0964	F-16A-15/ADF	61-557	USAF 184th FS/188th FW, Arkansas ANG, Fort Smith ANGB
82-0965	F-16A-15	61-558	Cr 23-May-89 (309th TFS)
82-0966	F-16A-15/ADF	61-559	AMARC, Davis-Monthan AFB, AZ [FG263]; arr 21-Oct-94
82-0967	F-16A-15/ADF	61-560	USAF 178th FS/119th FW, North Dakota ANG, Hector Field
82-0968	F-16A-15	61-561	AMARC, Davis-Monthan AFB, AZ [FG264]; arr 25-Oct-94
82-0969	F-16A-15/ADF	61-562	AMARC, Davis-Monthan AFB, AZ [FG301]; arr 13-Dec-94
82-0970	F-16A-15/ADF	61-563	USAF 184th FS/188th FW, Arkansas ANG, Fort Smith ANGB
82-0971	F-16A-15	61-564	Cr 25-Jun-84 (401st TFW)
82-0972	F-16A-15/ADF	61-565	USAF 186th FS/120th FW, Montana ANG, Great Falls IAP
82-0973	F-16A-15/ADF	61-566	AMARC, Davis-Monthan AFB, AZ [FG257]; arr 20-Oct-94
82-0974	F-16A-15/ADF	61-567	AMARC, Davis-Monthan AFB, AZ [FG136]; arr 08-Apr-94
82-0975	F-16A-15	61-568	AMARC, Davis-Monthan AFB, AZ [FG306]; arr 15-Dec-94
82-0976	F-16A-15	61-569	To NASA as N516NA
82-0977	F-16A-15/ADF	61-570	AMARC, Davis-Monthan AFB, AZ [FG259]; arr 21-Oct-94
82-0978	F-16A-15/ADF	61-571	AMARC, Davis-Monthan AFB, AZ [FG089]; arr 24-Feb-94
82-0979	F-16A-15/ADF	61-572	USAF 186th FS/120th FW, Montana ANG, Great Falls IAP
82-0980	F-16A-15	61-573	USAF 184th FS/188th FW, Arkansas ANG, Fort Smith ANGB
82-0981	F-16A-15/ADF	61-574	USAF 198th FS/156th FW, Puerto Rico ANG, Muniz ANGB
82-0982	F-16A-15	61-575	AMARC, Davis-Monthan AFB, AZ [FG175]; arr 28-Jun-94
82-0983	F-16A-15/ADF	61-576	USAF 178th FS/119th FW, North Dakota ANG, Hector Field
82-0984	F-16A-15/ADF	61-577	AMARC, Davis-Monthan AFB, AZ [FG389]; arr 29-Oct-96
82-0985	F-16A-15	61-578	Cr 30-Oct-92 (15th TS)
82-0986	F-16A-15	61-579	AMARC, Davis-Monthan AFB, AZ [FG254]; arr 17-Oct-94
82-0987	F-16A-15	61-580	AMARC, Davis-Monthan AFB, AZ [FG405]; arr 17-Dec-96
82-0988	F-16A-15	61-581	AMARC, Davis-Monthan AFB, AZ [FG277]; arr 07-Nov-94
82-0989	F-16A-15/ADF	61-582	AMARC, Davis-Monthan AFB, AZ [FG388]; arr 28-Oct-96
82-0990	F-16A-15/ADF	61-583	Cr 27-Aug-94 (134th FS)
82-0991	F-16A-15/ADF	61-584	AMARC, Davis-Monthan AFB, AZ [FG371]; arr 26-Jun-96
82-0992	F-16A-15/ADF	61-585	USAF 178th FS/119th FW, North Dakota ANG, Hector Field
82-0993	F-16A-15	61-586	USAF 162nd FW, Arizona ANG, Tucson IAP
82-0994	F-16A-15	61-587	Cr 13-Sep-88 (388th TFW)
82-0995	F-16A-15/ADF	61-588	USAF 198th FS/156th FW, Puerto Rico ANG, Muniz ANGB
82-0996	F-16A-15	61-589	AMARC, Davis-Monthan AFB, AZ [FG378]; arr 12-Jul-96
82-0997	F-16A-15	61-590	AMARC, Davis-Monthan AFB, AZ [FG390]; arr 30-Oct-96
82-0998	F-16A-15	61-591	Cr 09-Oct-86 (401st TFW)
82-0999	F-16A-15	61-592	AMARC, Davis-Monthan AFB, AZ [FG212]; arr 22-Aug-94
82-1000	F-16A-15/ADF	61-593	USAF 111st FS/147th FW, Texas ANG, Ellington ANGB
82-1001	F-16A-15/ADF	61-594	AMARC, Davis-Monthan AFB, AZ [FG391]; arr 30-Oct-96
82-1002	F-16A-15/ADF	61-595	AMARC, Davis-Monthan AFB, AZ [FG238]; arr 04-Oct-94
82-1003	F-16A-15/ADF	61-596	Cr 15-Mar-91 (194th FIS)
82-1004	F-16A-15	61-597	AMARC, Davis-Monthan AFB, AZ [FG302]; arr 13-Dec-94
82-1005	F-16A-15/ADF	61-598	AMARC, Davis-Monthan AFB, AZ [FG393]; arr 04-Nov-96
82-1006	F-16A-15/ADF	61-599	USAF 111st FS/147th FW, Texas ANG, Ellington ANGB
82-1007	F-16A-15	61-600	AMARC, Davis-Monthan AFB, AZ [FG220]; arr 12-Sep-94
82-1008	F-16A-15/ADF	61-601	USAF 198th FS/156th FW, Puerto Rico ANG, Muniz ANGB
82-1009	F-16A-15	61-602	USAF 184th FS/188th FW, Arkansas ANG, Fort Smith ANGB
82-1010	F-16A-15/ADF	61-603	AMARC, Davis-Monthan AFB, AZ [FG088]; arr 23-Feb-94
82-1011	F-16A-15	61-604	To R Danish AF as E-011
82-1012	F-16A-15/ADF	61-605	USAF 178th FS/119th FW, North Dakota ANG, Hector Field
82-1013	F-16A-15	61-606	USAF 184th FS/188th FW, Arkansas ANG, Fort Smith ANGB
82-1014	F-16A-15/ADF	61-607	USAF 114th FS/173rd FW, Oregon ANG, Klamath Falls
82-1015	F-16A-15	61-608	Cr 13-Jan-88 (401st TFW)
82-1016	F-16A-15/ADF	61-609	AMARC, Davis-Monthan AFB, AZ [FG053]; arr 21-Jan-94
82-1017	F-16A-15	61-610	AMARC, Davis-Monthan AFB, AZ [FG318]; arr 03-Mar-95
82-1018	F-16A-15	61-611	USAF 184th FS/188th FW, Arkansas ANG, Fort Smith ANGB
82-1019	F-16A-15/ADF	61-612	USAF 186th FS/120th FW, Montana ANG, Great Falls IAP
82-1020	F-16A-15	61-613	USAF 184th FS/188th FW, Arkansas ANG, Fort Smith ANGB
82-1021	F-16A-15/ADF	61-614	USAF 186th FS/120th FW, Montana ANG, Great Falls IAP
82-1022	F-16A-15	61-615	AMARC, Davis-Monthan AFB, AZ [FG222]; arr 12-Sep-94
82-1023	F-16A-15/ADF	61-616	USAF 186th FS/120th FW, Montana ANG, Great Falls IAP
82-1024	F-16A-15	61-617	To R Danish AF as E-024 08-Jul-94
82-1025	F-16A-15	61-618	USAF 184th FS/188th FW, Arkansas ANG, Fort Smith ANGB
82-1026	F-16B-15/ADF	62-92	USAF 178th FS/119th FW, North Dakota ANG, Hector Field
82-1027	F-16B-15/ADF	62-93	USAF 114th FS/173rd FW, Oregon ANG, Klamath Falls
82-1028	F-16B-15/ADF	62-94	AMARC, Davis-Monthan AFB, AZ [FG169]; arr 10-Jun-94
82-1029	F-16B-15	62-95	Cr 15-Nov-85 (57th FWW)
82-1030	F-16B-15/ADF	62-96	AMARC, Davis-Monthan AFB, AZ [FG332]; arr 14-Jul-95
82-1031	F-16B-15/ADF	62-97	USAF 114th FS/173rd FW, Oregon ANG, Klamath Falls
82-1032	F-16B-15/ADF	62-98	AMARC, Davis-Monthan AFB, AZ [FG312]; arr 02-Feb-95
82-1033	F-16B-15/ADF	62-99	USAF ANG/AFRes Test Center, Tucson ANGB, AZ
82-1034	F-16B-15/ADF	62-100	USAF 114th FS/173rd FW, Oregon ANG, Klamath Falls
82-1035	F-16B-15/ADF	62-101	USAF 162nd FW, Arizona ANG, Tucson IAP
82-1036	F-16B-15/ADF	62-102	USAF 178th FS/119th FW, North Dakota ANG, Hector Field
82-1037	F-16B-15	62-103	USAF 40th TES/46th TW, Eglin AFB, FL
82-1038	F-16B-15	62-104	Cr 23-May-86 (388th TFW)
82-1039	F-16B-15/ADF	62-105	USAF 114th FS/173rd FW, Oregon ANG, Klamath Falls
82-1040	F-16B-15/ADF	62-106	Cr 19-Dec-91 (179th FIS)
82-1041	F-16B-15/ADF	62-107	USAF 179th FS/148th FW, Minnesota ANG, Duluth IAP
82-1042	F-16B-15/ADF	62-108	Cr 23-Jun-94 (169th FS)
82-1043	F-16B-15	62-109/9F-8	To Egyptian AF as 9208 23-Feb-85
82-1044	F-16B-15/ADF	62-110	AMARC, Davis-Monthan AFB, AZ [FG279]; arr 07-Nov-94
82-1045	F-16B-15	62-111	Cr 02-May-84 (388th TFW)
82-1046	F-16B-15/ADF	62-112	USAF 114th FS/173rd FW, Oregon ANG, Klamath Falls
82-1047	F-16B-15	62-113	USAF 416th TS/412th TW, Edwards AFB, CA
82-1048	F-16B-15/ADF	62-114	AMARC, Davis-Monthan AFB, AZ [FG336]; arr 18-Oct-95
82-1049	F-16B-15/ADF	62-115	USAF 198th FS/156th FW, Puerto Rico ANG, Muniz ANGB
83-1066	F-16A-15/ADF	61-619	AMARC, Davis-Monthan AFB, AZ [FG248]; arr 13-Oct-94
83-1067	F-16A-15	61-620	Cr 17-Dec-87 (401st TFW)
83-1068	F-16A-15/ADF	61-621	AMARC, Davis-Monthan AFB, AZ [FG289]; arr 18-Nov-94
83-1069	F-16A-15	61-622	To R Danish AF as E-069
83-1070	F-16A-15	61-623	To R Danish AF as E-070
83-1071	F-16A-15	61-624	Cr 21-May-92 (704th FS)
83-1072	F-16A-15/ADF	61-625	AMARC, Davis-Monthan AFB, AZ [FG255]; arr 17-Oct-94
83-1073	F-16A-15/ADF	61-626	AMARC, Davis-Monthan AFB, AZ [FG260]; arr 21-Oct-94
83-1074	F-16A-15	61-627	To R Danish AF as E-074
83-1075	F-16A-15	61-628	To R Danish AF as E-075 08-Jul-94
83-1076	F-16A-15	61-629	AMARC, Davis-Monthan AFB, AZ [FG172]; arr 21-Jun-94
83-1077	F-16A-15/ADF	61-630	AMARC, Davis-Monthan AFB, AZ [FG303]; arr 14-Dec-94
83-1078	F-16A-15	61-631	Cr 17-Dec-92 (704th FS)
83-1079	F-16A-15	61-632	USAF 184th FS/188th FW, Arkansas ANG, Fort Smith ANGB
83-1080	F-16A-15	61-633	AMARC, Davis-Monthan AFB, AZ [FG221]; arr 12-Sep-94
83-1081	F-16A-15	61-634	AMARC, Davis-Monthan AFB, AZ [FG203]; arr 05-Aug-94
83-1082	F-16A-15	61-635	Cr 17-Nov-89 (31st TFW)
83-1083	F-16A-15/ADF	61-636	AMARC, Davis-Monthan AFB, AZ [FG237]; arr 04-Oct-94
83-1084	F-16A-15/ADF	61-637	AMARC, Davis-Monthan AFB, AZ [FG280]; arr 09-Nov-94
83-1085	F-16A-15/ADF	61-638	AMARC, Davis-Monthan AFB, AZ [FG375]; arr 11-Jul-96
83-1086	F-16A-15	61-639	Cr 27-Feb-86 (31st TFW)
83-1087	F-16A-15	61-640	USAF 184th FS/188th FW, Arkansas ANG, Fort Smith ANGB
83-1088	F-16A-15	61-641	AMARC, Davis-Monthan AFB, AZ [FG201]; arr 29-Jul-94
83-1089	F-16A-15	61-642	Cr 14-Jan-91 (31st TFW)
83-1090	F-16A-15	61-643	AMARC, Davis-Monthan AFB, AZ [FG178]; arr 05-Jul-94
83-1091	F-16A-15/ADF	61-644	USAF ANG/AFRes Test Center, Tucson ANGB, AZ
83-1092	F-16A-15/ADF	61-645	AMARC, Davis-Monthan AFB, AZ [FG311]; arr 02-Feb-95
83-1093	F-16A-15/ADF	61-646	AMARC, Davis-Monthan AFB, AZ [FG364]; arr 21-Jun-96
83-1094	F-16A-15	61-647	AMARC, Davis-Monthan AFB, AZ [FG208]; arr 12-Aug-94

Serial	Type/Code	c/n	Operator/location
83-1095	F-16A-15	61-648	USAF 184th FS/188th FW, Arkansas ANG, Fort Smith ANGB
83-1096	F-16A-15	61-649	AMARC, Davis-Monthan AFB, AZ [FG209]; arr 15-Aug-94
83-1097	F-16A-15/ADF	61-650	AMARC, Davis-Monthan AFB, AZ [FG363]; arr 21-Jun-96
83-1098	F-16A-15/ADF	61-651	AMARC, Davis-Monthan AFB, AZ [FG361]; arr 18-Jun-96
83-1099	F-16A-15	61-652	USAF 184th FS/188th FW, Arkansas ANG, Fort Smith ANGB
83-1100	F-16A-15/ADF	61-653	AMARC, Davis-Monthan AFB, AZ [FG374]; arr 11-Jul-96
83-1101	F-16A-15	61-654	AMARC, Davis-Monthan AFB, AZ [FG218]; arr 06-Sep-94
83-1102	F-16A-15	61-655	Cr 19-Feb-93 (182nd FS)
83-1103	F-16A-15/ADF	61-656	AMARC, Davis-Monthan AFB, AZ [FG366]; arr 26-Jun-96
83-1104	F-16A-15	61-657	AMARC, Davis-Monthan AFB, AZ [FG210]; arr 19-Aug-94
83-1105	F-16A-15/ADF	61-658	AMARC, Davis-Monthan AFB, AZ [FG370]; arr 26-Jun-96
83-1106	F-16A-15/ADF	61-659	AMARC, Davis-Monthan AFB, AZ [FG365]; arr 26-Jun-96
83-1107	F-16A-15	61-660	To R Danish AF as E-107 08-Jul-94
83-1108	F-16A-15/ADF	61-661	AMARC, Davis-Monthan AFB, AZ [FG362]; arr 18-Jun-96
83-1109	F-16A-15/ADF	61-662	AMARC, Davis-Monthan AFB, AZ [FG373]; arr 03-Jul-96
83-1110	F-16A-15/ADF	61-663	AMARC, Davis-Monthan AFB, AZ [FG367]; arr 26-Jun-96
83-1111	F-16A-15/ADF	61-664	AMARC, Davis-Monthan AFB, AZ [FG369]; arr 26-Jun-96
83-1112	F-16A-15/ADF	61-665	AMARC, Davis-Monthan AFB, AZ [FG288]; arr 18-Nov-94
83-1113	F-16A-15/ADF	61-666	AMARC, Davis-Monthan AFB, AZ [FG322]; arr 31-Mar-95
83-1114	F-16A-15/ADF	61-667	AMARC, Davis-Monthan AFB, AZ [FG376]; arr 11-Jul-96
83-1115	F-16A-15	61-668	Cr 22-Mar-87 (432nd TFW)
83-1116	F-16A-15	61-669	Cr 04-Jan-89 (31st TFW)
83-1117	F-16A-15	61-670	Cr 27-Apr-85 (363rd TFW)
83-1166	F-16B-15	62-116	USAF 184th FS/188th FW, Arkansas ANG, Fort Smith ANGB
83-1167	F-16B-15	62-117	AMARC, Davis-Monthan AFB, AZ [FG192]; arr 25-Jul-94
83-1168	F-16B-15/ADF	62-118	AMARC, Davis-Monthan AFB, AZ [FG299]; arr 09-Dec-94
83-1169	F-16B-15	62-119	USAF 85th TES/53rd Wg, Eglin AFB, FL
83-1170	F-16B-15/ADF	62-120	USAF 162nd FW, Arizona ANG, Tucson IAP
83-1171	F-16B-15	62-121	AMARC, Davis-Monthan AFB, AZ [FG204]; arr 05-Aug-94
83-1172	F-16B-15	62-122	USAF 416th TS/412th TW, Edwards AFB, CA
83-1173	F-16B-15/ADF	62-123	Cr 01-Jul-94 (182nd FS)
90-0942	F-16A-15	DG-1	AMARC, Davis-Monthan AFB, AZ [FG003]; arr 20-Apr-92 (Pak AF 91729)
90-0943	F-16A-15	DG-2	AMARC, Davis-Monthan AFB, AZ [FG001]; arr 10-Apr-92 (Pak AF 92730)
90-0944	F-16A-15	DG-3	AMARC, Davis-Monthan AFB, AZ [FG004]; arr 21-May-92 (Pak AF 92731)
90-0945	F-16A-15	DG-4	AMARC, Davis-Monthan AFB, AZ [FG005]; arr 21-May-92 (Pak AF 92732)
90-0946	F-16A-15	DG-5	AMARC, Davis-Monthan AFB, AZ [FG006]; arr 16-Jul-92 (Pak AF 92733)
90-0947	F-16A-15	DG-6	AMARC, Davis-Monthan AFB, AZ [FG009]; arr 22-Sep-92 (Pak AF 92734)
90-0948	F-16B-15	DH-1	AMARC, Davis-Monthan AFB, AZ [FG002]; arr 10-Apr-92 (Pak AF 91613)
90-0949	F-16B-15	DH-2	AMARC, Davis-Monthan AFB, AZ [FG008]; arr 04-Sep-92 (Pak AF 92614)
90-0950	F-16B-15	DH-3	AMARC, Davis-Monthan AFB, AZ [FG007]; arr 01-Sep-92 (Pak AF 92615)
90-0951	F-16B-15	DH-4	AMARC, Davis-Monthan AFB, AZ [FG025]; arr 25-Aug-93 (Pak AF 92616)
90-0952	F-16B-15	DH-5	AMARC, Davis-Monthan AFB, AZ [FG035]; arr 27-Sep-93 (Pak AF 92617)
92-0404	F-16A-15	DG-7	AMARC, Davis-Monthan AFB, AZ [FG010]; arr 23-Jun-93 (Pak AF 92735)
92-0405	F-16A-15	DG-8	AMARC, Davis-Monthan AFB, AZ [FG011]; arr 15-Jul-93 (Pak AF 92736)
92-0406	F-16A-15	DG-9	AMARC, Davis-Monthan AFB, AZ [FG034]; arr 21-Sep-93 (Pak AF 92737)
92-0407	F-16A-15	DG-10	AMARC, Davis-Monthan AFB, AZ [FG036]; arr 28-Sep-93 (Pak AF 92738)
92-0408	F-16A-15	DG-11	AMARC, Davis-Monthan AFB, AZ [FG037]; arr 29-Sep-93 (Pak AF 93739)
92-0409	F-16A-15	DG-12	AMARC, Davis-Monthan AFB, AZ [FG039]; arr 20-Dec-93 (Pak AF 93740)
92-0410	F-16A-15	DG-13	AMARC, Davis-Monthan AFB, AZ [FG040]; arr 21-May-92 (Pak AF 93741)
92-0452	F-16B-15	DH-6	AMARC, Davis-Monthan AFB, AZ [FG026]; arr 21-Dec-93 (Pak AF 92618)
92-0453	F-16B-15	DH-7	AMARC, Davis-Monthan AFB, AZ [FG038]; arr 02-Dec-93 (Pak AF 92619)
92-0454	F-16B-15	DH-8	AMARC, Davis-Monthan AFB, AZ [FG101]; arr 09-Mar-94 (Pak AF 93620)
92-0455	F-16B-15	DH-9	AMARC, Davis-Monthan AFB, AZ [FG102]; arr 09-Mar-94 (Pak AF 93621)

This two-seat F-16XL-2 was originally the third F-16A FSD aircraft, and is now with NASA as 848. LMTAS

NASA 516, an F-16A (82-0976) is used as a chase aircraft at Langley. BRIAN NICKLAS

Serial	Type/Code	c/n	Operator/location
92-0456	F-16B-15	DH-10	AMARC, Davis-Monthan AFB, AZ [FG183]; arr 20-Jul-94 (Pak AF 94622)
92-0457	F-16B-15	DH-11	AMARC, Davis-Monthan AFB, AZ [FG202]; arr 04-Aug-94 (Pak AF 94623)
92-0458	F-16B-15	DH-12	AMARC, Davis-Monthan AFB, AZ [FG239]; arr 04-Oct-94 (Pak AF...624)
92-0459	F-16B-15	DH-13	AMARC, Davis-Monthan AFB, AZ [FG271]; arr 02-Nov-94 (Pak AF...625)
92-0460	F-16B-15	DH-14	AMARC, Davis-Monthan AFB, AZ [FG270]; arr 01-Nov-94 (Pak AF...626)
92-0461	F-16B-15	DH-15	AMARC, Davis-Monthan AFB, AZ [FG298]; arr 07-Dec-94 (Pak AF...627)
93-0702	F-16A-20	TA-1	USAF 416th TS/412th TW, Edwards AFB, CA (RoCAF 6601)
93-0703	F-16A-20	TA-2	USAF 21st FS/56th FW, Luke AFB, AZ (RoCAF 6602)
93-0704	F-16A-20	TA-3	USAF 21st FS/56th FW, Luke AFB, AZ (RoCAF 6603)
93-0705	F-16A-20	TA-4	USAF 21st FS/56th FW, Luke AFB, AZ (RoCAF 6604)
93-0822	F-16B-20	TB-1	USAF 21st FS/56th FW, Luke AFB, AZ (RoCAF 6801)
93-0823	F-16B-20	TB-2	Lockheed Martin, Fort Worth, TX (RoCAF 6802)
93-0824	F-16B-20	TB-3	USAF 21st FS/56th FW, Luke AFB, AZ (RoCAF 6803)
93-0825	F-16B-20	TB-4	USAF 21st FS/56th FW, Luke AFB, AZ (RoCAF 6804)

Serial	Type/Code	c/n	Operator/location
NASA			
NASA 516	F-16A-15	61-569	NASA, Langley, VA
NASA 848	F-16XL-2	61-3	NASA Dryden, Edwards AFB, CA (was 847)
NASA 849	F-16XL-1	61-5	NASA, Langley, VA

2. Г-16C/D

Serial	Type/Code	c/n	Operator/location
83-1118	F-16C-25	5C-1	USAF 416th TS/412th TW, Edwards AFB, CA
83-1119	F-16C-25	5C-2	USAF 416th TS/412th TW, Edwards AFB, CA
83-1120	F-16C-25	5C-3	USAF 416th TS/412th TW, Edwards AFB, CA
83-1121	F-16C-25	5C-4	USAF 194th FS/144th FW, California ANG, Fresno
83-1122	F-16C-25	5C-5	USAF 194th FS/144th FW, California ANG, Fresno
83-1123	F-16C-25	5C-6	USAF 49th FTS/46th TW, Eglin AFB, FL
83-1124	F-16C-25/GF-16C	5C-7	USAF TTC/82nd TRW, Sheppard AFB, TX
83-1125	F-16C-25/GF-16C	5C-8	USAF TTC/82nd TRW, Sheppard AFB, TX
83-1126	F-16C-25	5C-9	USAF 309th FS/56th FW, Luke AFB, AZ
83-1127	F-16C-25/GF-16C	5C-10	USAF TTC/82nd TRW, Sheppard AFB, TX

F-16C Block 25 (83-1161) was operating with the 457th TFS AFRes from Fort Worth in 1991. PETER R MARCH

Serial	Type/Code	c/n	Operator/location
83-1128	F-16C-25	5C-11	USAF 309th FS/56th FW, Luke AFB, AZ
83-1129	F-16C-25	5C-12	USAF 309th FS/56th FW, Luke AFB, AZ
83-1130	F-16C-25	5C-13	USAF 163rd FS/122nd FW, Indiana ANG, Fort Wayne
83-1131	F-16C-25	5C-14	USAF 309th FS/56th FW, Luke AFB, AZ
83-1132	F-16C-25	5C-15	USAF 309th FS/56th FW, Luke AFB, AZ
83-1133	F-16C-25	5C-16	USAF 119th FS/177th FW, New Jersey ANG, Atlantic City
83-1134	F-16C-25	5C-17	Cr 28-Jan-97 (56th FW)
83-1135	F-16C-25	5C-18	USAF 194th FS/144th FW, California ANG, Fresno
83-1136	F-16C-25	5C-19	USAF 134th FS/158th FW, Vermont ANG, Burlington
83-1137	F-16C-25	5C-20	USAF 134th FS/158th FW, Vermont ANG, Burlington
83-1138	F-16C-25	5C-21	USAF 119th FS/177th FW, New Jersey ANG, Atlantic City
83-1139	F-16C-25	5C-22	Cr 01-Sep-92 (58th FW)
83-1140	F-16C-25	5C-23	USAF 61st FS/56th FW, Luke AFB, AZ
83-1141	F-16C-25	5C-24	USAF 182nd FS/149th FW, Texas ANG, Kelly AFB
83-1142	F-16C-25	5C-25	USAF 119th FS/177th FW, New Jersey ANG, Atlantic City
83-1143	F-16C-25/GF-16C	5C-26	USAF TTC/82nd TRW, Sheppard AFB, TX
83-1144	F-16C-25	5C-27	USAF 194th FS/144th FW, California ANG, Fresno
83-1145	F-16C-25	5C-28	USAF 62nd FS/56th FW, Luke AFB, AZ
83-1146	F-16C-25	5C-29	USAF 61st FS/56th FW, Luke AFB, AZ
83-1147	F-16C-25	5C-30	USAF 111st FS/147th FW, Texas ANG, Ellington ANGB
83-1148	F-16C-25	5C-31	USAF 119th FS/177th FW, New Jersey ANG, Atlantic City
83-1149	F-16C-25	5C-32	Cr 25-Jul-87 (363rd TFW)
83-1150	F-16C-25	5C-33	USAF 134th FS/158th FW, Vermont ANG, Burlington
83-1151	F-16C-25	5C-34	Cr 03-Sep-90 (363 TFW)
83-1152	F-16C-25	5C-35	USAF 61st FS/56th FW, Luke AFB, AZ
83-1153	F-16C-25	5C-36	USAF 309th FS/56th FW, Luke AFB, AZ
83-1154	F-16C-25	5C-37	USAF 61st FS/56th FW, Luke AFB, AZ
83-1155	F-16C-25	5C-38	USAF 182nd FS/149th FW, Texas ANG, Kelly AFB
83-1156	F-16C-25	5C-39	USAF 134th FS/158th FW, Vermont ANG, Burlington
83-1157	F-16C-25	5C-40	USAF 182nd FS/149th FW, Texas ANG, Kelly AFB
83-1158	F-16C-25	5C-41	USAF 62nd FS/56th FW, Luke AFB, AZ
83-1159	F-16C-25	5C-42	USAF 134th FS/158th FW, Vermont ANG, Burlington
83-1160	F-16C-25	5C-43	USAF 194th FS/144th FW, California ANG, Fresno
83-1161	F-16C-25	5C-44	USAF 61st FS/56th FW, Luke AFB, AZ
83-1162	F-16C-25	5C-45	USAF 182nd FS/149th FW, Texas ANG, Kelly AFB
83-1163	F-16C-25	5C-46	USAF 40th TES/46th TW, Eglin AFB, FL
83-1164	F-16C-25	5C-47	USAF 62nd FS/56th FW, Luke AFB, AZ
83-1165	F-16C-25	5C-48	USAF 134th FS/158th FW, Vermont ANG, Burlington
83-1174	F-16D-25	5D-1	USAF 62nd FS/56th FW, Luke AFB, AZ
83-1175	F-16D-25	5D-2	USAF 62nd FS/56th FW, Luke AFB, AZ
83-1176	F-16D-25	5D-3	USAF 416th TS/412th TW, Edwards AFB, CA
83-1177	F-16D-25	5D-4	USAF 309th FS/56th FW, Luke AFB, AZ
83-1178	F-16D-25	5D-5	USAF 61st FS/56th FW, Luke AFB, AZ
83-1179	F-16D-25	5D-6	USAF 61st FS/56th FW, Luke AFB, AZ
83-1180	F-16D-25	5D-7	USAF ANG/AFRes Test Center, Tucson IAP, AZ
83-1181	F-16D-25	5D-8	USAF 309th FS/56th FW, Luke AFB, AZ
83-1182	F-16D-25	5D-9	USAF 62nd FS/56th FW, Luke AFB, AZ
83-1183	F-16D-25	5D-10	USAF 194th FS/144th FW, California ANG, Fresno
83-1184	F-16D-25	5D-11	USAF 62nd FS/56th FW, Luke AFB, AZ
83-1185	F-16D-25	5D-12	USAF 309th FS/56th FW, Luke AFB, AZ
84-1212	F-16C-25	5C-49	USAF 134th FS/158th FW, Vermont ANG, Burlington
84-1213	F-16C-25	5C-50	USAF 309th FS/56th FW, Luke AFB, AZ
84-1214	F-16C-25	5C-51	USAF 182nd FS/149th FW, Texas ANG, Kelly AFB
84-1215	F-16C-25	5C-52	USAF 182nd FS/149th FW, Texas ANG, Kelly AFB

Serial	Type/Code	c/n	Operator/location
84-1216	F-16C-25	5C-53	USAF 93rd FS/482nd FW, AFRes, Homestead AFB, FL
84-1217	F-16C-25	5C-54	USAF 62nd FS/56th FW, Luke AFB, AZ
84-1218	F-16C-25	5C-55	Cr 17-Feb-91 (363rd TFW)
84-1219	F-16C-25	5C-56	USAF 62nd FS/56th FW, Luke AFB, AZ
84-1220	F-16C-25	5C-57	USAF 182nd FS/149th FW, Texas ANG, Kelly AFB
84-1221	F-16C-25	5C-58	Cr 02-Aug-88 (363rd TFW)
84-1222	F-16C-25	5C-59	USAF 62nd FS/56th FW, Luke AFB, AZ
84-1223	F-16C-25	5C-60	USAF 62nd FS/56th FW, Luke AFB, AZ
84-1224	F-16C-25	5C-61	Cr 11-Feb-86 (363rd TFW)
84-1225	F-16C-25	5C-62	USAF 182nd FS/149th FW, Texas ANG, Kelly AFB
84-1226	F-16C-25	5C-63	USAF 163rd FS/122nd FW, Indiana ANG, Fort Wayne
84-1227	F-16C-25	5C-64	USAF 182nd FS/149th FW, Texas ANG, Kelly AFB
84-1228	F-16C-25	5C-65	Cr 05-Jan-89 (363rd TFW)
84-1229	F-16C-25	5C-66	USAF 134th FS/158th FW, Vermont ANG, Burlington
84-1230	F-16C-25	5C-67	USAF 309th FS/56th FW, Luke AFB, AZ
84-1231	F-16C-25	5C-68	USAF 457th FS/301st FW, AFRes, NAS Fort Worth, TX
84-1232	F-16C-25	5C-69	Cr 25-Jul-88 (363rd TFW)
84-1233	F-16C-25	5C-70	Cr 12-Nov-86 (363rd TFW)
84-1234	F-16C-25	5C-71	USAF 194th FS/144th FW, California ANG, Fresno
84-1235	F-16C-25	5C-72	USAF 182nd FS/149th FW, Texas ANG, Kelly AFB
84-1236	F-16C-25	5C-73	USAF 163rd FS/122nd FW, Indiana ANG, Fort Wayne
84-1237	F-16C-25	5C-74	USAF 194th FS/144th FW, California ANG, Fresno
84-1238	F-16C-25	5C-75	USAF 163rd FS/122nd FW, Indiana ANG, Fort Wayne
84-1239	F-16C-25	5C-76	USAF 309th FS/56th FW, Luke AFB, AZ
84-1240	F-16C-25	5C-77	USAF 309th FS/56th FW, Luke AFB, AZ
84-1241	F-16C-25	5C-78	USAF 62nd FS/56th FW, Luke AFB, AZ
84-1242	F-16C-25	5C-79	USAF 182nd FS/149th FW, Texas ANG, Kelly AFB
84-1243	F-16C-25	5C-80	USAF 309th FS/56th FW, Luke AFB, AZ
84-1244	F-16C-25	5C-81	USAF 163rd FS/122nd FW, Indiana ANG, Fort Wayne
84-1245	F-16C-25	5C-82	USAF 182nd FS/149th FW, Texas ANG, Kelly AFB
84-1246	F-16C-25	5C-83	USAF 309th FS/56th FW, Luke AFB, AZ
84-1247	F-16C-25	5C-84	USAF 62nd FS/56th FW, Luke AFB, AZ
84-1248	F-16C-25	5C-85	USAF 182nd FS/149th FW, Texas ANG, Kelly AFB
84-1249	F-16C-25	5C-86	Cr 13-Sep-88 (363rd TFW)
84-1250	F-16C-25	5C-87	USAF 62nd FS/56th FW, Luke AFB, AZ
84-1251	F-16C-25	5C-88	USAF 309th FS/56th FW, Luke AFB, AZ
84-1252	F-16C-25	5C-89	USAF 309th FS/56th FW, Luke AFB, AZ
84-1253	F-16C-25	5C-90	USAF 182nd FS/149th FW, Texas ANG, Kelly AFB
84-1254	F-16C-25	5C-91	USAF 309th FS/56th FW, Luke AFB, AZ
84-1255	F-16C-25	5C-92	USAF 194th FS/144th FW, California ANG, Fresno
84-1256	F-16C-25	5C-93	USAF 309th FS/56th FW, Luke AFB, AZ
84-1257	F-16C-25	5C-94	USAF 163rd FS/122nd FW, Indiana ANG, Fort Wayne
84-1258	F-16C-25	5C-95	USAF 119th FS/177th FW, New Jersey ANG, Atlantic City
84-1259	F-16C-25	5C-96	Cr 09-Oct-86 (363rd TFW)
84-1260	F-16C-25	5C-97	USAF 119th FS/177th FW, New Jersey ANG, Atlantic City
84-1261	F-16C-25	5C-98	USAF 309th FS/56th FW, Luke AFB, AZ
84-1262	F-16C-25	5C-99	USAF ANG/AFRes Test Center, Tucson IAP, AZ
84-1263	F-16C-25	5C-100	Cr 18-Dec-89 (50 TFW)
84-1264	F-16C-25	5C-101	USAF 163rd FS/122nd FW, Indiana ANG, Fort Wayne
84-1265	F-16C-25	5C-102	USAF ANG/AFRes Test Center, Tucson IAP, AZ
84-1266	F-16C-25	5C-103	USAF 163rd FS/122nd FW, Indiana ANG, Fort Wayne
84-1267	F-16C-25	5C-104	Cr 13-Jan-92 (184th FG)
84-1268	F-16C-25	5C-105	USAF 93rd FS/482nd FW, AFRes, Homestead AFB, FL
84-1269	F-16C-25	5C-106	USAF 134th FS/158th FW, Vermont ANG, Burlington
84-1270	F-16C-25	5C-107	Cr 10-Oct-87 (363rd TFW)
84-1271	F-16C-25	5C-108	USAF 194th FS/144th FW, California ANG, Fresno
84-1272	F-16C-25	5C-109	USAF 309th FS/56th FW, Luke AFB, AZ
84-1273	F-16C-25	5C-110	USAF 62nd FS/56th FW, Luke AFB, AZ
84-1274	F-16C-25	5C-111	USAF 162nd FW, Arizona ANG, Tucson IAP
84-1275	F-16C-25	5C-112	USAF 134th FS/158th FW, Vermont ANG, Burlington
84-1276	F-16C-25	5C-113	USAF 119th FS/177th FW, New Jersey ANG, Atlantic City
84-1277	F-16C-25	5C-114	USAF 309th FS/56th FW, Luke AFB, AZ
84-1278	F-16C-25	5C-115	USAF ANG/AFRes Test Center, Tucson IAP, AZ
84-1279	F-16C-25	5C-116	USAF 194th FS/144th FW, California ANG, Fresno
84-1280	F-16C-25	5C-117	USAF 309th FS/56th FW, Luke AFB, AZ
84-1281	F-16C-25	5C-118	USAF 62nd FS/56th FW, Luke AFB, AZ
84-1282	F-16C-25	5C-119	USAF 194th FS/144th FW, California ANG, Fresno
84-1283	F-16C-25	5C-120	USAF 62nd FS/56th FW, Luke AFB, AZ
84-1284	F-16C-25	5C-121	USAF 119th FS/177th FW, New Jersey ANG, Atlantic City
84-1285	F-16C-25	5C-122	USAF 85th TES/53rd Wg, Eglin AFB, FL
84-1286	F-16C-25	5C-123	USAF 119th FS/177th FW, New Jersey ANG, Atlantic City
84-1287	F-16C-25	5C-124	USAF 134th FS/158th FW, Vermont ANG, Burlington
84-1288	F-16C-25	5C-125	USAF 119th FS/177th FW, New Jersey ANG, Atlantic City
84-1289	F-16C-25	5C-126	USAF NY ANG, Hancock Field, Syracuse (recruiting aid)
84-1290	F-16C-25	5C-127	USAF 182nd FS/149th FW, Texas ANG, Kelly AFB

Serial	Type/Code	c/n	Operator/location
84-1291	F-16C-25	5C-128	USAF 182nd FS/149th FW, Texas ANG, Kelly AFB
84-1292	F-16C-25	5C-129	USAF 119th FS/177th FW, New Jersey ANG, Atlantic City
84-1293	F-16C-25	5C-130	Cr 18-Dec-89 (50th TFW)
84-1294	F-16C-25	5C-131	USAF 134th FS/158th FW, Vermont ANG, Burlington
84-1295	F-16C-25	5C-132	USAF 119th FS/177th FW, New Jersey ANG, Atlantic City
84-1296	F-16C-25	5C-133	USAF 62nd FS/56th FW, Luke AFB, AZ
84-1297	F-16C-25	5C-134	USAF 62nd FS/56th FW, Luke AFB, AZ
84-1298	F-16C-25	5C-135	USAF 163rd FS/122nd FW, Indiana ANG, Fort Wayne
84-1299	F-16C-25	5C-136	USAF 119th FS/177th FW, New Jersey ANG, Atlantic City
84-1300	F-16C-25	5C-137	USAF 163rd FS/122nd FW, Indiana ANG, Fort Wayne
84-1301	F-16C-25	5C-138	USAF 457th FS/301st FW, AFRes, NAS Fort Worth, TX
84-1302	F-16C-25	5C-139	USAF 119th FS/177th FW, New Jersey ANG, Atlantic City
84-1303	F-16C-25	5C-140	USAF 182nd FS/149th FW, Texas ANG, Kelly AFB
84-1304	F-16C-25	5C-141	USAF 62nd FS/56th FW, Luke AFB, AZ
84-1305	F-16C-25	5C-142	USAF 162nd FW, Arizona ANG, Tucson IAP
84-1306	F-16C-25	5C-143	USAF 134th FS/158th FW, Vermont ANG, Burlington
84-1307	F-16C-25	5C-144	USAF 119th FS/177th FW, New Jersey ANG, Atlantic City
84-1308	F-16C-25	5C-145	USAF 62nd FS/56th FW, Luke AFB, AZ
84-1309	F-16C-25	5C-146	USAF 182nd FS/149th FW, Texas ANG, Kelly AFB
84-1310	F-16C-25	5C-147	USAF 163rd FS/122nd FW, Indiana ANG, Fort Wayne
84-1311	F-16C-25	5C-148	USAF 309th FS/56th FW, Luke AFB, AZ
84-1312	F-16C-25	5C-149	USAF 119th FS/177th FW, New Jersey ANG, Atlantic City
84-1313	F-16C-25	5C-150	USAF 182nd FS/149th FW, Texas ANG, Kelly AFB
84-1314	F-16C-25	5C-151	USAF 61st FS/56th FW, Luke AFB, AZ
84-1315	F-16C-25	5C-152	USAF 163rd FS/122nd FW, Indiana ANG, Fort Wayne
84-1316	F-16C-25	5C-153	USAF 194th FS/144th FW, California ANG, Fresno
84-1317	F-16C-25	5C-154	USAF 162nd FW, Arizona ANG, Tucson IAP
84-1318	F-16C-25	5C-155	USAF 194th FS/144th FW, California ANG, Fresno
84-1319	F-16D-25	5D-13	USAF 62nd FS/56th FW, Luke AFB, AZ
84-1320	F-16D-25	5D-14	USAF 119th FS/177th FW, New Jersey ANG, Atlantic City
84-1321	F-16D-25	5D-15	Cr 07-Aug-90 (363rd TFW)
84-1322	F-16D-25	5D-16	USAF 309th FS/56th FW, Luke AFB, AZ
84-1323	F-16D-25	5D-17	USAF 61st FS/56th FW, Luke AFB, AZ
84-1324	F-16D-25	5D-18	USAF 309th FS/56th FW, Luke AFB, AZ
84-1325	F-16D-25	5D-19	USAF 134th FS/158th FW, Vermont ANG, Burlington
84-1326	F-16D-25	5D-20	USAF 163rd FS/122nd FW, Indiana ANG, Fort Wayne
84-1327	F-16D-25	5D-21	USAF 309th FS/56th FW, Luke AFB, AZ
84-1328	F-16D-25	5D-22	USAF 62nd FS/56th FW, Luke AFB, AZ
84-1329	F-16D-25	5D-23	USAF 61st FS/56th FW, Luke AFB, AZ
84-1330	F-16D-25	5D-24	USAF 61st FS/56th FW, Luke AFB, AZ
84-1331	F-16D-25	5D-25	USAF 62nd FS/56th FW, Luke AFB, AZ
84-1374	F-16C-25	5C-156	USAF 163rd FS/122nd FW, Indiana ANG, Fort Wayne
84-1375	F-16C-25	5C-157	USAF 194th FS/144th FW, California ANG, Fresno
84-1376	F-16C-25	5C-158	USAF 194th FS/144th FW, California ANG, Fresno
84-1377	F-16C-25	5C-159	USAF 163rd FS/122nd FW, Indiana ANG, Fort Wayne
84-1378	F-16C-25	5C-160	USAF 309th FS/56th FW, Luke AFB, AZ
84-1379	F-16C-25	5C-161	Cr 16-Feb-91 (363rd TFW)
84-1380	F-16C-25	5C-162	USAF 134th FS/158th FW, Vermont ANG, Burlington
84-1381	F-16C-25	5C-163	USAF 62nd FS/56th FW, Luke AFB, AZ
84-1382	F-16C-25	5C-164	USAF 62nd FS/56th FW, Luke AFB, AZ
84-1383	F-16C-25	5C-165	USAF 119th FS/177th FW, New Jersey ANG, Atlantic City
84-1384	F-16C-25	5C-166	USAF 134th FS/158th FW, Vermont ANG, Burlington
84-1385	F-16C-25	5C-167	USAF 194th FS/144th FW, California ANG, Fresno
84-1386	F-16C-25	5C-168	USAF 61st FS/56th FW, Luke AFB, AZ
84-1387	F-16C-25	5C-169	USAF 194th FS/144th FW, California ANG, Fresno
84-1388	F-16C-25	5C-170	USAF 163rd FS/122nd FW, Indiana ANG, Fort Wayne
84-1389	F-16C-25	5C-171	Cr 31-Mar-88 (50th TFW)
84-1390	F-16C-25	5C-172	Cr 27-Feb-91 (50th TFW)
84-1391	F-16C-25	5C-173	USAF 194th FS/144th FW, California ANG, Fresno
84-1392	F-16C-25	5C-174	USAF 62nd FS/56th FW, Luke AFB, AZ
84-1393	F-16C-25	5C-175	USAF 162nd FW, Arizona ANG, Tucson IAP
84-1394	F-16C-25	5C-176	USAF 163rd FS/122nd FW, Indiana ANG, Fort Wayne
84-1395	F-16C-25	5C-177	Cr 29-Jun-88 (50th TFW)
84-1396	F-16D-25	5D-26	USAF 62nd FS/56th FW, Luke AFB, AZ
84-1397	F-16D-25	5D-27	USAF 62nd FS/56th FW, Luke AFB, AZ
85-1398	F-16C-25	5C-178	USAF 175th FS/114th FW, South Dakota ANG, Sioux Falls
85-1399	F-16C-25	5C-179	Cr 17-Sep-87 (50th TFW)
85-1400	F-16C-30	5C-180	USAF 121st FS/113th FW, DC ANG, Andrews AFB
85-1401	F-16C-25	5C-181	Cr 29-Jun-88 (50th TFW)
85-1402	F-16C-30	5C-182	USAF Ogden Air Logistics Center Hill AFB, UT
85-1403	F-16C-25	5C-183	USAF 134th FS/158th FW, Vermont ANG, Burlington
85-1404	F-16C-25	5C-184	USAF 194th FS/144th FW, California ANG, Fresno
85-1405	F-16C-25	5C-185	USAF ANG/AFRes Test Center, Tucson IAP, AZ
85-1406	F-16C-25	5C-186	USAF 134th FS/158th FW, Vermont ANG, Burlington
85-1407	F-16C-25	5C-187	USAF 162nd FW, Arizona ANG, Tucson IAP
85-1408	F-16C-30	5C-188	USAF 150th DSE/150th FW, New Mexico ANG, Kirtland AFB
85-1409	F-16C-25	5C-189	USAF ANG/AFRes Test Center, Tucson IAP, AZ
85-1410	F-16C-30	5C-190	USAF Ogden Air Logistics Centre Hill AFB, UT
85-1411	F-16C-25	5C-191	USAF 119th FS/177th FW, New Jersey ANG, Atlantic City
85-1412	F-16C-30	5C-192	USAF 457th FS/301st FW, AFRes, NAS Fort Worth, TX
85-1413	F-16C-25	5C-193	USAF 163rd FS/122nd FW, Indiana ANG, Fort Wayne
85-1414	F-16C-30	5C-194	Cr 01-Sep-88 (432nd FW)
85-1415	F-16C-25	5C-195	USAF 162nd FW, Arizona ANG, Tucson IAP
85-1416	F-16C-25	5C-196	USAF 163rd FS/122nd FW, Indiana ANG, Fort Wayne
85-1417	F-16C-25	5C-197	USAF 163rd FS/122nd FW, Indiana ANG, Fort Wayne
85-1418	F-16C-25	5C-198	USAF 163rd FS/122nd FW, Indiana ANG, Fort Wayne
85-1419	F-16C-25	5C-199	USAF ANG/AFRes Test Center, Tucson IAP, AZ
85-1420	F-16C-25	5C-200	USAF 457th FS/301st FW, AFRes, NAS Fort Worth, TX
85-1421	F-16C-25	5C-201	USAF 62nd FS/56th FW, Luke AFB, AZ
85-1422	F-16C-30	5C-202	USAF 121st FS/113th FW, DC ANG, Andrews AFB
85-1423	F-16C-25	5C-203	Cr 28-Jan-91 (57th FWW)
85-1424	F-16C-30	5C-204	Cr 23-Jun-87 (86th TFW)

A line up of F-16Cs of the 706th FS/926th FW at NAS New Orleans in December 1995. BOB ARCHER

One of the F-16Ds (86-0039) operated by the 57th FW at Nellis AFB, NV. JAMIE HUNTER

Serial	Type/Code	c/n	Operator/location	Serial	Type/Code	c/n	Operator/location
85-1425	F-16C-25	5C-205	USAF 61st FS/56th FW, Luke AFB, AZ	85-1472	F-16C-30	5C-252	USAF 121st FS/113th FW, DC ANG, Andrews AFB
85-1426	F-16C-30	5C-206	USAF 121st FS/113th FW, DC ANG, Andrews AFB	85-1473	F-16C-30	5C-253	USAF 175th FS/114th FW, South Dakota ANG, Sioux Falls
85-1427	F-16C-25	5C-207	USAF 61st FS/56th FW, Luke AFB, AZ	85-1474	F-16C-30	5C-254	USAF 121st FS/113th FW, DC ANG, Andrews AFB
85-1428	F-16C-30	5C-208	USAF 93rd FS/482nd FW, AFRes, Homestead AFB, FL	85-1475	F-16C-30	5C-255	USAF 457th FS/301st FW, AFRes, NAS Fort Worth, TX
85-1429	F-16C-25	5C-209	USAF 61st FS/56th FW, Luke AFB, AZ	85-1476	F-16C-30	5C-256	USAF 121st FS/113th FW, DC ANG, Andrews AFB
85-1430	F-16C-25	5C-210	USAF 61st FS/56th FW, Luke AFB, AZ	85-1477	F-16C-30	5C-257	USAF 121st FS/113th FW, DC ANG, Andrews AFB
85-1431	F-16C-25	5C-211	USAF 61st FS/56th FW, Luke AFB, AZ	85-1478	F-16C-30	5C-258	USAF 175th FS/114th FW, South Dakota ANG, Sioux Falls
85-1432	F-16C-30	5C-212	USAF 174th FS/185th FW, Iowa ANG, Sioux City	85-1479	F-16C-30	5C-259	USAF 457th FS/301st FW, AFRes, NAS Fort Worth, TX
85-1433	F-16C-25	5C-213	USAF 61st FS/56th FW, Luke AFB, AZ	85-1480	F-16C-30	5C-260	USAF 121st FS/113th FW, DC ANG, Andrews AFB
85-1434	F-16C-30	5C-214	USAF 175th FS/114th FW, South Dakota ANG, Sioux Falls	85-1481	F-16C-30	5C-261	USAF 121st FS/113th FW, DC ANG, Andrews AFB
85-1435	F-16C-25	5C-215	USAF 61st FS/56th FW, Luke AFB, AZ	85-1482	F-16C-30	5C-262	USAF 174th FS/185th FW, Iowa ANG, Sioux City
85-1436	F-16C-30	5C-216	USAF 113th FS/181st FW, Indiana ANG, Terre Haute	85-1483	F-16C-30	5C-263	USAF 174th FS/185th FW, Iowa ANG, Sioux City
85-1437	F-16C-25	5C-217	USAF 61st FS/56th FW, Luke AFB, AZ	85-1484	F-16C-30	5C-264	USAF 457th FS/301st FW, AFRes, NAS Fort Worth, TX
85-1438	F-16C-30	5C-218	USAF 121st FS/113th FW, DC ANG, Andrews AFB	85-1485	F-16C-30	5C-265	Cr 22-Oct-92 (86th Wg)
85-1439	F-16C-25	5C-219	USAF 61st FS/56th FW, Luke AFB, AZ	85-1486	F-16C-30	5C-266	USAF 175th FS/114th FW, South Dakota ANG, Sioux Falls
85-1440	F-16C-30	5C-220	USAF 175th FS/114th FW, South Dakota ANG, Sioux Falls	85-1487	F-16C-30	5C-267	USAF 107th FS/127th Wg, Michigan ANG, Selfridge ANGB
85-1441	F-16C-25	5C-221	USAF 61st FS/56th FW, Luke AFB, AZ	85-1488	F-16C-30	5C-268	USAF 107th FS/127th Wg, Michigan ANG, Selfridge ANGB
85-1442	F-16C-30	5C-222	USAF 175th FS/114th FW, South Dakota ANG, Sioux Falls	85-1489	F-16C-30	5C-269	USAF 113th FS/181st FW, Indiana ANG, Terre Haute
85-1443	F-16C-25	5C-223	USAF 61st FS/56th FW, Luke AFB, AZ	85-1490	F-16C-30	5C-270	USAF 107th FS/127th Wg, Michigan ANG, Selfridge ANGB
85-1444	F-16C-30	5C-224	USAF 457th FS/301st FW, AFRes, NAS Fort Worth, TX	85-1491	F-16C-30	5C-271	USAF 107th FS/127th Wg, Michigan ANG, Selfridge ANGB
85-1445	F-16C-25	5C-225	USAF 61st FS/56th FW, Luke AFB, AZ	85-1492	F-16C-30	5C-272	Cr 28-Apr-93 (432nd FW)
85-1446	F-16C-30	5C-226	USAF 175th FS/114th FW, South Dakota ANG, Sioux Falls	85-1493	F-16C-30	5C-273	USAF 107th FS/127th Wg, Michigan ANG, Selfridge ANGB
85-1447	F-16C-25	5C-227	USAF 61st FS/56th FW, Luke AFB, AZ	85-1494	F-16C-30	5C-274	USAF 107th FS/127th Wg, Michigan ANG, Selfridge ANGB
85-1448	F-16C-30	5C-228	USAF 175th FS/114th FW, South Dakota ANG, Sioux Falls	85-1495	F-16C-30	5C-275	USAF 113th FS/181st FW, Indiana ANG, Terre Haute
85-1449	F-16C-30	5C-229	USAF 457th FS/301st FW, AFRes, NAS Fort Worth, TX	85-1496	F-16C-30	5C-276	Cr 22-Jan-92 (432nd FW)
85-1450	F-16C-30	5C-230	USAF 121st FS/113th FW, DC ANG, Andrews AFB	85-1497	F-16C-30	5C-277	USAF 113th FS/181st FW, Indiana ANG, Terre Haute
85-1451	F-16C-30	5C-231	Cr 08-Sep-92 (86th FW)	85-1498	F-16C-30	5C-278	USAF 107th FS/127th Wg, Michigan ANG, Selfridge ANGB
85-1452	F-16C-25	5C-232	USAF 61st FS/56th FW, Luke AFB, AZ	85-1499	F-16C-30	5C-279	USAF 107th FS/127th Wg, Michigan ANG, Selfridge ANGB
85-1453	F-16C-30	5C-233	USAF 121st FS/113th FW, DC ANG, Andrews AFB	85-1500	F-16C-30	5C-280	USAF 113th FS/181st FW, Indiana ANG, Terre Haute
85-1454	F-16C-30	5C-234	USAF 175th FS/114th FW, South Dakota ANG, Sioux Falls	85-1501	F-16C-30	5C-281	USAF 107th FS/127th Wg, Michigan ANG, Selfridge ANGB
85-1455	F-16C-30	5C-235	USAF 121st FS/113th FW, DC ANG, Andrews AFB	85-1502	F-16C-30	5C-282	USAF 107th FS/127th Wg, Michigan ANG, Selfridge ANGB
85-1456	F-16C-30	5C-236	USAF 457th FS/301st FW, AFRes, NAS Fort Worth, TX	85-1503	F-16C-30	5C-283	USAF 107th FS/127th Wg, Michigan ANG, Selfridge ANGB
85-1457	F-16C-30	5C-237	USAF 113th FS/181st FW, Indiana ANG, Terre Haute	85-1504	F-16C-30	5C-284	USAF 107th FS/127th Wg, Michigan ANG, Selfridge ANGB
85-1458	F-16C-30	5C-238	USAF 457th FS/301st FW, AFRes, NAS Fort Worth, TX	85-1505	F-16C-30	5C-285	USAF 113th FS/181st FW, Indiana ANG, Terre Haute
85-1459	F-16C-30	5C-239	USAF 706th FS/926th FW NAS New Orleans, LA	85-1506	F-16D-25	5D-28	USAF 61st FS/56th FW, Luke AFB, AZ
85-1460	F-16C-30	5C-240	USAF 150th DSE/150th FW, New Mexico ANG, Kirtland AFB	85-1507	F-16D-25	5D-29	USAF 62nd FS/56th FW, Luke AFB, AZ
85-1461	F-16C-30	5C-241	USAF 121st FS/113th FW, DC ANG, Andrews AFB	85-1508	F-16D-25	5D-30	USAF 61st FS/56th FW, Luke AFB, AZ
85-1462	F-16C-30	5C-242	Cr 18-Apr-88 (86th TFW)	85-1509	F-16D-30	5D-31	USAF 121st FS/113th FW, DC ANG, Andrews AFB
85-1463	F-16C-30	5C-243	Cr 19-Oct-87 (86th TFW)	85-1510	F-16D-25	5D-32	Cr 20-Sep-90 (58th TTW)
85-1464	F-16C-30	5C-244	USAF 121st FS/113th FW, DC ANG, Andrews AFB	85-1511	F-16D-30	5D-33	USAF 113th FS/181st FW, Indiana ANG, Terre Haute
85-1465	F-16C-30	5C-245	USAF 121st FS/113th FW, DC ANG, Andrews AFB	85-1512	F-16D-25	5D-34	USAF 62nd FS/56th FW, Luke AFB, AZ
85-1466	F-16C-30	5C-246	USAF 175th FS/114th FW, South Dakota ANG, Sioux Falls	85-1513	F-16D-30	5D-35	USAF 150th DSE/150th FW, New Mexico ANG, Kirtland AFB
85-1467	F-16C-30	5C-247	USAF 457th FS/301st FW, AFRes, NAS Fort Worth, TX	85-1514	F-16D-25	5D-36	USAF 61st FS/56th FW, Luke AFB, AZ
85-1468	F-16C-30	5C-248	USAF 457th FS/301st FW, AFRes, NAS Fort Worth, TX	85-1515	F-16D-25	5D-37	USAF 309th FS/56th FW, Luke AFB, AZ
85-1469	F-16C-30	5C-249	USAF 175th FS/114th FW, South Dakota ANG, Sioux Falls	85-1516	F-16D-25	5D-38	USAF 61st FS/56th FW, Luke AFB, AZ
85-1470	F-16C-30	5C-250	USAF 175th FS/114th FW, South Dakota ANG, Sioux Falls	85-1517	F-16D-30	5D-39	Cr 27-Aug-87 (86th TFW)
85-1471	F-16C-30	5C-251	USAF 121st FS/113th FW, DC ANG, Andrews AFB	85-1544	F-16C-30	5C-286	USAF 113th FS/181st FW, Indiana ANG, Terre Haute

Serial	Type/Code	c/n	Operator/location
85-1545	F-16C-30	5C-285	USAF 174th FS/185th FW, Iowa ANG, Sioux City
85-1546	F-16C-30	5C-288	USAF 149th FS/192nd FW, Virginia ANG, Richmond
85-1547	F-16C-30	5C-289	USAF 174th FS/185th FW, Iowa ANG, Sioux City
85-1548	F-16C-30	5C-290	USAF 174th FS/185th FW, Iowa ANG, Sioux City
85-1549	F-16C-30	5C-291	USAF 457th FS/301st FW, AFRes, NAS Fort Worth, TX
85-1550	F-16C-30	5C-292	USAF 174th FS/185th FW, Iowa ANG, Sioux City
85-1551	F-16C-30	5C-293	USAF 174th FS/185th FW, Iowa ANG, Sioux City
85-1552	F-16C-30	5C-294	USAF 113th FS/181st FW, Indiana ANG, Terre Haute
85-1553	F-16C-30	5C-295	USAF 175th FS/114th FW, South Dakota ANG, Sioux Falls
85-1554	F-16C-30	5C-296	USAF 174th FS/185th FW, Iowa ANG, Sioux City
85-1555	F-16C-30	5C-297	USAF 113th FS/181st FW, Indiana ANG, Terre Haute
85-1556	F-16C-30	5C-298	USAF 174th FS/185th FW, Iowa ANG, Sioux City
85-1557	F-16C-30	5C-299	USAF 113th FS/181st FW, Indiana ANG, Terre Haute
85-1558	F-16C-30	5C-300	USAF 457th FS/301st FW, AFRes, NAS Fort Worth, TX
85-1559	F-16C-30	5C-301	USAF 175th FS/114th FW, South Dakota ANG, Sioux Falls
85-1560	F-16C-30	5C-302	USAF 174th FS/185th FW, Iowa ANG, Sioux City
85-1561	F-16C-30	5C-303	USAF 174th FS/185th FW, Iowa ANG, Sioux City
85-1562	F-16C-30	5C-304	USAF 113th FS/181st FW, Indiana ANG, Terre Haute
85-1563	F-16C-30	5C-305	USAF 174th FS/185th FW, Iowa ANG, Sioux City
85-1564	F-16C-30	5C-306	USAF 457th FS/301st FW, AFRes, NAS Fort Worth, TX
85-1565	F-16C-30	5C-307	USAF 174th FS/185th FW, Iowa ANG, Sioux City
85-1566	F-16C-30	5C-308	USAF 174th FS/185th FW, Iowa ANG, Sioux City
85-1567	F-16C-30	5C-309	USAF 150th DSE/150th FW, New Mexico ANG, Kirtland AFB
85-1568	F-16C-30	5C-310	USAF 174th FS/185th FW, Iowa ANG, Sioux City
85-1569	F-16C-30	5C-311	USAF 174th FS/185th FW, Iowa ANG, Sioux City
85-1570	F-16C-30	5C-312	USAF 174th FS/185th FW, Iowa ANG, Sioux City
85-1571	F-16D-30	5D-40	USAF 457th FS/301st FW, AFRes, NAS Fort Worth, TX
85-1572	F-16D-30	5D-41	USAF 149th FS/192nd FW, Virginia ANG, Richmond
85-1573	F-16D-30	5D-42	USAF 107th FS/127th Wg, Michigan ANG, Selfridge ANGB
86-0039	F-16D-32	5D-43	USAF 414th CTS/57th Wg, Nellis AFB, NV
86-0040	F-16D-32	5D-44	USAF 302nd FS/944th FW, AFRes, Luke AFB, AZ
86-0041	F-16D-32	5D-45	USAF Thunderbirds, Nellis AFB, NV
86-0042	F-16D-30	5D-46	USAF 174th FS/185th FW, Iowa ANG, Sioux City
86-0043	F-16D-30	5D-47	USAF 175th FS/114th FW, South Dakota ANG, Sioux Falls
86-0044	F-16D-30	5D-48	USAF 523rd FS/27th FW, Cannon AFB, NM
86-0045	F-16D-30	5D-49	Cr 17-Jul-91 (8th TFW)
86-0046	F-16D-30	5D-50	USAF 80th FS/8th FW, Kunsan AB, Republic of Korea
86-0047	F-16D-30	5D-51	USAF 162nd FS/178th FW, Ohio ANG, Springfield-Beckley A/P
86-0048	NF-16D (VISTA)	5D-52/1V-1	To Calspan 15-Jul-93
86-0049	F-16D-30	5D-53	USAF 170th FS/183rd FW, Illinois ANG, Springfield
86-0050	F-16D-30	5D-54	USAF 120th FS/140th FW, Colorado ANG, Buckley ANGB
86-0051	F-16D-30	5D-55	USAF 523rd FS/27th FW, Cannon AFB, NM
86-0052	F-16D-30	5D-56	USAF 176th FS/115th FW, Wisconsin ANG, Madison
86-0053	F-16D-30	5D-57	USAF 466th FS/419th FW, AFRes, Hill AFB, UT
86-0207	F-16C-30	5C-313	USAF 107th FS/127th Wg, Michigan ANG, Selfridge ANGB
86-0208	F-16C-30	5C-314	USAF 107th FS/127th Wg, Michigan ANG, Selfridge ANGB
86-0209	F-16C-30	5C-315	USAF 121st FS/113th FW, DC ANG, Andrews AFB
86-0210	F-16C-32	5C-316	USAF 93rd FS/482nd FW, AFRes, Homestead AFB, FL
86-0211	F-16C-32	5C-317	USAF 302nd FS/944th FW, AFRes, Luke AFB, AZ
86-0212	F-16C-32	5C-318	USAF 302nd FS/944th FW, AFRes, Luke AFB, AZ
86-0213	F-16C-32	5C-319	Cr 20-Feb-88 (302nd TFS)
86-0214	F-16C-32	5C-320	USAF 93rd FS/482nd FW, AFRes, Homestead AFB, FL
86-0215	F-16C-32	5C-321	USAF 93rd FS/482nd FW, AFRes, Homestead AFB, FL
86-0216	F-16C-30	5C-322	USAF 149th FS/192nd FW, Virginia ANG, Richmond
86-0217	F-16C-32	5C-323	USAF 302nd FS/944th FW, AFRes, Luke AFB, AZ
86-0218	F-16C-32	5C-324	USAF 93rd FS/482nd FW, AFRes, Homestead AFB, FL
86-0219	F-16C-30	5C-325	USAF 149th FS/192nd FW, Virginia ANG, Richmond
86-0220	F-16C-32	5C-326	USAF 414th CTS/57th Wg, Nellis AFB, NV
86-0221	F-16C-30	5C-327	USAF 107th FS/127th Wg, Michigan ANG, Selfridge ANGB
86-0222	F-16C-30	5C-328	USAF 149th FS/192nd FW, Virginia ANG, Richmond
86-0223	F-16C-30	5C-329	USAF 149th FS/192nd FW, Virginia ANG, Richmond
86-0224	F-16C-30	5C-330	USAF 150th DSE/150th FW, New Mexico ANG, Kirtland AFB
86-0225	F-16C-30	5C-331	USAF 149th FS/192nd FW, Virginia ANG, Richmond
86-0226	F-16C-30	5C-332	USAF 113th FS/181st FW, Indiana ANG, Terre Haute
86-0227	F-16C-30	5C-333	USAF 149th FS/192nd FW, Virginia ANG, Richmond
86-0228	F-16C-30	5C-334	USAF 149th FS/192nd FW, Virginia ANG, Richmond
86-0229	F-16C-30	5C-335	USAF 149th FS/192nd FW, Virginia ANG, Richmond
86-0230	F-16C-30	5C-336	USAF 149th FS/192nd FW, Virginia ANG, Richmond
86-0231	F-16C-30	5C-337	USAF 149th FS/192nd FW, Virginia ANG, Richmond
86-0232	F-16C-30	5C-338	USAF 149th FS/192nd FW, Virginia ANG, Richmond
86-0233	F-16C-30	5C-339	USAF 107th FS/127th Wg, Michigan ANG, Selfridge ANGB
86-0234	F-16C-30	5C-340	USAF 107th FS/127th Wg, Michigan ANG, Selfridge ANGB
86-0235	F-16C-30	5C-341	USAF 107th FS/127th Wg, Michigan ANG, Selfridge ANGB
86-0236	F-16C-32	5C-342	USAF 162nd FW, Arizona ANG, Tucson IAP
86-0237	F-16C-30	5C-343	USAF 175th FS/114th FW, South Dakota ANG, Sioux Falls
86-0238	F-16C-32	5C-344	USAF 93rd FS/482nd FW, AFRes, Homestead AFB, FL
86-0239	F-16C-32	5C-345	USAF 93rd FS/482nd FW, AFRes, Homestead AFB, FL
86-0240	F-16C-32	5C-346	USAF 302nd FS/944th FW, AFRes, Luke AFB, AZ
86-0241	F-16C-32	5C-347	USAF 302nd FS/944th FW, AFRes, Luke AFB, AZ
86-0242	F-16C-30	5C-348	USAF 149th FS/192nd FW, Virginia ANG, Richmond
86-0243	F-16C-30	5C-349	USAF 149th FS/192nd FW, Virginia ANG, Richmond
86-0244	F-16C-30	5C-350	USAF 149th FS/192nd FW, Virginia ANG, Richmond
86-0245	F-16C-30	5C-351	USAF 149th FS/192nd FW, Virginia ANG, Richmond
86-0246	F-16C-30	5C-352	USAF 149th FS/192nd FW, Virginia ANG, Richmond
86-0247	F-16C-30	5C-353	Cr 29-Jun-88 (52nd TFW)
86-0248	F-16C-30	5C-354	USAF 175th FS/114th FW, South Dakota ANG, Sioux Falls
86-0249	F-16C-30	5C-355	USAF 149th FS/192nd FW, Virginia ANG, Richmond
86-0250	F-16C-32	5C-356	USAF 414th CTS/57th Wg, Nellis AFB, NV
86-0251	F-16C-32	5C-357	USAF 302nd FS/944th FW, AFRes, Luke AFB, AZ
86-0252	F-16C-32	5C-358	USAF 302nd FS/944th FW, AFRes, Luke AFB, AZ
86-0253	F-16C-32	5C-359	USAF 302nd FS/944th FW, AFRes, Luke AFB, AZ
86-0254	F-16C-30	5C-360	USAF 149th FS/192nd FW, Virginia ANG, Richmond
86-0255	F-16C-30	5C-361	USAF 121st FS/113th FW, DC ANG, Andrews AFB
86-0256	F-16C-32	5C-362	USAF 302nd FS/944th FW, AFRes, Luke AFB, AZ
86-0257	F-16C-32	5C-363	USAF 93rd FS/482nd FW, AFRes, Homestead AFB, FL
86-0258	F-16C-30	5C-364	USAF 113th FS/181st FW, Indiana ANG, Terre Haute
86-0259	F-16C-30	5C-365	USAF 113th FS/181st FW, Indiana ANG, Terre Haute
86-0260	F-16C-30	5C-366	USAF 113th FS/181st FW, Indiana ANG, Terre Haute

F-16C of the short-lived 527th Adversary Squadron based at Bentwaters, UK in 1989. ANDREW MARCH

Another of the 57th FW's adversary aircraft, F-16C-32 (86-0272) landing at Nellis AFB.
BOB ARCHER

Serial	Type/Code	c/n	Operator/location
86-0261	F-16C-30	5C-367	USAF 113th FS/181st FW, Indiana ANG, Terre Haute
86-0262	F-16C-30	5C-368	USAF 162nd FS/178th FW, Ohio ANG, Springfield-Beckley A/P
86-0263	F-16C-30	5C-369	USAF 170th FS/183rd FW, Illinois ANG, Springfield
86-0264	F-16C-30	5C-370	USAF 35th FS/8th FW, Kunsan AB, Republic of Korea
86-0265	F-16C-30	5C-371	USAF 35th FS/8th FW, Kunsan AB, Republic of Korea
86-0266	F-16C-30	5C-372	USAF 35th FS/8th FW, Kunsan AB, Republic of Korea
86-0267	F-16C-30	5C-373	USAF 414th CTS/57th Wg, Nellis AFB, NV
86-0268	F-16C-30	5C-374	USAF 35th FS/8th FW, Kunsan AB, Republic of Korea
86-0269	F-16C-32	5C-375	USAF 414th CTS/57th Wg, Nellis AFB, NV
86-0270	F-16C-30	5C-376	USAF 138th FS/174th FW, NY ANG, Hancock Field, Syracuse
86-0271	F-16C-32	5C-377	USAF 414th CTS/57th Wg, Nellis AFB, NV
86-0272	F-16C-32	5C-378	USAF 414th CTS/57th Wg, Nellis AFB, NV
86-0273	F-16C-32	5C-379	USAF 302nd FS/944th FW, AFRes, Luke AFB, AZ
86-0274	F-16C-30	5C-380	Cr 13-Feb-89 (8th TFW)
86-0275	F-16C-30	5C-381	USAF 35th FS/8th FW, Kunsan AB, Republic of Korea
86-0276	F-16C-30	5C-382	Cr 13-Feb-89 (8th TFW)
86-0277	F-16C-30	5C-383	USAF 35th FS/8th FW, Kunsan AB, Republic of Korea
86-0278	F-16C-30	5C-384	USAF 35th FS/8th FW, Kunsan AB, Republic of Korea
86-0279	F-16C-32	5C-385	USAF 302nd FS/944th FW, AFRes, Luke AFB, AZ
86-0280	F-16C-32	5C-386	USAF 302nd FS/944th FW, AFRes, Luke AFB, AZ
86-0281	F-16C-32	5C-387	USAF 93rd FS/482nd FW, AFRes, Homestead AFB, FL
86-0282	F-16C-30	5C-388	USAF 35th FS/8th FW, Kunsan AB, Republic of Korea
86-0283	F-16C-32	5C-389	USAF 302nd FS/944th FW, AFRes, Luke AFB, AZ
86-0284	F-16C-30	5C-390	USAF 524th FS/27th FW, Cannon AFB, NM
86-0285	F-16C-32	5C-391	USAF 93rd FS/482nd FW, AFRes, Homestead AFB, FL
86-0286	F-16C-30	5C-392	USAF 35th FS/8th FW, Kunsan AB, Republic of Korea
86-0287	F-16C-30	5C-393	USAF 523rd FS/27th FW, Cannon AFB, NM
86-0288	F-16C-30	5C-394	USAF 523rd FS/27th FW, Cannon AFB, NM
86-0289	F-16C-30	5C-395	USAF 523rd FS/27th FW, Cannon AFB, NM
86-0290	F-16C-30	5C-396	USAF 302nd FS/944th FW, AFRes, Luke AFB, AZ
86-0291	F-16C-32	5C-397	USAF 302nd FS/944th FW, AFRes, Luke AFB, AZ
86-0292	F-16C-32	5C-398	USAF 302nd FS/944th FW, AFRes, Luke AFB, AZ
86-0293	F-16C-30	5C-399	USAF 302nd FS/944th FW, AFRes, Luke AFB, AZ
86-0294	F-16C-30	5C-400	USAF 170th FS/183rd FW, Illinois ANG, Springfield
86-0295	F-16C-30	5C-401	USAF 80th FS/8th FW, Kunsan AB, Republic of Korea
86-0296	F-16C-32	5C-402	USAF 302nd FS/944th FW, AFRes, Luke AFB, AZ
86-0297	F-16C-30	5C-403	Cr 29-Jan-89 (8th TFW)

Block 30 F-16C (86-0363) of the Illinois ANG flies with the 170th FS. RICHARD COOPER

Serial	Type/Code	c/n	Operator/location
86-0298	F-16C-30	5C-404	USAF 35th FS/8th FW, Kunsan AB, Republic of Korea
86-0299	F-16C-32	5C-405	USAF 302nd FS/944th FW, AFRes, Luke AFB, AZ
86-0300	F-16C-30	5C-406	Cr 26-Dec-89 (8th TFW)
86-0301	F-16C-30	5C-407	USAF 35th FS/8th FW, Kunsan AB, Republic of Korea
86-0302	F-16C-30	5C-408	USAF 162nd FS/178th FW, Ohio ANG, Springfield-Beckley A/P
86-0303	F-16C-30	5C-409	USAF 523rd FS/27th FW, Cannon AFB, NM
86-0304	F-16C-30	5C-410	USAF 80th FS/8th FW, Kunsan AB, Republic of Korea
86-0305	F-16C-30	5C-411	USAF 35th FS/8th FW, Kunsan AB, Republic of Korea
86-0306	F-16C-30	5C-412	USAF 35th FS/8th FW, Kunsan AB, Republic of Korea
86-0307	F-16C-30	5C-413	USAF 80th FS/8th FW, Kunsan AB, Republic of Korea
86-0308	F-16C-30	5C-414	USAF 80th FS/8th FW, Kunsan AB, Republic of Korea
86-0309	F-16C-30	5C-415	USAF 80th FS/8th FW, Kunsan AB, Republic of Korea
86-0310	F-16C-30	5C-416	USAF 80th FS/8th FW, Kunsan AB, Republic of Korea
86-0311	F-16C-30	5C-417	Cr 14-Mar-89 (401st TFW)
86-0312	F-16C-30	5C-418	Cr 14-Mar-89 (401st TFW)
86-0313	F-16C-30	5C-419	USAF 524th FS/27th FW, Cannon AFB, NM
86-0314	F-16C-30	5C-420	USAF 35th FS/8th FW, Kunsan AB, Republic of Korea
86-0315	F-16C-30	5C-421	USAF 162nd FS/178th FW, Ohio ANG, Springfield-Beckley A/P
86-0316	F-16C-30	5C-422	Cr 05-Dec-88 (401st TFW)
86-0317	F-16C-30	5C-423	USAF 80th FS/8th FW, Kunsan AB, Republic of Korea
86-0318	F-16C-30	5C-424	USAF 80th FS/8th FW, Kunsan AB, Republic of Korea
86-0319	F-16C-30	5C-425	USAF 80th FS/8th FW, Kunsan AB, Republic of Korea
86-0320	F-16C-30	5C-426	USAF 80th FS/8th FW, Kunsan AB, Republic of Korea
86-0321	F-16C-30	5C-427	USAF 80th FS/8th FW, Kunsan AB, Republic of Korea
86-0322	F-16C-30	5C-428	USAF 80th FS/8th FW, Kunsan AB, Republic of Korea
86-0323	F-16C-30	5C-429	USAF 80th FS/8th FW, Kunsan AB, Republic of Korea
86-0324	F-16C-30	5C-430	USAF 523rd FS/27th FW, Cannon AFB, NM
86-0325	F-16C-30	5C-431	Cr 09-Nov-93 (120th FS)
86-0326	F-16C-30	5C-432	USAF 160th FS/187th FW, Alabama ANG, Montgomery
86-0327	F-16C-30	5C-433	USAF 162nd FS/178th FW, Ohio ANG, Springfield-Beckley A/P
86-0328	F-16C-30	5C-434	USAF 523rd FS/27th FW, Cannon AFB, NM
86-0329	F-16C-30	5C-435	Cr 20-Feb-91 (401st TFW)
86-0330	F-16C-30	5C-436	USAF 523rd FS/27th FW, Cannon AFB, NM
86-0331	F-16C-30	5C-437	USAF 80th FS/8th FW, Kunsan AB, Republic of Korea
86-0332	F-16C-30	5C-438	USAF 522nd FS/27th FW, Cannon AFB, NM
86-0333	F-16C-30	5C-439	USAF 80th FS/8th FW, Kunsan AB, Republic of Korea
86-0334	F-16C-30	5C-440	USAF 80th FS/8th FW, Kunsan AB, Republic of Korea
86-0335	F-16C-30	5C-441	USAF 80th FS/8th FW, Kunsan AB, Republic of Korea
86-0336	F-16C-30	5C-442	USAF 80th FS/8th FW, Kunsan AB, Republic of Korea
86-0337	F-16C-30	5C-443	USAF 80th FS/8th FW, Kunsan AB, Republic of Korea
86-0338	F-16C-30	5C-444	USAF 120th FS/140th FW, Colorado ANG, Buckley ANGB
86-0339	F-16C-30	5C-445	USAF 120th FS/140th FW, Colorado ANG, Buckley ANGB
86-0340	F-16C-30	5C-446	USAF 523rd FS/27th FW, Cannon AFB, NM
86-0341	F-16C-30	5C-447	USAF 160th FS/187th FW, Alabama ANG, Montgomery
86-0342	F-16C-30	5C-448	USAF 523rd FS/27th FW, Cannon AFB, NM
86-0343	F-16C-30	5C-449	Cr 11-Aug-93 (52nd FW)
86-0344	F-16C-30	5C-450	Cr 18-Oct-88 (401st TFW)
86-0345	F-16C-30	5C-451	USAF 120th FS/140th FW, Colorado ANG, Buckley ANGB
86-0346	F-16C-30	5C-452	USAF 160th FS/187th FW, Alabama ANG, Montgomery
86-0347	F-16C-30	5C-453	USAF 523rd FS/27th FW, Cannon AFB, NM
86-0348	F-16C-30	5C-454	USAF 160th FS/187th FW, Alabama ANG, Montgomery
86-0349	F-16C-30	5C-455	USAF 523rd FS/27th FW, Cannon AFB, NM
86-0350	F-16C-30	5C-456	USAF 162nd FS/178th FW, Ohio ANG, Springfield-Beckley A/P
86-0351	F-16C-30	5C-457	USAF 80th FS/8th FW, Kunsan AB, Republic of Korea
86-0352	F-16C-30	5C-458	USAF 80th FS/8th FW, Kunsan AB, Republic of Korea
86-0353	F-16C-30	5C-459	USAF 80th FS/8th FW, Kunsan AB, Republic of Korea
86-0354	F-16C-30	5C-460	Cr 07-Nov-90 (8th TFW)
86-0355	F-16C-30	5C-461	USAF 522nd FS/27th FW, Cannon AFB, NM
86-0356	F-16C-30	5C-462	USAF 523rd FS/27th FW, Cannon AFB, NM
86-0357	F-16C-30	5C-463	USAF 522nd FS/27th FW, Cannon AFB, NM
86-0358	F-16C-30	5C-464	USAF 120th FS/140th FW, Colorado ANG, Buckley ANGB
86-0359	F-16C-30	5C-465	USAF 416th TS/412th TW, Edwards AFB, CA
86-0360	F-16C-30	5C-466	USAF 120th FS/140th FW, Colorado ANG, Buckley ANGB
86-0361	F-16C-30	5C-467	USAF 162nd FS/178th FW, Ohio ANG, Springfield-Beckley A/P
86-0362	F-16C-30	5C-468	USAF 170th FS/183rd FW, Illinois ANG, Springfield
86-0363	F-16C-30	5C-469	USAF 170th FS/183rd FW, Illinois ANG, Springfield
86-0364	F-16C-30	5C-470	USAF 162nd FS/178th FW, Ohio ANG, Springfield-Beckley A/P
86-0365	F-16C-30	5C-471	USAF 170th FS/183rd FW, Illinois ANG, Springfield
86-0366	F-16C-30	5C-472	USAF 523rd FS/27th FW, Cannon AFB, NM
86-0367	F-16C-30	5C-473	USAF 120th FS/140th FW, Colorado ANG, Buckley ANGB
86-0368	F-16C-30	5C-474	USAF 120th FS/140th FW, Colorado ANG, Buckley ANGB
86-0369	F-16C-30	5C-475	USAF 523rd FS/27th FW, Cannon AFB, NM
86-0370	F-16C-30	5C-476	USAF 120th FS/140th FW, Colorado ANG, Buckley ANGB
86-0371	F-16C-30	5C-477	USAF 170th FS/183rd FW, Illinois ANG, Springfield
87-0217	F-16C-30	5C-478	USAF 162nd FS/178th FW, Ohio ANG, Springfield-Beckley A/P

Block 30 F-16C (87-0246) carried 614 AMU titles in September 1991 while based at Torrejon, Spain. BOB ARCHER

Serial	Type/Code	c/n	Operator/location	Serial	Type/Code	c/n	Operator/location
87-0218	F-16C-30	5C-479	USAF 160th FS/187th FW, Alabama ANG, Montgomery	87-0265	F-16C-30	5C-526	USAF 170th FS/183rd FW, Illinois ANG, Springfield
87-0219	F-16C-30	5C-480	USAF 160th FS/187th FW, Alabama ANG, Montgomery	87-0266	F-16C-30	5C-527	USAF 176th FS/115th FW, Wisconsin ANG, Madison
87-0220	F-16C-30	5C-481	USAF 160th FS/187th FW, Alabama ANG, Montgomery	87-0267	F-16C-32	5C-528	USAF 414th CTS/57th Wg, Nellis AFB, NV
87-0221	F-16C-30	5C-482	USAF 160th FS/187th FW, Alabama ANG, Montgomery	87-0268	F-16C-30	5C-529	USAF 162nd FS/178th FW, Ohio ANG, Springfield-Beckley A/P
87-0222	F-16C-30	5C-483	USAF 162nd FS/178th FW, Ohio ANG, Springfield-Beckley A/P	87-0269	F-16C-32	5C-530	USAF 414th CTS/57th Wg, Nellis AFB, NV
87-0223	F-16C-30	5C-484	USAF 160th FS/187th FW, Alabama ANG, Montgomery	87-0270	F-16C-30	5C-531	Cr 26-Jan-94 (52nd FW)
87-0224	F-16C-30	5C-485	Cr 21-Jan-91 (401st TFW)	87-0271	F-16C-30	5C-532	USAF 162nd FS/178th FW, Ohio ANG, Springfield-Beckley A/P
87-0225	F-16C-30	5C-486	USAF 466th FS/419th FW, AFRes, Hill AFB, UT	87-0272	F-16C-30	5C-533	USAF 138th FS/174th FW, NY ANG, Hancock Field, Syracuse
87-0226	F-16C-30	5C-487	USAF 35th FS/8th FW, Kunsan AB, Republic of Korea	87-0273	F-16C-30	5C-534	Cr 25-Jun-95 (176th FS)
87-0227	F-16C-30	5C-488	USAF 523rd FS/27th FW, Cannon AFB, NM	87-0274	F-16C-30	5C-535	Cr 06-May-94 (8th FW)
87-0228	F-16C-30	5C-489	Cr 19-Jan-91 (401st TFW)	87-0275	F-16C-30	5C-536	USAF 138th FS/174th FW, NY ANG, Hancock Field, Syracuse
87-0229	F-16C-30	5C-490	USAF 120th FS/140th FW, Colorado ANG, Buckley ANGB	87-0276	F-16C-30	5C-537	USAF 162nd FS/178th FW, Ohio ANG, Springfield-Beckley A/P
87-0230	F-16C-30	5C-491	USAF 466th FS/419th FW, AFRes, Hill AFB, UT	87-0277	F-16C-30	5C-538	USAF 522nd FS/27th FW, Cannon AFB, NM
87-0231	F-16C-30	5C-492	USAF 120th FS/140th FW, Colorado ANG, Buckley ANGB	87-0278	F-16C-30	5C-539	USAF 176th FS/115th FW, Wisconsin ANG, Madison
87-0232	F-16C-30	5C-493	USAF 160th FS/187th FW, Alabama ANG, Montgomery	87-0279	F-16C-30	5C-540	USAF 138th FS/174th FW, NY ANG, Hancock Field, Syracuse
87-0233	F-16C-30	5C-494	USAF 466th FS/419th FW, AFRes, Hill AFB, UT	87-0280	F-16C-30	5C-541	USAF 176th FS/115th FW, Wisconsin ANG, Madison
87-0234	F-16C-30	5C-495	USAF 176th FS/115th FW, Wisconsin ANG, Madison	87-0281	F-16C-30	5C-542	USAF 466th FS/419th FW, AFRes, Hill AFB, UT
87-0235	F-16C-30	5C-496	USAF 138th FS/174th FW, NY ANG, Hancock Field, Syracuse	87-0282	F-16C-30	5C-543	USAF 160th FS/187th FW, Alabama ANG, Montgomery
87-0236	F-16C-30	5C-497	USAF 170th FS/183rd FW, Illinois ANG, Springfield	87-0283	F-16C-30	5C-544	USAF 162nd FS/178th FW, Ohio ANG, Springfield-Beckley A/P
87-0237	F-16C-30	5C-498	USAF 120th FS/140th FW, Colorado ANG, Buckley ANGB	87-0284	F-16C-30	5C-545	USAF 120th FS/140th FW, Colorado ANG, Buckley ANGB
87-0238	F-16C-30	5C-499	USAF 466th FS/419th FW, AFRes, Hill AFB, UT	87-0285	F-16C-30	5C-546	USAF 138th FS/174th FW, NY ANG, Hancock Field, Syracuse
87-0239	F-16C-30	5C-500	USAF 466th FS/419th FW, AFRes, Hill AFB, UT	87-0286	F-16C-30	5C-547	USAF 138th FS/174th FW, NY ANG, Hancock Field, Syracuse
87-0240	F-16C-30	5C-501	USAF 170th FS/183rd FW, Illinois ANG, Springfield	87-0287	F-16C-30	5C-548	USAF 466th FS/419th FW, AFRes, Hill AFB, UT
87-0241	F-16C-30	5C-502	USAF 120th FS/140th FW, Colorado ANG, Buckley ANGB	87-0288	F-16C-30	5C-549	USAF 176th FS/115th FW, Wisconsin ANG, Madison
87-0242	F-16C-30	5C-503	USAF 176th FS/115th FW, Wisconsin ANG, Madison	87-0289	F-16C-30	5C-550	USAF 176th FS/115th FW, Wisconsin ANG, Madison
87-0243	F-16C-30	5C-504	USAF 162nd FS/178th FW, Ohio ANG, Springfield-Beckley A/P	87-0290	F-16C-30	5C-551	USAF 466th FS/419th FW, AFRes, Hill AFB, UT
87-0244	F-16C-30	5C-505	USAF 170th FS/183rd FW, Illinois ANG, Springfield	87-0291	F-16C-30	5C-552	USAF 522nd FS/27th FW, Cannon AFB, NM
87-0245	F-16C-30	5C-506	USAF 162nd FS/178th FW, Ohio ANG, Springfield-Beckley A/P	87-0292	F-16C-30	5C-553	USAF 522nd FS/27th FW, Cannon AFB, NM
87-0246	F-16C-30	5C-507	USAF 523rd FS/27th FW, Cannon AFB, NM	87-0293	F-16C-32	5C-554	USAF 93rd FS/482nd FW, AFRes, Homestead AFB, FL
87-0247	F-16C-30	5C-508	USAF 466th FS/419th FW, AFRes, Hill AFB, UT	87-0294	F-16C-30	5C-555	USAF 170th FS/183rd FW, Illinois ANG, Springfield
87-0248	F-16C-30	5C-509	USAF 138th FS/174th FW, NY ANG, Hancock Field, Syracuse	87-0295	F-16C-32/GF-16C	5C-556	USAF TTC/82nd TRW, Sheppard AFB, TX
87-0249	F-16C-30	5C-510	USAF 170th FS/183rd FW, Illinois ANG, Springfield	87-0296	F-16C-30	5C-557	USAF 170th FS/183rd FW, Illinois ANG, Springfield
87-0250	F-16C-30	5C-511	USAF 466th FS/419th FW, AFRes, Hill AFB, UT	87-0297	F-16C-32	5C-558	USAF 93rd FS/482nd FW, AFRes, Homestead AFB, FL
87-0251	F-16C-30/GF-16C	5C-512	USAF TTC/82nd TRW, Sheppard AFB, TX	87-0298	F-16C-30	5C-559	USAF 176th FS/115th FW, Wisconsin AN
87-0252	F-16C-30	5C-513	USAF 176th FS/115th FW, Wisconsin ANG, Madison	87-0299	F-16C-32	5C-560	USAF 93rd FS/482nd FW, AFRes, Homestead AFB, FL
87-0253	F-16C-30	5C-514	USAF 138th FS/174th FW, NY ANG, Hancock Field, Syracuse	87-0300	F-16C-30	5C-561	USAF 176th FS/116th FW, Wisconsin ANG, Madison
87-0254	F-16C-30	5C-515	USAF 120th FS/140th FW, Colorado ANG, Buckley ANGB	87-0301	F-16C-32	5C-562	USAF 93rd FS/482nd FW, AFRes, Homestead AFB, FL
87-0255	F-16C-30	5C-516	USAF 138th FS/174th FW, NY ANG, Hancock Field, Syracuse	87-0302	F-16C-30	5C-563	Cr 07-May-91 (432nd FW)
87-0256	F-16C-30	5C-517	USAF 138th FS/174th FW, NY ANG, Hancock Field, Syracuse	87-0303	F-16C-32	5C-564	USAF Thunderbirds, Nellis AFB, NV
87-0257	F-16C-30	5C-518	Cr 19-Jan-91 (401st TFW)	87-0304	F-16C-30	5C-565	USAF 522nd FS/27th FW, Cannon AFB, NM
87-0258	F-16C-30	5C-519	USAF 466th FS/419th FW, AFRes, Hill AFB, UT	87-0305	F-16C-32	5C-566	USAF Thunderbirds, Nellis AFB, NV
87-0259	F-16C-30	5C-520	USAF 138th FS/174th FW, NY ANG, Hancock Field, Syracuse	87-0306	F-16C-30	5C-567	USAF 522nd FS/27th FW, Cannon AFB, NM
87-0260	F-16C-30	5C-521	USAF 176th FS/115th FW, Wisconsin ANG, Madison	87-0307	F-16C-32	5C-568	USAF 414th CTS/57th Wg, Nellis AFB, NV
87-0261	F-16C-30	5C-522	USAF 138th FS/174th FW, NY ANG, Hancock Field, Syracuse	87-0308	F-16C-30	5C-569	USAF 522nd FS/27th FW, Cannon AFB, NM
87-0262	F-16C-30	5C-523	USAF 176th FS/115th FW, Wisconsin ANG, Madison	87-0309	F-16C-32	5C-570	Cr 14-Feb-94 (Thunderbirds)
87-0263	F-16C-30	5C-524	USAF 160th FS/187th FW, Alabama ANG, Montgomery	87-0310	F-16C-30	5C-571	USAF 522nd FS/27th FW, Cannon AFB, NM
87-0264	F-16C-30	5C-525	USAF 138th FS/174th FW, NY ANG, Hancock Field, Syracuse	87-0311	F-16C-32	5C-572	USAF 302nd FS/944th FW, AFRes, Luke AFB, AZ

Thunderbirds F-16D (87-0381), one of a pair of two-seaters used by the team for familiarisation and publicity flights. PETER R MARCH

Serial	Type/Code	c/n	Operator/location	Serial	Type/Code	c/n	Operator/location
87-0312	F-16C-30	5C-573	USAF 170th FS/183rd FW, Illinois ANG, Springfield	87-0360	F-16C-42	1C-11	USAF 310th FS/56th FW, Luke AFB, AZ
87-0313	F-16C-32	5C-574	USAF Thunderbirds, Nellis AFB, NV	87-0361	F-16C-42	1C-12	USAF 162nd FW, Arizona ANG, Tucson IAP
87-0314	F-16C-30	5C-575	USAF 522nd FS/27th FW, Cannon AFB, NM	87-0362	F-16C-42	1C-13	USAF 422nd TES/53rd Wg, Nellis AFB, NV
87-0315	F-16C-32	5C-576	USAF 302nd FS/944th FW, AFRes, Luke AFB, AZ	87-0363	F-16D-30	5D-58	Cr 15-Mar-89 (56th TTW)
87-0316	F-16C-30	5C-577	USAF 522nd FS/27th FW, Cannon AFB, NM	87-0364	F-16D-30	5D-59	USAF 162nd FS/178th FW, Ohio ANG, Springfield-Beckley A/P
87-0317	F-16C-32	5C-578	USAF 93rd FS/482nd FW, AFRes, Homestead AFB, FL	87-0365	F-16D-30	5D-60	USAF 150th DSE/150th FW, New Mexico ANG, Kirtland AFB
87-0318	F-16C-30	5C-579	USAF 522nd FS/27th FW, Cannon AFB, NM	87-0366	F-16D-30	5D-61	USAF 523rd FS/27th FW, Cannon AFB, NM
87-0319	F-16C-32	5C-580	USAF Thunderbirds, Nellis AFB, NV	87-0367	F-16D-30	5D-62	USAF 160th FS/187th FW, Alabama ANG, Montgomery
87-0320	F-16C-30	5C-581	USAF 170th FS/183rd FW, Illinois ANG, Springfield	87-0368	F-16D-30	5D-63	USAF 120th FS/140th FW, Colorado ANG, Buckley ANGB
87-0321	F-16C-32	5C-582	USAF 414th CTS/57th Wg, Nellis AFB, NV	87-0369	F-16D-32	5D-64	Cr 15-Oct-89 (302nd TFS)
87-0322	F-16C-30	5C-583	USAF 170th FS/183rd FW, Illinois ANG, Springfield	87-0370	F-16D-30	5D-65	USAF 170th FS/183rd FW, Illinois ANG, Springfield
87-0323	F-16C-32	5C-584	USAF Thunderbirds, Nellis AFB, NV	87-0371	F-16D-30	5D-66	USAF 138th FS/174th FW, NY ANG, Hancock Field, Syracuse
87-0324	F-16C-30	5C-585	USAF 170th FS/183rd FW, Illinois ANG, Springfield	87-0372	F-16D-30	5D-67	USAF 162nd FS/178th FW, Ohio ANG, Springfield-Beckley A/P
87-0325	F-16C-32	5C-586	USAF Thunderbirds, Nellis AFB, NV	87-0373	F-16D-30	5D-68	USAF 160th FS/187th FW, Alabama ANG, Montgomery
87-0326	F-16C-30	5C-587	USAF 522nd FS/27th FW, Cannon AFB, NM	87-0374	F-16D-30	5D-69	USAF 188th FS/150th FW, New Mexico ANG, Kirtland AFB
87-0327	F-16C-32	5C-588	USAF Thunderbirds, Nellis AFB, NV	87-0375	F-16D-30	5D-70	USAF 523rd FS/27th FW, Cannon AFB, NM
87-0328	F-16C-30	5C-589	USAF 523rd FS/27th FW, Cannon AFB, NM	87-0376	F-16D-30	5D-71	USAF 176th FS/115th FW, Wisconsin ANG, Madison
87-0329	F-16C-32	5C-590	USAF Thunderbirds, Nellis AFB, NV	87-0377	F-16D-30	5D-72	USAF 522nd FS/27th FW, Cannon AFB, NM
87-0330	F-16C-30	5C-591	USAF 522nd FS/27th FW, Cannon AFB, NM	87-0378	F-16D-30	5D-73	USAF 176th FS/115th FW, Wisconsin ANG, Madison
87-0331	F-16C-32	5C-592	USAF Thunderbirds, Nellis AFB, NV	87-0379	F-16D-30	5D-74	USAF 62nd FS/347th Wg, Moody AFB, GA
87-0332	F-16C-30	5C-593	USAF 522nd FS/27th FW, Cannon AFB, NM	87-0380	F-16D-30	5D-75	USAF 522nd FS/27th FW, Cannon AFB, NM
87-0333	F-16C-32	5C-594	USAF 302nd FS/944th FW, AFRes, Luke AFB, AZ	87-0381	F-16D-32	5D-76	USAF Thunderbirds, Nellis AFB, NV
87-0334	F-16C-30	5C-595	USAF 522nd FS/27th FW, Cannon AFB, NM	87-0382	F-16D-30	5D-77	USAF 162nd FS/178th FW, Ohio ANG, Springfield-Beckley A/P
87-0335	F-16C-30	5C-596	Cr 02-Aug-93 (56th FW)	87-0383	F-16D-30	5D-78	USAF Ogden Air Logistics Centre Hill AFB, UT
87-0336	F-16C-30	5C-597	USAF 160th FS/187th FW, Alabama ANG, Montgomery	87-0384	F-16D-30	5D-79	USAF 138th FS/174th FW, NY ANG, Hancock Field, Syracuse
87-0337	F-16C-30	5C-598	USAF 120th FS/140th FW, Colorado ANG, Buckley ANGB	87-0385	F-16D-30	5D-80	USAF 466th FS/419th FW, AFRes, Hill AFB, UT
87-0338	F-16C-30	5C-599	USAF 466th FS/419th FW, AFRes, Hill AFB, UT	87-0386	F-16D-30	5D-81	USAF 170th FS/183rd FW, Illinois ANG, Springfield
87-0339	F-16C-30	5C-600	USAF 138th FS/174th FW, NY ANG, Hancock Field, Syracuse	87-0387	F-16D-30	5D-82	USAF 176th FS/115th FW, Wisconsin ANG, Madison
87-0340	F-16C-30	5C-601	USAF 466th FS/419th FW, AFRes, Hill AFB, UT	87-0388	F-16D-30	5D-83	USAF 466th FS/419th FW, AFRes, Hill AFB, UT
87-0341	F-16C-30	5C-602	USAF 138th FS/174th FW, NY ANG, Hancock Field, Syracuse	87-0389	F-16D-30	5D-84	USAF 522nd FS/27th FW, Cannon AFB, NM
87-0342	F-16C-30	5C-603	USAF 162nd FS/178th FW, Ohio ANG, Springfield-Beckley A/P	87-0390	F-16D-30	5D-85	USAF 62nd FS/347th Wg, Moody AFB, GA
87-0343	F-16C-30	5C-604	USAF 176th FS/115th FW, Wisconsin ANG, Madison	87-0391	F-16D-40	1D-1	USAF 34th FS/388th FW, Hill AFB, UT
87-0344	F-16C-30	5C-605	USAF 138th FS/174th FW, NY ANG, Hancock Field, Syracuse	87-0392	F-16D-42	1D-2	USAF 416th TS/412th TW, Edwards AFB, CA
87-0345	F-16C-30	5C-606	USAF 176th FS/115th FW, Wisconsin ANG, Madison	87-0393	F-16D-40	1D-3	USAF 34th FS/388th FW, Hill AFB, UT
87-0346	F-16C-30	5C-607	USAF 176th FS/115th FW, Wisconsin ANG, Madison	87-0394	F-16D-42	1D-4	USAF 310th FS/56th FW, Luke AFB, AZ
87-0347	F-16C-30	5C-608	USAF 466th FS/419th FW, AFRes, Hill AFB, UT	87-0395	F-16D-42	1D-5	USAF 310th FS/56th FW, Luke AFB, AZ
87-0348	F-16C-30	5C-609	USAF 176th FS/115th FW, Wisconsin ANG, Madison	87-0396	F-16D-42	1D-6	USAF 422nd TES/53rd Wg, Nellis AFB, NV
87-0349	F-16C-30	5C-610	USAF 523rd FS/27th FW, Cannon AFB, NM	88-0150	F-16D-30	5D-86	USAF 85th TES/53rd Wg, Eglin AFB, FL
87-0350	F-16C-40	1C-1	USAF 555th FS/31st FW, Aviano AB, Italy	88-0151	F-16D-30	5D-87	USAF 176th FS/115th FW, Wisconsin ANG, Madison
87-0351	F-16C-40	1C-2	USAF 555th FS/31st FW, Aviano AB, Italy	88-0152	F-16D-30	5D-88	USAF 310th FS/56th FW, Luke AFB, AZ
87-0352	F-16C-40	1C-3	USAF 170th FS/183rd FW, Illinois ANG, Springfield	88-0153	F-16D-42	1D-7	USAF 524th FS/27th FW, Cannon AFB, NM
87-0353	F-16C-40	1C-4	USAF 40th TES/46th TW, Eglin AFB, FL	88-0154	F-16D-42	1D-8	USAF 310th FS/56th FW, Luke AFB, AZ
87-0354	F-16C-40	1C-5	USAF 34th FS/388th FW, Hill AFB, UT	88-0155	F-16D-42	1D-9	USAF 310th FS/56th FW, Luke AFB, AZ
87-0355	F-16C-40	1C-6	USAF 510th FS/31st FW, Aviano AB, Italy	88-0156	F-16D-42	1D-10	USAF 425th FS/56th FW, Luke AFB, AZ
87-0356	F-16C-42	1C-7	USAF 310th FS/56th FW, Luke AFB, AZ	88-0157	F-16D-42	1D-11	USAF 310th FS/56th FW, Luke AFB, AZ
87-0357	F-16C-40	1C-8	USAF 34th FS/388th FW, Hill AFB, UT	88-0158	F-16D-42	1D-12	USAF 310th FS/56th FW, Luke AFB, AZ
87-0358	F-16C-42	1C-9	USAF 310th FS/56th FW, Luke AFB, AZ	88-0159	F-16D-42	1D-13	USAF 310th FS/56th FW, Luke AFB, AZ
87-0359	F-16C-40	1C-10	USAF 555th FS/31st FW, Aviano AB, Italy	88-0160	F-16D-42	1D-14	Cr 02-Jun-92 (58th FW)

Serial	Type/Code	c/n	Operator/location
88-0161	F-16D-42	1D-15	USAF 310th FS/56th FW, Luke AFB, AZ
88-0162	F-16D-42	1D-16	USAF 310th FS/56th FW, Luke AFB, AZ
88-0163	F-16D-42	1D-17	USAF 308th FS/56th FW, Luke AFB, AZ
88-0164	F-16D-42	1D-18	USAF 308th FS/56th FW, Luke AFB, AZ
88-0165	F-16D-42	1D-19	USAF 308th FS/56th FW, Luke AFB, AZ
88-0166	F-16D-40	1D-20	USAF 421st FS/388th FW, Hill AFB, UT
88-0167	F-16D-42	1D-21	USAF 308th FS/56th FW, Luke AFB, AZ
88-0168	F-16D-40	1D-22	Cr 30-Jul-91 (388th TFW)
88-0169	F-16D-42	1D-23	USAF 308th FS/56th FW, Luke AFB, AZ
88-0170	F-16D-40	1D-24	USAF 524th FS/27th FW, Cannon AFB, NM
88-0171	F-16D-40	1D-25	Cr 23-Mar-94 (23rd Wg)
88-0172	F-16D-42	1D-26	USAF 308th FS/56th FW, Luke AFB, AZ
88-0173	F-16D-42	1D-27	USAF 162nd FW, Arizona ANG, Tucson IAP
88-0174	F-16D-40	1D-28	USAF 188th FS/150th FW, New Mexico ANG, Kirtland AFB
88-0175	F-16D-42	1D-29	USAF 308th FS/56th FW, Luke AFB, AZ
88-0397	F-16C-30	5C-611	USAF 466th FS/419th FW, AFRes, Hill AFB, UT
88-0398	F-16C-30	5C-612	USAF 160th FS/187th FW, Alabama ANG, Montgomery
88-0399	F-16C-30	5C-613	USAF 160th FS/187th FW, Alabama ANG, Montgomery
88-0400	F-16C-30	5C-614	USAF 160th FS/187th FW, Alabama ANG, Montgomery
88-0401	F-16C-30	5C-615	USAF 120th FS/140th FW, Colorado ANG, Buckley ANGB
88-0402	F-16C-30	5C-616	USAF 80th FS/8th FW, Kunsan AB, Republic of Korea
88-0403	F-16C-30	5C-617	USAF 80th FS/8th FW, Kunsan AB, Republic of Korea
88-0404	F-16C-30	5C-618	USAF 35th FS/8th FW, Kunsan AB, Republic of Korea
88-0405	F-16C-30	5C-619	USAF 35th FS/8th FW, Kunsan AB, Republic of Korea
88-0406	F-16C-30	5C-620	USAF 35th FS/8th FW, Kunsan AB, Republic of Korea
88-0407	F-16C-30	5C-621	USAF 35th FS/8th FW, Kunsan AB, Republic of Korea
88-0408	F-16C-30	5C-622	Cr 03-Apr-90 (8th TFW)
88-0409	F-16C-30	5C-623	USAF 138th FS/174th FW, NY ANG, Hancock Field, Syracuse
88-0410	F-16C-30	5C-624	USAF 466th FS/419th FW, AFRes, Hill AFB, UT
88-0411	F-16C-30	5C-625	Cr 30-Mar-94 (176th FS)
88-0412	F-16C-42	1C-14	USAF 310th FS/56th FW, Luke AFB, AZ
88-0413	F-16C-40	1C-15	USAF 510th FS/31st FW, Aviano AB, Italy
88-0414	F-16C-42	1C-16	USAF 310th FS/56th FW, Luke AFB, AZ
88-0415	F-16C-40	1C-17	USAF 188th FS/150th FW, New Mexico ANG, Kirtland AFB
88-0416	F-16C-40	1C-18	USAF 421st FS/388th FW, Hill AFB, UT
88-0417	F-16C-42	1C-19	USAF 425th FS/56th FW, Luke AFB, AZ
88-0418	F-16C-40	1C-20	USAF 421st FS/388th FW, Hill AFB, UT
88-0419	F-16C-40	1C-21	USAF 4th FS/388th FW, Hill AFB, UT
88-0420	F-16C-42	1C-22	USAF 422nd TES/53rd Wg, Nellis AFB, NV
88-0421	F-16C-40	1C-23	USAF 421st FS/388th FW, Hill AFB, UT
88-0422	F-16C-40	1C-24	USAF 421st FS/388th FW, Hill AFB, UT
88-0423	F-16C-42	1C-25	USAF 422nd TES/53rd Wg, Nellis AFB, NV
88-0424	F-16C-40	1C-26	USAF 421st FS/388th FW, Hill AFB, UT
88-0425	F-16C-40	1C-27	USAF 555th FS/31st FW, Aviano AB, Italy
88-0426	F-16C-40	1C-28	USAF 421st FS/388th FW, Hill AFB, UT
88-0427	F-16C-42	1C-29	USAF 425th FS/56th FW, Luke AFB, AZ
88-0428	F-16C-40	1C-30	USAF 421st FS/388th FW, Hill AFB, UT

This Block 40 F-16C (88-0436) is operated from Hill AFB by the 34th FS of the 388th FW. MIKE CRUTCH

Serial	Type/Code	c/n	Operator/location
88-0429	F-16C-40	1C-31	USAF 524th FS/27th FW, Cannon AFB, NM
88-0430	F-16C-40	1C-32	USAF 34th FS/388th FW, Hill AFB, UT
88-0431	F-16C-40	1C-33	USAF 421st FS/388th FW, Hill AFB, UT
88-0432	F-16C-40	1C-34	USAF 34th FS/388th FW, Hill AFB, UT
88-0433	F-16C-40	1C-35	USAF 524th FS/27th FW, Cannon AFB, NM
88-0434	F-16C-42	1C-36	USAF 310th FS/56th FW, Luke AFB, AZ
88-0435	F-16C-40	1C-37	USAF 555th FS/31st FW, Aviano AB, Italy
88-0436	F-16C-40	1C-38	USAF 34th FS/388th FW, Hill AFB, UT
88-0437	F-16C-40	1C-39	USAF 34th FS/388th FW, Hill AFB, UT
88-0438	F-16C-40	1C-40	USAF 34th FS/388th FW, Hill AFB, UT
88-0439	F-16C-40	1C-41	USAF 524th FS/27th FW, Cannon AFB, NM
88-0440	F-16C-40	1C-42	USAF 36th FS/51st FW, Osan AB, Republic of Korea
88-0441	F-16C-40	1C-43	USAF 40th TES/46th TW, Eglin AFB, FL
88-0442	F-16C-42	1C-44	USAF 422nd TES/53rd Wg, Nellis AFB, NV
88-0443	F-16C-40	1C-45	USAF 510th FS/31st FW, Aviano AB, Italy
88-0444	F-16C-40	1C-46	USAF 510th FS/31st FW, Aviano AB, Italy
88-0445	F-16C-42	1C-47	Cr 21-Aug-95 (56th FW)
88-0446	F-16C-40	1C-48	USAF 510th FS/31st FW, Aviano AB, Italy
88-0447	F-16C-40	1C-49	USAF 421st FS/388th FW, Hill AFB, UT
88-0448	F-16C-42	1C-50	Cr 08-Nov-93 (57th Wg)
88-0449	F-16C-40	1C-51	USAF 421st FS/388th FW, Hill AFB, UT
88-0450	F-16C-40	1C-52	USAF 421st FS/388th FW, Hill AFB, UT
88-0451	F-16C-42	1C-53	USAF 310th FS/56th FW, Luke AFB, AZ
88-0452	F-16C-40	1C-54	USAF 34th FS/388th FW, Hill AFB, UT
88-0453	F-16C-40	1C-55	Cr 13-Mar-91 (388th FW)
88-0454	F-16C-40	1C-56	USAF 34th FS/388th FW, Hill AFB, UT
88-0455	F-16C-42	1C-57	Cr 21-Aug-95 (56th FW)

Photographed in August 1994, this F-16D (88-0150) carries Air Warfare Center markings. DANIEL MARCH

F-16C (88-0457) operated by the New Mexico ANG from Kirkland AFB, seen here in February 1994. PETER R MARCH

Serial	Type/Code	c/n	Operator/location
88-0456	F-16C-40	1C-58	USAF 416th TS/412th TW, Edwards AFB, CA
88-0457	F-16C-40	1C-59	USAF 4th FS/388th FW, Hill AFB, UT
88-0458	F-16C-42	1C-60	USAF 310th FS/56th FW, Luke AFB, AZ
88-0459	F-16C-40	1C-61	USAF 34th FS/388th FW, Hill AFB, UT
88-0460	F-16C-40	1C-62	USAF 34th FS/388th FW, Hill AFB, UT
88-0461	F-16C-42	1C-63	Cr 01-Dec-90 (58th TFW)
88-0462	F-16C-40	1C-64	USAF 524th FS/27th FW, Cannon AFB, NM
88-0463	F-16C-40	1C-65	USAF 4th FS/388th FW, Hill AFB, UT
88-0464	F-16C-42	1C-66	USAF 308th FS/56th FW, Luke AFB, AZ
88-0465	F-16C-40	1C-67	USAF 68th FS/347th Wg, Moody AFB, GA
88-0466	F-16C-40	1C-68	USAF 4th FS/388th FW, Hill AFB, UT
88-0467	F-16C-40	1C-69	USAF 34th FS/388th FW, Hill AFB, UT
88-0468	F-16C-40	1C-70	USAF 69th FS/347th Wg, Moody AFB, GA
88-0469	F-16C-42	1C-71	USAF 85th TES/53rd Wg, Eglin AFB, FL
88-0470	F-16C-40	1C-72	Cr 14-Jan-92 (388th FW)
88-0471	F-16C-40	1C-73	USAF 421st FS/388th FW, Hill AFB, UT
88-0472	F-16C-42	1C-74	USAF 308th FS/56th FW, Luke AFB, AZ
88-0473	F-16C-40	1C-75	USAF 188th FS/150th FW, New Mexico ANG, Kirtland AFB
88-0474	F-16C-40	1C-76	USAF 4th FS/388th FW, Hill AFB, UT
88-0475	F-16C-42	1C-77	USAF 308th FS/56th FW, Luke AFB, AZ
88-0476	F-16C-40	1C-78	USAF 4th FS/388th FW, Hill AFB, UT
88-0477	F-16C-40	1C-79	USAF 188th FS/150th FW, New Mexico ANG, Kirtland AFB
88-0478	F-16C-42	1C-80	Cr 10-Feb-95 (56th FW)
88-0479	F-16C-40	1C-81	USAF 4th FS/388th FW, Hill AFB, UT
88-0480	F-16C-40	1C-82	USAF 188th FS/150th FW, New Mexico ANG, Kirtland AFB
88-0481	F-16C-42	1C-83	USAF 308th FS/56th FW, Luke AFB, AZ
88-0482	F-16C-40	1C-84	USAF 188th FS/150th FW, New Mexico ANG, Kirtland AFB
88-0483	F-16C-40	1C-85	Cr 08-Jan-91 (388th TFW)
88-0484	F-16C-42	1C-86	USAF 308th FS/56th FW, Luke AFB, AZ
88-0485	F-16C-40	1C-87	USAF 421st FS/388th FW, Hill AFB, UT
88-0486	F-16C-40	1C-88	USAF 524th FS/27th FW, Cannon AFB, NM
88-0487	F-16C-42	1C-89	USAF 308th FS/56th FW, Luke AFB, AZ
88-0488	F-16C-40	1C-90	Cr 20-Sep-94 (388th FW)
88-0489	F-16C-40	1C-91	USAF 188th FS/150th FW, New Mexico ANG, Kirtland AFB
88-0490	F-16C-42	1C-92	USAF 308th FS/56th FW, Luke AFB, AZ
88-0491	F-16C-40	1C-93	USAF 510th FS/31st FW, Aviano AB, Italy
88-0492	F-16C-40	1C-94	USAF 4th FS/388th FW, Hill AFB, UT
88-0493	F-16C-42	1C-95	USAF 308th FS/56th FW, Luke AFB, AZ
88-0494	F-16C-40	1C-96	USAF 36th FS/51st FW, Osan AB, Republic of Korea
88-0495	F-16C-40	1C-97	USAF 4th FS/388th FW, Hill AFB, UT
88-0496	F-16C-42	1C-98	USAF 308th FS/56th FW, Luke AFB, AZ
88-0497	F-16C-40	1C-99	USAF 524th FS/27th FW, Cannon AFB, NM
88-0498	F-16C-40	1C-100	USAF 34th FS/388th FW, Hill AFB, UT
88-0499	F-16C-42	1C-101	USAF 422nd TES/53rd Wg, Nellis AFB, NV
88-0500	F-16C-40	1C-102	USAF 34th FS/388th FW, Hill AFB, UT
88-0501	F-16C-40	1C-103	USAF 421st FS/388th FW, Hill AFB, UT
88-0502	F-16C-42	1C-104	USAF 124th FS/132nd FW, Iowa ANG, Des Moines
88-0503	F-16C-40	1C-105	USAF 188th FS/150th FW, New Mexico ANG, Kirtland AFB
88-0504	F-16C-40	1C-106	USAF 188th FS/150th FW, New Mexico ANG, Kirtland AFB
88-0505	F-16C-42	1C-107	USAF 308th FS/56th FW, Luke AFB, AZ
88-0506	F-16C-40	1C-108	USAF 188th FS/150th FW, New Mexico ANG, Kirtland AFB
88-0507	F-16C-40	1C-109	USAF 4th FS/388th FW, Hill AFB, UT
88-0508	F-16C-42	1C-110	USAF 63 FS/56 FW, Luke AFB, AZ
88-0509	F-16C-40	1C-111	USAF 34th FS/388th FW, Hill AFB, UT
88-0510	F-16C-40	1C-112	USAF 421st FS/388th FW, Hill AFB, UT

Serial	Type/Code	c/n	Operator/location
88-0511	F-16C-42	1C-113	USAF 308th FS/56th FW, Luke AFB, AZ
88-0512	F-16C-40	1C-114	USAF 524th FS/27th FW, Cannon AFB, NM
88-0513	F-16C-40	1C-115	USAF 188th FS/150th FW, New Mexico ANG, Kirtland AFB
88-0514	F-16C-42	1C-116	USAF 308th FS/56th FW, Luke AFB, AZ
88-0515	F-16C-40	1C-117	USAF 69th FS/347th Wg, Moody AFB, GA
88-0516	F-16C-40	1C-118	USAF 524th FS/27th FW, Cannon AFB, NM
88-0517	F-16C-42	1C-119	USAF 308th FS/56th FW, Luke AFB, AZ
88-0518	F-16C-40	1C-120	USAF 524th FS/27th FW, Cannon AFB, NM
88-0519	F-16C-40	1C-121	USAF 36th FS/51st FW, Osan AB, Republic of Korea
88-0520	F-16C-42	1C-122	USAF 425th FS/56th FW, Luke AFB, AZ
88-0521	F-16C-40	1C-123	USAF 4th FS/388th FW, Hill AFB, UT
88-0522	F-16C-40	1C-124	USAF 69th FS/347th Wg, Moody AFB, GA
88-0523	F-16C-40	1C-125	Cr 23-Feb-93 (347th FW)
88-0524	F-16C-42	1C-126	USAF 310th FS/56th FW, Luke AFB, AZ
88-0525	F-16C-40	1C-127	USAF 510th FS/31st FW, Aviano AB, Italy
88-0526	F-16C-40	1C-128	USAF 555th FS/31st FW, Aviano AB, Italy
88-0527	F-16C-42	1C-129	USAF 124th FS/132nd FW, Iowa ANG, Des Moines
88-0528	F-16C-40	1C-130	USAF 69th FS/347th Wg, Moody AFB, GA
88-0529	F-16C-40	1C-131	USAF 510th FS/31st FW, Aviano AB, Italy
88-0530	F-16C-42	1C-132	USAF 125 FS/138 FW, Oklahoma ANG, Tulsa
88-0531	F-16C-40	1C-133	USAF 36th FS/51st FW, Osan AB, Republic of Korea
88-0532	F-16C-40	1C-134	USAF 555th FS/31st FW, Aviano AB, Italy
88-0533	F-16C-40	1C-135	USAF 421st FS/388th FW, Hill AFB, UT
88-0534	F-16C-42	1C-136	USAF 124th FS/132nd FW, Iowa ANG, Des Moines
88-0535	F-16C-40	1C-137	USAF 555th FS/31st FW, Aviano AB, Italy
88-0536	F-16C-40	1C-138	USAF 36th FS/51st FW, Osan AB, Republic of Korea
88-0537	F-16C-40	1C-139	USAF 4th FS/388th FW, Hill AFB, UT
88-0538	F-16C-40	1C-140	USAF 36th FS/51st FW, Osan AB, Republic of Korea
88-0539	F-16C-42	1C-141	USAF 124th FS/132nd FW, Iowa ANG, Des Moines
88-0540	F-16C-42	1C-142	USAF 36th FS/51st FW, Osan AB, Republic of Korea
88-0541	F-16C-40	1C-143	USAF 510th FS/31st FW, Aviano AB, Italy
88-0542	F-16C-42	1C-144	USAF 422nd TES/53rd Wg, Nellis AFB, NV
88-0543	F-16C-40	1C-145	USAF 188th FS/150th FW, New Mexico ANG, Kirtland AFB
88-0544	F-16C-40	1C-146	USAF 524th FS/27th FW, Cannon AFB, NM
88-0545	F-16C-42	1C-147	USAF 124th FS/132nd FW, Iowa ANG, Des Moines
88-0546	F-16C-40	1C-148	USAF 69th FS/347th Wg, Moody AFB, GA
88-0547	F-16C-40	1C-149	USAF 36th FS/51st FW, Osan AB, Republic of Korea
88-0548	F-16C-42	1C-150	USAF 125 FS/138 FW, Oklahoma ANG, Tulsa
88-0549	F-16C-40	1C-151	USAF 524th FS/27th FW, Cannon AFB, NM
88-0550	F-16C-40	1C-152	USAF 555th FS/31st FW, Aviano AB, Italy
89-2000	F-16C-40	1C-153	Cr 05-Feb-95 (188th FS)
89-2001	F-16C-40	1C-154	USAF 555th FS/31st FW, Aviano AB, Italy
89-2002	F-16C-42	1C-155	USAF 425th FS/56th FW, Luke AFB, AZ
89-2003	F-16C-40	1C-156	USAF 69th FS/347th Wg, Moody AFB, GA
89-2004	F-16C-42	1C-157	USAF 308th FS/56th FW, Luke AFB, AZ
89-2005	F-16C-40	1C-158	USAF 69th FS/347th Wg, Moody AFB, GA
89-2006	F-16C-40	1C-159	USAF 524th FS/27th FW, Cannon AFB, NM
89-2007	F-16C-42	1C-160	USAF 425th FS/56th FW, Luke AFB, AZ
89-2008	F-16C-40	1C-161	USAF 524th FS/27th FW, Cannon AFB, NM
89-2009	F-16C-40	1C-162	USAF 510th FS/31st FW, Aviano AB, Italy
89-2010	F-16C-42	1C-163	USAF 125th FS/138th FW, Oklahoma ANG, Tulsa
89-2011	F-16C-40	1C-164	USAF 510th FS/31st FW, Aviano AB, Italy
89-2012	F-16C-42	1C-165	USAF 425th FS/56th FW, Luke AFB, AZ
89-2013	F-16C-40	1C-166	USAF 69th FS/347th Wg, Moody AFB, GA
89-2014	F-16C-40	1C-167	USAF 36th FS/51st FW, Osan AB, Republic of Korea
89-2015	F-16C-40	1C-168	USAF 188th FS/150th FW, New Mexico ANG, Kirtland AFB
89-2016	F-16C-40	1C-169	USAF 555th FS/31st FW, Aviano AB, Italy
89-2017	F-16C-42	1C-170	USAF 125th FS/138th FW, Oklahoma ANG, Tulsa
89-2018	F-16C-42	1C-171	USAF 85th TES/53rd Wg, Eglin AFB, FL
89-2019	F-16C-40	1C-172	USAF 124th FS/132nd FW, Iowa ANG, Des Moines
89-2020	F-16C-40	1C-173	USAF 36th FS/51st FW, Osan AB, Republic of Korea
89-2021	F-16C-40	1C-174	USAF 188th FS/150th FW, New Mexico ANG, Kirtland AFB
89-2022	F-16C-42	1C-175	USAF 425th FS/56th FW, Luke AFB, AZ
89-2023	F-16C-40	1C-176	USAF 555th FS/31st FW, Aviano AB, Italy
89-2024	F-16C-40	1C-177	USAF 555th FS/31st FW, Aviano AB, Italy
89-2025	F-16C-40	1C-178	USAF 124th FS/132nd FW, Iowa ANG, Des Moines
89-2026	F-16C-40	1C-179	USAF 510th FS/31st FW, Aviano AB, Italy
89-2027	F-16C-40	1C-180	Cr 19-Sep-90 (347th TFW)
89-2028	F-16C-42	1C-181	USAF 425th FS/56th FW, Luke AFB, AZ
89-2029	F-16C-40	1C-182	USAF 510th FS/31st FW, Aviano AB, Italy
89-2030	F-16C-40	1C-183	USAF 510th FS/31st FW, Aviano AB, Italy
89-2031	F-16C-42	1C-184	USAF 125th FS/138th FW, Oklahoma ANG, Tulsa
89-2032	F-16C-40	1C-185	Cr 02-Jun-95 (31st FW)
89-2033	F-16C-40	1C-186	USAF 36th FS/51st FW, Osan AB, Republic of Korea
89-2034	F-16C-42	1C-187	USAF 425th FS/56th FW, Luke AFB, AZ

F-16C (89-2001) of the 555th/31st FW based at Aviano, Italy. TIM RIPLEY

Serial	Type/Code	c/n	Operator/location
89-2035	F-16C-40	1C-188	USAF 555th FS/31st FW, Aviano AB, Italy
89-2036	F-16C-40	1C-189	Cr 26-Jan-95 (31st FW)
89-2037	F-16C-42	1C-190	USAF 124th FS/132nd FW, Iowa ANG, Des Moines
89-2038	F-16C-40	1C-191	USAF 555th FS/31st FW, Aviano AB, Italy
89-2039	F-16C-40	1C-192	USAF 555th FS/31st FW, Aviano AB, Italy
89-2040	F-16C-42	1C-193	USAF 125th FS/138th FW, Oklahoma ANG, Tulsa
89-2041	F-16C-40	1C-194	USAF 188th FS/150th FW, New Mexico ANG, Kirtland AFB
89-2042	F-16C-40	1C-195	USAF 524th FS/27th FW, Cannon AFB, NM
89-2043	F-16C-40	1C-196	USAF 36th FS/51st FW, Osan AB, Republic of Korea
89-2044	F-16C-40	1C-197	USAF 510th FS/31st FW, Aviano AB, Italy
89-2045	F-16C-42	1C-198	USAF 124th FS/132nd FW, Iowa ANG, Des Moines
89-2046	F-16C-40	1C-199	USAF 510th FS/31st FW, Aviano AB, Italy
89-2047	F-16C-40	1C-200	USAF 510th FS/31st FW, Aviano AB, Italy
89-2048	F-16C-42	1C-201	USAF 422nd TES/53rd Wg, Nellis AFB, NV
89-2049	F-16C-40	1C-202	USAF 510th FS/31st FW, Aviano AB, Italy
89-2050	F-16C-40	1C-203	USAF 510th FS/31st FW, Aviano AB, Italy
89-2051	F-16C-42	1C-204	USAF 124th FS/132nd FW, Iowa ANG, Des Moines
89-2052	F-16C-40	1C-205	USAF 36th FS/51st FW, Osan AB, Republic of Korea
89-2053	F-16C-42	1C-206	USAF 125th FS/138th FW, Oklahoma ANG, Tulsa
89-2054	F-16C-40	1C-207	USAF 524th FS/27th FW, Cannon AFB, NM
89-2055	F-16C-40	1C-208	USAF 69th FS/347th Wg, Moody AFB, GA
89-2056	F-16C-42	1C-209	USAF 63rd FS/56th FW, Luke AFB, AZ
89-2057	F-16C-40	1C-210	USAF 555th FS/31st FW, Aviano AB, Italy
89-2058	F-16C-40	1C-211	USAF 69th FS/347th Wg, Moody AFB, GA
89-2059	F-16C-42	1C-212	Cr 07-Oct-91 (57th Wg)
89-2060	F-16C-40	1C-213	USAF 69th FS/347th Wg, Moody AFB, GA
89-2061	F-16C-40	1C-214	Cr 04-Apr-91 (347th TFW)
89-2062	F-16C-40	1C-215	USAF 69th FS/347th Wg, Moody AFB, GA
89-2063	F-16C-40	1C-216	USAF 69th FS/347th Wg, Moody AFB, GA
89-2064	F-16C-40	1C-217	USAF 4th FS/388th FW, Hill AFB, UT
89-2065	F-16C-40	1C-218	USAF 4th FS/388th FW, Hill AFB, UT
89-2066	F-16C-40	1C-219	USAF 18th FS/354th FW, Eielson AFB, AK
89-2067	F-16C-40	1C-220	USAF 4th FS/388th FW, Hill AFB, UT
89-2068	F-16C-40	1C-221	USAF 68th FS/347th Wg, Moody AFB, GA
89-2069	F-16C-40	1C-222	Cr 18-May-93 (343th Wg)
89-2070	F-16C-42	1C-223	USAF 85th TES/53rd Wg, Eglin AFB, FL
89-2071	F-16C-40	1C-224	USAF 69th FS/347th Wg, Moody AFB, GA

Serial	Type/Code	c/n	Operator/location
89-2072	F-16C-40	1C-225	USAF 421st FS/388th FW, Hill AFB, UT
89-2073	F-16C-42	1C-226	USAF 125th FS/138th FW, Oklahoma ANG, Tulsa
89-2074	F-16C-42	1C-227	USAF 4th FS/388th FW, Hill AFB, UT
89-2075	F-16C-40	1C-228	USAF 4th FS/388th FW, Hill AFB, UT
89-2076	F-16C-42	1C-229	USAF 524th FS/27th FW, Cannon AFB, NM
89-2077	F-16C-40	1C-230	USAF 18th FS/354th FW, Eielson AFB, AK
89-2078	F-16C-40	1C-231	USAF 18th FS/354th FW, Eielson AFB, AK
89-2079	F-16C-42	1C-232	USAF 112nd FS/180th FG, Ohio ANG, Toledo
89-2080	F-16C-40	1C-233	USAF 36th FS/51st FW, Osan AB, Republic of Korea
89-2081	F-16C-40	1C-234	USAF 4th FS/388th FW, Hill AFB, UT
89-2082	F-16C-42	1C-235	USAF 425th FS/56th FW, Luke AFB, AZ
89-2083	F-16C-40	1C-236	USAF 524th FS/27th FW, Cannon AFB, NM
89-2084	F-16C-40	1C-237	USAF 68th FS/347th Wg, Moody AFB, GA
89-2085	F-16C-42	1C-238	USAF 112nd FS/180th FG, Ohio ANG, Toledo
89-2086	F-16C-40	1C-239	USAF 4th FS/388th FW, Hill AFB, UT
89-2087	F-16C-40	1C-240	USAF 4th FS/388th FW, Hill AFB, UT
89-2088	F-16C-42	1C-241	USAF 125th FS/138th FW, Oklahoma ANG, Tulsa

Block 40 F-16C (89-2067) was operated from Eielson AFB, Alaska in 1992. PETER R FOSTER

Serial	Type/Code	c/n	Operator/location	Serial	Type/Code	c/n	Operator/location
89-2089	F-16C-42	1C-242	Cr 16-Dec-91 (363rd TFW)	89-2133	F-16C-40	1C-286	USAF 36th FS/51st FW, Osan AB, Republic of Korea
89-2090	F-16C-40	1C-243	USAF 69th FS/347th Wg, Moody AFB, GA	89-2134	F-16C-40	1C-287	Cr 16-Feb-94 (86th FW)
89-2091	F-16C-42	1C-244	USAF 162nd FW, Arizona ANG, Tucson IAP	89-2135	F-16C-42	1C-288	USAF 162nd FW, Arizona ANG, Tucson IAP
89-2092	F-16C-40	1C-245	USAF 4th FS/388th FW, Hill AFB, UT	89-2136	F-16C-40	1C-289	USAF 36th FS/51st FW, Osan AB, Republic of Korea
89-2093	F-16C-40	1C-246	Cr 31-Jul-96 (347th Wg)	89-2137	F-16C-40	1C-290	USAF 510th FS/31st FW, Aviano AB, Italy
89-2094	F-16C-42	1C-247	USAF 63rd FS/56th FW, Luke AFB, AZ	89-2138	F-16C-42	1C-291	USAF 125th FS/138th FW, Oklahoma ANG, Tulsa
89-2095	F-16C-40	1C-248	USAF 68th FS/347th Wg, Moody AFB, GA	89-2139	F-16C-40	1C-292	USAF 36th FS/51st FW, Osan AB, Republic of Korea
89-2096	F-16C-40	1C-249	USAF 69th FS/347th Wg, Moody AFB, GA	89-2140	F-16C-40	1C-293	USAF 36th FS/51st FW, Osan AB, Republic of Korea
89-2097	F-16C-42	1C-250	USAF 63rd FS/56th FW, Luke AFB, AZ	89-2141	F-16C-42	1C-294	USAF 125th FS/138th FW, Oklahoma ANG, Tulsa
89-2098	F-16C-42	1C-251	USAF 112nd FS/180th FG, Ohio ANG, Toledo	89-2142	F-16C-42	1C-295	USAF 124th FS/132nd FW, Iowa ANG, Des Moines
89-2099	F-16C-40	1C-252	USAF 69th FS/347th Wg, Moody AFB, GA	89-2143	F-16C-40	1C-296	USAF 68th FS/347th Wg, Moody AFB, GA
89-2100	F-16C-42	1C-253	USAF 162nd FW, Arizona ANG, Tucson IAP	89-2144	F-16C-40	1C-297	USAF 34th FS/388th FW, Hill AFB, UT
89-2101	F-16C-40	1C-254	USAF 34th FS/388th FW, Hill AFB, UT	89-2145	F-16C-42	1C-298	USAF 125th FS/138th FW, Oklahoma ANG, Tulsa
89-2102	F-16C-40	1C-255	USAF 68th FS/347th Wg, Moody AFB, GA	89-2146	F-16C-40/GF-16C	1C-299	USAF TTC/82nd TRW, Sheppard AFB, TX
89-2103	F-16C-42	1C-256	USAF 308th FS/56th FW, Luke AFB, AZ	89-2147	F-16C-40	1C-300	USAF 69th FS/347th Wg, Moody AFB, GA
89-2104	F-16C-40	1C-257	USAF 68th FS/347th Wg, Moody AFB, GA	89-2148	F-16C-42	1C-301	USAF 124th FS/132nd FW, Iowa ANG, Des Moines
89-2105	F-16C-40	1C-258	USAF 68th FS/347th Wg, Moody AFB, GA	89-2149	F-16C-40	1C-302	USAF 68th FS/347th Wg, Moody AFB, GA
89-2106	F-16C-42	1C-259	USAF 112nd FS/180th FG, Ohio ANG, Toledo	89-2150	F-16C-40	1C-303	USAF 69th FS/347th Wg, Moody AFB, GA
89-2107	F-16C-42	1C-260	USAF 308th FS/56th FW, Luke AFB, AZ	89-2151	F-16C-42	1C-304	USAF 425th FS/56th FW, Luke AFB, AZ
89-2108	F-16C-40	1C-261	USAF 4th FS/388th FW, Hill AFB, UT	89-2152	F-16C-40	1C-305	USAF 4th FS/388th FW, Hill AFB, UT
89-2109	F-16C-42	1C-262	USAF 112nd FS/180th FG, Ohio ANG, Toledo	89-2153	F-16C-40	1C-306	USAF 524th FS/27th FW, Cannon AFB, NM
89-2110	F-16C-40	1C-263	Cr 24-Aug-92 (31st FW)	89-2154	F-16C-42	1C-307	USAF 63rd FS/56th FW, Luke AFB, AZ
89-2111	F-16C-40	1C-264	USAF 68th FS/347th Wg, Moody AFB, GA	89-2155	F-16D-42	1D-30	USAF 162nd FW, Arizona ANG, Tucson IAP
89-2112	F-16C-42	1C-265	USAF 112nd FS/180th FG, Ohio ANG, Toledo	89-2156	F-16D-42	1D-31	USAF 162nd FW, Arizona ANG, Tucson IAP
89-2113	F-16C-40	1C-266	USAF 18th FS/354th FW, Eielson AFB, AK	89-2157	F-16D-42	1D-32	USAF 310th FS/56th FW, Luke AFB, AZ
89-2114	F-16C-42	1C-267	USAF 112nd FS/180th FG, Ohio ANG, Toledo	89-2158	F-16D-42	1D-33	USAF 63rd FS/56th FW, Luke AFB, AZ
89-2115	F-16C-40	1C-268	USAF 68th FS/347th Wg, Moody AFB, GA	89-2159	F-16D-42	1D-34	USAF 310th FS/56th FW, Luke AFB, AZ
89-2116	F-16C-40	1C-269	USAF 69th FS/347th Wg, Moody AFB, GA	89-2160	F-16D-42	1D-35	USAF 310th FS/56th FW, Luke AFB, AZ
89-2117	F-16C-42	1C-270	USAF 162nd FW, Arizona ANG, Tucson IAP	89-2161	F-16D-42	1D-36	USAF 308th FS/56th FW, Luke AFB, AZ
89-2118	F-16C-40	1C-271	USAF 188th FS/150th FW, New Mexico ANG, Kirtland AFB	89-2162	F-16D-42	1D-37	USAF 308th FS/56th FW, Luke AFB, AZ
89-2119	F-16C-40	1C-272	USAF 34th FS/388th FW, Hill AFB, UT	89-2163	F-16D-42	1D-38	USAF 162nd FW, Arizona ANG, Tucson IAP
89-2120	F-16C-42	1C-273	USAF 63rd FS/56th FW, Luke AFB, AZ	89-2164	F-16D-42	1D-39	USAF 310th FS/56th FW, Luke AFB, AZ
89-2121	F-16C-40	1C-274	USAF 18th FS/354th FW, Eielson AFB, AK	89-2165	F-16D-42	1D-40	USAF 112nd FS/180th FG, Ohio ANG, Toledo
89-2122	F-16C-40	1C-275	USAF 18th FS/354th FW, Eielson AFB, AK	89-2166	F-16D-40	1D-41	USAF 69th FS/347th Wg, Moody AFB, GA
89-2123	F-16C-42	1C-276	USAF 162nd FW, Arizona ANG, Tucson IAP	89-2167	F-16D-42	1D-42	USAF 125th FS/138th FW, Oklahoma ANG, Tulsa
89-2124	F-16C-40	1C-277	USAF 188th FS/150th FW, New Mexico ANG, Kirtland AFB	89-2168	F-16D-40	1D-43	USAF 36th FS/51st FW, Osan AB, Republic of Korea
89-2125	F-16C-40	1C-278	USAF 524th FS/27th FW, Cannon AFB, NM	89-2169	F-16D-40	1D-44	USAF 524th FS/27th FW, Cannon AFB, NM
89-2126	F-16C-42	1C-279	USAF 422nd TES/53rd Wg, Nellis AFB, NV	89-2170	F-16D-42	1D-45	USAF 310th FS/56th FW, Luke AFB, AZ
89-2127	F-16C-40	1C-280	USAF 524th FS/27th FW, Cannon AFB, NM	89-2171	F-16D-40	1D-46	USAF 69th FS/347th Wg, Moody AFB, GA
89-2128	F-16C-40	1C-281	USAF 112nd FS/180th FG, Ohio ANG, Toledo	89-2172	F-16D-40	1D-47	USAF 18th FS/354th FW, Eielson AFB, AK
89-2129	F-16C-42	1C-282	USAF 112nd FS/180th FG, Ohio ANG, Toledo	89-2173	F-16D-40	1D-48	USAF 188th FS/150th FW, New Mexico ANG, Kirtland AFB
89-2130	F-16C-40	1C-283	USAF 36th FS/51st FW, Osan AB, Republic of Korea	89-2174	F-16D-40	1D-49	USAF 4th FS/388th FW, Hill AFB, UT
89-2131	F-16C-40	1C-284	USAF 34th FS/388th FW, Hill AFB, UT	89-2175	F-16D-42	1D-50	USAF 63rd FS/56th FW, Luke AFB, AZ
89-2132	F-16C-42	1C-285	USAF 112nd FS/180th FG, Ohio ANG, Toledo	89-2176	F-16D-40	1D-51	USAF 524th FS/27th FW, Cannon AFB, NM

Eight F-16Cs of the 112th FS, Ohio ANG, based at Toledo Express Airport, including a Block 42 aircraft (90-0704). BOB ARCHER

Serial	Type/Code	c/n	Operator/location
89-2177	F-16D-42	1D-52	USAF 310th FS/56th FW, Luke AFB, AZ
89-2178	F-16D-40	1D-53	USAF 510th FS/31st FW, Aviano AB, Italy
89-2179	F-16D-42	1D-54	USAF 188th FS/150th FW, New Mexico ANG, Kirtland AFB
90-0700	F-16C-42	1C-308	USAF 112nd FS/180th FG, Ohio ANG, Toledo
90-0701	F-16C-42	1C-309	USAF 112nd FS/180th FG, Ohio ANG, Toledo
90-0702	F-16C-42	1C-310	USAF 112nd FS/180th FG, Ohio ANG, Toledo
90-0703	F-16C-40	1C-311	USAF 69th FS/347th Wg, Moody AFB, GA
90-0704	F-16C-42	1C-312	USAF 112nd FS/180th FG, Ohio ANG, Toledo
90-0705	F-16C-42	1C-313	USAF 63rd FS/56th FW, Luke AFB, AZ
90-0706	F-16C-42	1C-314	USAF 112nd FS/180th FG, Ohio ANG, Toledo
90-0707	F-16C-42	1C-315	USAF 422nd TES/53rd Wg, Nellis AFB, NV
90-0708	F-16C-42	1C-316	USAF 162nd FW, Arizona ANG, Tucson IAP
90-0709	F-16C-40	1C-317	USAF 510th FS/31st FW, Aviano AB, Italy
90-0710	F-16C-40	1C-318	USAF 36th FS/51st FW, Osan AB, Republic of Korea
90-0711	F-16C-40	1C-319	USAF 18th FS/354th FW, Eielson AFB, AK
90-0712	F-16C-42	1C-320	USAF 63rd FS/56th FW, Luke AFB, AZ
90-0713	F-16C-42	1C-321	USAF 162nd FW, Arizona ANG, Tucson IAP
90-0714	F-16C-40	1C-322	USAF 18th FS/354th FW, Eielson AFB, AK
90-0715	F-16C-42	1C-323	USAF 162nd FW, Arizona ANG, Tucson IAP
90-0716	F-16C-42	1C-324	USAF 162nd FW, Arizona ANG, Tucson IAP
90-0717	F-16C-40	1C-325	USAF 18th FS/354th FW, Eielson AFB, AK
90-0718	F-16C-40	1C-326	USAF 18th FS/354th FW, Eielson AFB, AK
90-0719	F-16C-42	1C-327	USAF 125th FS/138th FW, Oklahoma ANG, Tulsa
90-0720	F-16C-42	1C-328	USAF 162nd FW, Arizona ANG, Tucson IAP
90-0721	F-16C-42	1C-329	USAF 422nd TES/53rd Wg, Nellis AFB, NV
90-0722	F-16C-42	1C-330	USAF 63rd FS/56th FW, Luke AFB, AZ
90-0723	F-16C-40	1C-331	USAF 18th FS/354th FW, Eielson AFB, AK
90-0724	F-16C-40	1C-332	USAF 18th FS/354th FW, Eielson AFB, AK
90-0725	F-16C-40	1C-333	USAF 68th FS/347th Wg, Moody AFB, GA
90-0726	F-16C-42	1C-334	USAF 85th TES/53rd Wg, Eglin AFB, FL
90-0727	F-16C-42	1C-335	USAF 422nd TES/53rd Wg, Nellis AFB, NV
90-0728	F-16C-42	1C-336	USAF 422nd TES/53rd Wg, Nellis AFB, NV
90-0729	F-16C-42	1C-337	USAF 422nd TES/53rd Wg, Nellis AFB, NV
90-0730	F-16C-42	1C-338	USAF 310th FS/56th FW, Luke AFB, AZ
90-0731	F-16C-42	1C-339	USAF 124th FS/132nd FW, Iowa ANG, Des Moines
90-0732	F-16C-42	1C-340	USAF 308th FS/56th FW, Luke AFB, AZ
90-0733	F-16C-40	1C-341	USAF 18th FS/354th FW, Eielson AFB, AK
90-0734	F-16C-40	1C-342	USAF 18th FS/354th FW, Eielson AFB, AK
90-0735	F-16C-40	1C-343	USAF 18th FS/354th FW, Eielson AFB, AK
90-0736	F-16C-40	1C-344	USAF 18th FS/354th FW, Eielson AFB, AK
90-0737	F-16C-42	1C-345	USAF 308th FS/56th FW, Luke AFB, AZ
90-0738	F-16C-42	1C-346	USAF 125th FS/138th FW, Oklahoma ANG, Tulsa
90-0739	F-16C-42	1C-347	USAF 422nd TES/53rd Wg, Nellis AFB, NV
90-0740	F-16C-42	1C-348	USAF 422nd TES/53rd Wg, Nellis AFB, NV
90-0741	F-16C-42	1C-349	USAF 162nd FW, Arizona ANG, Tucson IAP
90-0742	F-16C-40	1C-350	USAF 18th FS/354th FW, Eielson AFB, AK
90-0743	F-16C-40	1C-351	USAF 36th FS/51st FW, Osan AB, Republic of Korea
90-0744	F-16C-40	1C-352	USAF 18th FS/354th FW, Eielson AFB, AK
90-0745	F-16C-40	1C-353	USAF 18th FS/354th FW, Eielson AFB, AK
90-0746	F-16C-42	1C-354	USAF 422nd TES/53rd Wg, Nellis AFB, NV
90-0747	F-16C-42	1C-355	USAF 422nd TES/53rd Wg, Nellis AFB, NV
90-0748	F-16C-42	1C-356	USAF 124th FS/132nd FW, Iowa ANG, Des Moines
90-0749	F-16C-42	1C-357	Cr 31-May-92 (363rd FW)
90-0750	F-16C-42	1C-358	USAF 422nd TES/53rd Wg, Nellis AFB, NV
90-0751	F-16C-42	1C-359	USAF 422nd TES/53rd Wg, Nellis AFB, NV
90-0752	F-16C-42	1C-360	USAF 63rd FS/56th FW, Luke AFB, AZ
90-0753	F-16C-40	1C-361	USAF 68th FS/347th Wg, Moody AFB, GA
90-0754	F-16C-42	1C-362	USAF 63rd FS/56th FW, Luke AFB, AZ
90-0755	F-16C-42	1C-363	USAF 63rd FS/56th FW, Luke AFB, AZ
90-0756	F-16C-40	1C-364	USAF 68th FS/347th Wg, Moody AFB, GA
90-0757	F-16C-42	1C-365	USAF 63rd FS/56th FW, Luke AFB, AZ
90-0758	F-16C-42	1C-366	USAF 310th FS/56th FW, Luke AFB, AZ
90-0759	F-16C-42	1C-367	USAF 63rd FS/56th FW, Luke AFB, AZ
90-0760	F-16C-42	1C-368	USAF 63rd FS/56th FW, Luke AFB, AZ
90-0761	F-16C-42	1C-369	Cr 27-Oct-92 (363rd FW)
90-0762	F-16C-42	1C-370	USAF 63rd FS/56th FW, Luke AFB, AZ
90-0763	F-16C-40	1C-371	USAF 68th FS/347th Wg, Moody AFB, GA
90-0764	F-16C-42	1C-372	Cr 07-Feb-94 (125th FS)
90-0765	F-16C-42	1C-373	USAF 63rd FS/56th FW, Luke AFB, AZ
90-0766	F-16C-42	1C-374	USAF 308th FS/56th FW, Luke AFB, AZ
90-0767	F-16C-42	1C-375	USAF 422nd TES/53rd Wg, Nellis AFB, NV
90-0768	F-16C-42	1C-376	USAF 63rd FS/56th FW, Luke AFB, AZ
90-0769	F-16C-42	1C-377	USAF 63rd FS/56th FW, Luke AFB, AZ
90-0770	F-16C-42	1C-378	USAF 310th FS/56th FW, Luke AFB, AZ
90-0771	F-16C-40	1C-379	USAF 36th FS/51st FW, Osan AB, Republic of Korea

A WSF (weapons School Falcon) F-16C (90-0751) landing at Nellis AFB. DANIEL MARCH

Serial	Type/Code	c/n	Operator/location
90-0772	F-16C-40	1C-380	USAF 68th FS/347th Wg, Moody AFB, GA
90-0773	F-16C-40	1C-381	USAF 68th FS/347th Wg, Moody AFB, GA
90-0774	F-16C-40	1C-382	USAF 36th FS/51st FW, Osan AB, Republic of Korea
90-0775	F-16C-40	1C-383	USAF 36th FS/51st FW, Osan AB, Republic of Korea
90-0776	F-16C-40	1C-384	USAF 524th FS/27th FW, Cannon AFB, NM
90-0777	F-16D-40	1D-55	USAF 188th FS/150th FW, New Mexico ANG, Kirtland AFB
90-0778	F-16D-42	1D-56	USAF 63rd FS/56th FW, Luke AFB, AZ
90-0779	F-16D-40	1D-57	USAF 36th FS/51st FW, Osan AB, Republic of Korea
90-0780	F-16D-40	1D-58	USAF /57th Wg, Nellis AFB, NV
90-0781	F-16D-42	1D-59	USAF 63rd FS/56th FW, Luke AFB, AZ
90-0782	F-16D-40	1D-60	USAF 421st FS/388th FW, Hill AFB, UT
90-0783	F-16D-42	1D-61	USAF 63rd FS/56th FW, Luke AFB, AZ
90-0784	F-16D-40	1D-62	Cr 18-Feb-93 (343rd Wg)
90-0785	F-16D-42	1D-63	USAF 162nd FW, Arizona ANG, Tucson IAP
90-0786	F-16D-42	1D-64	USAF 63rd FS/56th FW, Luke AFB, AZ
90-0787	F-16D-42	1D-65	USAF 63rd FS/56th FW, Luke AFB, AZ
90-0788	F-16D-42	1D-66	USAF 63rd FS/56th FW, Luke AFB, AZ
90-0789	F-16D-42	1D-67	USAF 310th FS/56th FW, Luke AFB, AZ
90-0790	F-16D-42	1D-68	USAF 162nd FW, Arizona ANG, Tucson IAP
90-0791	F-16D-40	1D-69	USAF 18th FS/354th FW, Eielson AFB, AK
90-0792	F-16D-40	1D-70	USAF 36th FS/51st FW, Osan AB, Republic of Korea
90-0793	F-16D-42	1D-71	USAF 63rd FS/56th FW, Luke AFB, AZ
90-0794	F-16D-40	1D-72	USAF 68th FS/347th Wg, Moody AFB, GA
90-0795	F-16D-40	1D-73	USAF 555th FS/31st FW, Aviano AB, Italy
90-0796	F-16D-40	1D-74	USAF 510th FS/31st FW, Aviano AB, Italy
90-0797	F-16D-40	1D-75	USAF 4th FS/388th FW, Hill AFB, UT
90-0798	F-16D-40	1D-76	USAF 68th FS/347th Wg, Moody AFB, GA
90-0799	F-16D-40	1D-77	USAF 68th FS/347th Wg, Moody AFB, GA
90-0800	F-16D-40	1D-78	USAF 555th FS/31st FW, Aviano AB, Italy
90-0801	F-16C-50	CC-1	USAF 14th FS/35th FW, Misawa AB, Japan
90-0802	F-16C-50	CC-2	USAF 14th FS/35th FW, Misawa AB, Japan
90-0803	F-16C-50	CC-3	USAF 14th FS/35th FW, Misawa AB, Japan
90-0804	F-16C-50	CC-4	USAF 14th FS/35th FW, Misawa AB, Japan
90-0805	F-16C-50	CC-5	USAF 14th FS/35th FW, Misawa AB, Japan
90-0806	F-16C-50	CC-6	USAF 77th FS/20th FW, Shaw AFB, SC
90-0807	F-16C-50	CC-7	USAF 14th FS/35th FW, Misawa AB, Japan
90-0808	F-16C-50	CC-8	USAF 14th FS/35th FW, Misawa AB, Japan
90-0809	F-16C-52	CC-9	USAF 422nd TES/53rd Wg, Nellis AFB, NV
90-0810	F-16C-50	CC-10	USAF 162nd FW, Arizona ANG, Tucson IAP
90-0811	F-16C-50	CC-11	USAF 14th FS/35th FW, Misawa AB, Japan
90-0812	F-16C-50	CC-12	USAF 14th FS/35th FW, Misawa AB, Japan
90-0813	F-16C-50	CC-13	USAF 22nd FS/52nd FW, Spangdahlem AB, Germany
90-0814	F-16C-50	CC-14	Cr 25-Oct-94 (388th FW)
90-0815	F-16C-50	CC-15	USAF 77th FS/20th FW, Shaw AFB, SC
90-0816	F-16C-50	CC-16	USAF 13th FS/36th FW, Misawa AB, Japan
90-0817	F-16C-50	CC-17	USAF 14th FS/35th FW, Misawa AB, Japan
90-0818	F-16C-50	CC-18	USAF 22nd FS/52nd FW, Spangdahlem AB, Germany
90-0819	F-16C-50	CC-19	USAF 14th FS/35th FW, Misawa AB, Japan
90-0820	F-16C-50	CC-20	USAF 14th FS/35th FW, Misawa AB, Japan
90-0821	F-16C-50	CC-21	USAF 77th FS/20th FW, Shaw AFB, SC
90-0822	F-16C-50	CC-22	USAF 14th FS/35th FW, Misawa AB, Japan
90-0823	F-16C-50	CC-23	Cr 08-Feb-94 (20th FW)
90-0824	F-16C-50	CC-24	USAF 14th FS/35th FW, Misawa AB, Japan
90-0825	F-16C-50	CC-25	USAF 14th FS/35th FW, Misawa AB, Japan
90-0826	F-16C-50	CC-26	USAF 77th FS/20th FW, Shaw AFB, SC
90-0827	F-16C-50	CC-27	USAF 22nd FS/52nd FW, Spangdahlem AB, Germany

This Shaw based F-16C is operated by the 20th FW's 'Tiger' squadron, the 79th FS. DANIEL MARCH

Serial	Type/Code	c/n	Operator/location
90-0828	F-16C-50	CC-28	USAF 22nd FS/52nd FW, Spangdahlem AB, Germany
90-0829	F-16C-50	CC-29	USAF 22nd FS/52nd FW, Spangdahlem AB, Germany
90-0830	F-16C-50	CC-30	USAF 77th FS/20th FW, Shaw AFB, SC
90-0831	F-16C-50	CC-31	USAF 22nd FS/52nd FW, Spangdahlem AB, Germany
90-0832	F-16C-50	CC-32	Cr 24-May-93 (Lockheed)
90-0833	F-16C-50	CC-33	USAF 22nd FS/52nd FW, Spangdahlem AB, Germany
90-0834	F-16D-50	CD-1	USAF 14th FS/35th FW, Misawa AB, Japan
90-0835	F-16D-50	CD-2	USAF 416th TS/412th TW, Edwards AFB, CA
90-0836	F-16D-50	CD-3	USAF 40th TES/46th TW, Eglin AFB, FL
90-0837	F-16D-50	CD-4	USAF 14th FS/35th FW, Misawa AB, Japan
90-0838	F-16D-50	CD-5	USAF 13th FS/35th FW, Misawa AB, Japan
90-0839	F-16D-52	CD-6	USAF 422nd TES/53rd Wg, Nellis AFB, NV
90-0840	F-16D-50	CD-7	USAF 85th TES/53rd Wg, Eglin AFB, FL
90-0841	F-16D-50	CD-8	USAF 85th TES/53rd Wg, Eglin AFB, FL
90-0842	F-16D-50	CD-9	USAF 85th TES/53rd Wg, Eglin AFB, FL
90-0843	F-16D-50	CD-10	USAF 22nd FS/52nd FW, Spangdahlem AB, Germany
90-0844	F-16D-50	CD-11	USAF 85th TES/53rd Wg, Eglin AFB, FL
90-0845	F-16D-50	CD-12	USAF 77th FS/20th FW, Shaw AFB, SC
90-0846	F-16D-50	CD-13	USAF 22nd FS/52nd FW, Spangdahlem AB, Germany
90-0847	F-16D-50	CD-14	USAF 77th FS/20th FW, Shaw AFB, SC
90-0848	F-16D-50	CD-15	Lockheed Martin, Fort Worth, TX
90-0849	F-16D-50	CD-16	Cr 13-Jan-95 (52nd FW)
91-0336	F-16C-50	CC-34	USAF 22nd FS/52nd FW, Spangdahlem AB, Germany
91-0337	F-16C-50	CC-35	USAF 22nd FS/52nd FW, Spangdahlem AB, Germany
91-0338	F-16C-50	CC-36	USAF 22nd FS/52nd FW, Spangdahlem AB, Germany
91-0339	F-16C-50	CC-37	USAF 22nd FS/52nd FW, Spangdahlem AB, Germany
91-0340	F-16C-50	CC-38	USAF 22nd FS/52nd FW, Spangdahlem AB, Germany
91-0341	F-16C-50	CC-39	USAF 22nd FS/52nd FW, Spangdahlem AB, Germany
91-0342	F-16C-50	CC-40	USAF 22nd FS/52nd FW, Spangdahlem AB, Germany
91-0343	F-16C-50	CC-41	USAF 22nd FS/52nd FW, Spangdahlem AB, Germany
91-0344	F-16C-50	CC-42	USAF 22nd FS/52nd FW, Spangdahlem AB, Germany
91-0345	F-16C-50	CC-43	USAF 77th FS/20th FW, Shaw AFB, SC
91-0346	F-16C-50	CC-44	USAF 77th FS/20th FW, Shaw AFB, SC
91-0347	F-16C-50	CC-45	USAF 77th FS/20th FW, Shaw AFB, SC
91-0348	F-16C-50	CC-46	USAF 77th FS/20th FW, Shaw AFB, SC
91-0349	F-16C-50	CC-47	USAF 77th FS/20th FW, Shaw AFB, SC
91-0350	F-16C-50	CC-48	Cr 08-Oct-93 (on delivery)
91-0351	F-16C-50	CC-49	USAF 22nd FS/52nd FW, Spangdahlem AB, Germany
91-0352	F-16C-50	CC-50	USAF 22nd FS/52nd FW, Spangdahlem AB, Germany
91-0353	F-16C-50	CC-51	USAF 77th FS/20th FW, Shaw AFB, SC
91-0354	F-16C-50	CC-52	USAF 77th FS/20th FW, Shaw AFB, SC
91-0355	F-16C-50	CC-53	USAF 77th FS/20th FW, Shaw AFB, SC
91-0356	F-16C-50	CC-54	USAF 77th FS/20th FW, Shaw AFB, SC
91-0357	F-16C-50	CC-55	USAF 77th FS/20th FW, Shaw AFB, SC
91-0358	F-16C-50	CC-56	USAF 77th FS/20th FW, Shaw AFB, SC
91-0359	F-16C-50	CC-57	USAF 77th FS/20th FW, Shaw AFB, SC
91-0360	F-16C-50	CC-58	USAF 79th FS/20th FW, Shaw AFB, SC
91-0361	F-16C-50	CC-59	USAF 79th FS/20th FW, Shaw AFB, SC
91-0362	F-16C-52	CC-60	USAF 422nd TES/53rd Wg, Nellis AFB, NV
91-0363	F-16C-50	CC-61	USAF 78th FS/20th FW, Shaw AFB, SC
91-0364	F-16C-50	CC-62	USAF 79th FS/20th FW, Shaw AFB, SC
91-0365	F-16C-50	CC-63	USAF 79th FS/20th FW, Shaw AFB, SC
91-0366	F-16C-50	CC-64	USAF 79th FS/20th FW, Shaw AFB, SC
91-0367	F-16C-50	CC-65	USAF 79th FS/20th FW, Shaw AFB, SC
91-0368	F-16C-50	CC-66	USAF 79th FS/20th FW, Shaw AFB, SC
91-0369	F-16C-50	CC-67	USAF 79th FS/20th FW, Shaw AFB, SC
91-0370	F-16C-52	CC-68	USAF 389th FS/366th Wg, Mountain Home AFB, ID
91-0371	F-16C-50	CC-69	USAF 79th FS/20th FW, Shaw AFB, SC
91-0372	F-16C-50	CC-70	USAF 79th FS/20th FW, Shaw AFB, SC
91-0373	F-16C-50	CC-71	USAF 79th FS/20th FW, Shaw AFB, SC
91-0374	F-16C-52	CC-72	USAF 422nd TES/53rd Wg, Nellis AFB, NV
91-0375	F-16C-50	CC-73	USAF 79th FS/20th FW, Shaw AFB, SC
91-0376	F-16C-50	CC-74	USAF 79th FS/20th FW, Shaw AFB, SC
91-0377	F-16C-50	CC-75	USAF 78th FS/20th FW, Shaw AFB, SC
91-0378	F-16C-50	CC-76	USAF 78th FS/20th FW, Shaw AFB, SC
91-0379	F-16C-50	CC-77	USAF 79th FS/20th FW, Shaw AFB, SC
91-0380	F-16C-50	CC-78	USAF 78th FS/20th FW, Shaw AFB, SC
91-0381	F-16C-50	CC-79	USAF 78th FS/20th FW, Shaw AFB, SC
91-0382	F-16C-50	CC-80	USAF 79th FS/20th FW, Shaw AFB, SC
91-0383	F-16C-50	CC-81	USAF 78th FS/20th FW, Shaw AFB, SC

Block 50 F-16D operated by the 52nd FW at Spangdahlem AB, Germany. GRAHAM FINCH

Serial	Type/Code	c/n	Operator/location	Serial	Type/Code	c/n	Operator/location
91-0384	F-16C-50	CC-82	USAF 78th FS/20th FW, Shaw AFB, SC	91-0465	F-16D-50	CD-20	USAF 77th FS/20th FW, Shaw AFB, SC
91-0385	F-16C-50	CC-83	USAF 78th FS/20th FW, Shaw AFB, SC	91-0466	F-16D-52	CD-21	USAF 389th FS/366th Wg, Mountain Home AFB, ID
91-0386	F-16C-52	CC-84	USAF 389th FS/366th Wg, Mountain Home AFB, ID	91-0467	F-16D-52	CD-22	USAF 422nd TES/53rd Wg, Nellis AFB, NV
91-0387	F-16C-50	CC-85	USAF 78th FS/20th FW, Shaw AFB, SC	91-0468	F-16D-50	CD-23	USAF 79th FS/20th FW, Shaw AFB, SC
91-0388	F-16C-50	CC-86	USAF 78th FS/20th FW, Shaw AFB, SC	91-0469	F-16D-50	CD-24	USAF 78th FS/20th FW, Shaw AFB, SC
91-0389	F-16C-50	CC-87	USAF 78th FS/20th FW, Shaw AFB, SC	91-0470	F-16D-52	CD-25	USAF 422nd TES/53rd Wg, Nellis AFB, NV
91-0390	F-16C-50	CC-88	USAF 78th FS/20th FW, Shaw AFB, SC	91-0471	F-16D-50	CD-26	USAF 13th FS/35th FW, Misawa AB, Japan
91-0391	F-16C-50	CC-89	USAF 78th FS/20th FW, Shaw AFB, SC	91-0472	F-16D-50	CD-27	USAF 23rd FS/52nd FW, Spangdahlem AB, Germany
91-0392	F-16C-52	CC-90	USAF 389th FS/366th Wg, Mountain Home AFB, ID	91-0473	F-16D-52	CD-28	USAF 422nd TES/53rd Wg, Nellis AFB, NV
91-0393	F-16C-52	CC-91	USAF 389th FS/366th Wg, Mountain Home AFB, ID	91-0474	F-16D-50	CD-29	USAF 23rd FS/52nd FW, Spangdahlem AB, Germany
91-0394	F-16C-50	CC-92	USAF 78th FS/20th FW, Shaw AFB, SC	91-0475	F-16D-52	CD-30	USAF 422nd TES/53rd Wg, Nellis AFB, NV
91-0395	F-16C-50	CC-93	USAF 78th FS/20th FW, Shaw AFB, SC	91-0476	F-16D-50	CD-31	USAF 78th FS/20th FW, Shaw AFB, SC
91-0396	F-16C-50	CC-94	USAF 78th FS/20th FW, Shaw AFB, SC	91-0477	F-16D-50	CD-32	USAF 13th FS/35th FW, Misawa AB, Japan
91-0397	F-16C-50	CC-95	USAF 78th FS/20th FW, Shaw AFB, SC	91-0478	F-16D-52	CD-33	USAF 422nd TES/53rd Wg, Nellis AFB, NV
91-0398	F-16C-50	CC-96	USAF 79th FS/20th FW, Shaw AFB, SC	91-0479	F-16D-52	CD-34	USAF 389th FS/366th Wg, Mountain Home AFB, ID
91-0399	F-16C-50	CC-97	USAF 14th FS/35th FW, Misawa AB, Japan	91-0480	F-16D-50	CD-35	USAF 79th FS/20th FW, Shaw AFB, SC
91-0400	F-16C-50	CC-98	USAF 13th FS/35th FW, Misawa AB, Japan	91-0481	F-16D-50	CD-36	USAF 85th TES/53rd Wg, Eglin AFB, FL
91-0401	F-16C-52	CC-99	USAF 389th FS/366th Wg, Mountain Home AFB, ID	92-3880	F-16C-52	CC-122	USAF 389th FS/366th Wg, Mountain Home AFB, ID
91-0402	F-16C-50	CC-100	USAF 23rd FS/52nd FW, Spangdahlem AB, Germany	92-3881	F-16C-52	CC-123	USAF 389th FS/366th Wg, Mountain Home AFB, ID
91-0403	F-16C-50	CC-101	USAF 23rd FS/52nd FW, Spangdahlem AB, Germany	92-3882	F-16C-52	CC-124	USAF 422nd TES/53rd Wg, Nellis AFB, NV
91-0404	F-16C-52	CC-102	USAF 422nd TES/53rd Wg, Nellis AFB, NV	92-3883	F-16C-50	CC-125	USAF 14th FS/35th FW, Misawa AB, Japan
91-0405	F-16C-50	CC-103	USAF 23rd FS/52nd FW, Spangdahlem AB, Germany	92-3884	F-16C-50	CC-126	USAF 13th FS/35th FW, Misawa AB, Japan
91-0406	F-16C-50	CC-104	USAF 23rd FS/52nd FW, Spangdahlem AB, Germany	92-3885	F-16C-52	CC-127	USAF 389th FS/366th Wg, Mountain Home AFB, ID
91-0407	F-16C-50	CC-105	USAF 23rd FS/52nd FW, Spangdahlem AB, Germany	92-3886	F-16C-50	CC-128	USAF 13th FS/35th FW, Misawa AB, Japan
91-0408	F-16C-50	CC-106	USAF 23rd FS/52nd FW, Spangdahlem AB, Germany	92-3887	F-16C-50	CC-129	USAF 13th FS/35th FW, Misawa AB, Japan
91-0409	F-16C-50	CC-107	USAF 23rd FS/52nd FW, Spangdahlem AB, Germany	92-3888	F-16C-50	CC-130	USAF 389th FS/366th Wg, Mountain Home AFB, ID
91-0410	F-16C-50	CC-108	USAF 23rd FS/52nd FW, Spangdahlem AB, Germany	92-3889	F-16C-52	CC-131	USAF 389th FS/366th Wg, Mountain Home AFB, ID
91-0411	F-16C-50	CC-109	USAF 14th FS/35th FW, Misawa AB, Japan	92-3890	F-16C-52	CC-132	USAF 389th FS/366th Wg, Mountain Home AFB, ID
91-0412	F-16C-50	CC-110	USAF 23rd FS/52nd FW, Spangdahlem AB, Germany	92-3891	F-16C-50	CC-133	USAF 13th FS/35th FW, Misawa AB, Japan
91-0413	F-16C-52	CC-111	USAF 389th FS/366th Wg, Mountain Home AFB, ID	92-3892	F-16C-50	CC-134	USAF 13th FS/35th FW, Misawa AB, Japan
91-0414	F-16C-50	CC-112	USAF 23rd FS/52nd FW, Spangdahlem AB, Germany	92-3893	F-16C-50	CC-135	USAF 13th FS/35th FW, Misawa AB, Japan
91-0415	F-16C-50	CC-113	USAF 23rd FS/52nd FW, Spangdahlem AB, Germany	92-3894	F-16C-50	CC-136	USAF 13th FS/35th FW, Misawa AB, Japan
91-0416	F-16C-50	CC-114	USAF 23rd FS/52nd FW, Spangdahlem AB, Germany	92-3895	F-16C-50	CC-137	USAF 13th FS/35th FW, Misawa AB, Japan
91-0417	F-16C-50	CC-115	USAF 23rd FS/52nd FW, Spangdahlem AB, Germany	92-3896	F-16C-52	CC-138	USAF 389th FS/366th Wg, Mountain Home AFB, ID
91-0418	F-16C-50	CC-116	USAF 23rd FS/52nd FW, Spangdahlem AB, Germany	92-3897	F-16C-50	CC-139	USAF 13th FS/35th FW, Misawa AB, Japan
91-0419	F-16C-50	CC-117	USAF 23rd FS/52nd FW, Spangdahlem AB, Germany	92-3898	F-16C-52	CC-140	USAF 389th FS/366th Wg, Mountain Home AFB, ID
91-0420	F-16C-50	CC-118	USAF 23rd FS/52nd FW, Spangdahlem AB, Germany	92-3899	F-16C-52	CC-141	USAF 389th FS/366th Wg, Mountain Home AFB, ID
91-0421	F-16C-50	CC-119	USAF 23rd FS/52nd FW, Spangdahlem AB, Germany	92-3900	F-16C-50	CC-142	USAF 14th FS/35th FW, Misawa AB, Japan
91-0422	F-16C-50	CC-120	USAF 13th FS/35th FW, Misawa AB, Japan	92-3901	F-16C-50	CC-143	USAF 14th FS/35th FW, Misawa AB, Japan
91-0423	F-16C-50	CC-121	USAF 13th FS/35th FW, Misawa AB, Japan	92-3902	F-16C-52	CC-144	USAF 157th FS/169th FW, SC ANG, McEntire ANGS
91-0462	F-16D-50	CD-17	USAF 85th TES/53rd Wg, Eglin AFB, FL	92-3903	F-16C-52	CC-145	USAF 157th FS/169th FW, SC ANG, McEntire ANGS
91-0463	F-16D-50	CD-18	USAF 77th FS/20th FW, Shaw AFB, SC	92-3904	F-16C-50	CC-146	USAF 79th FS/20th FW, Shaw AFB, SC
91-0464	F-16D-50	CD-19	USAF 22nd FS/52nd FW, Spangdahlem AB, Germany	92-3905	F-16C-52	CC-147	USAF 157th FS/169th FW, SC ANG, McEntire ANGS

A 'Red Force' F-16C (of the 414th CTS) comes in to land at Nellis AFB during a Green Flag *exercise.* RICHARD COOPER

Serial	Type/Code	c/n	Operator/location
92-3906	F-16C-50	CC-148	USAF 78th FS/20th FW, Shaw AFB, SC
92-3907	F-16C-50	CC-149	USAF 78th FS/20th FW, Shaw AFB, SC
92-3908	F-16C-52	CC-150	USAF 389th FS/366th Wg, Mountain Home AFB, ID
92-3909	F-16C-52	CC-151	USAF 157th FS/169th FW, SC ANG, McEntire ANGS
92-3910	F-16C-50	CC-152	USAF 79th FS/20th FW, Shaw AFB, SC
92-3911	F-16C-52	CC-153	USAF 157th FS/169th FW, SC ANG, McEntire ANGS
92-3912	F-16C-50	CC-154	USAF 14th FS/35th FW, Misawa AB, Japan
92-3913	F-16C-50	CC-155	USAF 14th FS/35th FW, Misawa AB, Japan
92-3914	F-16C-52	CC-156	USAF 157th FS/169th FW, SC ANG, McEntire ANGS
92-3915	F-16C-50	CC-157	USAF 23rd FS/52nd FW, Spangdahlem AB, Germany
92-3916	F-16C-52	CC-158	USAF 157th FS/169th FW, SC ANG, McEntire ANGS
92-3917	F-16C-52	CC-159	USAF 157th FS/169th FW, SC ANG, McEntire ANGS
92-3918	F-16C-50	CC-160	USAF 23rd FS/52nd FW, Spangdahlem AB, Germany
92-3919	F-16C-50	CC-161	USAF 14th FS/35th FW, Misawa AB, Japan
92-3920	F-16C-50	CC-162	USAF 79th FS/20th FW, Shaw AFB, SC
92-3921	F-16C-50	CC-163	USAF 79th FS/20th FW, Shaw AFB, SC
92-3922	F-16C-52	CC-164	USAF 157th FS/169th FW, SC ANG, McEntire ANGS
92-3923	F-16C-50	CC-165	USAF 79th FS/20th FW, Shaw AFB, SC
92-3924	F-16D-52	CD-37	USAF 422nd TES/53rd Wg, Nellis AFB, NV
92-3925	F-16D-52	CD-38	USAF 157th FS/169th FW, SC ANG, McEntire ANGS
92-3926	F-16D-52	CD-39	USAF 422nd TES/53rd Wg, Nellis AFB, NV
92-3927	F-16D-52	CD-40	USAF 422nd TES/53rd Wg, Nellis AFB, NV
93-0531	F-16C-52	CC-166	USAF 157th FS/169th FW, SC ANG, McEntire ANGS
93-0532	F-16C-50	CC-167	USAF 78th FS/20th FW, Shaw AFB, SC
93-0533	F-16C-52	CC-168	USAF 157th FS/169th FW, SC ANG, McEntire ANGS
93-0534	F-16C-50	CC-169	USAF 78th FS/20th FW, Shaw AFB, SC
93-0535	F-16C-52	CC-170	USAF 157th FS/169th FW, SC ANG, McEntire ANGS
93-0536	F-16C-50	CC-171	USAF 79th FS/20th FW, Shaw AFB, SC
93-0537	F-16C-52	CC-172	USAF 157th FS/169th FW, SC ANG, McEntire ANGS
93-0538	F-16C-50	CC-173	USAF 78th FS/20th FW, Shaw AFB, SC
93-0539	F-16C-52	CC-174	USAF 157th FS/169th FW, SC ANG, McEntire ANGS
93-0540	F-16C-50	CC-175	USAF 78th FS/20th FW, Shaw AFB, SC
93-0541	F-16C-52	CC-176	USAF 389th FS/366th Wg, Mountain Home AFB, ID
93-0542	F-16C-50	CC-177	USAF 78th FS/20th FW, Shaw AFB, SC
93-0543	F-16C-52	CC-178	USAF 157th FS/169th FW, SC ANG, McEntire ANGS
93-0544	F-16C-50	CC-179	USAF 78th FS/20th FW, Shaw AFB, SC
93-0545	F-16C-52	CC-180	USAF 389th FS/366th Wg, Mountain Home AFB, ID
93-0546	F-16C-50	CC-181	USAF 78th FS/20th FW, Shaw AFB, SC
93-0547	F-16C-52	CC-182	USAF 389th FS/366th Wg, Mountain Home AFB, ID
93-0548	F-16C-50	CC-183	USAF 78th FS/20th FW, Shaw AFB, SC
93-0549	F-16C-52	CC-184	USAF 157th FS/169th FW, SC ANG, McEntire ANGS
93-0550	F-16C-50	CC-185	USAF 78th FS/20th FW, Shaw AFB, SC
93-0551	F-16C-52	CC-186	USAF 389th FS/366th Wg, Mountain Home AFB, ID
93-0552	F-16C-50	CC-187	USAF 78th FS/20th FW, Shaw AFB, SC
93-0553	F-16C-52	CC-188	USAF 422nd TES/53rd Wg, Nellis AFB, NV
93-0554	F-16C-50	CC-189	USAF 78th FS/20th FW, Shaw AFB, SC
94-0038	F-16C-50	CC-190	USAF 77th FS/20th FW, Shaw AFB, SC

Serial	Type/Code	c/n	Operator/location
94-0039	F-16C-50	CC-191	USAF ? FS/20th FW, Shaw AFB, SC
94-0040	F-16C-50	CC-192	USAF ? FS/20th FW, Shaw AFB, SC
94-0041	F-16C-50	CC-193	USAF ? FS/20th FW, Shaw AFB, SC
94-0042	F-16C-50	CC-194	USAF ? FS/20th FW, Shaw AFB, SC
94-0043	F-16C-50	CC-195	USAF ? FS/20th FW, Shaw AFB, SC
94-0044	F-16C-50	CC-196	USAF ? FS/20th FW, Shaw AFB, SC
94-0045	F-16C-50	CC-197	USAF ? FS/20th FW, Shaw AFB, SC
94-0046	F-16C-50	CC-198	USAF
94-0047	F-16C-50	CC-199	USAF
94-0048	F-16C-50	CC-200	USAF
94-0049	F-16C-50	CC-201	USAF
96-0080	F-16C-50	CC-202	USAF
96-0081	F-16C-50	CC-203	USAF
96-0082	F-16C-50	CC-204	USAF
96-0083	F-16C-50	CC-205	USAF
96-0084	F-16C-50	CC-206	USAF
96-0085	F-16C-50	CC-207	USAF

3. US NAVY

Serial	Type/Code	c/n	ex	Operator/location
163268	F-16N-30	3M-1	85-1369	AMARC, Davis-Monthan AFB, AZ [1F0013]; arr 11-Jan-95
163269	F-16N-30	3M-2	85-1370	San Diego Aerospace Museum, El Cajon, CA
163270	F-16N-30	3M-3	85-1371	AMARC, Davis-Monthan AFB, AZ [1F0017]; arr 12-Jan-95
163271	F-16N-30	3M-4	85-1372	On display, Santa Rosa, CA
163272	F-16N-30	3M-5	85-1373	AMARC, Davis-Monthan AFB, AZ [1F0003]; arr 30-Jun-94
163273	F-16N-30	3M-6	85-1374	AMARC, Davis-Monthan AFB, AZ [1F0004]; arr 30-Jun-94
163274	F-16N-30	3M-7	85-1375	AMARC, Davis-Monthan AFB, AZ [1F0001]; arr 21-Jun-94
163275	F-16N-30	3M-8	85-1376	AMARC, Davis-Monthan AFB, AZ [1F0011]; arr 10-Jan-95
163276	F-16N-30	3M-9	85-1377	AMARC, Davis-Monthan AFB, AZ [1F0006]; arr 06-Oct-94
163277	F-16N-30	3M-10	85-1378	On display, NAS Miramar, CA
163278	TF-16N-30	3N-1	85-1379	AMARC, Davis-Monthan AFB, AZ [1F0008]; arr 08-Dec-94
163279	TF-16N-30	3N-2	85-1380	AMARC, Davis-Monthan AFB, AZ [1F0015]; arr 11-Jan-95
163280	TF-16N-30	3N-3	85-1381	AMARC, Davis-Monthan AFB, AZ [1F0018]; arr 12-Jan-95
163281	TF-16N-30	3N-4	85-1382	AMARC, Davis-Monthan AFB, AZ [1F0009]; arr 15-Dec-94
163566	F-16N-30	3M-11	86-1684	AMARC, Davis-Monthan AFB, AZ [1F0014]; arr 11-Jan-95
163567	F-16N-30	3M-12	86-1685	AMARC, Davis-Monthan AFB, AZ [1F0005]; arr 06-Oct-94
163568	F-16N-30	3M-13	86-1686	Cr 17-Dec-92 (VF-126)
163569	F-16N-30	3M-14	86-1687	On display, NAS Fort Worth, TX
163570	F-16N-30	3M-15	86-1688	AMARC, Davis-Monthan AFB, AZ [1F0010]; arr 10-Jan-95
163571	F-16N-30	3M-16	86-1689	AMARC, Davis-Monthan AFB, AZ [1F0007]; arr 29-Nov-94
163572	F-16N-30	3M-17	86-1690	On display, USN Museum, NAS Pensacola, FL
163573	F-16N-30	3M-18	86-1691	Wreck at NAS Key West, FL, Feb-95
163574	F-16N-30	3M-19	86-1692	AMARC, Davis-Monthan AFB, AZ [1F0002]; arr 21-Jun-94
163575	F-16N-30	3M-20	86-1693	AMARC, Davis-Monthan AFB, AZ [1F0016]; arr 12-Jan-95
163576	F-16N-30	3M-21	86-1694	On display, NAS Fallon, NV
163577	F-16N-30	3M-22	86-1695	AMARC, Davis-Monthan AFB, AZ [1F0012]; arr 10-Jan-95

Photographed in April 1994, this F-16N (163575) was then operated by VF-43 at NAS Oceana. PETER R FOSTER

Belgian Air Force F-16A FA-18 was painted in 350 Sqn anniversary colours in 1987. BOB ARCHER

1. EUROPE

BELGIUM – Belgian Air Force – Force Aerienne Belge/Belgische Luchtmacht (FAB)

Serial	Type/Code	c/n	ex	Operator/location
FA01	S-GD F-16A-01	6H-1	78-0116	Brussels Air Museum
FA02	S-GD F-16A-01	6H-2	78-0117	FAB stored, Weelde
FA03	S-GD F-16A-01	6H-3	78-0118	Royal Technical School, Saffraanberg
FA04	S-GD F-16A-01	6H-4	78-0119	FAB stored, Weelde
FA05	S-GD F-16A-01	6H-5	78-0120	FAB stored, Weelde
FA06	S-GD F-16A-01	6H-6	78-0121	Cr 02-Sep-85 (350 Sm)
FA07	S-GD F-16A-01	6H-7	78-0122	Cr 10-Nov-83 (350 Sm)
FA08	S-GD F-16A-01	6H-8	78-0123	Cr 28-Jul-80 (350 Sm)
FA09	S-GD F-16A-01	6H-9	78-0124	FAB stored, Weelde
FA10	S-GD F-16A-01	6H-10	78-0125	FAB stored, Weelde
FA11	S-GD F-16A-01	6H-11	78-0126	Cr 12-Mar-81 (350 Sm)
FA12	S-GD F-16A-01	6H-12	78-0127	Cr 18-Oct-89 (350 Sm)
FA13	S-GD F-16A-01	6H-13	78-0128	Cr 10-May-83 (349 Sm)
FA14	S-GD F-16A-01	6H-14	78-0129	Cr 19-Jan-82 (1 Wg)
FA15	S-GD F-16A-01	6H-15	78-0130	Cr 17-Nov-88 (350 Sm)
FA16	S-GD F-16A-01	6H-16	78-0131	FAB stored, Weelde
FA17	S-GD F-16A-01	6H-17	78-0132	FAB stored, Weelde
FA18	S-GD F-16A-05	6H-18	78-0133	FAB stored, Weelde
FA19	S-GD F-16A-05	6H-19	78-0134	FAB stored, Weelde
FA20	S-GD F-16A-05	6H-20	78-0135	FAB stored, Weelde
FA21	S-GD F-16A-05	6H-21	78-0136	FAB stored, Weelde
FA22	S-GD F-16A-05	6H-22	78-0137	FAB stored, Weelde
FA23	S-GD F-16A-05	6H-23	78-0138	FAB stored, Weelde
FA24	S-GD F-16A-05	6H-24	78-0139	Cr 29-Apr-85 (1 Wg)
FA25	S-GD F-16A-05	6H-25	78-0140	FAB stored, Weelde
FA26	S-GD F-16A-10	6H-26	78-0141	FAB stored, Weelde
FA27	S-GD F-16A-10	6H-27	78-0142	FAB (Carapace test aircraft)
FA28	S-GD F-16A-10	6H-28	78-0143	FAB stored, Weelde
FA29	S-GD F-16A-10	6H-29	78-0144	Cr 22-Oct-81 (1 Wg)
FA30	S-GD F-16A-10	6H-30	78-0145	FAB stored, Weelde
FA31	S-GD F-16A-10	6H-31	78-0146	FAB stored, Weelde
FA32	S-GD F-16A-10	6H-32	78-0147	FAB stored, Weelde
FA33	S-GD F-16A-10	6H-33	78-0148	Cr 19-Aug-86 (349 Sm)
FA34	S-GD F-16A-10	6H-34	78-0149	FAB stored, Weelde
FA35	S-GD F-16A-10	6H-35	78-0150	Cr 19-Oct-82 (1 Wg)
FA36	S-GD F-16A-10	6H-36	78-0151	FAB stored, Weelde
FA37	S-GD F-16A-10	6H-37	78-0152	FAB stored, Weelde
FA38	S-GD F-16A-10	6H-38	78-0153	FAB stored, Weelde
FA39	S-GD F-16A-10	6H-39	78-0154	FAB 23 Sm (10 Wg), Kleine-Brogel
FA40	S-GD F-16A-10	6H-40	78-0155	FAB stored, Weelde
FA41	S-GD F-16A-10	6H-41	78-0156	Cr 10-Nov-83 (350 Sm)
FA42	S-GD F-16A-10	6H-42	78-0157	Cr 09-Oct-86 (1 Wg)
FA43	S-GD F-16A-10	6H-43	78-0158	FAB stored, Weelde
FA44	S-GD F-16A-10	6H-44	78-0159	FAB stored, Weelde
FA45	S-GD F-16A-10	6H-45	78-0160	FAB stored, Weelde
FA46	S-GD F-16A-10	6H-46	78-0161	FAB stored, Weelde
FA47	S-GD F-16A-10	6H-47	80-3538	FAB 349 Sm (10 Wg), Kleine-Brogel
FA48	S-GD F-16A-10(MLU)	6H-48	80-3539	FAB/SABCA, Gosselies
FA49	S-GD F-16A-10	6H-49	80-3540	FAB 349 Sm (10 Wg), Kleine-Brogel
FA50	S-GD F-16A-10	6H-50	80-3541	FAB 350 Sm (2 Wg), Florennes
FA51	S-GD F-16A-10	6H-51	80-3542	FAB stored, Weelde
FA52	S-GD F-16A-10	6H-52	80-3543	Cr 19-Sep-87 (350 Sm)
FA53	S-GD F-16A-10	6H-53	80-3544	FAB 349 Sm (10 Wg), Kleine-Brogel
FA54	S-GD F-16A-10	6H-54	80-3545	Cr 18-Oct-89 (350 Sm)
FA55	S-GD F-16A-10	6H-55	80-3546	FAB 349 Sm (10 Wg), Kleine-Brogel
FA56	S-GD F-16A-15	6H-56	80-3547	FAB 23 Sm (10 Wg), Kleine-Brogel
FA57	S-GD F-16A-15	6H-57	80-3548	FAB 23 Sm (10 Wg), Kleine-Brogel
FA58	S-GD F-16A-15	6H-58	80-3549	FAB 23 Sm (10 Wg), Kleine-Brogel
FA59	S-GD F-16A-15	6H-59	80-3550	Cr 20-Sep-83 (10 Wg)
FA60	S-GD F-16A-15	6H-60	80-3551	FAB 23 Sm (10 Wg), Kleine-Brogel
FA61	S-GD F-16A-15	6H-61	80-3552	FAB 349 Sm (10 Wg), Kleine-Brogel
FA62	S-GD F-16A-15	6H-62	80-3553	Cr 17-Nov-88 (31 Sm)
FA63	S-GD F-16A-15	6H-63	80-3554	Cr 14-Sep-87 (23 Sm)
FA64	S-GD F-16A-15	6H-64	80-3555	Cr 07-Sep-93 (31 Sm)
FA65	S-GD F-16A-15	6H-65	80-3556	FAB 23 Sm (10 Wg), Kleine-Brogel
FA66	S-GD F-16A-15	6H-66	80-3557	FAB 31 Sm (10 Wg), Kleine-Brogel
FA67	S-GD F-16A-15	6H-67	80-3558	FAB 23 Sm (10 Wg), Kleine-Brogel
FA68	S-GD F-16A-15	6H-68	80-3559	FAB 2 Sm (2 Wg), Florennes
FA69	S-GD F-16A-15	6H-69	80-3560	FAB 1 Sm (2 Wg), Florennes
FA70	S-GD F-16A-15	6H-70	80-3561	FAB 2 Sm (2 Wg), Florennes
FA71	S-GD F-16A-15	6H-71	80-3562	FAB 23 Sm (10 Wg), Kleine-Brogel
FA72	S-GD F-16A-15	6H-72	80-3563	FAB 31 Sm (10 Wg), Kleine-Brogel

Another colourful Belgian AF F-16A was FA-49, this time marking the anniversary of 349 Sqn. JEREMY FLACK/API

Serial	Type/Code	c/n	ex	Operator/location	Serial	Type/Code	c/n	ex	Operator/location
FA73	S-GD F-16A-15	6H-73	80-3564	FAB 23 Sm (10 Wg), Kleine-Brogel	FA94	S-GD F-16A-15/F-16A(R)	6H-94	80-3585	FAB 1 Sm (2 Wg), Florennes
FA74	S-GD F-16A-15	6H-74	80-3565	FAB 31 Sm (10 Wg), Kleine-Brogel	FA95	S-GD F-16A-15	6H-95	80-3586	FAB 349 Sm (10 Wg), Kleine-Brogel
FA75	S-GD F-16A-15	6H-75	80-3566	FAB 350 Sm (2 Wg), Florennes	FA96	S-GD F-16A-15	6H-96	80-3587	FAB 1 Sm (2 Wg), Florennes
FA76	S-GD F-16A-15	6H-76	80-3567	FAB 350 Sm (2 Wg), Florennes	FA97	S-GD F-16A-15	6H-97	86-0073	FAB 349 Sm (10 Wg), Kleine-Brogel
FA77	S-GD F-16A-15	6H-77	80-3568	FAB 1 Sm (2 Wg), Florennes	FA98	S-GD F-16A-15	6H-98	86-0074	FAB 2 Sm (2 Wg), Florennes
FA78	S-GD F-16A-15	6H-78	80-3569	FAB 31 Sm (10 Wg), Kleine-Brogel	FA99	S-GD F-16A-15	6H-99	86-0075	FAB 349 Sm (10 Wg), Kleine-Brogel
FA79	S-GD F-16A-15	6H-79	80-3570	Cr 30-Jun-86 (31 Sm)	FA100	S-GD F-16A-15	6H-100	86-0076	FAB 349 Sm (10 Wg), Kleine-Brogel
FA80	S-GD F-16A-15	6H-80	80-3571	FAB 349 Sm (10 Wg), Kleine-Brogel	FA101	S-GD F-16A-15	6H-101	86-0077	FAB 1 Sm (2 Wg), Florennes
FA81	S-GD F-16A-15	6H-81	80-3572	FAB 1 Sm (2 Wg), Florennes	FA102	S-GD F-16A-15	6H-102	87-0046	FAB 2 Sm (2 Wg), Florennes
FA82	S-GD F-16A-15/F-16A(R)	6H-82	80-3573	FAB 1 Sm (2 Wg), Florennes	FA103	S-GD F-16A-15	6H-103	87-0047	FAB 350 Sm (2 Wg), Florennes
FA83	S-GD F-16A-15	6H-83	80-3574	FAB 349 Sm (10 Wg), Kleine-Brogel	FA104	S-GD F-16A-15	6H-104	87-0048	FAB 2 Sm (2 Wg), Florennes
FA84	S-GD F-16A-15	6H-84	80-3575	FAB (2 Wg), Florennes	FA105	S-GD F-16A-15	6H-105	87-0049	Cr 05-Sep-89 (1 Sm)
FA85	S-GD F-16A-15	6H-85	80-3576	Cr 25-Oct-89 (23 Sm)	FA106	S-GD F-16A-15	6H-106	87-0050	FAB 2 Sm (2 Wg), Florennes
FA86	S-GD F-16A-15	6H-86	80-3577	FAB 31 Sm (10 Wg), Kleine-Brogel	FA107	S-GD F-16A-15	6H-107	87-0051	FAB 1 Sm (2 Wg), Florennes
FA87	S-GD F-16A-15	6H-87	80-3578	FAB 23 Sm (10 Wg), Kleine-Brogel	FA108	S-GD F-16A-15	6H-108	87-0052	FAB 2 Sm (2 Wg), Florennes
FA88	S-GD F-16A-15	6H-88	80-3579	FAB 350 Sm (2 Wg), Florennes	FA109	S-GD F-16A-15	6H-109	87-0053	FAB 1 Sm (2 Wg), Florennes
FA89	S-GD F-16A-15	6H-89	80-3580	FAB 1 Sm (2 Wg), Florennes	FA110	S-GD F-16A-15	6H-110	87-0054	FAB 350 Sm (2 Wg), Florennes
FA90	S-GD F-16A-15	6H-90	80-3581	FAB 31 Sm (10 Wg), Kleine-Brogel	FA111	S-GD F-16A-15	6H-111	87-0055	FAB 1 Sm (2 Wg), Florennes
FA91	S-GD F-16A-15	6H-91	80-3582	FAB 349 Sm (10 Wg), Kleine-Brogel	FA112	S-GD F-16A-15	6H-112	87-0056	FAB 2 Sm (2 Wg), Florennes
FA92	S-GD F-16A-15/F-16A(R)	6H-92	80-3583	FAB 31 Sm (10 Wg), Kleine-Brogel	FA113	S-GD F-16A-15	6H-113	88-0038	Cr 12-May-95 (23 Sm)
FA93	S-GD F-16A-15(MLU)	6H-93	80-3584	FAB/F-16 MLU Test Team, Leeuwarden	FA114	S-GD F-16A-15	6H-114	88-0039	FAB 349 Sm (10 Wg), Kleine-Brogel
					FA115	S-GD F-16A-15(MLU)	6H-115	88-0040	FAB 2 Wg, Florennes
					FA116	S-GD F-16A-15	6H-116	88-0041	FAB 350 Sm (2 Wg), Florennes
					FA117	S-GD F-16A-15	6H-117	88-0042	FAB 349 Sm (10 Wg), Kleine-Brogel
					FA118	S-GD F-16A-15	6H-118	88-0043	FAB 2 Sm (2 Wg), Florennes
					FA119	S-GD F-16A-15	6H-119	88-0044	FAB 1 Sm (2 Wg), Florennes
					FA120	S-GD F-16A-15	6H-120	88-0045	FAB 31 Sm (10 Wg), Kleine-Brogel
					FA121	S-GD F-16A-15	6H-121	88-0046	FAB 1 Sm (2 Wg), Florennes
					FA122	S-GD F-16A-15	6H-122	88-0047	FAB 2 Sm (2 Wg), Florennes
					FA123	S-GD F-16A-15	6H-123	89-0001	FAB 349 Sm (10 Wg), Kleine-Brogel
					FA124	S-GD F-16A-15	6H-124	89-0002	FAB 23 Sm (10 Wg), Kleine-Brogel
					FA125	S-GD F-16A-15	6H-125	89-0003	FAB 1 Sm (2 Wg), Florennes
					FA126	S-GD F-16A-15	6H-126	89-0004	FAB 349 Sm (10 Wg), Kleine-Brogel
					FA127	S-GD F-16A-15	6H-127	89-0005	FAB 1 Sm (2 Wg), Florennes
					FA128	S-GD F-16A-15	6H-128	89-0006	FAB 2 Sm (2 Wg), Florennes
					FA129	S-GD F-16A-15	6H-129	89-0007	FAB 1 Sm (2 Wg), Florennes
					FA130	S-GD F-16A-15	6H-130	89-0008	FAB 2 Sm (2 Wg), Florennes
					FA131	S-GD F-16A-15	6H-131	89-0009	FAB 1 Sm (2 Wg), Florennes
					FA132	S-GD F-16A-15	6H-132	89-0010	FAB 2 Sm (2 Wg), Florennes
					FA133	S-GD F-16A-15	6H-133	89-0011	FAB 349 Sm (10 Wg), Kleine-Brogel

F-16A FA-115 carried Kleine-Brogel 50th anniversary colours in 1995. PETER R MARCH

Serial	Type/Code	c/n	ex	Operator/location
FA134	S-GD F-16A-15	6H-134	90-0025	FAB 2 Sm (2 Wg), Florennes
FA135	S-GD F-16A-15	6H-135	90-0026	FAB 1 Sm (2 Wg), Florennes
FA136	S-GD F-16A-15	6H-136	90-0027	FAB 23 Sm (10 Wg), Kleine-Brogel
FB01	S-GD F-16B-01	6J-1	78-0162	FAB OCU (10 Wg), Kleine-Brogel
FB02	S-GD F-16B-01	6J-2	78-0163	FAB OCU (10 Wg), Kleine-Brogel
FB03	S-GD F-16B-01	6J-3	78-0164	FAB stored, Weelde
FB04	S-GD F-16B-01	6J-4	78-0165	FAB OCU (10 Wg), Kleine-Brogel
FB05	S-GD F-16B-01	6J-5	78-0166	FAB OCU (10 Wg), Kleine-Brogel
FB06	S-GD F-16B-01	6J-6	78-0167	Cr 14-Jul-89 (1 Wg)
FB07	S-GD F-16B-05	6J-7	78-0168	FAB OCU (10 Wg), Kleine-Brogel
FB08	S-GD F-16B-05	6J-8	78-0169	FAB OCU (10 Wg), Kleine-Brogel
FB09	S-GD F-16B-05	6J-9	78-0170	FAB OCU (10 Wg), Kleine-Brogel
FB10	S-GD F-16B-05	6J-10	78-0171	FAB OCU (10 Wg), Kleine-Brogel
FB11	S-GD F-16B-10	6J-11	78-0172	Cr 23-Jun-93 (SABCA)
FB12	S-GD F-16B-10	6J-12	78-0173	FAB 2 Sm (2 Wg), Florennes
FB13	S-GD F-16B-15	6J-13	80-3588	Cr 09-Jan-92 (10 Wg)
FB14	S-GD F-16B-15	6J-14	80-3589	FAB 2 Wg, Florennes
FB15	S-GD F-16B-15	6J-15	80-3590	FAB 1 Sm (2 Wg), Florennes
FB16	S-GD F-16B-15	6J-16	80-3591	Cr 19-Sep-84 (10 Wg)
FB17	S-GD F-16B-15	6J-17	80-3592	FAB OCU (10 Wg), Kleine-Brogel
FB18	S-GD F-16B-15	6J-18	80-3593	FAB OCU (10 Wg), Kleine-Brogel
FB19	S-GD F-16B-15	6J-19	80-3594	FAB 350 Sm (2 Wg), Florennes
FB20	S-GD F-16B-15	6J-20	80-3595	FAB 2 Wg, Florennes
FB21	S-GD F-16B-15(MLU)	6J-21	87-0001	FAB/F-16 MLU Test Team, Leeuwarden
FB22	S-GD F-16B-15(MLU)	6J-22	88-0048	FAB/SABCA, Gosselies
FB23	S-GD F-16B-15	6J-23	88-0049	FAB 1 Sm (2 Wg), Florennes
FB24	S-GD F-16B-15	6J-24	89-0012	FAB 2 Sm (2 Wg), Florennes

DENMARK – Royal Danish Air Force – Kongelige Danske Flyvevaabnet (KDF)

Serial	Type/Code	c/n	ex	Operator/location
E-004	S-GD F-16A-15	6F-47	87-0004	KDF Esk 726, Aalborg
E-005	S-GD F-16A-15	6F-48	87-0005	KDF Esk 726, Aalborg
E-006	S-GD F-16A-15	6F-49	87-0006	KDF Esk 726, Aalborg
E-007	S-GD F-16A-15	6F-50	87-0007	KDF Esk 726, Aalborg
E-008	S-GD F-16A-15	6F-51	87-0008	KDF Esk 726, Aalborg
E-011	GD F-16A-15	61-604	82-1011	KDF, Aalborg
E-016	S-GD F-16A-15	6F-52	88-0016	KDF Esk 726, Aalborg
E-017	S-GD F-16A-15	6F-53	88-0017	KDF Esk 726, Aalborg
E-018	S-GD F-16A-15	6F-54	88-0018	KDF Esk 726, Aalborg
E-024	GD F-16A-15	61-617/M12-1	82-1024	KDF Esk 723, Aalborg
E-069	GD F-16A-15	61-622	83-1069	KDF, Aalborg
E-070	GD F-16A-15	61-623	83-1070	KDF, Aalborg
E-074	GD F-16A-15	61-627	83-1074	KDF, Aalborg
E-075	GD F-16A-15	61-628/M12-2	83-1075	KDF, Aalborg
E-107	GD F-16A-15	61-660/M12-3	83-1107	KDF, Aalborg
E-174	S-GD F-16A-01	6F-1	78-0174	KDF Esk 727, Skrydstrup
E-175	S-GD F-16A-01	6F-2	78-0175	Cr 05-Apr-83 (Esk 730)
E-176	S-GD F-16A-01	6F-3	78-0176	KDF Esk 723, Aalborg
E-177	S-GD F-16A-05	6F-4	78-0177	KDF/F-16 MLU Test Team, Leeuwarden
E-178	S-GD F-16A-05	6F-5	78-0178	KDF Esk 730, Skrydstrup
E-179	S-GD F-16A-05	6F-6	78-0179	Cr 01-Apr-85 (Esk 730)
E-180	S-GD F-16A-05	6F-7	78-0180	KDF Esk 726, Aalborg
E-181	S-GD F-16A-05	6F-8	78-0181	KDF Esk 723, Aalborg
E-182	S-GD F-16A-05	6F-9	78-0182	KDF Esk 730, Skrydstrup
E-183	S-GD F-16A-05	6F-10	78-0183	KDF Esk 723, Aalborg
E-184	S-GD F-16A-05	6F-11	78-0184	KDF Esk 723, Aalborg
E-185	S-GD F-16A-05	6F-12	78-0185	Cr 10-Dec-87 (Esk 730)
E-186	S-GD F-16A-05	6F-13	78-0186	Cr 01-Apr-85 (Esk 730)
E-187	S-GD F-16A-05	6F-14	78-0187	KDF Esk 727, Skrydstrup
E-188	S-GD F-16A-05	6F-15	78-0188	KDF Esk 723, Aalborg
E-189	S-GD F-16A-10	6F-16	78-0189	KDF Esk 723, Aalborg
E-190	S-GD F-16A-10	6F-17	78-0190	KDF Esk 723, Aalborg
E-191	S-GD F-16A-10	6F-18	78-0191	KDF Esk 730, Skrydstrup
E-192	S-GD F-16A-10	6F-19	78-0192	KDF Esk 730, Skrydstrup
E-193	S-GD F-16A-10	6F-20	78-0193	KDF Esk 727, Skrydstrup
E-194	S-GD F-16A-10	6F-21	78-0194	KDF Esk 730, Skrydstrup
E-195	S-GD F-16A-10	6F-22	78-0195	KDF Esk 723, Aalborg
E-196	S-GD F-16A-10	6F-23	78-0196	KDF Esk 723, Aalborg
E-197	S-GD F-16A-10	6F-24	78-0197	KDF Esk 723, Aalborg
E-198	S-GD F-16A-10	6F-25	78-0198	KDF Esk 730, Skrydstrup
E-199	S-GD F-16A-10	6F-26	78-0199	KDF Esk 723, Aalborg
E-200	S-GD F-16A-10	6F-27	78-0200	KDF Esk 723, Aalborg
E-201	S-GD F-16A-10	6F-28	78-0201	Cr 07-Dec-87 (Esk 723)
E-202	S-GD F-16A-10	6F-29	78-0202	KDF Esk 730, Skrydstrup
E-203	S-GD F-16A-10	6F-30	78-0203	KDF Esk 723, Aalborg
E-596	S-GD F-16A-15	6F-31	80-3596	KDF Esk 723, Aalborg
E-597	S-GD F-16A-15	6F-32	80-3597	KDF Esk 730, Skrydstrup
E-598	S-GD F-16A-15	6F-33	80-3598	KDF Esk 730, Skrydstrup
E-599	S-GD F-16A-15	6F-34	80-3599	KDF Esk 730, Skrydstrup
E-600	S-GD F-16A-15	6F-35	80-3600	KDF Esk 727, Skrydstrup
E-601	S-GD F-16A-15	6F-36	80-3601	KDF Esk 727, Skrydstrup
E-602	S-GD F-16A-15	6F-37	80-3602	KDF Esk 730, Skrydstrup
E-603	S-GD F-16A-15	6F-38	80-3603	KDF Esk 727, Skrydstrup
E-604	S-GD F-16A-15	6F-39	80-3604	KDF Esk 726, Aalborg
E-605	S-GD F-16A-15	6F-40	80-3605	KDF Esk 727, Skrydstrup
E-606	S-GD F-16A-15	6F-41	80-3606	KDF Esk 730, Skrydstrup
E-607	S-GD F-16A-15	6F-42	80-3607	KDF Esk 723, Aalborg
E-608	S-GD F-16A-15	6F-43	80-3608	KDF Esk 723, Aalborg
E-609	S-GD F-16A-15	6F-44	80-3609	KDF Esk 727, Skrydstrup
E-610	S-GD F-16A-15	6F-45	80-3610	KDF Esk 727, Skrydstrup
E-611	S-GD F-16A-15	6F-46	80-3611	KDF Esk 727, Skrydstrup
ET-022	F-GD F-16B-15	6G-16	87-0022	KDF Esk 730, Skrydstrup
ET-197	F-GD F-16B-15	6G-13	86-0197	KDF Esk 726, Aalborg
ET-198	F-GD F-16B-15	6G-14	86-0198	KDF Esk 726, Aalborg
ET-199	F-GD F-16B-15	6G-15	86-0199	KDF Esk 726, Aalborg
ET-204	S-GD F-16B-01(MLU)	6G-1	78-0204	KDF Esk 727, Skrydstrup
ET-205	S-GD F-16B-01	6G-2	78-0205	Cr 11-Dec-96 (Esk 730)
ET-206	S-GD F-16B-05	6G-3	78-0206	KDF Esk 730, Skrydstrup
ET-207	S-GD F-16B-05	6G-4	78-0207	KDF Esk 727, Skrydstrup
ET-208	S-GD F-16B-05	6G-5	78-0208	KDF Esk 730, Skrydstrup

Royal Danish Air Force F-16B ET-206 remains in service with Esk 727 at Skrydstrup. GRAHAM FINCH

F-16A E-177 is the first RDAF single-seater to have the Mid Life Update. GRAHAM FINCH

Serial	Type/Code	c/n	ex	Operator/location
ET-209	S-GD F-16B-10	6G-6	78-0209	Cr 19-Jun-84 (Esk 730)
ET-210	S-GD F-16B-10	6G-7	78-0210	KDF Esk 726, Aalborg
ET-211	S-GD F-16B-10	6G-8	78-0211	Cr 19-Jun-84 (Esk 723)
ET-612	S-GD F-16B-15	6G-9	80-3612	KDF Esk 727, Skrydstrup
ET-613	S-GD F-16B-15	6G-10	80-3613	MLU conversion
ET-614	S-GD F-16B-15	6G-11	80-3614	KDF Esk 723, Aalborg
ET-615	S-GD F-16B-15	6G-12	80-3615	KDF Esk 727, Skrydstrup
J-234	F-GD F-16A-05	6D-23	78-0234	KDF, Aalborg, spares use (ex KLu)

GREECE – Hellenic Air Force – Elliniki Aeroporia (EA)

Serial	Type/Code	c/n	ex	Operator/location
110	GD F-16C-30	2Y-1	88-0110	EA 346 Mira, Nea Ankhialos
111	GD F-16C-30	2Y-2	88-0111	EA 330 Mira, Nea Ankhialos
112	GD F-16C-30	2Y-3	88-0112	EA 346 Mira, Nea Ankhialos
113	GD F-16C-30	2Y-4	88-0113	EA 330 Mira, Nea Ankhialos
114	GD F-16C-30	2Y-5	88-0114	EA 346 Mira, Nea Ankhialos
115	GD F-16C-30	2Y-6	88-0115	EA 330 Mira, Nea Ankhialos
116	GD F-16C-30	2Y-7	88-0116	EA 346 Mira, Nea Ankhialos

Serial	Type/Code	c/n	ex	Operator/location
117	GD F-16C-30	2Y-8	88-0117	EA 330 Mira, Nea Ankhialos
118	GD F-16C-30	2Y-9	88-0118	EA 346 Mira, Nea Ankhialos
119	GD F-16C-30	2Y-10	88-0119	EA 330 Mira, Nea Ankhialos
120	GD F-16C-30	2Y-11	88-0120	EA 346 Mira, Nea Ankhialos
121	GD F-16C-30	2Y-12	88-0121	EA 330 Mira, Nea Ankhialos
122	GD F-16C-30	2Y-13	88-0122	EA 346 Mira, Nea Ankhialos
123	GD F-16C-30	2Y-14	88-0123	EA 330 Mira, Nea Ankhialos
124	GD F-16C-30	2Y-15	88-0124	EA 346 Mira, Nea Ankhialos
125	GD F-16C-30	2Y-16	88-0125	EA 330 Mira, Nea Ankhialos
126	GD F-16C-30	2Y-17	88-0126	EA 346 Mira, Nea Ankhialos
127	GD F-16C-30	2Y-18	88-0127	EA 330 Mira, Nea Ankhialos
128	GD F-16C-30	2Y-19	88-0128	EA 346 Mira, Nea Ankhialos
129	GD F-16C-30	2Y-20	88-0129	EA 330 Mira, Nea Ankhialos
130	GD F-16C-30	2Y-21	88-0130	EA 346 Mira, Nea Ankhialos
131	GD F-16C-30	2Y-22	88-0131	EA 330 Mira, Nea Ankhialos
132	GD F-16C-30	2Y-23	88-0132	EA 346 Mira, Nea Ankhialos
133	GD F-16C-30	2Y-24	88-0133	EA 330 Mira, Nea Ankhialos
134	GD F-16C-30	2Y-25	88-0134	EA 346 Mira, Nea Ankhialos
135	GD F-16C-30	2Y-26	88-0135	Cr 15-Jul-93 (330 Mira)
136	GD F-16C-30	2Y-27	88-0136	EA 346 Mira, Nea Ankhialos
137	GD F-16C-30	2Y-28	88-0137	Cr 26-Nov-92 (330 Mira)
138	GD F-16C-30	2Y-29	88-0138	EA 330 Mira, Nea Ankhialos
139	GD F-16C-30	2Y-30	88-0139	EA 330 Mira, Nea Ankhialos
140	GD F-16C-30	2Y-31	88-0140	EA 346 Mira, Nea Ankhialos
141	GD F-16C-30	2Y-32	88-0141	EA 330 Mira, Nea Ankhialos
142	GD F-16C-30	2Y-33	88-0142	Cr 06-Oct-95
143	GD F-16C-30	2Y-34	88-0143	EA 330 Mira, Nea Ankhialos
144	GD F-16D-30	2Z-1	88-0144	EA 346 Mira, Nea Ankhialos
145	GD F-16D-30	2Z-2	88-0145	EA 330 Mira, Nea Ankhialos
146	GD F-16D-30	2Z-3	88-0146	EA 346 Mira, Nea Ankhialos
147	GD F-16D-30	2Z-4	88-0147	EA 330 Mira, Nea Ankhialos
148	GD F-16D-30	2Z-5	88-0148	EA 346 Mira, Nea Ankhialos
149	GD F-16D-30	2Z-6	88-0149	EA 330 Mira, Nea Ankhialos

On order: 32 LMTAS F-16C-50s (c/n TC-1 to TC-32, ex 93-1045 to 93-1076), plus 8 LMTAS F-16D-50s (c/n TD-1 to TD-8, ex 93-1077 to 93-1084)

The penultimate F-16D (148) in service with the Hellenic Air Force at Nea Ankhialos. PETER R FOSTER

NETHERLANDS – Royal Netherlands Air Force – Koninklijke Luchtmacht (KLu)

Serial	Type/Code	c/n	ex	Operator/location
J-001	F-GD F-16A-15	6D-157	88-0001	KLu 312 Sqn, Volkel
J-002	F-GD F-16A-15	6D-158	88-0002	KLu 315 Sqn, Twenthe
J-003	F-GD F-16A-15	6D-159	88-0003	KLu 312 Sqn, Volkel
J-004	F-GD F-16A-15	6D-160	88-0004	KLu 311 Sqn, Volkel
J-005	F-GD F-16A-15	6D-161	88-0005	KLu 315 Sqn, Twenthe
J-006	F-GD F-16A-15	6D-162	88-0006	KLu 315 Sqn, Twenthe
J-007	F-GD F-16A-15	6D-163	88-0007	Cr 10-Jan-92 (313 Sqn)
J-008	F-GD F-16A-15	6D-164	88-0008	KLu 315 Sqn, Twenthe
J-009	F-GD F-16A-15	6D-165	88-0009	KLu 315 Sqn, Twenthe
J-010	F-GD F-16A-15	6D-166	88-0010	KLu 312 Sqn, Volkel
J-011	F-GD F-16A-15	6D-167	88-0011	KLu 315 Sqn, Twenthe
J-012	F-GD F-16A-15	6D-168	88-0012	Cr 10-Jan-96 (315 Sqn)
J-013	F-GD F-16A-15	6D-169	89-0013	KLu 312 Sqn, Volkel
J-014	F-GD F-16A-15	6D-170	89-0014	KLu 315 Sqn, Twenthe
J-015	F-GD F-16A-15	6D-171	89-0015	KLu 312 Sqn, Volkel
J-016	F-GD F-16A-15	6D-172	89-0016	KLu 311 Sqn, Volkel
J-017	F-GD F-16A-15	6D-173	89-0017	KLu 315 Sqn, Twenthe
J-018	F-GD F-16A-15	6D-174	89-0018	KLu 311 Sqn, Volkel
J-019	F-GD F-16A-15	6D-175	89-0019	KLu 311 Sqn, Volkel
J-020	F-GD F-16A-15	6D-176	89-0020	KLu 315 Sqn, Twenthe
J-021	F-GD F-16A-15	6D-177	89-0021	KLu 312 Sqn, Volkel
J-054	F-GD F-16A-15	6D-137	86-0054	Cr 11-Feb-92 (315 Sqn)
J-055	F-GD F-16A-15	6D-138	86-0055	MLU conversion, Woensdrecht
J-056	F-GD F-16A-15	6D-139	86-0056	Cr 19-Apr-89 (315 Sqn)
J-057	F-GD F-16A-15	6D-140	86-0057	MLU conversion, Woensdrecht
J-058	F-GD F-16A-15	6D-141	86-0058	KLu 311 Sqn, Volkel
J-059	F-GD F-16A-15	6D-142	86-0059	KLu 315 Sqn, Twenthe
J-060	F-GD F-16A-15	6D-143	86-0060	KLu 306 Sqn, Volkel
J-061	F-GD F-16A-15	6D-144	86-0061	KLu 311 Sqn, Volkel
J-062	F-GD F-16A-15	6D-145	86-0062	KLu 312 Sqn, Volkel
J-063	F-GD F-16A-15	6D-146	86-0063	KLu 312 Sqn, Volkel
J-064	F-GD F-16B-15	6E-33	86-0064	KLu 312 Sqn, Volkel
J-065	F-GD F-16B-15	6E-34	86-0065	KLu 311 Sqn, Volkel
J-066	F-GD F-16B-15	6E-35	87-0066	KLu 311 Sqn, Volkel
J-067	F-GD F-16B-15	6E-36	87-0067	KLu 312 Sqn, Volkel
J-068	F-GD F-16B-15	6E-37	87-0068	KLu 312 Sqn, Volkel
J-135	F-GD F-16A-15	6D-125	85-0135	KLu 315 Sqn, Twenthe
J-136	F-GD F-16A-15	6D-126	85-0136	KLu 322 Sqn, Leeuwarden
J-137	F-GD F-16A-15	6D-127	85-0137	KLu 322 Sqn, Leeuwarden
J-138	F-GD F-16A-15	6D-128	85-0138	KLu 323 Sqn, Leeuwarden
J-139	F-GD F-16A-15	6D-129	85-0139	KLu 323 Sqn, Leeuwarden
J-140	F-GD F-16A-15	6D-130	85-0140	KLu 322 Sqn, Leeuwarden
J-141	F-GD F-16A-15	6D-131	85-0141	KLu 323 Sqn, Leeuwarden
J-142	F-GD F-16A-15	6D-132	85-0142	KLu 323 Sqn, Leeuwarden
J-143	F-GD F-16A-15	6D-133	85-0143	KLu 323 Sqn, Leeuwarden
J-144	F-GD F-16A-15	6D-134	85-0144	KLu 323 Sqn, Leeuwarden
J-145	F-GD F-16A-15	6D-135	85-0145	KLu 315 Sqn, Twenthe
J-146	F-GD F-16A-15	6D-136	85-0146	KLu 315 Sqn, Twenthe
J-192	F-GD F-16A-15	6D-99	83-1192	KLu 322 Sqn, Leeuwarden
J-193	F-GD F-16A-15	6D-100	83-1193	KLu 312 Sqn, Volkel
J-194	F-GD F-16A-15	6D-101	83-1194	KLu 322 Sqn, Leeuwarden
J-195	F-GD F-16A-15	6D-102	83-1195	Cr 10-Feb-93 (311 Sqn)
J-196	F-GD F-16A-15	6D-103	83-1196	KLu 323 Sqn, Leeuwarden
J-197	F-GD F-16A-15	6D-104	83-1197	KLu 322 Sqn, Leeuwarden
J-198	F-GD F-16A-15	6D-105	83-1198	KLu 311 Sqn, Volkel
J-199	F-GD F-16A-15	6D-106	83-1199	KLu 322 Sqn, Leeuwarden
J-200	F-GD F-16A-15	6D-107	83-1200	Cr 28-Feb-91 (323 Sqn)
J-201	F-GD F-16A-15	6D-108	83-1201	KLu 312 Sqn, Volkel
J-202	F-GD F-16A-15	6D-109	83-1202	KLu 322 Sqn, Leeuwarden
J-203	F-GD F-16A-15	6D-110	83-1203	KLu 322 Sqn, Leeuwarden
J-204	F-GD F-16A-15	6D-111	83-1204	KLu 322 Sqn, Leeuwarden
J-205	F-GD F-16A-15	6D-112	83-1205	KLu 322 Sqn, Leeuwarden
J-206	F-GD F-16A-15	6D-113	83-1206	KLu 312 Sqn, Volkel
J-207	F-GD F-16A-15	6D-114	83-1207	KLu 322 Sqn, Leeuwarden
J-208	F-GD F-16B-15	6E-27	83-1208	KLu 322 Sqn, Leeuwarden
J-209	F-GD F-16B-15	6E-28	83-1209	KLu 322 Sqn, Leeuwarden
J-210	F-GD F-16B-15	6E-29	83-1210	KLu 323 Sqn, Twenthe
J-211	F-GD F-16B-15	6E-30	83-1211	KLu 323 Sqn, Twenthe
J-212	F-GD F-16A-01	6D-1	78-0212	KLu, Volkel, spares use
J-213	F-GD F-16A-01	6D-2	78-0213	KLu 312 Sqn, Volkel
J-214	F-GD F-16A-01	6D-3	78-0214	KLu 311 Sqn, Volkel
J-215	F-GD F-16A-01	6D-4	78-0215	KLu 312 Sqn, Volkel
J-216	F-GD F-16A-01	6D-5	78-0216	Cr 10-Mar-80 (TCA)
J-217	F-GD F-16A-01	6D-6	78-0217	Cr 17-Jul-81 (322 Sqn)

J-213 – one of a number of specially painted F-16A display aircraft flown by the Royal Netherlands AF. PETER R MARCH

Serial	Type/Code	c/n	ex	Operator/location
J-218	F-GD F-16A-01	6D-7	78-0218	KLu 313 Sqn, Twenthe
J-219	F-GD F-16A-01	6D-8	78-0219	Leeuwarden, instructional use
J-220	F-GD F-16A-01	6D-9	78-0220	KLu 311 Sqn, Volkel
J-221	F-GD F-16A-01	6D-10	78-0221	Twenthe, instructional use
J-222	F-GD F-16A-01	6D-11	78-0222	Volkel, instructional use
J-223	F-GD F-16A-01	6D-12	78-0223	Volkel, spares use
J-224	F-GD F-16A-05	6D-13	78-0224	Cr 26-Apr-83 (322 Sqn)
J-225	F-GD F-16A-05	6D-14	78-0225	Cr 21-Mar-83 (322 Sqn)
J-226	F-GD F-16A-05	6D-15	78-0226	KLu 312 Sqn, Volkel
J-227	F-GD F-16A-05	6D-16	78-0227	Cr 26-Apr-83 (322 Sqn)
J-228	F-GD F-16A-05	6D-17	78-0228	KLu 312 Sqn, Volkel
J-229	F-GD F-16A-05	6D-18	78-0229	Volkel, instructional use
J-230	F-GD F-16A-05	6D-19	78-0230	KLu 313 Sqn, Twenthe
J-231	F-GD F-16A-05	6D-20	78-0231	KLu 312 Sqn, Volkel
J-232	F-GD F-16A-05	6D-21	78-0232	KLu 315 Sqn, Twenthe
J-233	F-GD F-16A-05	6D-22	78-0233	Cr 22-Oct-81 (323 Sqn)
J-234	F-GD F-16A-05	6D-23	78-0234	To RDanish AF for spares use, 1996
J-235	F-GD F-16A-05	6D-24	78-0235	KLu 323 Sqn, Leeuwarden
J-236	F-GD F-16A-05	6D-25	78-0236	KLu 312 Sqn, Volkel
J-237	F-GD F-16A-05	6D-26	78-0237	Cr 03-Jul-81 (322 Sqn)
J-238	F-GD F-16A-10	6D-27	78-0238	LETS, Schaarsbergen, instructional use
J-239	F-GD F-16A-10	6D-28	78-0239	KLu 313 Sqn, Twenthe
J-240	F-GD F-16A-10	6D-29	78-0240	Volkel, spares use
J-241	F-GD F-16A-10	6D-30	78-0241	KLu 311 Sqn, Volkel
J-242	F-GD F-16A-10	6D-31	78-0242	Volkel, instructional use
J-243	F-GD F-16A-10	6D-32	78-0243	KLu 311 Sqn, Volkel
J-244	F-GD F-16A-10	6D-33	78-0244	Cr 17-Nov-86 (322 Sqn)
J-245	F-GD F-16A-10	6D-34	78-0245	Leeuwarden, instructional use
J-246	F-GD F-16A-10	6D-35	78-0246	KLu 315 Sqn, Twenthe
J-247	F-GD F-16A-10	6D-36	78-0247	Twenthe, instructional use
J-248	F-GD F-16A-10	6D-37	78-0248	KLu 312 Sqn, Volkel
J-249	F-GD F-16A-10	6D-38	78-0249	KLu 306 Sqn, Volkel
J-250	F-GD F-16A-10	6D-39	78-0250	KLu 311 Sqn, Volkel
J-251	F-GD F-16A-10	6D-40	78-0251	KLu/F-16 MLU Test Team, Leeuwarden
J-252	F-GD F-16A-10	6D-41	78-0252	Cr 04-Oct-83 (322 Sqn)
J-253	F-GD F-16A-10	6D-42	78-0253	KLu 315 Sqn, Twenthe
J-254	F-GD F-16A-10	6D-43	78-0254	KLu 312 Sqn, Volkel
J-255	F-GD F-16A-10	6D-44	78-0255	KLu 315 Sqn, Twenthe
J-256	F-GD F-16A-10	6D-45	78-0256	KLu 311 Sqn, Volkel
J-257	F-GD F-16A-10	6D-46	78-0257	KLu 315 Sqn, Twenthe
J-258	F-GD F-16A-15	6D-47	78-0258	Cr 10-May-90 (322 Sqn)
J-259	F-GD F-16B-01	6E-1	78-0259	KLu 313 Sqn, Twenthe
J-260	F-GD F-16B-01	6E-2	78-0260	LETS, Schaarsbergen, instructional use
J-261	F-GD F-16B-01	6E-3	78-0261	KLu 313 Sqn, Twenthe
J-262	F-GD F-16B-01	6E-4	78-0262	KLu 313 Sqn, Twenthe
J-263	F-GD F-16B-01	6E-5	78-0263	LETS, Schaarsbergen, instructional use
J-264	F-GD F-16B-01	6E-6	78-0264	KLu 313 Sqn, Twenthe
J-265	F-GD F-16B-05	6E-7	78-0265	KLu 313 Sqn, Twenthe
J-266	F-GD F-16B-05	6E-8	78-0266	KLu 313 Sqn, Twenthe
J-267	F-GD F-16B-10	6E-9	78-0267	KLu 315 Sqn, Twenthe
J-268	F-GD F-16B-10	6E-10	78-0268	KLu 313 Sqn, Twenthe
J-269	F-GD F-16B-10	6E-11	78-0269	KLu 313 Sqn, Twenthe
J-270	F-GD F-16B-10	6E-12	78-0270	KLu 313 Sqn, Twenthe
J-271	F-GD F-16B-10	6E-13	78-0271	Cr 11-Dec-84 (TCA)

F-16A J-252 carried 322 Sqn 40th anniversary colours. GRAHAM FINCH

Serial	Type/Code	c/n	ex	Operator/location
J-358	F-GD F-16A-15	6D-115	84-1358	Cr 10-May-90 (323 Sqn)
J-359	F-GD F-16A-15	6D-116	84-1359	Cr 24-Sep-92 (323 Sqn)
J-360	F-GD F-16A-15	6D-117	84-1360	KLu 322 Sqn, Leeuwarden
J-361	F-GD F-16A-15	6D-118	84-1361	KLu 322 Sqn, Leeuwarden
J-362	F-GD F-16A-15	6D-119	84-1362	KLu 322 Sqn, Leeuwarden
J-363	F-GD F-16A-15	6D-120	84-1363	KLu 322 Sqn, Leeuwarden
J-364	F-GD F-16A-15	6D-121	84-1364	KLu 322 Sqn, Leeuwarden
J-365	F-GD F-16A-15	6D-122	84-1365	KLu 322 Sqn, Leeuwarden
J-366	F-GD F-16A-15	6D-123	84-1366	KLu 322 Sqn, Leeuwarden
J-367	F-GD F-16A-15	6D-124	84-1367	KLu 322 Sqn, Leeuwarden
J-368	F-GD F-16B-15	6E-31	84-1368	KLu 315 Sqn, Twenthe
J-369	F-GD F-16B-15	6E-32	84-1369	KLu 323 Sqn, Leeuwarden
J-508	F-GD F-16A-15	6D-147	87-0508	KLu 312 Sqn, Volkel
J-509	F-GD F-16A-15	6D-148	87-0509	KLu 315 Sqn, Twenthe
J-510	F-GD F-16A-15	6D-149	87-0510	KLu 315 Sqn, Twenthe
J-511	F-GD F-16A-15	6D-150	87-0511	KLu 311 Sqn, Volkel

Serial	Type/Code	c/n	ex	Operator/location
J-512	F-GD F-16A-15	6D-151	87-0512	KLu 311 Sqn, Volkel
J-513	F-GD F-16A-15	6D-152	87-0513	KLu 312 Sqn, Volkel
J-514	F-GD F-16A-15	6D-153	87-0514	KLu 315 Sqn, Twenthe
J-515	F-GD F-16A-15	6D-154	87-0515	KLu 315 Sqn, Twenthe
J-516	F-GD F-16A-15	6D-155	87-0516	KLu 315 Sqn, Twenthe
J-616	F-GD F-16A-15	6D-48	80-3616	KLu 322 Sqn, Leeuwarden
J-617	F-GD F-16A-15	6D-49	80-3617	KLu 323 Sqn, Leeuwarden
J-618	F-GD F-16A-15	6D-50	80-3618	Cr 26-May-92 (311 Sqn)
J-619	F-GD F-16A-15	6D-51	80-3619	KLu 311 Sqn, Volkel
J-620	F-GD F-16A-15	6D-52	80-3620	KLu 322 Sqn, Leeuwarden
J-621	F-GD F-16A-15	6D-53	80-3621	Cr 03-Jun-85 (311 Sqn)
J-622	F-GD F-16A-15	6D-54	80-3622	KLu 311 Sqn, Volkel
J-623	F-GD F-16A-15	6D-55	80-3623	KLu 322 Sqn, Leeuwarden
J-624	F-GD F-16A-15	6D-56	80-3624	KLu 322 Sqn, Leeuwarden
J-625	F-GD F-16A-15	6D-57	80-3625	Cr 04-Jun-88 (311 Sqn)
J-626	F-GD F-16A-15	6D-58	80-3626	Cr 13-Jun-86 (311 Sqn)
J-627	F-GD F-16A-15/F-16A(R)	6D-59	80-3627	KLu 306 Sqn, Volkel
J-628	F-GD F-16A-15/F-16A(R)	6D-60	80-3628	KLu 306 Sqn, Volkel
J-629	F-GD F-16A-15/F-16A(R)	6D-61	80-3629	Cr 15-Apr-86 (306 Sqn)
J-630	F-GD F-16A-15/F-16A(R)	6D-62	80-3630	KLu 306 Sqn, Volkel
J-631	F-GD F-16A-15/F-16A(R)	6D-63	80-3631	KLu 306 Sqn, Volkel
J-632	F-GD F-16A-15/F-16A(R)	6D-64	80-3632	KLu 306 Sqn, Volkel
J-633	F-GD F-16A-15/F-16A(R)	6D-65	80-3633	KLu 306 Sqn, Volkel
J-634	F-GD F-16A-15/F-16A(R)	6D-66	80-3634	Cr 28-May-84 (311 Sqn)
J-635	F-GD F-16A-15/F-16A(R)	6D-67	80-3635	KLu 306 Sqn, Volkel
J-636	F-GD F-16A-15/F-16A(R)	6D-68	80-3636	KLu 306 Sqn, Volkel
J-637	F-GD F-16A-15/F-16A(R)	6D-69	80-3637	KLu 306 Sqn, Volkel
J-638	F-GD F-16A-15/F-16A(R)	6D-70	80-3638	KLu 306 Sqn, Volkel
J-639	F-GD F-16A-15/F-16A(R)	6D-71	80-3639	Cr 11-Feb-88 (306 Sqn)
J-640	F-GD F-16A-15/F-16A(R)	6D-72	80-3640	KLu 306 Sqn, Volkel
J-641	F-GD F-16A-15/F-16A(R)	6D-73	80-3641	KLu 306 Sqn, Volkel
J-642	F-GD F-16A-15/F-16A(R)	6D-74	80-3642	KLu 306 Sqn, Volkel
J-643	F-GD F-16A-15/F-16A(R)	6D-75	80-3643	KLu 306 Sqn, Volkel
J-644	F-GD F-16A-15/F-16A(R)	6D-76	80-3644	KLu 306 Sqn, Volkel

F-16A J-864 was painted in 1988 with R Neth AF 75th anniversary markings. ANDREW MARCH

Royal Norwegian Air Force F-16B photographed in July 1983. ANDREW MARCH

Serial	Type/Code	c/n	ex	Operator/location
J-645	F-GD F-16A-15/F-16A(R)	6D-77	80-3645	Cr 09-Aug-93 (306 Sqn)
J-646	F-GD F-16A-15/F-16A(R)	6D-78	80-3646	KLu 306 Sqn, Volkel
J-647	F-GD F-16A-15/F-16A(R)	6D-79	80-3647	KLu 306 Sqn, Volkel
J-648	F-GD F-16A-15/F-16A(R)	6D-80	80-3648	KLu 306 Sqn, Volkel
J-649	F-GD F-16B-15	6E-14	80-3649	KLu 306 Sqn, Volkel
J-650	F-GD F-16B-15(MLU)	6E-15	80-3650	KLu F-16 MLU Test Team, Leeuwarden
J-651	F-GD F-16B-15	6E-16	80-3651	KLu 306 Sqn, Volkel
J-652	F-GD F-16B-15	6E-17	80-3652	KLu 306 Sqn, Volkel
J-653	F-GD F-16B-15	6E-18	80-3653	KLu Test Groep, Volkel
J-654	F-GD F-16B-15	6E-19	80-3654	KLu 323 Sqn, Leeuwarden
J-655	F-GD F-16B-15	6E-20	80-3655	KLu 323 Sqn, Leeuwarden
J-656	F-GD F-16B-15	6E-21	80-3656	KLu 323 Sqn, Leeuwarden
J-657	F-GD F-16B-15	6E-22	80-3657	KLu 323 Sqn, Leeuwarden
J-710	F-GD F-16A-15	6D-156	87-0710	Cr 21-Nov-90 (315 Sqn)
J-864	F-GD F-16A-15/F-16A(R)	6D-81	81-0864	KLu 306 Sqn, Volkel
J-865	F-GD F-16A-15	6D-82	81-0865	Cr 03-Jun-85 (311 Sqn)
J-866	F-GD F-16A-15/F-16A(R)	6D-83	81-0866	KLu 306 Sqn, Volkel
J-867	F-GD F-16A-15/F-16A(R)	6D-84	81-0867	KLu 306 Sqn, Volkel
J-868	F-GD F-16A-15	6D-85	81-0868	KLu 323 Sqn, Leeuwarden
J-869	F-GD F-16A-15	6D-86	81-0869	KLu 323 Sqn, Leeuwarden
J-870	F-GD F-16A-15	6D-87	81-0870	KLu 323 Sqn, Leeuwarden
J-871	F-GD F-16A-15	6D-88	81-0871	KLu 323 Sqn, Leeuwarden
J-872	F-GD F-16A-15	6D-89	81-0872	KLu 323 Sqn, Leeuwarden
J-873	F-GD F-16A-15	6D-90	81-0873	KLu 323 Sqn, Leeuwarden
J-874	F-GD F-16A-15	6D-91	81-0874	KLu 323 Sqn, Leeuwarden
J-875	F-GD F-16A-15	6D-92	81-0875	KLu 323 Sqn, Leeuwarden
J-876	F-GD F-16A-15	6D-93	81-0876	KLu 323 Sqn, Leeuwarden
J-877	F-GD F-16A-15	6D-94	81-0877	KLu 322 Sqn, Leeuwarden
J-878	F-GD F-16A-15	6D-95	81-0878	KLu 323 Sqn, Leeuwarden
J-879	F-GD F-16A-15	6D-96	81-0879	KLu 312 Sqn, Volkel
J-880	F-GD F-16A-15	6D-97	81-0880	Cr 21-May-91 (312 Sqn)
J-881	F-GD F-16A-15	6D-98	81-0881	KLu 323 Sqn, Leeuwarden
J-882	F-GD F-16A-15	6E-23	81-0882	KLu 323 Sqn, Leeuwarden
J-883	F-GD F-16B-15	6E-24	81-0883	To Egyptian AF as 9207
J-884	F-GD F-16B-15	6E-25	81-0884	KLu 323 Sqn, Leeuwarden
J-885	F-GD F-16B-15	6E-26	81-0885	KLu 311 Sqn, Volkel

NORWAY – Royal Norwegian Air Force – Kongelige Norske Luftforsvaret (KNL)

Serial	Type/Code	c/n	ex	Operator/location
272	F-GD F-16A-01	6K-1	78-0272	KNL 332 Skv, Rygge
273	F-GD F-16A-01	6K-2	78-0273	KNL 332 Skv, Rygge
274	F-GD F-16A-01	6K-3	78-0274	KNL 332 Skv, Rygge
275	F-GD F-16A-05	6K-4	78-0275	KNL 332 Skv, Rygge
276	F-GD F-16A-05	6K-5	78-0276	KNL 332 Skv, Rygge
277	F-GD F-16A-05	6K-6	78-0277	KNL 332 Skv, Rygge
278	F-GD F-16A-05	6K-7	78-0278	Cr 23-Mar-92 (332 Skv)
279	F-GD F-16A-05	6K-8	78-0279	KNL 332 Skv, Rygge

Serial	Type/Code	c/n	ex	Operator/location
280	F-GD F-16A-05	6K-9	78-0280	Cr 02-Jul-81 (332 Skv)
281	F-GD F-16A-05	6K-10	78-0281	KNL 332 Skv, Rygge
282	F-GD F-16A-05	6K-11	78-0282	KNL 332 Skv, Rygge
283	F-GD F-16A-05	6K-12	78-0283	Cr 31-Jan-83 (331 Skv)
284	F-GD F-16A-05	6K-13	78-0284	KNL 332 Skv, Rygge
285	F-GD F-16A-10	6K-14	78-0285	KNL 332 Skv, Rygge
286	F-GD F-16A-10	6K-15	78-0286	Cr
287	F-GD F-16A-10	6K-16	78-0287	Cr 05-Apr-89 (338 Skv)
288	F-GD F-16A-10	6K-17	78-0288	KNL 338 Skv, Ørland
289	F-GD F-16A-10	6K-18	78-0289	KNL 338 Skv, Ørland
290	F-GD F-16A-10	6K-19	78-0290	Cr 15-Sep-87 (338 Skv)
291	F-GD F-16A-10	6K-20	78-0291	KNL 338 Skv, Ørland
292	F-GD F-16A-10	6K-21	78-0292	KNL 338 Skv, Ørland
293	F-GD F-16A-10	6K-22	78-0293	KNL 338 Skv, Ørland
294	F-GD F-16A-10	6K-23	78-0294	Cr 05-Apr-89 (338 Skv)
295	F-GD F-16A-10	6K-24	78-0295	KNL 338 Skv, Ørland
296	F-GD F-16A-10	6K-25	78-0296	Cr 22-May-90 (332 Skv)
297	F-GD F-16A-10	6K-26	78-0297	KNL 338 Skv, Ørland
298	F-GD F-16A-10	6K-27	78-0298	KNL 338 Skv, Ørland
299	F-GD F-16A-10	6K-28	78-0299	KNL F-16 MLU Test Team, Leeuwarden
300	F-GD F-16A-15	6K-29	78-0300	Cr 05-Jul-88 (334 Skv)
301	F-GD F-16B-01	6L-1	78-0301	Cr 13-Nov-84 (332 Skv)
302	F-GD F-16B-01	6L-2	78-0302	KNL 332 Skv, Rygge
303	F-GD F-16B-05	6L-3	78-0303	Cr 12-Jun-85 (332 Skv)
304	F-GD F-16B-05	6L-4	78-0304	KNL 332 Skv, Rygge
305	F-GD F-16B-05	6L-5	78-0305	KNL 332 Skv, Rygge
306	F-GD F-16B-10	6L-6	78-0306	KNL/F-16 MLU Test Team, Leeuwarden
307	F-GD F-16B-10	6L-7	78-0307	Cr 04-May-95 (332 Skv)

Operated by 338 Skv, this R Nor AF F-16A (297) is based at Ørland. BOB ARCHER

New-build Portuguese Air Force F-16A Block 15 15104 is flown by Esq 201 at Monte Real. PETER R FOSTER

Serial	Type/Code	c/n	ex	Operator/location
658	F-GD F-16A-15	6K-30	80-3658	KNL 334 Skv, Bodø
659	F-GD F-16A-15	6K-31	80-3659	KNL 334 Skv, Bodø
660	F-GD F-16A-15	6K-32	80-3660	KNL 334 Skv, Bodø
661	F-GD F-16A-15	6K-33	80-3661	KNL 334 Skv, Bodø
662	F-GD F-16A-15	6K-34	80-3662	KNL 334 Skv, Bodø
663	F-GD F-16A-15	6K-35	80-3663	KNL 334 Skv, Bodø
664	F-GD F-16A-15	6K-36	80-3664	KNL 334 Skv, Bodø
665	F-GD F-16A-15	6K-37	80-3665	KNL 334 Skv, Bodø
666	F-GD F-16A-15	6K-38	80-3666	KNL 334 Skv, Bodø
667	F-GD F-16A-15	6K-39	80-3667	KNL 334 Skv, Bodø
668	F-GD F-16A-15	6K-40	80-3668	KNL 334 Skv, Bodø
669	F-GD F-16A-15	6K-41	80-3669	KNL 334 Skv, Bodø
670	F-GD F-16A-15	6K-42	80-3670	KNL 334 Skv, Bodø
671	F-GD F-16A-15	6K-43	80-3671	KNL 338 Skv, Ørland
672	F-GD F-16A-15	6K-44	80-3672	KNL 331 Skv, Bodø
673	F-GD F-16A-15	6K-45	80-3673	KNL 331 Skv, Bodø
674	F-GD F-16A-15	6K-46	80-3674	KNL 331 Skv, Bodø
675	F-GD F-16A-15	6K-47	80-3675	KNL 331 Skv, Bodø
676	F-GD F-16A-15	6K-48	80-3676	Cr 10-Jan-89 (331 Skv)
677	F-GD F-16A-15	6K-49	80-3677	KNL 331 Skv, Bodø
678	F-GD F-16A-15	6K-50	80-3678	KNL 331 Skv, Bodø
679	F-GD F-16A-15	6K-51	80-3679	Cr 14-Mar-88 (331 Skv)
680	F-GD F-16A-15(MLU)	6K-52	80-3680	KNL/SABCA, Gosselies, Belgium
681	F-GD F-16A-15	6K-53	80-3681	KNL 331 Skv, Bodø
682	F-GD F-16A-15	6K-54	80-3682	KNL 331 Skv, Bodø
683	F-GD F-16A-15	6K-55	80-3683	KNL 331 Skv, Bodø
684	F-GD F-16A-15	6K-56	80-3684	Cr 10-Jul-86 (331 Skv)
685	F-GD F-16A-15	6K-57	80-3685	Cr 06-Jun-89 (331 Skv)
686	F-GD F-16A-15	6K-58	80-3686	KNL 331 Skv, Bodø
687	F-GD F-16A-15	6K-59	80-3687	KNL 331 Skv, Bodø
688	F-GD F-16A-15	6K-60	80-3688	KNL 331 Skv, Bodø
689	F-GD F-16B-15	6L-8	80-3689	KNL 338 Skv, Ørland
690	F-GD F-16B-15	6L-9	80-3690	KNL 338 Skv, Ørland
691	F-GD F-16B-15	6L-10	80-3691	KNL 334 Skv, Bodø
692	F-GD F-16B-15	6L-11	80-3692	KNL 334 Skv, Bodø
693	F-GD F-16B-15	6L-12	80-3693	KNL 338 Skv, Ørland
711	GD F-16B-15	6L-13	87-0711	KNL 331 Skv, Bodø
712	GD F-16B-15	6L-14	87-0712	KNL 331 Skv, Bodø

PORTUGAL – Portuguese Air Force – Forca Aerea Portuguesa (FAP)

Serial	Type/Code	c/n	ex	Operator/location
15101	LMTAS F-16A-15	AA-1	93-0465	FAP Esq 201, Monte Real
15102	LMTAS F-16A-15	AA-2	93-0466	FAP Esq 201, Monte Real
15103	LMTAS F-16A-15	AA-3	93-0467	FAP Esq 201, Monte Real
15104	LMTAS F-16A-15	AA-4	93-0468	FAP Esq 201, Monte Real
15105	LMTAS F-16A-15	AA-5	93-0469	FAP Esq 201, Monte Real
15106	LMTAS F-16A-15	AA-6	93-0470	FAP Esq 201, Monte Real

Serial	Type/Code	c/n	ex	Operator/location
15107	LMTAS F-16A-15	AA-7	93-0471	FAP Esq 201, Monte Real
15108	LMTAS F-16A-15	AA-8	93-0472	FAP Esq 201, Monte Real
15109	LMTAS F-16A-15	AA-9	93-0473	FAP Esq 201, Monte Real
15110	LMTAS F-16A-15	AA-10	93-0474	FAP Esq 201, Monte Real
15111	LMTAS F-16A-15	AA-11	93-0475	FAP Esq 201, Monte Real
15112	LMTAS F-16A-15	AA-12	93-0476	FAP Esq 201, Monte Real
15113	LMTAS F-16A-15	AA-13	93-0477	FAP Esq 201, Monte Real
15114	LMTAS F-16A-15	AA-14	93-0478	FAP Esq 201, Monte Real
15115	LMTAS F-16A-15	AA-15	93-0479	FAP Esq 201, Monte Real
15116	LMTAS F-16A-15	AA-16	93-0480	FAP Esq 201, Monte Real
15117	LMTAS F-16A-15	AA-17	93-0481	FAP Esq 201, Monte Real
15118	LMTAS F-16B-15	AB-1	93-0482	FAP Esq 201, Monte Real
15119	LMTAS F-16B-15	AB-2	93-0483	FAP Esq 201, Monte Real
15120	LMTAS F-16B-15	AB-3	93-0484	FAP Esq 201, Monte Real

Portugal has a further 25 F-16A/B on order (15121 to 15145).

TURKEY – Turkish Air Force – Turk Hava Kuvvetleri (THK)

Serial	Type/Code	c/n	Operator/location
86-0066	GD F-16C-30	4R-1	THK Öncel Filo (4 AJÜ), Mürted
86-0067	GD F-16C-30	4R-2	Cr 05-Jul-91 (Öncel Filo)
86-0068	TUSAS-GD F-16C-30	4R-3	THK Öncel Filo (4 AJÜ), Mürted
86-0069	TUSAS-GD F-16C-30	4R-4	THK Öncel Filo (4 AJÜ), Mürted
86-0070	TUSAS-GD F-16C-30	4R-5	THK Öncel Filo (4 AJÜ), Mürted
86-0071	TUSAS-GD F-16C-30	4R-6	THK Öncel Filo (4 AJÜ), Mürted
86-0072	TUSAS-GD F-16C-30	4R-7	THK Öncel Filo (4 AJÜ), Mürted
86-0191	GD F-16D-30	4S-1	THK Öncel Filo (4 AJÜ), Mürted
86-0192	GD F-16D-30	4S-2	THK 191 Filo (9 AJÜ), Balikesir
86-0193	GD F-16D-30	4S-3	THK 191 Filo (9 AJÜ), Balikesir
86-0194	GD F-16D-30	4S-4	THK Öncel Filo (4 AJÜ), Mürted
86-0195	GD F-16D-30	4S-5	THK Öncel Filo (4 AJÜ), Mürted
86-0196	GD F-16D-30	4S-6	THK Öncel Filo (4 AJÜ), Mürted
87-0002	TUSAS-GD F-16D-30	4S-7	THK 142 Filo (4 AJÜ), Mürted
87-0003	TUSAS-GD F-16D-30	4S-8	THK 142 Filo (4 AJÜ), Mürted
87-0009	TUSAS-GD F-16C-30	4R-8	THK Öncel Filo (4 AJÜ), Mürted
87-0010	TUSAS-GD F-16C-30	4R-9	THK Öncel Filo (4 AJÜ), Mürted
87-0011	TUSAS-GD F-16C-30	4R-10	THK Öncel Filo (4 AJÜ), Mürted
87-0012	TUSAS-GD F-16C-30	4R-11	Cr 25-Jun-92 (Öncel Filo)
87-0013	TUSAS-GD F-16C-30	4R-12	THK 141 Filo (4 AJÜ), Mürted
87-0014	TUSAS-GD F-16C-30	4R-13	THK Öncel Filo (4 AJÜ), Mürted
87-0015	TUSAS-GD F-16C-30	4R-14	THK Öncel Filo (4 AJÜ), Mürted
87-0016	TUSAS-GD F-16C-30	4R-15	THK Öncel Filo (4 AJÜ), Mürted
87-0017	TUSAS-GD F-16C-30	4R-16	THK 141 Filo (4 AJÜ), Mürted
87-0018	TUSAS-GD F-16C-30	4R-17	THK 142 Filo (4 AJÜ), Mürted
87-0019	TUSAS-GD F-16C-30	4R-18	THK Öncel Filo (4 AJÜ), Mürted
87-0020	TUSAS-GD F-16C-30	4R-19	THK Öncel Filo (4 AJÜ), Mürted
87-0021	TUSAS-GD F-16C-30	4R-20	THK 191 Filo (9 AJÜ), Balikesir
88-0013	TUSAS-GD F-16D-30	4S-9	THK Öncel Filo (4 AJÜ), Mürted

Serial	Type/Code	c/n	Operator/location		Serial	Type/Code	c/n	Operator/location
88-0014	TUSAS-GD F-16D-40	4S-10	THK 141 Filo (4 AJÜ), Mürted		89-0032	TUSAS-GD F-16C-40	4R-50	THK 141 Filo (4 AJÜ), Mürted
88-0015	TUSAS-GD F-16D-40	4S-11	THK 141 Filo (4 AJÜ), Mürted		89-0033	TUSAS-GD F-16C-40	4R-51	Cr 29-Sep-95 (142 Filo)
88-0019	TUSAS-GD F-16C-30	4R-21	THK Öncel Filo (4 AJÜ), Mürted		89-0034	TUSAS-GD F-16C-40	4R-52	THK 162 Filo (6 AJÜ), Bandirma
88-0020	TUSAS-GD F-16C-30	4R-22	THK 191 Filo (9 AJÜ), Balikesir		89-0035	TUSAS-GD F-16C-40	4R-53	THK 162 Filo (6 AJÜ), Bandirma
88-0021	TUSAS-GD F-16C-30	4R-23	THK Öncel Filo (4 AJÜ), Mürted		89-0036	TUSAS-GD F-16C-40	4R-54	THK 161 Filo (6 AJÜ), Bandirma
88-0022	TUSAS-GD F-16C-30	4R-24	Cr 07-May-91 (142 Filo)		89-0037	TUSAS-GD F-16C-40	4R-55	THK 162 Filo (6 AJÜ), Bandirma
88-0023	TUSAS-GD F-16C-30	4R-25	Cr 11-Oct-95 (Öncel Filo)		89-0038	TUSAS-GD F-16C-40	4R-56	THK 162 Filo (6 AJÜ), Bandirma
88-0024	TUSAS-GD F-16C-30	4R-26	THK Öncel Filo (4 AJÜ), Mürted		89-0039	TUSAS-GD F-16C-40	4R-57	THK 162 Filo (6 AJÜ), Bandirma
88-0025	TUSAS-GD F-16C-30	4R-27	THK Öncel Filo (4 AJÜ), Mürted		89-0040	TUSAS-GD F-16C-40	4R-58	THK 162 Filo (6 AJÜ), Bandirma
88-0026	TUSAS-GD F-16C-30	4R-28	THK 191 Filo (9 AJÜ), Balikesir		89-0041	TUSAS-GD F-16C-40	4R-59	THK 162 Filo (6 AJÜ), Bandirma
88-0027	TUSAS-GD F-16C-30	4R-29	THK 191 Filo (9 AJÜ), Balikesir		89-0042	TUSAS-GD F-16D-40	4S-12	THK 181 Filo (8 AJÜ), Diyarbakir
88-0028	TUSAS-GD F-16C-30	4R-30	THK 191 Filo (9 AJÜ), Balikesir		89-0043	TUSAS-GD F-16D-40	4S-13	THK 162 Filo (6 AJÜ), Bandirma
88-0029	TUSAS-GD F-16C-30	4R-31	THK Öncel Filo (4 AJÜ), Mürted		89-0044	TUSAS-GD F-16D-40	4S-14	THK 162 Filo (6 AJÜ), Bandirma
88-0030	TUSAS-GD F-16C-30	4R-32	THK 191 Filo (9 AJÜ), Balikesir		89-0045	TUSAS-GD F-16D-40	4S-15	THK 162 Filo (6 AJÜ), Bandirma
88-0031	TUSAS-GD F-16C-30	4R-33	THK 191 Filo (9 AJÜ), Balikesir		90-0001	TUSAS-GD F-16C-40	4R-60	THK 162 Filo (6 AJÜ), Bandirma
88-0032	TUSAS-GD F-16C-30	4R-34	THK 141 Filo (4 AJÜ), Mürted		90-0002	TUSAS-GD F-16C-40	4R-61	Cr 01-Apr-93 (162 Filo)
88-0033	TUSAS-GD F-16C-40	4R-35	THK Öncel Filo (4 AJÜ), Mürted		90-0003	TUSAS-GD F-16C-40	4R-62	THK 162 Filo (6 AJÜ), Bandirma
88-0034	TUSAS-GD F-16C-40	4R-36	THK 141 Filo (4 AJÜ), Mürted		90-0004	TUSAS-GD F-16C-40	4R-63	THK 162 Filo (6 AJÜ), Bandirma
88-0035	TUSAS-GD F-16C-40	4R-37	THK 141 Filo (4 AJÜ), Mürted		90-0005	TUSAS-GD F-16C-40	4R-64	THK 162 Filo (6 AJÜ), Bandirma
88-0036	TUSAS-GD F-16C-40	4R-38	THK 141 Filo (4 AJÜ), Mürted		90-0006	TUSAS-GD F-16C-40	4R-65	THK 162 Filo (6 AJÜ), Bandirma
88-0037	TUSAS-GD F-16C-40	4R-39	THK 141 Filo (4 AJÜ), Mürted		90-0007	TUSAS-GD F-16C-40	4R-66	THK 162 Filo (6 AJÜ), Bandirma
89-0022	TUSAS-GD F-16C-40	4R-40	THK 141 Filo (4 AJÜ), Mürted		90-0008	TUSAS-GD F-16C-40	4R-67	THK 162 Filo (6 AJÜ), Bandirma
89-0023	TUSAS-GD F-16C-40	4R-41	THK 141 Filo (4 AJÜ), Mürted		90-0009	TUSAS-GD F-16C-40	4R-68	THK 162 Filo (6 AJÜ), Bandirma
89-0024	TUSAS-GD F-16C-40	4R-42	THK 141 Filo (4 AJÜ), Mürted		90-0010	TUSAS-GD F-16C-40	4R-69	THK 161 Filo (6 AJÜ), Bandirma
89-0025	TUSAS-GD F-16C-40	4R-43	THK 141 Filo (4 AJÜ), Mürted		90-0011	TUSAS-GD F-16C-40	4R-70	THK 162 Filo (6 AJÜ), Bandirma
89-0026	TUSAS-GD F-16C-40	4R-44	THK 141 Filo (4 AJÜ), Mürted		90-0012	TUSAS-GD F-16C-40	4R-71	THK 161 Filo (6 AJÜ), Bandirma
89-0027	TUSAS-GD F-16C-40	4R-45	THK 141 Filo (4 AJÜ), Mürted		90-0013	TUSAS-GD F-16C-40	4R-72	THK 161 Filo (6 AJÜ), Bandirma
89-0028	TUSAS-GD F-16C-40	4R-46	THK 141 Filo (4 AJÜ), Mürted		90-0014	TUSAS-GD F-16C-40	4R-73	THK 192 Filo (9 AJÜ), Balikesir
89-0029	TUSAS-GD F-16C-40	4R-47	Cr 28-Apr-93 (141 Filo)		90-0015	TUSAS-GD F-16C-40	4R-74	THK 162 Filo (6 AJÜ), Bandirma
89-0030	TUSAS-GD F-16C-40	4R-48	THK 142 Filo (4 AJÜ), Mürted		90-0016	TUSAS-GD F-16C-40	4R-75	THK 162 Filo (6 AJÜ), Bandirma
89-0031	TUSAS-GD F-16C-40	4R-49	THK 142 Filo (4 AJÜ), Mürted		90-0017	TUSAS-GD F-16C-40	4R-76	THK 161 Filo (6 AJÜ), Bandirma

The first Turkish Air Force F-16C Block 30 (86-0066) flying from Mürted AB. VIA PETER R FOSTER

Serial	Type/Code	c/n	Operator/location
90-0018	TUSAS-GD F-16C-40	4R-77	THK 161 Filo (6 AJÜ), Bandirma
90-0019	TUSAS-GD F-16C-40	4R-78	THK 161 Filo (6 AJÜ), Bandirma
90-0020	TUSAS-GD F-16C-40	4R-79	THK 161 Filo (6 AJÜ), Bandirma
90-0021	TUSAS-GD F-16C-40	4R-80	THK 161 Filo (6 AJÜ), Bandirma
90-0022	TUSAS-GD F-16D-40	4S-16	THK 142 Filo (4 AJÜ), Mürted
90-0023	TUSAS-GD F-16D-40	4S-17	THK 161 Filo (6 AJÜ), Bandirma
90-0024	TUSAS-GD F-16D-40	4S-18	THK 161 Filo (6 AJÜ), Bandirma
91-0001	TUSAS-GD F-16C-40	4R-81	THK 162 Filo (6 AJÜ), Bandirma
91-0002	TUSAS-GD F-16C-40	4R-82	THK 162 Filo (6 AJÜ), Bandirma
91-0003	TUSAS-GD F-16C-40	4R-83	THK 161 Filo (6 AJÜ), Bandirma
91-0004	TUSAS-GD F-16C-40	4R-84	THK 161 Filo (6 AJÜ), Bandirma
91-0005	TUSAS-GD F-16C-40	4R-85	THK 162 Filo (6 AJÜ), Bandirma
91-0006	TUSAS-GD F-16C-40	4R-86	THK 192 Filo (9 AJÜ), Balikesir
91-0007	TUSAS-GD F-16C-40	4R-87	THK 192 Filo (9 AJÜ), Balikesir
91-0008	TUSAS-GD F-16C-40	4R-88	THK 192 Filo (9 AJÜ), Balikesir
91-0009	TUSAS-GD F-16C-40	4R-89	Cr 03-Jan-94 (192 Filo)
91-0010	TUSAS-GD F-16C-40	4R-90	THK 192 Filo (9 AJÜ), Balikesir
91-0011	TUSAS-GD F-16C-40	4R-91	THK 192 Filo (9 AJÜ), Balikesir
91-0012	TUSAS-GD F-16C-40	4R-92	THK 192 Filo (9 AJÜ), Balikesir
91-0013	TUSAS-GD F-16C-40	4R-93	THK 192 Filo (9 AJÜ), Balikesir
91-0014	TUSAS-GD F-16C-40	4R-94	THK 192 Filo (9 AJÜ), Balikesir
91-0015	TUSAS-GD F-16C-40	4R-95	THK 191 Filo (9 AJÜ), Balikesir
91-0016	TUSAS-GD F-16C-40	4R-96	THK 192 Filo (9 AJÜ), Balikesir
91-0017	TUSAS-GD F-16C-40	4R-97	THK 192 Filo (9 AJÜ), Balikesir
91-0018	TUSAS-GD F-16C-40	4R-98	THK 192 Filo (9 AJÜ), Balikesir
91-0019	TUSAS-GD F-16C-40	4R-99	THK 192 Filo (9 AJÜ), Balikesir
91-0020	TUSAS-GD F-16C-40	4R-100	THK 192 Filo (9 AJÜ), Balikesir
91-0021	TUSAS-GD F-16C-40	4R-101	Cr 08-Feb-95 (192 Filo)
91-0022	TUSAS-GD F-16D-40	4S-19	THK 192 Filo (9 AJÜ), Balikesir
91-0023	TUSAS-GD F-16D-40	4S-20	Cr 08-Oct-96 (192 Filo)
91-0024	TUSAS-GD F-16D-40	4S-21	THK 192 Filo (9 AJÜ), Balikesir
92-0001	TUSAS-GD F-16C-40	4R-102	THK 192 Filo (9 AJÜ), Balikesir
92-0002	TUSAS-GD F-16C-40	4R-103	THK 192 Filo (9 AJÜ), Balikesir
92-0003	TUSAS-GD F-16C-40	4R-104	THK 182 Filo (8 AJÜ), Diyarbakir
92-0004	TUSAS-GD F-16C-40	4R-105	THK 192 Filo (9 AJÜ), Balikesir
92-0005	TUSAS-GD F-16C-40	4R-106	THK 192 Filo (9 AJÜ), Balikesir
92-0006	TUSAS-GD F-16C-40	4R-107	THK 192 Filo (9 AJÜ), Balikesir
92-0007	TUSAS-GD F-16C-40	4R-108	THK 192 Filo (9 AJÜ), Balikesir
92-0008	TUSAS-GD F-16C-40	4R-109	THK 192 Filo (9 AJÜ), Balikesir
92-0009	TUSAS-GD F-16C-40	4R-110	THK 192 Filo (9 AJÜ), Balikesir
92-0010	TUSAS-GD F-16C-40	4R-111	THK 142 Filo (4 AJÜ), Mürted
92-0011	TUSAS-GD F-16C-40	4R-112	THK 142 Filo (4 AJÜ), Mürted
92-0012	TUSAS-GD F-16C-40	4R-113	THK 192 Filo (9 AJÜ), Balikesir
92-0013	TUSAS-GD F-16C-40	4R-114	THK 192 Filo (9 AJÜ), Balikesir
92-0014	TUSAS-GD F-16C-40	4R-115	THK 192 Filo (9 AJÜ), Balikesir
92-0015	TUSAS-GD F-16C-40	4R-116	THK 142 Filo (4 AJÜ), Mürted
92-0016	TUSAS-GD F-16C-40	4R-117	THK 142 Filo (4 AJÜ), Mürted
92-0017	TUSAS-GD F-16C-40	4R-118	THK 142 Filo (4 AJÜ), Mürted
92-0018	TUSAS-GD F-16C-40	4R-119	THK 142 Filo (4 AJÜ), Mürted
92-0019	TUSAS-GD F-16C-40	4R-120	THK 142 Filo (4 AJÜ), Mürted
92-0020	TUSAS-GD F-16C-40	4R-121	THK 142 Filo (4 AJÜ), Mürted
92-0021	TUSAS-GD F-16C-40	4R-122	THK 181 Filo (8 AJÜ), Diyarbakir
92-0022	TUSAS-GD F-16D-40	4S-22	THK 181 Filo (8 AJÜ), Diyarbakir
92-0023	TUSAS-GD F-16D-40	4S-23	THK 161 Filo (6 AJÜ), Bandirma
92-0024	TUSAS-GD F-16D-40	4S-24	THK 191 Filo (9 AJÜ), Balikesir
93-0001	TUSAS-GD F-16C-40	4R-123	THK 181 Filo (8 AJÜ), Diyarbakir
93-0002	TUSAS-GD F-16C-40	4R-124	THK 181 Filo (8 AJÜ), Diyarbakir
93-0003	TUSAS-GD F-16C-40	4R-125	THK 181 Filo (8 AJÜ), Diyarbakir
93-0004	TUSAS-GD F-16C-40	4R-126	THK 181 Filo (8 AJÜ), Diyarbakir
93-0005	TUSAS-GD F-16C-40	4R-127	THK 181 Filo (8 AJÜ), Diyarbakir
93-0006	TUSAS-GD F-16C-40	4R-128	THK 181 Filo (8 AJÜ), Diyarbakir
93-0007	TUSAS-GD F-16C-40	4R-129	THK 142 Filo (4 AJÜ), Mürted
93-0008	TUSAS-GD F-16C-40	4R-130	THK 181 Filo (8 AJÜ), Diyarbakir
93-0009	TUSAS-GD F-16C-40	4R-131	THK 181 Filo (8 AJÜ), Diyarbakir
93-0010	TUSAS-GD F-16C-40	4R-132	THK 181 Filo (8 AJÜ), Diyarbakir
93-0011	TUSAS-GD F-16C-40	4R-133	THK 181 Filo (8 AJÜ), Diyarbakir
93-0012	TUSAS-GD F-16C-40	4R-134	THK 181 Filo (8 AJÜ), Diyarbakir
93-0013	TUSAS-GD F-16C-40	4R-135	THK 181 Filo (8 AJÜ), Diyarbakir
93-0014	TUSAS-GD F-16C-40	4R-136	THK 181 Filo (8 AJÜ), Diyarbakir
93-0657	TUSAS-GD F-16C-50	HC-1	THK 141 Filo (4 AJÜ), Mürted
93-0658	TUSAS-GD F-16C-50	HC-2	THK, on order
	TUSAS-GD F-16C-50	HC-3 to HC-78	THK, on order
	TUSAS-GD F-16D-50	HD-1 to HD-12	THK, on order

Aircraft are known to have crashed as follows:
22-Nov-94 (F-16C, 192 Filo), 08-Oct-96 (F-16D, 192 Filo) & 15-Oct-96 (F-16D, 192 Filo)

2. REST OF THE WORLD

BAHRAIN – Bahrain Amiri Air Force (BAAF)

Serial	Type/Code	c/n	ex	Operator/location
101	GD F-16C-40	AC-1	90-0028	BAAF, Sheikh Isa AB
103	GD F-16C-40	AC-2	90-0029	BAAF, Sheikh Isa AB
105	GD F-16C-40	AC-3	90-0030	BAAF, Sheikh Isa AB
107	GD F-16C-40	AC-4	90-0031	BAAF, Sheikh Isa AB
109	GD F-16C-40	AC-5	90-0032	BAAF, Sheikh Isa AB
111	GD F-16C-40	AC-6	90-0033	BAAF, Sheikh Isa AB
113	GD F-16C-40	AC-7	90-0034	BAAF, Sheikh Isa AB
115	GD F-16C-40	AC-8	90-0035	BAAF, Sheikh Isa AB
150	GD F-16D-40	AD-1	90-0036	BAAF, Sheikh Isa AB
152	GD F-16D-40	AD-2	90-0037	BAAF, Sheikh Isa AB
154	GD F-16D-40	AD-3	90-0038	BAAF, Sheikh Isa AB
156	GD F-16D-40	AD-4	90-0039	BAAF, Sheikh Isa AB

EGYPT – Egyptian Air Force – Al Quwwat al Jawwiya Ilmisriya (EAF)

Serial	Type/Code	c/n	ex	Operator/location
9201	GD F-16B-15	9F-1	80-0644	EAF
9202	GD F-16B-15	9F-2	80-0645	EAF
9203	GD F-16B-15	9F-3	80-0646	EAF
9204	GD F-16B-15	9F-4	80-0647	Cr 20-Jan-83
9205	GD F-16B-15	9F-5	80-0648	EAF
9206	GD F-16B-15	9F-6	81-0662	EAF
9207	F-GD F-16B-15	6E-24/9F-7	81-0883	EAF
9208	GD F-16B-15	62-109/9F-8	82-1043	EAF
9301	GD F-16A-15	9E-1	80-0639	EAF
9302	GD F-16A-15	9E-2	80-0640	EAF
9303	GD F-16A-15	9E-3	80-0641	EAF
9304	GD F-16A-15	9E-4	80-0642	EAF
9305	GD F-16A-15	9E-5	80-0643	EAF
9306	GD F-16A-15	9E-6	81-0643	EAF
9307	GD F-16A-15	9E-7	81-0644	EAF
9308	GD F-16A-15	9E-8	81-0645	EAF
9309	GD F-16A-15	9E-9	81-0646	EAF
9310	GD F-16A-15	9E-10	81-0647	EAF
9311	GD F-16A-15	9E-11	81-0648	Cr 06-Nov-90
9312	GD F-16A-15	9E-12	81-0649	Cr 02-Oct-91
9313	GD F-16A-15	9E-13	81-0650	Cr 06-Nov-90
9314	GD F-16A-15	9E-14	81-0651	EAF
9315	GD F-16A-15	9E-15	81-0652	EAF
9316	GD F-16A-15	9E-16	81-0653	Cr 21-May-87
9317	GD F-16A-15	9E-17	81-0654	EAF
9318	GD F-16A-15	9E-18	81-0655	EAF
9319	GD F-16A-15	9E-19	81-0656	EAF
9320	GD F-16A-15	9E-20	81-0657	Cr 03-Aug-92
9321	GD F-16A-15	9E-21	81-0658	EAF
9322	GD F-16A-15	9E-22	81-0659	EAF
9323	GD F-16A-15	9E-23	81-0660	EAF
9324	GD F-16A-15	9E-24	81-0661	EAF
9325	GD F-16A-15	9E-25	82-1056	EAF
9326	GD F-16A-15	9E-26	82-1057	Cr 12-Jul-93
9327	GD F-16A-15	9E-27	82-1058	Cr 15-Mar-95
9328	GD F-16A-15	9E-28	82-1059	EAF
9329	GD F-16A-15	9E-29	82-1060	EAF
9330	GD F-16A-15	9E-30	82-1061	EAF
9331	GD F-16A-15	9E-31	82-1062	EAF
9332	GD F-16A-15	9E-32	82-1063	Cr 03-Aug-92
9333	GD F-16A-15	9E-33	82-1064	EAF
9334	GD F-16A-15	9E-34	82-1065	EAF
9401	GD F-16D-32	4H-1	84-1340	EAF
9402	GD F-16D-32	4H-2	84-1341	EAF
9403	GD F-16D-32	4H-3	84-1342	EAF
9404	GD F-16D-32	4H-4	84-1343	EAF
9405	GD F-16D-32	4H-5	84-1344	EAF
9406	GD F-16D-32	4H-6	84-1345	EAF
9501	GD F-16C-32	4G-1	84-1332	EAF
9502	GD F-16C-32	4G-2	84-1333	EAF
9503	GD F-16C-32	4G-3	84-1334	EAF
9504	GD F-16C-32	4G-4	84-1335	EAF
9505	GD F-16C-32	4G-5	84-1336	EAF
9506	GD F-16C-32	4G-6	84-1337	EAF
9507	GD F-16C-32	4G-7	84-1338	EAF
9508	GD F-16C-32	4G-8	84-1339	EAF

The second F-167A (9302) delivered to the Egyptian Air Force in 1992. LMTAS

Serial	Type/Code	c/n	ex	Operator/location	Serial	Type/Code	c/n	ex	Operator/location
9509	GD F-16C-32	4G-9	85-1518	EAF	9855	T-GD F-16D-40	BD-17	93-0517	EAF
9510	GD F-16C-32	4G-10	85-1519	EAF	9856	T-GD F-16D-40	BD-18	93-0518	EAF
9511	GD F-16C-32	4G-11	85-1520	EAF	9857	T-GD F-16D-40	BD-19	93-0519	EAF
9512	GD F-16C-32	4G-12	85-1521	EAF	9858	T-GD F-16D-40	BD-20	93-0520	EAF
9513	GD F-16C-32	4G-13	85-1522	EAF	9859	T-GD F-16D-40	BD-21	93-0521	EAF
9514	GD F-16C-32	4G-14	85-1523	EAF	9860	T-GD F-16D-40	BD-22	93-0522	EAF
9515	GD F-16C-32	4G-15	85-1524	EAF	9861	T-GD F-16D-40	BD-23	93-0523	EAF
9516	GD F-16C-32	4G-16	85-1525	EAF	9862	T-GD F-16D-40	BD-24	93-0524	EAF
9517	GD F-16C-32	4G-17	85-1526	EAF	9901	GD F-16C-40	BC-1	89-0278	EAF
9518	GD F-16C-32	4G-18	85-1527	EAF	9902	GD F-16C-40	BC-2	89-0279	EAF
9519	GD F-16C-32	4G-19	85-1528	EAF	9903	GD F-16C-40	BC-3	90-0899	EAF
9520	GD F-16C-32	4G-20	85-1529	Cr 10-May-94	9904	GD F-16C-40	BC-4	90-0900	EAF
9521	GD F-16C-32	4G-21	85-1530	Cr 23-May-95	9905	GD F-16C-40	BC-5	90-0901	EAF
9522	GD F-16C-32	4G-22	85-1531	EAF	9906	GD F-16C-40	BC-6	90-0902	EAF
9523	GD F-16C-32	4G-23	85-1532	EAF	9907	GD F-16C-40	BC-7	90-0903	EAF
9524	GD F-16C-32	4G-24	85-1533	EAF	9908	GD F-16C-40	BC-8	90-0904	EAF
9525	GD F-16C-32	4G-25	85-1534	EAF	9909	GD F-16C-40	BC-9	90-0905	EAF
9526	GD F-16C-32	4G-26	85-1535	EAF	9910	GD F-16C-40	BC-10	90-0906	EAF
9527	GD F-16C-32	4G-27	85-1536	EAF	9911	GD F-16C-40	BC-11	90-0907	EAF
9528	GD F-16C-32	4G-28	85-1537	EAF	9912	GD F-16C-40	BC-12	90-0908	EAF
9529	GD F-16C-32	4G-29	85-1538	EAF	9913	GD F-16C-40	BC-13	90-0909	EAF
9530	GD F-16C-32	4G-30	85-1539	EAF	9914	GD F-16C-40	BC-14	90-0910	EAF
9531	GD F-16C-32	4G-31	85-1540	EAF	9915	GD F-16C-40	BC-15	90-0911	EAF
9532	GD F-16C-32	4G-32	85-1541	EAF	9916	GD F-16C-40	BC-16	90-0912	EAF
9533	GD F-16C-32	4G-33	85-1542	EAF	9917	GD F-16C-40	BC-17	90-0913	Cr 04-Oct-94
9534	GD F-16C-32	4G-34	85-1543	EAF	9918	GD F-16C-40	BC-18	90-0914	EAF
9801	GD F-16D-40	BD-1	90-0931	EAF	9919	GD F-16C-40	BC-19	90-0915	EAF
9802	GD F-16D-40	BD-2	90-0932	EAF	9920	GD F-16C-40	BC-20	90-0916	EAF
9803	GD F-16D-40	BD-3	90-0933	EAF	9921	GD F-16C-40	BC-21	90-0917	EAF
9804	GD F-16D-40	BD-4	90-0934	EAF	9922	GD F-16C-40	BC-22	90-0918	EAF
9805	GD F-16D-40	BD-5	90-0935	EAF	9923	GD F-16C-40	BC-23	00-0010	EAF
9806	GD F-16D-40	BD-6	90-0936	EAF	9924	GD F-16C-40	BC-24	90-0920	EAF
9807	GD F-16D-40	BD-7	90-0937	EAF	9925	GD F-16C-40	BC-25	90-0921	EAF
9808	GD F-16D-40	BD-8	90-0954	EAF	9926	GD F-16C-40	BC-26	90-0922	EAF
9809	GD F-16D-40	BD-9	90-0955	EAF	9927	GD F-16C-40	BC-27	90-0923	EAF
9810	GD F-16D-40	BD-10	90-0956	EAF	9928	GD F-16C-40	BC-28	90-0924	Cr 09-Sep-93
9811	GD F-16D-40	BD-11	90-0957	EAF	9929	GD F-16C-40	BC-29	90-0925	EAF
9812	GD F-16D-40	BD-12	90-0958	EAF	9930	GD F-16C-40	BC-30	90-0926	EAF
9851	T-GD F-16D-40	BD-13	93-0513	EAF	9931	GD F-16C-40	BC-31	90-0927	EAF
9852	T-GD F-16D-40	BD-14	93-0514	Cr 14-Jul-94	9932	GD F-16C-40	BC-32	90-0928	EAF
9853	T-GD F-16D-40	BD-15	93-0515	EAF	9933	GD F-16C-40	BC-33	90-0929	EAF
9854	T-GD F-16D-40	BD-16	93-0516	EAF	9934	GD F-16C-40	BC-34	90-0930	EAF

Serial	Type/Code	c/n	ex	Operator/location
9935	GD F-16C-40	BC-35	90-0953	EAF
9951	T-GD F-16C-40	BC-36	93-0485	EAF
9952	T-GD F-16C-40	BC-37	93-0486	EAF
9953	T-GD F-16C-40	BC-38	93-0487	EAF
9954	T-GD F-16C-40	BC-39	93-0488	EAF
9955	T-GD F-16C-40	BC-40	93-0489	EAF
9956	T-GD F-16C-40	BC-41	93-0490	EAF
9957	T-GD F-16C-40	BC-42	93-0491	EAF
9958	T-GD F-16C-40	BC-43	93-0492	EAF
9959	T-GD F-16C-40	BC-44	93-0493	EAF
9960	T-GD F-16C-40	BC-45	93-0494	EAF
9961	T-GD F-16C-40	BC-46	93-0495	EAF
9962	T-GD F-16C-40	BC-47	93-0496	EAF
9963	T-GD F-16C-40	BC-48	93-0497	EAF
9964	T-GD F-16C-40	BC-49	93-0498	EAF
9965	T-GD F-16C-40	BC-50	93-0499	EAF
9966	T-GD F-16C-40	BC-51	93-0500	EAF
9967	T-GD F-16C-40	BC-52	93-0501	EAF
9968	T-GD F-16C-40	BC-53	93-0502	EAF
9969	T-GD F-16C-40	BC-54	93-0503	EAF
9970	T-GD F-16C-40	BC-55	93-0504	EAF
9971	T-GD F-16C-40	BC-56	93-0505	EAF
9972	T-GD F-16C-40	BC-57	93-0506	EAF
9973	T-GD F-16C-40	BC-58	93-0507	EAF
9974	T-GD F-16C-40	BC-59	93-0508	EAF
9975	T-GD F-16C-40	BC-60	93-0509	EAF
9976	T-GD F-16C-40	BC-61	93-0510	EAF
9977	T-GD F-16C-40	BC-62	93-0511	EAF
9978	T-GD F-16C-40	BC-63	93-0512	EAF
9979	T-GD F-16C-40	BC-64	93-0525	EAF
9980	T-GD F-16C-40	BC-65	93-0526	EAF
9981	T-GD F-16C-40	BC-66	93-0527	EAF
9982	T-GD F-16C-40	BC-67	93-0528	EAF
9983	T-GD F-16C-40	BC-68	93-0529	EAF
9984	T-GD F-16C-40	BC-69	93-0530	EAF

Aircraft are known to have crashed as follows:
20-Nov-90 (F-16A), Nov-90 (F-16), Nov-90 (F-16), 09-Sep-93 (F-16B), 18-Jul-94 (F-16) & Oct-94 (F-16C)
A further 21 F-16C/F-16D are on order.

INDONESIA – Indonesian National Defence – Air Force – Tentara Nasional Indonesia – Angkatan Udara (TNI-AU)

Serial	Type/Code	c/n	ex	Operator/location
TS-1601	GD F-16B-15	1B-1	87-0721	TNI-AU 3 Sqn, Maidun-Iswahyudi
TS-1602	GD F-16B-15	1B-2	87-0722	TNI-AU 3 Sqn, Maidun-Iswahyudi
TS-1603	GD F-16B-15	1B-3	87-0723	TNI-AU 3 Sqn, Maidun-Iswahyudi
TS-1604	GD F-16B-15	1B-4	87-0724	TNI-AU 3 Sqn, Maidun-Iswahyudi
TS-1605	GD F-16A-15	1A-1	87-0713	TNI-AU 3 Sqn, Maidun-Iswahyudi
TS-1606	GD F-16A-15	1A-2	87-0714	TNI-AU 3 Sqn, Maidun-Iswahyudi
TS-1607	GD F-16A-15	1A-3	87-0715	Cr 11-Mar-97
TS-1608	GD F-16A-15	1A-4	87-0716	TNI-AU 3 Sqn, Maidun-Iswahyudi
TS-1609	GD F-16A-15	1A-5	87-0717	TNI-AU 3 Sqn, Maidun-Iswahyudi
TS-1610	GD F-16A-15	1A-6	87-0718	TNI-AU 3 Sqn, Maidun-Iswahyudi
TS-1611	GD F-16A-15	1A-7	87-0719	TNI-AU 3 Sqn, Maidun-Iswahyudi
TS-1612	GD F-16A-15	1A-8	87-0720	TNI-AU 3 Sqn, Maidun-Iswahyudi

ISRAEL – Israel Defence Force/Air Force – Tsvah Haganah Le Israeli – Heyl Ha'Avir (IDF/AF)

Serial	Type/Code	c/n	ex	Operator/location
001	GD F-16B-05	6W-1	78-0355	IDF/AF
003	GD F-16B-05	6W-2	78-0356	Cr
004	GD F-16B-05	6W-3	78-0357	IDF/AF
006	GD F-16B-05	6W-4	78-0358	IDF/AF
008	GD F-16B-05	6W-5	78-0359	Cr
010	GD F-16B-05	6W-6	78-0360	IDF/AF
015	GD F-16B-05	6W-7	78-0361	Cr
017	GD F-16B-05	6W-8	78-0362	IDF/AF
020	GD F-16D-30	4K-1	87-1694	IDF/AF
022	GD F-16D-30	4K-7	87-1700	IDF/AF
023	GD F-16D-30	4K-3	87-1696	IDF/AF
027	GD F-16D-30	4K-4	87-1697	IDF/AF
031	GD F-16D-30	4K-2	87-1695	IDF/AF 109 Sqn, Ramat-David AB
034	GD F-16D-30	4K-5	87-1698	IDF/AF
036	GD F-16D-30	4K-6	87-1699	IDF/AF 109 Sqn, Ramat-David AB
039	GD F-16D-30	4K-10	87-1703	IDF/AF 109 Sqn, Ramat-David AB
041	GD F-16D-30	4K-8	87-1701	IDF/AF 101 Sqn, Hatzor-Qastina AB
045	GD F-16D-30	4K-9	87-1702	IDF/AF

Serial	Type/Code	c/n	ex	Operator/location
046	GD F-16D-30	4K-11	87-1704	IDF/AF 109 Sqn, Ramat-David AB
050	GD F-16D-30	4K-12	87-1705	IDF/AF 109 Sqn, Ramat-David AB
055	GD F-16D-30	4K-15	87-1708	IDF/AF
057	GD F-16D-30	4K-13	87-1706	IDF/AF 109 Sqn, Ramat-David AB
061	GD F-16D-30	4K-14	87-1707	IDF/AF 109 Sqn, Ramat-David AB
063	GD F-16D-30	4K-17	88-1713	IDF/AF
069	GD F-16D-30	4K-18	88-1714	IDF/AF 101 Sqn, Hatzor-Qastina AB
072	GD F-16D-30	4K-16	88-1712	IDF/AF 109 Sqn, Ramat-David AB
074	GD F-16D-30	4K-20	88-1716	IDF/AF
075	GD F-16D-30	4K-22	88-1718	IDF/AF
077	GD F-16D-30	4K-19	88-1715	IDF/AF 109 Sqn, Ramat-David AB
079	GD F-16D-30	4K-21	88-1717	IDF/AF
083	GD F-16D-30	4K-24	88-1720	IDF/AF 109 Sqn, Ramat-David AB
088	GD F-16D-30	4K-23	88-1719	IDF/AF 109 Sqn, Ramat-David AB
100	GD F-16A-05	6V-1	78-0308	IDF/AF
102	GD F-16A-05	6V-2	78-0309	IDF/AF
105	GD F-16A-05	6V-3	78-0310	IDF/AF
107	GD F-16A-05	6V-4	78-0311	IDF/AF
109	GD F-16A-05	6V-5	78-0312	IDF/AF
111	GD F-16A-05	6V-6	78-0313	IDF/AF
112	GD F-16A-05	6V-7	78-0314	IDF/AF
113	GD F-16A-05	6V-8	78-0315	IDF/AF
114	GD F-16A-05	6V-9	78-0316	IDF/AF
116	GD F-16A-05	6V-10	78-0317	IDF/AF
118	GD F-16A-05	6V-11	78-0318	IDF/AF
121	GD F-16A-05	6V-12	78-0319	Cr
124	GD F-16A-05	6V-13	78-0320	IDF/AF
126	GD F-16A-05	6V-14	78-0321	IDF/AF
129	GD F-16A-05	6V-15	78-0322	IDF/AF
131	GD F-16A-05	6V-16	78-0323	IDF/AF
135	GD F-16A-05	6V-17	78-0324	IDF/AF
138	GD F-16A-05	6V-18	78-0325	IDF/AF
219	GD F-16A-10	6V-19	78-0326	IDF/AF
220	GD F-16A-10	6V-20	78-0327	IDF/AF
222	GD F-16A-10	6V-21	78-0328	Cr
223	GD F-16A-10	6V-22	78-0329	Cr 20-Jan-81
225	GD F-16A-10	6V-23	78-0330	Cr
227	GD F-16A-10	6V-24	78-0331	IDF/AF
228	GD F-16A-10	6V-25	78-0332	IDF/AF
230	GD F-16A-10	6V-26	78-0333	IDF/AF
232	GD F-16A-10	6V-27	78-0334	IDF/AF
233	GD F-16A-10	6V-28	78-0335	IDF/AF
234	GD F-16A-10	6V-29	78-0336	IDF/AF
236	GD F-16A-10	6V-30	78-0337	IDF/AF
237	GD F-16A-10	6V-31	78-0338	IDF/AF
239	GD F-16A-10	6V-32	78-0339	IDF/AF
240	GD F-16A-10	6V-33	78-0340	Cr
242	GD F-16A-10	6V-34	78-0341	IDF/AF
243	GD F-16A-10	6V-35	78-0342	IDF/AF
246	GD F-16A-10	6V-36	78-0343	IDF/AF
248	GD F-16A-10	6V-37	78-0344	IDF/AF
249	GD F-16A-10	6V-38	78-0345	IDF/AF
250	GD F-16A-10	6V-39	78-0346	IDF/AF
252	GD F-16A-10	6V-40	78-0347	IDF/AF
254	GD F-16A-10	6V-41	78-0348	IDF/AF
255	GD F-16A-10	6V-42	78-0349	IDF/AF
257	GD F-16A-10	6V-43	78-0350	Cr
258	GD F-16A-10	6V-44	78-0351	Cr 20-Jan-81
260	GD F-16A-10	6V-45	78-0352	IDF/AF
261	GD F-16A-10	6V-46	78-0353	IDF/AF
264	GD F-16A-10	6V-47	78-0354	IDF/AF
265	GD F-16A-10	6V-48	80-0649	IDF/AF
266	GD F-16A-10	6V-49	80-0650	IDF/AF
267	GD F-16A-10	6V-50	80-0651	IDF/AF
269	GD F-16A-10	6V-51	80-0652	IDF/AF
272	GD F-16A-10	6V-52	80-0653	IDF/AF
273	GD F-16A-10	6V-53	80-0654	IDF/AF
274	GD F-16A-10	6V-54	80-0655	IDF/AF
275	GD F-16A-10	6V-55	80-0656	IDF/AF
276	GD F-16A-10	6V-56	80-0657	IDF/AF
277	GD F-16A-10	6V-57	80-0658	IDF/AF
281	GD F-16A-10	6V-58	80-0659	IDF/AF
282	GD F-16A-10	6V-59	80-0660	IDF/AF
284	GD F-16A-10	6V-60	80-0661	IDF/AF
285	GD F-16A-10	6V-61	80-0662	IDF/AF

Serial	Type/Code	c/n	ex	Operator/location
287	GD F-16A-10	6V-62	80-0663	IDF/AF
290	GD F-16A-10	6V-63	80-0664	IDF/AF
292	GD F-16A-10	6V-64	80-0665	IDF/AF
296	GD F-16A-10	6V-65	80-0666	IDF/AF
298	GD F-16A-10	6V-66	80-0667	IDF/AF
299	GD F-16A-10	6V-67	80-0668	IDF/AF Test Centre, Tel Nof
301	GD F-16C-30	4J-1	86-1598	IDF/AF Test Centre, Tel Nof
304	GD F-16C-30	4J-2	86-1599	IDF/AF 117 Sqn, Ramat-David AB
305	GD F-16C-30	4J-3	86-1600	IDF/AF 117 Sqn, Ramat-David AB
307	GD F-16C-30	4J-4	86-1601	IDF/AF 117 Sqn, Ramat-David AB
309	GD F-16C-30	4J-5	86-1602	IDF/AF
310	GD F-16C-30	4J-6	86-1603	IDF/AF 117 Sqn, Ramat-David AB
313	GD F-16C-30	4J-50	88-1710	IDF/AF
315	GD F-16C-30	4J-7	86-1604	IDF/AF 117 Sqn, Ramat-David AB
317	GD F-16C-30	4J-8	86-1605	IDF/AF 117 Sqn, Ramat-David AB
318	GD F-16C-30	4J-9	86-1606	IDF/AF
321	GD F-16C-30	4J-10	86-1607	IDF/AF
324	GD F-16C-30	4J-11	86-1608	IDF/AF
326	GD F-16C-30	4J-12	86-1609	IDF/AF 117 Sqn, Ramat-David AB
329	GD F-16C-30	4J-51	88-1711	IDF/AF
332	GD F-16C-30	4J-13	86-1610	IDF/AF 117 Sqn, Ramat-David AB
333	GD F-16C-30	4J-14	86-1611	IDF/AF 117 Sqn, Ramat-David AB
337	GD F-16C-30	4J-15	86-1612	IDF/AF
340	GD F-16C-30	4J-16	87-1661	IDF/AF
341	GD F-16C-30	4J-17	87-1662	IDF/AF
344	GD F-16C-30	4J-18	87-1663	IDF/AF
345	GD F-16C-30	4J-19	87-1664	IDF/AF
348	GD F-16C-30	4J-20	87-1665	IDF/AF 117 Sqn, Ramat-David AB
349	GD F-16C-30	4J-21	87-1666	IDF/AF
350	GD F-16C-30	4J-22	87-1667	IDF/AF
353	GD F-16C-30	4J-23	87-1668	IDF/AF
355	GD F-16C-30	4J-24	87-1669	IDF/AF
356	GD F-16C-30	4J-25	87-1670	IDF/AF
359	GD F-16C-30	4J-49	88-1709	IDF/AF
360	GD F-16C-30	4J-26	87-1671	IDF/AF
364	GD F-16C-30	4J-27	87-1672	IDF/AF
367	GD F-16C-30	4J-28	87-1673	IDF/AF
368	GD F-16C-30	4J-29	87-1674	IDF/AF
371	GD F-16C-30	4J-30	87-1675	IDF/AF
373	GD F-16C-30	4J-31	87-1676	IDF/AF 110 Sqn, Ramat-David AB
374	GD F-16C-30	4J-32	87-1677	IDF/AF
376	GD F-16C-30	4J-48	87-1693	IDF/AF
377	GD F-16C-30	4J-33	87-1678	IDF/AF
378	GD F-16C-30	4J-34	87-1679	IDF/AF 110 Sqn, Ramat-David AB
381	GD F-16C-30	4J-35	87-1680	IDF/AF
383	GD F-16C-30	4J-46	87-1691	IDF/AF
384	GD F-16C-30	4J-36	87-1681	IDF/AF
385	GD F-16C-30	4J-47	87-1692	IDF/AF
386	GD F-16C-30	4J-37	87-1682	IDF/AF
388	GD F-16C-30	4J-38	87-1683	IDF/AF 110 Sqn, Ramat-David AB
389	GD F-16C-30	4J-39	87-1684	IDF/AF 110 Sqn, Ramat-David AB
391	GD F-16C-30	4J-40	87-1685	IDF/AF
392	GD F-16C-30	4J-43	87-1688	IDF/AF 110 Sqn, Ramat-David AB
393	GD F-16C-30	4J-41	87-1686	IDF/AF
394	GD F-16C-30	4J-42	87-1687	IDF/AF
397	GD F-16C-30	4J-44	87-1689	IDF/AF
399	GD F-16C-30	4J-45	87-1690	IDF/AF
502	GD F-16C-40	CJ-1	89-0277	IDF/AF 101 Sqn, Hatzor-Qastina AB
503	GD F-16C-40	CJ-2	90-0850	IDF/AF 105 Sqn, Hatzor-Qastina AB
506	GD F-16C-40	CJ-3	90-0851	IDF/AF 101 Sqn, Hatzor-Qastina AB
508	GD F-16C-40	CJ-4	90-0852	IDF/AF 101 Sqn, Hatzor-Qastina AB
511	GD F-16C-40	CJ-5	90-0853	IDF/AF 105 Sqn, Hatzor-Qastina AB
512	GD F-16C-40	CJ-6	90-0854	IDF/AF 101 Sqn, Hatzor-Qastina AB
514	GD F-16C-40	CJ-7	90-0855	IDF/AF 101 Sqn, Hatzor-Qastina AB
516	GD F-16C-40	CJ-8	90-0856	IDF/AF 101 Sqn, Hatzor-Qastina AB
519	GD F-16C-40	CJ-9	90-0857	IDF/AF 105 Sqn, Hatzor-Qastina AB
520	GD F-16C-40	CJ-10	90-0858	IDF/AF 101 Sqn, Hatzor-Qastina AB
522	GD F-16C-40	CJ-11	90-0859	IDF/AF 101 Sqn, Hatzor-Qastina AB
523	GD F-16C-40	CJ-12	90-0860	IDF/AF 105 Sqn, Hatzor-Qastina AB
525	GD F-16C-40	CJ-13	90-0861	IDF/AF 105 Sqn, Hatzor-Qastina AB
527	GD F-16C-40	CJ-14	90-0862	IDF/AF 105 Sqn, Hatzor-Qastina AB
528	GD F-16C-40	CJ-15	90-0863	IDF/AF 101 Sqn, Hatzor-Qastina AB
530	GD F-16C-40	CJ-16	90-0864	IDF/AF 101 Sqn, Hatzor-Qastina AB
531	GD F-16C-40	CJ-17	90-0865	IDF/AF 105 Sqn, Hatzor-Qastina AB
534	GD F-16C-40	CJ-18	90-0866	IDF/AF 101 Sqn, Hatzor-Qastina AB

F-16C 528 on delivery to Israel in August 1992. PETER R FOSTER

Serial	Type/Code	c/n	ex	Operator/location
535	GD F-16C-40	CJ-19	90-0867	IDF/AF
536	GD F-16C-40	CJ-20	90-0868	IDF/AF
538	GD F-16C-40	CJ-21	90-0869	IDF/AF
539	GD F-16C-40	CJ-22	90-0870	IDF/AF
542	GD F-16C-40	CJ-23	90-0871	IDF/AF
543	GD F-16C-40	CJ-24	90-0872	IDF/AF
546	GD F-16C-40	CJ-25	90-0873	IDF/AF
547	GD F-16C-40	CJ-26	90-0874	IDF/AF 101 Sqn, Hatzor-Qastina AB
551	GD F-16C-40	CJ-27	91-0486	IDF/AF
554	GD F-16C-40	CJ-28	91-0487	IDF/AF
557	GD F-16C-40	CJ-29	91-0488	IDF/AF
558	GD F-16C-40	CJ-30	91-0489	IDF/AF
601	GD F-16D-40	CK-1	90-0875	IDF/AF
603	GD F-16D-40	CK-2	90-0876	IDF/AF
606	GD F-16D-40	CK-3	90-0877	IDF/AF 101 Sqn, Hatzor-Qastina AB
610	GD F-16D-40	CK-4	90-0878	IDF/AF 105 Sqn, Hatzor-Qastina AB
612	GD F-16D-40	CK-5	90-0879	IDF/AF 101 Sqn, Hatzor-Qastina AB
615	GD F-16D-40	CK-6	90-0880	IDF/AF 105 Sqn, Hatzor-Qastina AB
619	GD F-16D-40	CK-7	90-0881	IDF/AF 101 Sqn, Hatzor-Qastina AB
621	GD F-16D-40	CK-8	90-0882	IDF/AF 105 Sqn, Hatzor-Qastina AB
624	GD F-16D-40	CK-9	90-0883	IDF/AF 101 Sqn, Hatzor-Qastina AB
628	GD F-16D-40	CK-10	90-0884	IDF/AF 105 Sqn, Hatzor-Qastina AB
630	GD F-16D-40	CK-11	90-0885	IDF/AF 105 Sqn, Hatzor-Qastina AB
633	GD F-16D-40	CK-12	90-0886	IDF/AF
637	GD F-16D-40	CK-13	90-0887	IDF/AF
638	GD F-16D-40	CK-14	90-0888	IDF/AF 105 Sqn, Hatzor-Qastina AB
642	GD F-16D-40	CK-15	90-0889	IDF/AF 105 Sqn, Hatzor-Qastina AB
647	GD F-16D-40	CK-16	90-0890	IDF/AF
648	GD F-16D-40	CK-17	90-0891	IDF/AF 101 Sqn, Hatzor-Qastina AB
651	GD F-16D-40	CK-18	90-0892	IDF/AF 105 Sqn, Hatzor-Qastina AB
652	GD F-16D-40	CK-19	90-0893	IDF/AF
656	GD F-16D-40	CK-20	90-0894	IDF/AF
660	GD F-16D-40	CK-21	90-0895	IDF/AF 101 Sqn, Hatzor-Qastina AB
664	GD F-16D-40	CK-22	90-0896	IDF/AF 105 Sqn, Hatzor-Qastina AB
666	GD F-16D-40	CK-23	90-0897	IDF/AF 105 Sqn, Hatzor-Qastina AB
667	GD F-16D-40	CK-24	90-0898	IDF/AF 105 Sqn, Hatzor-Qastina AB
673	GD F-16D-40	CK-25	91-0490	IDF/AF
676	GD F-16D-40	CK-26	91-0491	IDF/AF 101 Sqn, Hatzor-Qastina AB
678	GD F-16D-40	CK-27	91-0492	IDF/AF
682	GD F-16D-40	CK-28	91-0493	IDF/AF 101 Sqn, Hatzor-Qastina AB
684	GD F-16D-40	CK-29	91-0494	IDF/AF 105 Sqn, Hatzor-Qastina AB
687	GD F-16D-40	CK-30	91-0495	IDF/AF 101 Sqn, Hatzor-Qastina AB
712	GD F-16A	61-		IDF/AF
721	GD F-16A	61-		IDF/AF
724	GD F-16A	61-		IDF/AF
735	GD F-16A	61-		IDF/AF, Haifa Technical School
740	GD F-16A	61-		IDF/AF 111 Sqn, Hatzor-Nevatim AB
750	GD F-16A	61-		IDF/AF
752	GD F-16A	61-		IDF/AF 144 Sqn, Hatzor Nevatim AB
755	GD F-16A	61-		IDF/AF 144 Sqn, Hatzor-Nevatim AB
759	GD F-16A	61-		IDF/AF
760	GD F-16A	61-		IDF/AF 111 Sqn, Hatzor-Nevatim AB
769	GD F-16A	61-		IDF/AF
777	GD F-16A	61-		IDF/AF 111 Sqn, Hatzor-Nevatim AB
981	GD F-16B	62-		IDF/AF 111 Sqn, Hatzor-Nevatim AB
993	GD F-16B	62-		IDF/AF FTC, Hatzor-Qastina AB
995	GD F-16B	62-		IDF/AF 111 Sqn, Hatzor-Nevatim AB
996	GD F-16B	62-		IDF/AF 111 Sqn, Hatzor-Nevatim AB
	LMTAS F-16C-40	CJ-31 to CJ-60		IDF/AF, on order
	LMTAS F-16D-40	CK-31 to CK-60		IDF/AF, on order

In addition, the following are known to have been supplied from USAF stocks:

Serial	Type/Code	c/n	ex	Operator/location
	GD F-16A-01	61-18/M10-1	78-0012	IDF/AF
	GD F-16A-01	61-20/M10-2	78-0014	IDF/AF
	GD F-16A-01	61-24/M10-3	78-0018	IDF/AF
	GD F-16A-05	61-73/M10-4	79-0288	IDF/AF
	GD F-16A-10	61-74/M10-5	79-0289	IDF/AF
	GD F-16A-10	61-76/M10-6	79-0291	IDF/AF
	GD F-16A-10	61-77/M10-7	79-0292	IDF/AF
	GD F-16A-10	61-78/M10-8	79-0293	IDF/AF
	GD F-16A-10	61-80/M10-9	79-0295	IDF/AF
	GD F-16A-10	61-82/M10-10	79-0297	IDF/AF
	GD F-16A-10	61-84/M10-11	79-0299	IDF/AF
	GD F-16A-10	61-87/M10-12	79-0302	IDF/AF
	GD F-16A-10	61-89/M10-13	79-0304	IDF/AF
	GD F-16A-10	61-90/M10-14	79-0305	IDF/AF
	GD F-16A-10	61-104/M10-15	79-0319	IDF/AF
	GD F-16A-10	61-105/M10-16	79-0320	IDF/AF
	GD F-16A-10	61-106/M10-17	79-0321	IDF/AF
	GD F-16A-10	61-110/M10-18	79-0325	IDF/AF
	GD F-16A-10	61-113/M10-19	79-0328	IDF/AF
	GD F-16A-10	61-118/M10-20	79-0333	IDF/AF
	GD F-16A-10	61-124/M10-21	79-0339	IDF/AF
	GD F-16A-10	61-132/M10-22	79-0347	IDF/AF
	GD F-16A-10	61-141/M10-23	79-0356	IDF/AF
	GD F-16A-10	61-143/M10-24	79-0358	IDF/AF
	GD F-16A-10	61-146/M10-25	79-0361	IDF/AF
	GD F-16A-10	61-154/M10-26	79-0369	IDF/AF
	GD F-16A-10	61-162/M10-27	79-0377	IDF/AF
	Cr GD F-16A-10	61-212/M10-28	80-0491	IDF/AF
	GD F-16A-10	61-222/M10-29	80-0501	IDF/AF
	GD F-16A-10	61-223/M10-30	80-0502	IDF/AF
	GD F-16A-10	61-224/M10-31	80-0503	IDF/AF
	GD F-16A-10	61-235/M10-32	80-0514	IDF/AF
	GD F-16A-10	61-237/M10-33	80-0516	IDF/AF
	GD F-16A-10	61-238/M10-34	80-0517	IDF/AF
	GD F-16A-10	61-253/M10-35	80-0532	IDF/AF
	GD F-16A-10	61-255/M10-36	80-0534	IDF/AF
	GD F-16B-01	62-12/M11-1	78-0086	IDF/AF
	GD F-16B-01	62-21/M11-2	78-0095	IDF/AF
	GD F-16B-05	62-32/M11-3	78-0106	IDF/AF
	GD F-16B-05	62-34/M11-4	78-0108	IDF/AF
	GD F-16B-05	62-35/M11-5	78-0109	IDF/AF
	GD F-16B-05	62-37/M11-6	78-0111	IDF/AF
	GD F-16B-05	62-40/M11-7	78-0114	IDF/AF
	GD F-16B-05	62-41/M11-8	78-0115	IDF/AF
	GD F-16B-05	62-42/M11-9	79-0410	IDF/AF
	GD F-16B-10	62-55/M11-10	79-0423	IDF/AF
	GD F-16B-10	62-56/M11-11	79-0424	IDF/AF
	GD F-16B-10	62-57/M11-12	79-0425	IDF/AF
	GD F-16B-10	62-74/M11-13	80-0624	IDF/AF
	GD F-16B-10	62-74/M11-14	80-0632	IDF/AF

Aircraft are also known to have crashed as follows: 10-Jul-86 (F-16A), 05-Oct-87 (F-16), Oct-94 (F-16C), 17-Jan-95 (F-16), 17-Jan-95 (F-16), 29-Jul-96 (F-16D, 110 Sqn) & 29-Jul-96 (F-16D, 110 Sqn)

JORDAN – Royal Jordanian Air Force
– Al Quwwat Al Jawwiya Al Malakiya Al Urduniya (RJAF)
12 GD F-16A and 4 F-16B Royal Jordanian AF, on order

PAKISTAN – Pakistan Air Force – Pakistan Fiza'Ya (PAF)

Serial	Type/Code	c/n	ex	Operator/location
82601	GD F-16B-15	5H-1	81-0931	PAF 38 Wing, Sargodha
82602	GD F-16B-15	5H-2	81-0932	PAF 38 Wing, Sargodha
82603	GD F-16B-15	5H-3	81-0933	PAF 38 Wing, Sargodha
82604	GD F-16B-15	5H-4	81-0934	PAF 38 Wing, Sargodha
82701	GD F-16A-15	5G-1	81-0899	PAF 38 Wing, Sargodha
82702	GD F-16A-15	5G-2	81-0900	PAF 38 Wing, Sargodha
83605	GD F-16B-15	5H-5	81-0935	PAF 38 Wing, Sargodha
83703	GD F-16A-15	5G-3	81-0901	PAF 11 Sqn/38 Wing, Sargodha
84606	GD F-16B-15	5H-6	81-0936	PAF 38 Wing, Sargodha
84607	GD F-16B-15	5H-7	81-0937	PAF 38 Wing, Sargodha
84608	GD F-16B-15	5H-8	81-0938	PAF 38 Wing, Sargodha
84704	GD F-16A-15	5G-4	81-0902	PAF 11 Sqn/38 Wing, Sargodha
84705	GD F-16A-15	5G-5	81-0903	PAF 11 Sqn/38 Wing, Sargodha
84706	GD F-16A-15	5G-6	81-0904	PAF 38 Wing, Sargodha
84707	GD F-16A-15	5G-7	81-0905	PAF 38 Wing, Sargodha

Pakistan AF F-16B 85610 of 9 Sqn landing at Sargodha. PETER R FOSTER

Serial	Type/Code	c/n	ex	Operator/location
84708	GD F-16A-15	5G-8	81-0906	PAF 38 Wing, Sargodha
84709	GD F-16A-15	5G-9	81-0907	PAF 38 Wing, Sargodha
84710	GD F-16A-15	5G-10	81-0908	PAF 38 Wing, Sargodha
84711	GD F-16A-15	5G-11	81-0909	PAF 38 Wing, Sargodha
84712	GD F-16A-15	5G-12	81-0910	PAF 38 Wing, Sargodha
84713	GD F-16A-15	5G-13	81-0911	PAF 38 Wing, Sargodha
84714	GD F-16A-15	5G-14	81-0912	PAF 38 Wing, Sargodha
84715	GD F-16A-15	5G-15	81-0913	PAF 38 Wing, Sargodha
84716	GD F-16A-15	5G-16	81-0914	PAF 38 Wing, Sargodha
84717	GD F-16A-15	5G-17	81-0915	PAF 38 Wing, Sargodha
84718	GD F-16A-15	5G-18	81-0916	PAF 38 Wing, Sargodha
84719	GD F-16A-15	5G-19	81-0917	PAF 38 Wing, Sargodha
85609	GD F-16B-15	5H-9	81-1504	Cr 30-Dec-86 (38 Wing)
85610	GD F-16B-15	5H-10	81-1505	PAF 38 Wing, Sargodha
85611	GD F-16B-15	5H-11	81-1506	PAF 38 Wing, Sargodha
85612	GD F-16B-15	5H-12	81-1507	PAF 38 Wing, Sargodha
85720	GD F-16A-15	5G-20	81-0918	PAF 38 Wing, Sargodha
85721	GD F-16A-15	5G-21	81-0919	PAF 38 Wing, Sargodha
85722	GD F-16A-15	5G-22	81-0920	PAF 38 Wing, Sargodha
85723	GD F-16A-15	5G-23	81-0921	PAF 38 Wing, Sargodha
85724	GD F-16A-15	5G-24	81-0922	PAF 11 Sqn/38 Wing, Sargodha
85725	GD F-16A-15	5G-25	81-0923	PAF 38 Wing, Sargodha
85726	GD F-16A-15	5G-26	81-0924	PAF 38 Wing, Sargodha
85727	GD F-16A-15	5G-27	81-0925	PAF 38 Wing, Sargodha
85728	GD F-16A-15	5G-28	81-0926	PAF 38 Wing, Sargodha
91613	GD F-16B-15	DH-1	90-0948	Not delivered
91729	GD F-16A-15	DG-1	90-0942	Not delivered
92614	GD F-16B-15	DH-2	90-0949	Not delivered
92615	GD F-16B-15	DH-3	90-0950	Not delivered
92616	GD F-16B-15	DH-4	90-0951	Not delivered
92617	GD F-16B-15	DH-5	90-0952	Not delivered
92618	GD F-16B-15	DH-6	92-0452	Not delivered
92619	GD F-16B-15	DH-7	92-0453	Not delivered
92730	GD F-16A-15	DG-2	90-0943	Not delivered
92731	GD F-16A-15	DG-3	90-0944	Not delivered
92732	GD F-16A-15	DG-4	90-0945	Not delivered
92733	GD F-16A-15	DG-5	90-0946	Not delivered
92734	GD F-16A-15	DG-6	90-0947	Not delivered
92735	GD F-16A-15	DG-7	92-0404	Not delivered
92736	GD F-16A-15	DG-8	92-0405	Not delivered
92737	GD F-16A-15	DG-9	92-0406	Not delivered
92738	GD F-16A-15	DG-10	92-0407	Not delivered
93620	GD F-16B-15	DH-8	92-0454	Not delivered

The second F-16A delivered to the Pakistan AF is currently with 11 Sqn. PETER R FOSTER

Serial	Type/Code	c/n	ex	Operator/location
93621	GD F-16B-15	DH-9	92-0455	Not delivered
93739	GD F-16A-15	DG-11	92-0408	Not delivered
93740	GD F-16A-15	DG-12	92-0409	Not delivered
93741	GD F-16A-15	DG-13	92-0410	Not delivered
..742 to 782	GD F-16A-15	DG-14 to DG-54	92-0411 to 92-0451	Ordered but not built
94622	GD F-16B-15	DH-10	92-0456	Not delivered
94623	GD F-16B-15	DH-11	92-0457	Not delivered
..624 to 629	GD F-16B-15	DH-12 to DH-17	92-0458 to 92-0463	Not delivered
..629	GD F-16B-15	DH-17	92-0463	Ordered but not built

Aircraft are also known to have crashed as follows:
29-Apr-87 (F-16A), 28-Oct-91 (F-16A), 06-Sep-93 (F-16), 26-Apr-94 (F-16A) & 22-Oct-94 (F-16A)

SINGAPORE – Republic of Singapore Air Force (RoSAF)

Serial	Type/Code	c/n	ex	Operator/location
880	GD F-16A-15	27-1	87-0397	RoSAF 140 Sqn, Tengah
881	GD F-16A-15	27-2	87-0398	RoSAF 140 Sqn, Tengah
882	GD F-16A-15	27-3	87-0399	RoSAF 140 Sqn, Tengah
883	GD F-16A-15	27-4	87-0400	Cr 08-Jul-91 (140 Sqn)
884	GD F-16B-15	28-1	87-0401	RoSAF 140 Sqn, Tengah
885	GD F-16B-15	28-2	87-0402	RoSAF 140 Sqn, Tengah
886	GD F-16B-15	28-3	87-0403	RoSAF 140 Sqn, Tengah
887	GD F-16B-15	28-4	87-0404	RoSAF 140 Sqn, Tengah
	LMTAS F-16C-52	DA-1 to DA-8		RoSAF, on order
	LMTAS F-16D-52	DB-1 to DB-10		RoSAF, on order

SOUTH KOREA – Republic of Korea Air Force – Han-Guk Kong Goon (RoKAF)

Serial	Type/Code	c/n	ex	Operator/location
84-370	GD F-16D-30	5B-1	84-1370	RoKAF 11 TFW, Taegu
84-371	GD F-16D-30	5B-2	84-1371	RoKAF 11 TFW, Taegu
84-372	GD F-16D-30	5B-3	84-1372	RoKAF 11 TFW, Taegu
84-373	GD F-16D-30	5B-4	84-1373	RoKAF 11 TFW, Taegu
85-574	GD F-16C-32	5A-1	85-1574	RoKAF 11 TFW, Taegu
85-575	GD F-16C-32	5A-2	85-1575	RoKAF 11 TFW, Taegu
85-576	GD F-16C-32	5A-3	85-1576	RoKAF 11 TFW, Taegu
85-577	GD F-16C-32	5A-4	85-1577	RoKAF 11 TFW, Taegu
85-578	GD F-16C-32	5A-5	85-1578	RoKAF 11 TFW, Taegu
85-579	GD F-16C-32	5A-6	85-1579	RoKAF 11 TFW, Taegu
85-580	GD F-16C-32	5A-7	85-1580	RoKAF 11 TFW, Taegu
85-581	GD F-16C-32	5A-8	85-1581	RoKAF 11 TFW, Taegu
85-582	GD F-16C-32	5A-9	85-1582	RoKAF 11 TFW, Taegu
85-583	GD F-16C-32	5A-10	85-1583	RoKAF 11 TFW, Taegu
84-584	GD F-16D-32	5B-5	85-1584	RoKAF 11 TFW, Taegu
84-585	GD F-16D-32	5B-6	85-1585	RoKAF 11 TFW, Taegu
85-586	GD F-16C-32	5A-11	85-1586	RoKAF 11 TFW, Taegu
85-587	GD F-16C-32	5A-12	85-1587	RoKAF 11 TFW, Taegu

Serial	Type/Code	c/n	ex	Operator/location
85-588	GD F-16C-32	5A-13	85-1588	RoKAF 11 TFW, Taegu
85-589	GD F-16C-32	5A-14	85-1589	RoKAF 11 TFW, Taegu
85-590	GD F-16C-32	5A-15	85-1590	RoKAF 11 TFW, Taegu
85-591	GD F-16C-32	5A-16	85-1591	RoKAF 11 TFW, Taegu
85-592	GD F-16C-32	5A-17	85-1592	RoKAF 11 TFW, Taegu
85-593	GD F-16C-32	5A-18	85-1593	RoKAF 11 TFW, Taegu
85-594	GD F-16C-32	5A-19	85-1594	RoKAF 11 TFW, Taegu
85-595	GD F-16C-32	5A-20	85-1595	RoKAF 11 TFW, Taegu
85-596	GD F-16C-32	5A-21	85-1596	RoKAF 11 TFW, Taegu
85-597	GD F-16C-32	5A-22	85-1597	RoKAF 11 TFW, Taegu
87-653	GD F-16C-32	5A-23	87-1653	RoKAF 11 TFW, Taegu
87-654	GD F-16C-32	5A-24	87-1654	RoKAF 11 TFW, Taegu
87-655	GD F-16C-32	5A-25	87-1655	RoKAF 11 TFW, Taegu
87-656	GD F-16C-32	5A-26	87-1656	RoKAF 11 TFW, Taegu
87-657	GD F-16C-32	5A-27	87-1657	RoKAF 11 TFW, Taegu
87-658	GD F-16C-32	5A-28	87-1658	RoKAF 11 TFW, Taegu
87-659	GD F-16C-32	5A-29	87-1659	RoKAF 11 TFW, Taegu
87-660	GD F-16C-32	5A-30	87-1660	RoKAF 11 TFW, Taegu
90-938	GD F-16D-32	5B-7	90-0938	RoKAF 11 TFW, Taegu
90-939	GD F-16D-32	5B-8	90-0939	RoKAF 11 TFW, Taegu
90-940	GD F-16D-32	5B-9	90-0940	RoKAF 11 TFW, Taegu
90-941	GD F-16D-32	5B-10	90-0941	RoKAF 11 TFW, Taegu
92-000	LMTAS F-16C-52	KC-1	92-4000	RoKAF 11 TFW, Taegu
92-001	LMTAS F-16C-52	KC-2	92-4001	RoKAF 11 TFW, Taegu
92-002	LMTAS F-16C-52	KC-3	92-4002	RoKAF 11 TFW, Taegu
92-003	LMTAS F-16C-52	KC-4	92-4003	RoKAF 11 TFW, Taegu
92-004	LMTAS F-16C-52	KC-5	92-4004	RoKAF 11 TFW, Taegu
92-005	LMTAS F-16C-52	KC-6	92-4005	RoKAF 11 TFW, Taegu
92-006	LMTAS F-16C-52	KC-7	92-4006	RoKAF 11 TFW, Taegu
92-007	LMTAS F-16C-52	KC-8	92-4007	RoKAF 11 TFW, Taegu
92-008	LMTAS F-16C-52	KC-9	92-4008	RoKAF 11 TFW, Taegu
92-009	LMTAS F-16C-52	KC-10	92-4009	RoKAF 11 TFW, Taegu
92-010	LMTAS F-16C-52	KC-11	92-4010	RoKAF 11 TFW, Taegu
92-011	LMTAS F-16C-52	KC-12	92-4011	RoKAF 11 TFW, Taegu
92-012	LMTAS F-16C-52	KC-13	92-4012	RoKAF 11 TFW, Taegu
92-013	LMTAS F-16C-52	KC-14	92-4013	RoKAF 11 TFW, Taegu
92-014	LMTAS F-16C-52	KC-15	92-4014	RoKAF 11 TFW, Taegu
92-015	LMTAS F-16C-52	KC-16	92-4015	RoKAF 11 TFW, Taegu
92-016	LMTAS F-16C-52	KC-17	92-4016	RoKAF 11 TFW, Taegu
92-017	LMTAS F-16C-52	KC-18	92-4017	RoKAF 11 TFW, Taegu
92-018	LMTAS F-16C-52	KC-19	92-4018	RoKAF 11 TFW, Taegu
92-019	LMTAS F-16C-52	KC-20	92-4019	RoKAF 11 TFW, Taegu
92-020	LMTAS F-16C-52	KC-21	92-4020	RoKAF 11 TFW, Taegu
92-021	LMTAS F-16C-52	KC-22	92-4021	RoKAF 11 TFW, Taegu
92-022	LMTAS F-16C-52	KC-23	92-4022	RoKAF 11 TFW, Taegu

F-16C Block 32 85-575, one of 30 supplied to the RoKAF to replace Phantoms in 1986. LMTAS

Serial	Type/Code	c/n	ex	Operator/location
92-023	LMTAS F-16C-52	KC-24	92-4023	RoKAF 11 TFW, Taegu
92-024	LMTAS F-16C-52	KC-25	92-4024	RoKAF 11 TFW, Taegu
92-025	LMTAS F-16C-52	KC-26	92-4025	RoKAF 11 TFW, Taegu
92-026	LMTAS F-16C-52	KC-27	92-4026	RoKAF 11 TFW, Taegu
92-027	LMTAS F-16C-52	KC-28	92-4027	RoKAF 11 TFW, Taegu
92-028	LMTAS F-16D-52	KD-1	92-4028	RoKAF 11 TFW, Taegu
92-029	LMTAS F-16D-52	KD-2	92-4029	RoKAF 11 TFW, Taegu
92-030	LMTAS F-16D-52	KD-3	92-4030	RoKAF 11 TFW, Taegu
92-031	LMTAS F-16D-52	KD-4	92-4031	RoKAF 11 TFW, Taegu
92-032	LMTAS F-16D-52	KD-5	92-4032	RoKAF 11 TFW, Taegu
92-033	LMTAS F-16D-52	KD-6	92-4033	RoKAF 11 TFW, Taegu
92-034	LMTAS F-16D-52	KD-7	92-4034	RoKAF 11 TFW, Taegu
92-035	LMTAS F-16D-52	KD-8	92-4035	RoKAF 11 TFW, Taegu
92-036	LMTAS F-16D-52	KD-9	92-4036	RoKAF 11 TFW, Taegu
92-037	LMTAS F-16D-52	KD-10	92-4037	RoKAF 11 TFW, Taegu
92-038	LMTAS F-16D-52	KD-11	92-4038	RoKAF 11 TFW, Taegu
92-039	LMTAS F-16D-52	KD-12	92-4039	RoKAF 11 TFW, Taegu
92-040	LMTAS F-16D-52	KD-13	92-4040	RoKAF 11 TFW, Taegu
92-041	LMTAS F-16D-52	KD-14	92-4041	RoKAF 11 TFW, Taegu
92-042	LMTAS F-16D-52	KD-15	92-4042	RoKAF 11 TFW, Taegu
92-043	LMTAS F-16D-52	KD-16	92-4043	RoKAF 11 TFW, Taegu
92-044	LMTAS F-16D-52	KD-17	92-4044	RoKAF 11 TFW, Taegu
92-045	LMTAS F-16D-52	KD-18	92-4045	RoKAF 11 TFW, Taegu
92-046	LMTAS F-16D-52	KD-19	92-4046	RoKAF 11 TFW, Taegu
92-047	LMTAS F-16D-52	KD-20	92-4047	RoKAF 11 TFW, Taegu
	LMTAS F-16C-52	KC-29 to KC-80		RoKAF, on order (built by Samsung)
	LMTAS F-16D-52	KD-21 to KD-40		RoKAF, on order

An aircraft crashed on 08-Apr-93 (F-16C)

TAIWAN – Republic of China Air Force – Chung-Kuo Kung Chuan (RoCAF)

Serial	Type/Code	c/n	ex	Operator/location
6601	LMTAS F-16A-20	TA-1	93-0702	RoCAF, on order
to		to	to	
6720	LMTAS F-16A-20	TA-120	93-0821	RoCAF, on order
6801	LMTAS F-16B-20	TB-1	93-0822	RoCAF, on order
to		to	to	
6830	LMTAS F-16B-20	TB-30	93-0851	RoCAF, on order

THAILAND – Royal Thai Air Force (RTAF)

Serial	Type/Code	c/n	ex	Operator/location
86378	GD F-16A-15 [10305]	2J-1	86-0378	RTAF 103 Sqn, Khorat
86379	GD F-16B-15 [10301]	2K-1	86-0379	RTAF 103 Sqn, Khorat
86380	GD F-16B-15 [10302]	2K-2	86-0380	RTAF 103 Sqn, Khorat
86381	GD F-16B-15 [10303]	2K-3	86-0381	RTAF 103 Sqn, Khorat
87702	GD F-16A-15 [10306]	2J-2	87-0702	RTAF 103 Sqn, Khorat
87703	GD F-16A-15 [10307]	2J-3	87-0703	RTAF 103 Sqn, Khorat
87704	GD F-16A-15 [10308]	2J-4	87-0704	RTAF 103 Sqn, Khorat
87705	GD F-16A-15 [10309]	2J-5	87-0705	RTAF 103 Sqn, Khorat
87706	GD F-16A-15 [10310]	2J-6	87-0706	RTAF 103 Sqn, Khorat
87707	GD F-16A-15 [10311]	2J-7	87-0707	RTAF 103 Sqn, Khorat
87708	GD F-16A-15 [10312]	2J-8	87-0708	RTAF 103 Sqn, Khorat
87709	GD F-16B-15 [10304]	2K-4	87-0709	RTAF 103 Sqn, Khorat
90020	GD F-16A-15 [40307]	HN-1	90-7020	RTAF 403 Sqn, Ta Khli
90021	GD F-16A-15 [40308]	HN-2	90-7021	RTAF 403 Sqn, Ta Khli
90022	GD F-16A-15 [40309]	HN-3	90-7022	RTAF 403 Sqn, Ta Khli
90023	GD F-16A-15 [40310]	HN-4	90-7023	RTAF 403 Sqn, Ta Khli
90024	GD F-16A-15 [40311]	HN-5	90-7024	RTAF 403 Sqn, Ta Khli
90025	GD F-16A-15 [40312]	HN-6	90-7025	RTAF 403 Sqn, Ta Khli
90026	GD F-16A-15 [40313]	HN-7	90-7026	RTAF 403 Sqn, Ta Khli
90027	GD F-16A-15 [40314]	HN-8	90-7027	RTAF 403 Sqn, Ta Khli
90028	GD F-16A-15 [40315]	HN-9	90-7028	RTAF 403 Sqn, Ta Khli
90029	GD F-16A-15 [40316]	HN-10	90-7029	RTAF 403 Sqn, Ta Khli
90030	GD F-16A-15 [40317]	HN-11	90-7030	RTAF 403 Sqn, Ta Khli
90031	GD F-16A-15 [40318]	HN-12	90-7031	RTAF 403 Sqn, Ta Khli
90032	GD F-16B-15 [40301]	HP-1	90-7032	RTAF 403 Sqn, Ta Khli
90033	GD F-16B-15 [40302]	HP-2	90-7033	RTAF 403 Sqn, Ta Khli
90034	GD F-16B-15 [40303]	HP-3	90-7034	RTAF 403 Sqn, Ta Khli
90035	GD F-16B-15 [40304]	HP-4	90-7035	RTAF 403 Sqn, Ta Khli
90036	GD F-16B-15 [40305]	HP-5	90-7036	RTAF 403 Sqn, Ta Khli
90037	GD F-16B-15 [40306]	HP-6	90-7037	RTAF 403 Sqn, Ta Khli
91062	GD F-16A-15 [10313]	2J-9	91-0062	RTAF 103 Sqn, Khorat
91063	GD F-16A-15 [10314]	2J-10	91-0063	RTAF 103 Sqn, Khorat
91064	GD F-16A-15 [10315]	2J-11	91-0064	RTAF 103 Sqn, Khorat
91065	GD F-16A-15 [10316]	2J-12	91-0065	RTAF 103 Sqn, Khorat
91066	GD F-16A-15 [10317]	2J-13	91-0066	RTAF 103 Sqn, Khorat
91067	GD F-16A-15 [10318]	2J-14	91-0067	RTAF 103 Sqn, Khorat

The first Royal Thai Air Force F-16A (86378) is now in service with 103 Sqn at Khorat. LMTAS

Venezuelan Air Force F-16B 2337 is operated by 162 Esc, Grupo 16 from El Libertador. PETER R FOSTER

FAV F-16A Block 15 7268 landing at El Libertador in October 1990. PETER R FOSTER

VENEZUELA – Venezuelan Air Force – Fuerza Aerea Venezolanas (FAV)

Serial	Type/Code	c/n	ex	Operator/location
0049	GD F-16A-15	9P-5	83-1187	FAV 161 Esc, El Libertador
0051	CD F 16A 15	9P-2	82-1051	FAV 161 Esc, El Libertador
0220	GD F-16A-15	9P-18	84-1357	FAV 161 Esc, El Libertador
0678	GD F-16A-15	9P-6	83-1188	FAV 161 Esc, El Libertador
1041	GD F-16A-15	9P-1	82-1050	FAV 161 Esc, El Libertador
1715	GD F-16B-15	9Q-1	82-1053	FAV 162 Esc, El Libertador
2179	GD F-16B-15	9Q-2	82-1054	FAV 162 Esc, El Libertador
2337	GD F-16B-15	9Q-4	83-1189	FAV 162 Esc, El Libertador
3260	GD F-16A-15	9P-12	84-1351	FAV 161 Esc, El Libertador
3648	GD F-16A-15	9P-17	84-1356	FAV 161 Esc, El Libertador
4226	GD F-16A-15	9P-13	84-1352	FAV 161 Esc, El Libertador
4827	GD F-16A-15	9P-15	84-1354	FAV 161 Esc, El Libertador
5422	GD F-16A-15	9P-		FAV 161 Esc, El Libertador
6023	GD F-16A-15	9P-11	84-1350	FAV 161 Esc, El Libertador
6426	GD F-16A-15	9P-14	84-1353	FAV 161 Esc, El Libertador
6611	GD F-16A-15	9P-3	82-1052	FAV 161 Esc, El Libertador
7268	GD F-16A-15	9P-7	84-1346	FAV 161 Esc, El Libertador
7635	GD F-16B-15	9Q-5	83-1190	FAV 162 Esc, El Libertador
8900	GD F-16A-15	9P-10	84-1349	FAV 161 Esc, El Libertador
8924	GD F-16A-15	9P-9	84-1348	FAV 161 Esc, El Libertador
9068	GD F-16A-15	9P-		FAV 161 Esc, El Libertador
9581	GD F-16B-15	9Q-3	82-1055	FAV 162 Esc, El Libertador
9583	GD F-16B-15	9Q-6	83-1191	FAV 162 Esc, El Libertador
9864	GD F-16A-15	9P-8	84-1347	FAV 161 Esc, El Libertador

Some confusion exists over the exact tie-up between the FAV serials and FMS serials; the FMS serial batches are known to be 82-1050 to 82-1052, 83-1186 to 83-1188 and 84-1346 to 84-1357 for the F-16A and 82-1053 to 82-1055 with 83-1189 to 83-1191 for the F-16B.

Aircraft have crashed as follows: Aug-95 (F-16A) & 16-Nov-95 (F-16B)

The Royal Air Force Benevolent Fund Enterprises

BOOK COLLECTION

HARRIER – The Vertical Reality
£14.95 +p&p
Ref 780560

An authoritative look at the history of this remarkable V/STOL aircraft, illustrated throughout with pictures and diagrams – many previously unseen – and including fascinating first-hand accounts by the early test pilots.

'Highly recommended'.
ROYAL AIR FORCE NEWS

MIGHTY HERCULES – The First Four Decades
£10.95 +p&p
Ref 780515

A detailed history of the first 40 years of this venerable, highly versatile transport aircraft with colourful photographs throughout.

'Well produced and lavishly illustrated'. FOCUS

HAWK Comes of Age
£10.95 +p&p
Ref 780520

Superbly illustrated with over 250 colour photographs, this is a detailed look at the development and production of the world's most successful jet trainer. Includes operation by the *Red Arrows*.

'Excellent value for money'. AIR FORCES MONTHLY

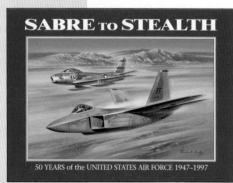

SABRE to STEALTH
50 years of the United States Air Force 1947-1997
A tribute in words and pictures
£30.00 +p&p
Ref 780586

A year-by-year history of the United States Air Force, detailing the principal events, people and planes that have played important roles during 50 years of the world's greatest air arm – with superb colour paintings by some of the world's leading aviation artists.

For more information, please contact:
The RAF Benevolent Fund Enterprises
PO Box 1940, RAF Fairford, Glos, GL7 4NA, England
Tel +44 (0)1285 713456 or fax: +44 (0)1285 713999